The Boxing Filmography

The Boxing Filmography

American Features, 1920–2003

Frederick V. Romano

McFarland & Company, Inc., Publishers
Jefferson, North Carolina, and London

LIBRARY OF CONGRESS CATALOGUING-IN-PUBLICATION DATA

Romano, Frederick V.
The boxing filmography : American features, 1920–2003 / Frederick V. Romano.
p. cm.
Includes bibliographical references and index.

ISBN 0-7864-1793-5 (softcover : 50# alkaline paper) ∞

1. Boxing in motion pictures — Catalogs.
I. Title.
PN1995.9.B69R66   2004   016.79143′657 — dc22   2004012470

British Library cataloguing data are available

©2004 Frederick V. Romano. All rights reserved

No part of this book may be reproduced or transmitted in any form or by any means, electronic or mechanical, including photocopying or recording, or by any information storage and retrieval system, without permission in writing from the publisher.

Cover photograph: ©2004 CREATAS

Manufactured in the United States of America

*McFarland & Company, Inc., Publishers
Box 611, Jefferson, North Carolina 28640
www.mcfarlandpub.com*

To my grandfathers,
Joseph Falcone and Frederick Romano, Sr.

To Joseph for introducing me to the seminal days of film —
including the Biograph Studios in the Bronx, the Gish sisters,
and Bronco Billy and reviving the ring exploits
of Jack Johnson, Stanley Ketchel, and Jack Dempsey.

And to Frederick, who related the tales of Johnny Dundee,
Luis Angel Firpo, Georges Carpentier and other
boxing heroes of the golden age of sport.

Acknowledgments

All my love to my sister, Lisa Romano Licht, who served as my pre-submission editor. The completion of this book would not have been possible without her friendship and assistance.

Special thanks to my confidant, Anthony Morgante, and my parents for their unwavering support and patience. My gratitude to Christian Ambrosio and Greg Licht for his computer tutelage.

Thank you to the staff of the New York Public Library for the Performing Arts, Billy Rose Theater Collection and the staff of the Eastchester Public Library for their assistance in the research of this book.

Table of Contents

Acknowledgments vii
Preface 1

Abbott & Costello Meet the Invisible Man	5
Against the Ropes	6
Ali	8
Battling Butler	10
Body and Soul (1947)	12
Body and Soul (1981)	15
Body and Soul (1998)	17
Born to Fight	18
Bowery Blitzkrieg	19
Cain and Mabel	22
The Champ (1931)	24
The Champ (1979)	26
Champion	28
City for Conquest	32
City Lights	34
City of Bad Men	36
Conflict	38
The Contender	41
The Crowd Roars	43
Dempsey	46
Diggstown	48
Don King: Only in America	50
Eastside Westside	53
Ex-Champ	54
Fat City	56
The Fighter	58
Flesh and Blood	60
Gentleman Jim	62
Girlfight	65
Golden Boy	67
The Golden Gloves Story	69
The Great John L.	71
The Great White Hope	73
The Great White Hype	75
The Greatest	78
Hard Times	80
The Harder They Fall	82
Heart of a Champion: The Ray Mancini Story	85
Heart Punch	87
Here Comes Mr. Jordan	88
Honey Boy	89
The Hurricane	91
The Irish in Us	95
The Iron Man (1931)	97
Joe and Max	99
The Joe Louis Story	101
Joe Palooka, Champ	102
Keep Punching	105
The Kid from Brooklyn	107
The Kid from Kokomo	108
Kid Galahad (1937)	110
Kid Nightingale	113
The Killers	115
Killer's Kiss	117

King for a Night	119	Ringside Maisie	163
The Leather Pushers	120	Rocky	165
The Life of Jimmy Dolan	122	Rocky II	168
Madison Square Garden	124	Rocky III	170
The Main Event	125	Rocky IV	172
The Man from Down Under	128	Rocky V	174
Marciano	130	Rocky Marciano	177
Matilda	131	The Set-Up	179
The Milky Way	133	Snake Eyes	182
The Miracle Kid	135	Somebody Up There Likes Me	184
Monkey on My Back	137	Spirit of Youth	187
Muhammad Ali: King of the World	138	The Square Jungle	189
		The Sting II	192
Night and the City	139	Streets of Gold	193
Off Limits	141	The Superfight	195
Palooka	143	They Made Me a Criminal	198
The Patent Leather Kid	145	Triumph of the Spirit	200
Play It to the Bone	147	Undisputed	202
The Power of One	148	When's Your Birthday	203
The Prize Fighter	150	When We Were Kings	205
The Prizefighter and the Lady	152	Winner Take All	207
Raging Bull	155	Woman-Wise	209
Requiem for a Heavyweight	158	Wonderman	211
Ring of Passion	161		

Selected Bibliography   213
Index   219

Preface

This book covers American full-length motion pictures in which boxing is central to the film's theme or the leading character is a boxer. It is comprehensive through 2003 and covers one film released in 2004. Since the overwhelming majority of boxing movies have been made in the United States, this volume includes virtually every significant boxing feature.

I provide a synopsis of each film, production information, and cast and production credits. However, the lifeblood of this book is the focus on the relationship between actors and boxing, the behind-the-scenes information about casting and filming, and the often amusing, biting reviews. The work also serves as a social mirror in that it imparts long-forgotten colloquialisms, slang, and virulent racial and ethnic prejudices of the past that serve as reminders of just how far we have come.

The love affair between boxing and Hollywood began in the seminal days of film. As early as the days of Chaplin, the "boxing film" quickly assumed its place as a subgenre, and ever since has dutifully served as a vehicle for biographies, dramas, romances, and even musicals and westerns. Curiously, despite the wealth of celluloid as fodder for a work of this kind, the subject has previously never received thorough treatment. In fact, this book is a one-of-a-kind volume for interested readers who have not had the opportunity to immerse themselves in the subject matter — until now.

This project was born of my deep passion for boxing, movies and writing. From an early age, writing provided an important means of personal expression. My interest in both boxing and film began almost simultaneously, at the age of fifteen, and my passion for both has steadily grown over the past quarter-century.

The vast majority of the research for this book was conducted within the walls of that venerable institution the New York Public Library. Principal research was made at this library's branch located at the Lincoln Center for Performing Arts, in the Billy Rose Theater Collection, which includes a vast film library of book, film reviews, and magazine and newspaper articles. I also relied heavily on my personal collection of hundreds of boxing books, magazines and movies, as well as my library of countless film books.

It is with great admiration and respect for both actors and boxers that I share this book. I hope that the participants and fans of both endeavors will enjoy it for many years to come.

THE FILMOGRAPHY

Abbott & Costello Meet the Invisible Man (1951)

Universal, Comedy, B & W, 82 minutes

Producer: Howard Christie. *Director:* Charles Lamont. *Screenplay:* Robert Lees, Frederic I. Rinaldo, John Grant, from the story by Hugh Wedlock, Jr., and Howard Snyder, suggested by H.G. Wells' *The Invisible Man*.

Bud Abbott (Bud Alexander), Lou Costello (Lou Francis), Nancy Guild (Helen Gray), Arthur Franz (Tommy Nelson), Adele Jergens (Boots Marsden), Sheldon Leonard (Morgan), William Frawley (Detective Roberts), Gavin Muir (Dr. Philip Gray), Sam Balter (Radio Announcer), John Day (Rocky Hanlon).

As a teenager, Lou Costello fancied athletics. Among his favorite sports were baseball and basketball. Costello, impressed with a local fighter named Johnny Lane, also developed an interest in boxing. Without the knowledge or consent of his family, he began a ring career under the alias of Lou King. Lou King rattled off ten bouts, and was developing into a prospect. One evening, while fighting in a local New Jersey ring, Costello was viewed by two unexpected spectators, his Uncle Mike and his father. The next morning, Lou sat down at the breakfast table with a black eye. His boxing career was about to end. "Good morning, Lou King," his father said.[1]

Several decades later, Lou Costello made a ring comeback of sorts in *Abbott and Costello Meet the Invisible Man*. In the film, Bud Alexander (Abbott) and Lou Francis (Costello) are recent graduates of a detective agency. The middleweight champion Tommy Nelson (Franz) has been accused of murdering his manager. He needs time to clear his name, so he injects himself with an experimental drug which makes him invisible. Initially, Bud and Lou pursue Nelson to collect a reward, but soon they join Nelson to assist in securing his vindication.

Nelson hatches a plan to have Lou impersonate a boxer while the unseen Nelson does the actual fighting. A gym incident builds Lou's reputation as "Louie the Looper." Described by the press as half Tony Galento, half Benny Leonard, he is matched with contender Rocky Hanlon. The fight-fixers who are actually responsible for Nelson's manager's death also attempt to fix the bout against Hanlon. But despite the fact that Lou is to lay down, the invisible man wins the bout for him. The fight-fixers are ultimately exposed and Tommy Nelson's good name is restored.

Abbott and Costello Meet the Invisible Man is one of the better efforts of Bud and Lou. The repartee between the boys is humorous, the invisible gags are enjoyable, and the ring antics, while not uproarious, are at least good fun. In the ring, the tubby Costello gallops, prances, whirls and mugs, as the invisible man does the blocking and punching. Joe Pihodna of the *New York-Herald Tribune* found the boxing vignette to be "a bright spot in the film."[2] Gilb of *Variety* concurred, writing that the film has a "flock of amusing sequences ... best of these is a scene in which Costello KOs the champ (with the invisible man's help)."[3] A bit in the gym, which finds Lou working the speed bag with his elbows, the back of his head, even his breathing, is also good.

Costello was eventually given the opportunity to work with a real fighter onscreen, in *Jack and the Beanstalk*, when he was teamed with former heavyweight contender Buddy Baer. Baer is best remembered for knocking Joe Louis out of the ring in one of his two losing efforts to win the championship. Naturally, Bud played Jack, while the six foot, six inch Baer assumed the role of the giant.[4]

Around the time of the making of the *Invisible Man* the relationship of the famed pair was in trouble, and they did a bit of fighting on their own. The duo would frequently argue on the set, sometimes ending with Bud giving Lou a slap before shooting a scene. Some thought the slaps were more like blows, but the angered ex-boxer would not retaliate, as he was sure that doing so would bring their relationship to an end.[5] On July 14, 1957, after twenty-one years, the great comic team finally called it quits, leaving a legacy which is still present almost a half-century later.[6]

1. Chris Costello with Raymond Strait, *Lou's on First* (New York: St. Martin's Press, 1981), 6–7.
2. Joe Pihodna, Review of *Abbott & Costello Meet the Invisible Man* (Universal Pictures movie), *New York Herald-Tribune*, 13 April 1951.
3. Gilb, Review of *Abbott & Costello Meet the Invisible Man* (Universal Pictures movie), *Variety*, 7 March 1951.
4. Costello and Strait, *Lou's on First*, 198.
5. *Ibid.*, 188–189.
6. *Ibid.*, 232.

Against the Ropes (2004)

Paramount Pictures, Drama, Color, 111 minutes

Producer: Robert W. Cort, David Madden. *Director:* Charles S. Dutton. *Screenplay:* Cheryl Edwards. *Film Editor:* Eric L. Beason. *Cinemaphotography:* Jack Green. *Music:* Michael Kamen.

Meg Ryan (Jackie Kallen), Omar Epps (Luther Shaw), Tony Shalhoub (Sam LaRocca), Tim Daly (Gavin Resse), Kerry Washington (Renee), Charles S. Dutton (Felix Reynolds).

Despite all its machismo, chauvinistic airs, and Neanderthal-like image, boxing has always had a feminine side. Behind the rise of light-heavyweight champion Young Stribling during the 1920s was "Ma" Stribling, who managed her son to more knockout victories than any other professional fighter in the history of the sport. More recently, Eileen Eaton successfully promoted major boxing contests at the Olympic Auditorium in Los Angeles and was a major force in the continued advancement of the popularity of fighters in the lower weight classifications.

Unquestionably, a prerequisite for women to succeed in the male-dominated world of boxing is that they possess qualities of strength, including courage, self-confidence, and persistence. The most successful of these contemporary boxing Joan of Arcs is Jackie Kallen, who was twice nominated for boxing manager of the year during the 1990s.

Kallen's entree into boxing began in 1977, when she conducted a newspaper interview with Thomas "Hit Man" Hearns. This spawned an unlikely career change for the feisty, well-groomed, and often provocatively dressed Detroitite.[1] After a decade of frequenting Hearns' haunt, the now famous Kronk gym, and its fabled trainer Emanuel Stewart, Kallen obtained her own boxing manager's license. Within six months, she had signed her second fighter, James Toney, with whom she forged a close but often tempestuous relationship. However, her managerial style, which combined the coddling of a Jewish mother with a no-nonsense business approach, led Toney to a 1991 victory over Michael Nunn, and the title of IBF Middleweight Championship of the World.[2]

Toney, who has recently rejuvenated his career in the higher weight classifications, lost his championship in 1994 to burgeoning superstar Roy Jones, Jr. Shortly thereafter, the fighter had an acrimonious split with Kallen. Kallen later wrote a book about her experiences entitled *Hit Me with Your Best Shot*, and Hollywood soon took the bait, which led to the film *Against the Ropes*.[3]

Against the Ropes is not a biography of Jackie Kallen. As the film credits clearly state, the film was "inspired by" and not "based upon" the life of the boxing manager. While the screenplay maintains Kallen's gruff talk and tight skirts, it ignores her family life, making its protagonist a single woman. The character of Luther Shaw, supposedly a composite of Kallen's fighters, is essentially based upon Toney.

Meg Ryan was an unlikely casting choice to play the lead. Ryan told Kallen that she wanted this film to be her *Erin Brockovich*, a movie that could really showcase her acting ability. Kallen felt that Ryan did find the essence of her character, noting that she captured "the spirit, the perseverance, the tenacity" of her journey.[4] The critics, however, were much less sure that Ryan, the cute, girl-next door type, had convincingly projected the hardness and flash of Kallen.

The critic for the *New York Post* wrote that "Ryan gives a self-conscious performance" and that her "desire to stretch is admirable, but this *Erin Brockovich* clone is not the place to do it."[5] Ann Hornaday, writing for *The Washington Post*, concurred: "Ryan looks uncomfortably out of place throughout."[6] Ryan co-star Omar Epps did receive more favorable notices, including one by Hornaday, who wrote that his Luther Shaw "is a genuinely appealing character whose problematic relationship with Kallen is never mined for its rich emotional or symbolic potential."[7]

Despite Ryan's earnest, if unsuccessful efforts, and Epp's good work, the story of a female manager who battles her own growing celebrity, and overcomes the odds to succeed in the paternal world of boxing, is yet another boxing movie whose plot is patent and banal. "The film is so anemic you should probably order iron supplements with your popcorn, its plot so predictable it makes falling dominoes seem like a white-knuckle thrill ride," wrote Michael O'Sullivan of *The Washington Post*, in his review of the film.[8] Kenneth Turan of *The Los Angeles Times*, writing with less venom but equal resignation, described the film as "a workmanlike production that's simply too predictable and too preposterous to hold our interest."[9]

While *Against the Ropes* is another Hollywood foray into the boxing world which did not live up to expectations, Kallen, now a 57-year-old grandmother, continues to both endure and inspire. Kallen is not resting on her laurels as a four-time manager of World Champions, but continues to reach for new horizons in the most contradictory and unpredictable of sports. After recently signing junior middleweight Mohammad Ali Diab, she quipped, "He's an Arab — managed by a Jew. I think together we can solve the problem of peace in the Middle East."[10]

1. Fred Bierman, "Up Against the Ropes, Giving It Her Best," Review of *Against the Ropes* (Paramount Pictures Movie), *New York Times*, 23 February 2004.
2. Ibid.
3. Ibid.
4. Hank Rosenfeld, "In the sport of boxing, she's a real heavyweight; Against the Ropes' inspiration Jackie Kallen made a mark with four world champs. 'I have a good chin,' she says," *Los Angeles Times*, 21 February 2004, E22.
5. "Ryan Ko'd," Review of *Against the Ropes* (Paramount Pictures Movie), *New York Post*, 20 February 2004.
6. Ann Hornaday, "The Sickly Sweet Science; Meg Ryan Is No Knockout in *Against the Ropes*." Review of *Against the Ropes* (Paramount Pictures Movie), *The Washington Post*, 20 February 2003.
7. Ibid.
8. Michael O'Sullivan, "Ropes: Down for the Count," Review of *Against the Ropes* (Paramount Pictures Movie), *The Washington Post*, 20 February 2003.
9. Kenneth Turan, "This is a punch you see coming; *Against the Ropes*, starring Meg Ryan as a boxing manager and directed by Charles S. Dutton, is workmanlike and predictable," Review of *Against the Ropes* (Paramount Pictures Movie), *Los Angeles Times*, 20 February 2003.
10. Hank Rosenfeld.

Ali (2001)

Columbia Pictures, Biography, Color, 157 minutes

Producer: Michael Waxman, John D. Schofield. *Director:* Michael Mann. *Screenplay:* Stephen J. Rivele, Christopher Wilkinson, Eric Roth, based upon a story by Gregory Allen Howard. *Film Editor:* William Goldberg. *Director of Photography:* Emmanuel Lubezki. *Music:* Lisa Gerrad, Pieter Bourke.

Will Smith (Cassius Clay/Muhammad Ali), Jamie Foxx (Drew "Bundini " Brown), Jon Voight (Howard Cosell), Mario Van Peebles (Malcom X), Ron Silver (Angelo Dundee), Jeffrey Wright (Howard Bingham), Mykeiti Williamson (Don King), Jada Pinkett Smith (Sonji), Nona Gaye (Belinda), Michael Michele (Veronica), Joe Morton (Chancy Eskridge), Paul Rodriguez (Dr. Ferdie Pacheco), Bruce McGill (Bradley), Barry Shabaka Henley (Herbert Muhammad), Giancarlo Esposito (Cassius Clay, Sr.), Laurence Mason (Luis Sarria), Le Var Burton (Martin Luther King, Jr.), Albert Hall (Elijah Muhammad), David Cubitt (Robert Lipsyte), Ted Levine (Joe Smiley), Candy Brown Houston (Odessa), David Elliot (Sam Cooke), Shari Watson (Woman Singer), Malick Bowens (Joseph Mobutu), Michael Bentt (Sonny Liston), James N. Toney (Joe Frazier), Alfred Cole (Ernie Terrell), George Foreman (Charles Shufford).

Arguably the most controversial sports figure of all time, Muhammad Ali is also one of the most recognized men in the world. Ten years ago, the *Guinness Book of World Records* reported the astounding statistic that more books and periodicals had been written about Ali than Abraham Lincoln or Jesus Christ.[1]

A figure of such Herculean dimensions, Ali is often difficult to put in perspective. Perhaps one of his opponents, former heavyweight champion Floyd Patterson, best summed up Ali's relative status when he said, "I came to see that I was a fighter and Ali was history."[2]

The gigantic challenge of reducing the multi-faceted political, social, religious and athletic experiences of Muhammad Ali into a single motion picture was painfully evident to filmmakers. But Hollywood has never lacked risk-takers. Martin Scorsese had already attempted the unthinkable when he brought his own unique interpretation of Christ to the screen in *The Last Temptation of Christ*, and director Richard Attenborough proved equal to the daunting task of exploring the life of Gandhi.

Still, it had been many years since Ali had portrayed himself in the 1976 bio-pic, *The Greatest*, and it was many more years before a successful Ali project would get off the ground. Eric Roth, whose screenplay for *Forrest Gump* had won him an Oscar in 1994, had written a serviceable draft of the Ali tale, but Sony Pictures considered several directors before settling on Michael Mann, winner of the 1999 best director Academy Award for *The Insider*.

The issue of who would portray Ali loomed larger than all others, and the only man for whom Muhammad Ali would offer his stamp of approval was the television comedian turned action-movie hero Will Smith. Smith admitted the naïveté of his generation regarding Ali, noting that "most people my age just know him as the funny boxer."[3] However, after hearing the regimen of physical, spiritual, and political awareness that Mann had planned for Smith to bring him closer to his subject, the actor quickly realized the dimensions of the man he was to portray. After undergoing his own metamorphosis, Smith would later explain, "I am just profoundly changed after making this film. I have a greater understanding of greatness."[4]

For director Mann there were no illusions about the enormity of the task he had chosen. In particular, the film's running time created limitations which he would be obliged to work within. He compared making final cuts to the film to "cutting off appendages."[5] Partially for this reason Mann chose to tell only a portion of Ali's life, covering the period from 1964 — when a young Cassius Clay upset Sonny Liston to win the heavyweight championship — until his redemptive victory over George Foreman in Zaire in which he re-captured the heavyweight crown.

Mann, aware of the existing body of work on Ali, instinctively knew that another Ali documentary was not needed, and thus sought to show Ali from the inside. "This is about the real Ali, the one the public saw, but also about the one they didn't see, and have never seen."[6] Ali wanted to avoid a storybook version of his life and told Smith, "Don't idolize me, don't sanitize me, tell the truth."[7]

It is perhaps because Mann was so acutely aware of the need to offer the public a new perspective on Ali that the final product will disappoint some. Certain aspects of the film, which are intended to be illuminating, are simply old hat. Ali's infidelity is already common knowledge, and his siding with Elijah Muhammad in favor of Malcom X is replete in the record. In *Ali*, Mann also falls victim to the same trappings which seem to ensnarl all other Ali pieces. The issues of racism and religion cannot be appropriately addressed as subthemes, but, alas, Mann inevitably limits them to summarized treatments. In sum, Mann offers some good strong details regarding his subject, but is unable to create a full composite picture.

Putting aside Mann's substantial ambitions, *Ali* is still a good movie, and better than most boxing films. What Mann did achieve with his $100 million plus budget was a polished piece of Hollywood entertainment that serves as a taste of the many interesting facets of Muhammad Ali's experiences during the prime of his prizefighting career.

Will Smith also proved to be a smart choice for the lead role. Smith did not seek to impersonate Ali, but to create an interpretation — an Ali-like character that expressed his internal motivations.[8] What the actor achieved was credibility, reaching a high-water mark for believability, both in and out of the ring. However, revelations of the Ali persona or new insights into Ali's motivations — clearly part of Mann's intentions — are never quite realized. Critic Joe Morgenstern, writing for *The Wall Street Journal*, offered a careful analysis of the *Ali* produced by Mann and Smith when he wrote, "*Ali* nails its subject's anger and courage, but not his lilt; his swaggering boasts but not his sly self-irony, his power but not his grace; and his inner turmoil, but not the outward joyousness that had made us come to love him."[9]

And while Smith failed to master all of the aspects of Ali's mercurial and often contradictory nature, he realized the importance of capturing Ali's voice — its rhythm, its tone, and its cadence. It is this element of the Ali persona that Smith is most successful in replicating — an effort undoubtedly facilitated by the careful scriptwriting that masterfully recreated Ali's grammatical usage and phraseology.

In as much as Mann sought to disclose the inner Ali, he placed an equal emphasis on Ali's physicality and his experience in the ring, as evidenced by the film's lengthy and detailed fight scenes. Turning Smith's lean body into a physique befitting of the heavyweight champion was essential to the picture's success. Smith's physical metamorphosis was put in the hands of ex-boxer and trainer Darrel Foster. Under his tutelage, Smith beefed up 30 pounds, to Ali's fighting weight of 215-220 pounds.[10] "We put Will in the ring with real fighters," Mann explained, "and he had to be able to take a punch."[11] Ali's trainer Angelo Dundee designed a regimen for Smith that included torturous sit-ups.[12] Workouts consumed up to six hours per day and were filled with lifting weights, punching the bag, sparring, and eating seven times a day.[13]

Countless hours of Ali fight footage and other footage of "The Greatest" was processed by Smith, including some invaluable film provided by Leon Gast, producer of the award-winning Ali documentary entitled *When We Were Kings*. "I'd sit in a dark room and watch tapes before I went to bed and again as soon as I got up in the morning," Smith explained.[14] Angelo Dundee gave Smith a passing grade when he explained, "I'm from Philly, and I can spot legitimate. Will is from Philly."[15]

To simulate the Rumble in the Jungle, Mann utilized a Mozambican soccer stadium filled with 20,000 volunteers, paid extras, and even some cardboard cut-outs to round out the crowd.[16] Mann focused on each detail of the actual fight to create the impression that you were watching a film replay of the original Ali-Foreman bout. While Martin Scorsese had utilized an interpretive method of portraying boxing, bringing the art to new heights in *Raging Bull*, Mann was no less diligent in using his re-creative approach to simulate each punch, dodge, feint and drop of sweat from both Ali and Foreman.

Attention to detail is also the strength of the reenactment of the Clay-Liston bout, but in this vignette Mann also sought to create mood through the use of muted sound. Both bouts are excellent for their realism, and while heightened drama can sometimes be achieved through the appropriate exploitation of artistic license, that was not Mann's intention here. These scenes are well-grounded, doggedly avoid the artifice, and skillfully deliver the director's vision.

Ali was the most expensive biography made in the history of film. While the film's budget was representative of the effort expended, it is questionable whether the results can justify the price tag. The accountants for Sony Pictures will assuredly be the final arbitrator on that issue. Nevertheless, the boxing fan should be thankful that there are still filmmakers like Michael Mann who are not afraid to make big-budget boxing movies.

1. Allen Barra, "Michael Mann and Will Smith in the Ring with Ali," *New York Times*, 9 September 2001, sec 2, p. 56.
2. Mark Hale, "A King's World," *New York Post*, Sunday, 23 December 2001, p. 63.
3. Patrick Goldstein, "Putting on the Gloves," *Newsday*, Sunday, 9 December 2001, D6.
4. Ray Pride, "Raging Bulls," *Time Out New York*, 13–17 December 2001, 145.
5. David Hinkley, "Sparring with a Myth," *New York Daily News*, Sunday, 16 December 2001, p. 4.
6. Barra, "Michael Mann," 56.
7. *New York Amsterdam News*, 20 December 2001.
8. Barra, "Michael Mann," 59.
9. Joe Morgenstern, "Lavish, Disjointed 'Ali' Might Be the Prettiest, But It Isn't the Greatest," Review of *Ali* (Columbia Pictures movie), *Wall Street Journal*.
10. Barra, "Michael Mann," 59.
11. Hinkley, "Sparring with a Myth," 4.
12. *Ibid*.
13. Barbara Hoffman, *New York Post*, 17 October 2001.
14. Goldstein, "Putting on the Gloves," D6.
15. Barra, "Michael Mann," 59.
16. *Ibid*.

Battling Butler (1926)

Metro-Goldwyn Mayer, Comedy, B&W, Silent, 6970 feet.

Producer: Joseph M. Schenck. *Director:* Buster Keaton. *Screenplay:* Al Boasberg, Lex Neal, Charles H. Smith, Paul Gerard Smith. *Film Editor:* _____. *Cinematography:* Bert Haines, J.D. Jennings.

Buster Keaton (Alfred Butler), Sally O'Neil (Mountain Girl), Walter James (Sally's Father), Budd Fine (Sally's Brother-Bud Fine), Francis McDonald (Alfred Battling Butler), Mary O'Brien (Battling's Wife), Tom Wilson (Battling's Trainer), Eddie Borden (Battling's Manager), Snitz Edwards (Alfred's Valet).

At least in one respect, *Raging Bull* can be considered the legacy of Buster Keaton's *Battling Butler*. Director Martin Scorsese remembered Keaton's picture from childhood and followed its pattern of avoiding crowd shots during fight scenes when he filmed those in *Raging Bull*. "The only person who had the right attitude about boxing in movies for me was Buster Keaton," said Scorsese, who is universally recognized as creating the best fight scenes in film history.[1]

Before being brought to the screen, *Battling Butler* first appeared on the stage. The English musical-comedy, which featured Charles Ruggles in the leading role, had a successful run on Broadway of 288 performances.[2] Buster Keaton purchased the play and hired a team of writers including Paul Gerard Smith, Al Boasberg, Charles H. Smith and Lex Neal to retool it to his liking.[3] The film adaptation eliminated the song-and-dance routines, and other aspects of the plot were trimmed, leaving Keaton with a straight comedic vehicle.[4]

In *Battling Butler*, Keaton portrays a spoiled dandy named Alfred Butler. Desiring that he break his idleness, Alfred's parents send him to the mountains. There he meets a lovely girl portrayed by Sally O'Neil. To impress the girl and her family and to win the girl's hand in marriage, Alfred claims that he is Alfred "Battling" Butler, the famed world lightweight champion boxer, who coincidentally shares the same name.

After marrying the girl, however, Alfred is forced to continue the deception by fighting a contender named the Alabama Murderer. Believing he has Battling's consent to fight as his substitute, a nervous Alfred suffers through pre-fight jitters. Unbeknownst to Alfred, the real Battling, who has always intended to fight himself, defeats the Alabama Murderer in the ring. After the match, Battling seeks out Alfred to avenge him for his earlier flirtation with his wife. Alfred puts his training to use and defeats Battling in a gloved fist-fight held in the dressing room, regaining his own wife's confidence and securing the future of his marriage.

The picture, which premiered at the Capitol in New York, was Keaton's biggest money-maker, grossing nearly three-quarters of a million dollars. Always in fine physical condition, Keaton took the boxing aspects of the picture seriously and supplemented his workout routine by increasing roadwork and adopting a special training diet. Despite careful preparation, injuries did occur. Production was forced to a halt when Keaton fell out of a ring and landed on his head, resulting in head and body bruises. Another injury occurred when Keaton failed to properly execute his reentry into the ring in a scene in which he was knocked out of the squared circle.[5]

To enhance the realism of the fight scenes, ring-worn boxers were collected from boxing gyms throughout the state. To simulate Madison Square Garden, the fictitious venue of the fight finale, the famed Olympic Auditorium in Los Angeles was rented, and hundreds of extras placed in the ringside seats, with the balance of the crowd being comprised of those who provided their services free of charge for the privilege of participating in the filmmaking process.[6]

Keaton was one of the pioneers in using the squared circle in cinema for comic effect. In one scene, Alfred observes the real Battling Butler from ringside, all the while ducking the arms and elbows of the fan sitting beside him. The use of the overzealous fan to supplement the comedic ring antics was soon to become a staple of the boxing comedy film.

Keaton's best boxing-related comedic efforts are seen in a lengthy ring training sequence. No ring comedy is without the obligatory entanglement of the fighter in the ring ropes, but Keaton achieves the trick with a deftness which defies its difficulty and danger, each time ending up with his head hilariously bound by a pair of ring ropes. In another sequence marked by its originality, Keaton keeps his eyes glued on his instructor, who feeds him blocking and hitting techniques, as he simultaneously executes them with increasing effectiveness against a sparring mate with whom he never makes eye contact.

While Keaton would often claim that *Battling Butler* was his favorite picture, it was actually one of his weaker efforts.[7] Detractors have noted the poor production values including obvious changes in lighting. Slow by modern standards, the picture also has a repetitive soundtrack that grates on viewers' nerves. Nevertheless, the film has a few classic Keaton moments, clever in premise and skilled in execution — and there are the several memorable ring antics.

1. Marion Meade, *Buster Keaton: Cut to the Chase* (New York: HarperCollins, 1995), 160.
2. *Ibid.*
3. David Robinson, *Buster Keaton* (Bloomington and London: Indiana University Press, 1969), 136.
4. Meade, *Cut to the Chase*, 160.
5. *Ibid.*, 160–61.
6. *Ibid.*, 160.
7. *Ibid.*, 161.

Body and Soul (1947)

The Enterprise Studios, released by United Artists, Drama, B & W, 104 minutes

Producer: Bob Roberts. *Director*: Robert Rossen. *Screenplay*: Abraham Polonsky. *Supervising Editor*: Francis Lyon. *Film Editor*: Robert Parrish. *Photography*: James Wong Howe. *Musical Director*: Rudolph Polk.

John Garfield (Charlie Davis), Lili Palmer (Peg Born), Hazel Brooks (Alice), Anne Revere (Anna Davis), William Conrad (Quinn), Joseph Pevney (Shorty Polaski), Canada Lee (Ben Chapman), Lloyd Goff (Roberts), Art Smith (David Davis), James Burke (Arnold), Virginia Gregg (Irma), Peter Virgo (Drummer), Joe Devlin (Prince), Shimin Ruskin (Grocer), Mary Currier (Miss Tedd), Milton Kibbie (Dan), Tim Ryan (Shelton), Artie Dorrell (Jack Marlowe), Cy Ring (Victor), Glenn Lee (Marine), Dan Tobey (Ring Announcer).

While Warner Brothers was grooming their new talent John Garfield as a boxer in *They Made Me a Criminal,* Columbia Pictures entertained notions of starring the actor in a boxing film of their own. The acclaimed Clifford Odets play *Golden Boy* was being brought to the screen by Columbia, and studio boss Harry Cohn naturally sought Garfield, the man for whom Odet had specifically penned the lead. Destiny had once been defied when the Garfield role for the stage performance was politically steered to Luther Adler.[1] Warner's fledgling star desperately wanted this injustice atoned, but his studio flatly refused Cohn's request for a loan out.[2] As a consequence, Odets' vision of Garfield as boxer Joe Bonaparte was never realized.

Warner Brothers, in fact, had other plans for Garfield in boxing trunks and scheduled to star him in a remake of the silent film *The Patent Leather Kid*. However, when the production of the picture was postponed, Garfield was redirected toward other studio objectives. *The Patent Leather Kid* was eventually re-titled *Knockout,* with fellow newcomer Arthur Kennedy cast in the lead.[3]

Several years later, in 1946, Garfield and Bob Roberts formed The Enterprise Productions.[4] An independent company, Enterprise unshackled the actor from Hollywood's systematic bondage, leaving him free rein to determine the content of his films. Not surprisingly, Garfield used his new freedom to realize unfilled ambitions. For one of his early projects Garfield chose Abraham Polonsky's *Body and Soul*. While a lofty production, *Body and Soul* was, at its core, a thinly veiled retooling of *Golden Boy*. However, with *Golden Boy* reincarnated in the form of Polonsky's script, Garfield would finally be afforded an opportunity to mirror the soul of Joe Bonaparte, albeit now cast in the body of Polonsky's Johnny Davis.

In *Body and Soul*, Charlie Davis (Garfield), reaches a metaphorical fork in the road where he must choose between two paths: one which leads to money and fame, symbolized by the body, and a second which leads to friendship and love, symbolized by the soul. Sensing that the paths are divergent, but still desiring to reach both destinations, Davis attempts to traverse the brush in between, ultimately suffering the consequences.

Having lost his father (Smith), through a senseless killing, the cynical Davis embraces boxing as a means to support his mother and to obtain "lots of clothes, lots of money, lots of everything." However, the price paid for these items and for winning the middleweight championship is Davis's soul, which must be surrendered to Roberts (Goff), a devilish racketeer who controls the fight game. Davis becomes Roberts's chattel, and is swallowed by his world and all its trappings. Fight manager Quinn (Conrad) taints Davis with greed and slovenliness, and infidelity beckons in the form of a gold digger named Alice (Brooks). Entangled in Roberts's thicket, Davis vainly struggles to find the clearing back to his loved ones, but is unable to commit to them when the opportunities arise. As a consequence, Davis's mother (Revere), who urges her son "to fight for something, but not for money," becomes alienated from her materialistic son. Fiancée Peg (Palmer) is unable to marry the fighter, who has come to embody the traits of his gangster boss. Davis's friendships suffer equally, with his loyal friend Shorty (Peveney) being beaten by Roberts's crowd, leading to his untimely death.

Roberts had already drained his previous champ Chapman (Lee), fighting him well beyond his capacity. When Chapman dies of a blood clot resulting from Roberts's abuse, Davis begins to see the depth of his misjudgment. The surrender of Davis's soul is to come in the form of a fixed fight in which Davis relinquishes his crown to satisfy Roberts's betting interests. Davis bets against himself in an effort to capitalize on his own moral demise, but finally reaches his true path and redemption when he fights on the level, winning both the match and the respect of his loved ones.

Garfield's performance in *Body and Soul* as Johnny Davis, the prizefighter with the embattled conscience, earned him a second Academy Award nomination. Bosley Crowther of *The New York Times* found Garfield "trim, taut and full of vitality," and wrote that he gives "a rattling good performance." Others in the cast were well received. Crowther noted that "Lloyd Goff also does a withering job," and that "William Conrad is revolting as a punk and Joseph Pevney is appropriately tinhorn, but good-hearted, as a small-time hanger-on."[5] The *Time* magazine critic observed that "Canada Lee plays with dignity and fervor one of the few thoroughly unpatronizing screen roles ever given a Negro."[6] Interestingly, Lee and the film's technical advisor, John Indrisano, were both former professional boxers who once fought each other in the ring.[7]

The Davis character, now considered Garfield's greatest role, has become protypical of the fighter seduced by fame and fortune. The film's sustained notoriety has made *Body and Soul* one of the most identifiable movies of the boxing subgenera. If the average person were asked to name five boxing movies (limiting their selection to only one *Rocky* entry), all but the cinematic neophyte would likely include the Rossen film. Remade in 1981, with Leon Isaac Kennedy in the lead, the vacuous revival has already been forgotten, but the Garfield version continues to endure.

Unlike the remake, the original had benefited from its timely subject matter. Several months prior to the film's release, the New York District Attorney's office launched a probe of the Jake La Motta–Billy Fox fight on the grounds that the match had been fixed by New York's "underworld." Indeed La Motta had thrown the fight, though the allegation went unproved. La Motta was fined $1,000 and suspended for seven months for concealment of an injury which he fabricated and used to excuse his poor performance.[8] Only years later would La Motta go public with the truth; his full story was later told in another film classic, Martin Scorsese's *Raging Bull*.[9]

The initial development of the fight scenes in *Body and Soul* were made by Garfield, Roberts, and director Robert Rossen. The trio poured over 50,000 feet of fight film footage, beginning with the Dempsey-Carpentier fight, and continuing up through contemporary matches.[10] To assist photographer James Wong Howe in the actual production of his stylized fight scenes, the photography unit utilized an advanced speed film processing method called the Duplex Perimeter Developing System. Originally designed for the rapid development of film shot by pilots on reconnaissance missions during World War II, the new system enabled the development of film negatives within 30 minutes. A portable laboratory was established on the set of *Body and Soul*, and after the negatives were developed, positives were quickly run off to allow near-simultaneous reviews of the day's filming. If retakes of the fight scenes were necessary, they could be shot before the set was dismantled and hundreds of extras were sent home.[11]

The fight scenes in *Body and Soul* are superlative. "Magnificent," applauded Sondra Gonley of *The Daily Worker*.[12] In many respects they are the best to be filmed before or during that time. Photographer Howe firmly resisted the temptation to use the close-up as a panacea, and then masterfully exploited his zoom lenses, selectively applying them to intensify the collision of leather and bone. Howe pointed his camera from ringside level, through the ropes and upward, capturing plumes of smoke accentuated by the shafts of light from the ring bulbs above, grafting a texture to the ring encounter enmeshed within. Howe, who filmed several of the shots while traversing the ring on roller skates, used a mixture of distant shots, upward angles and imprecise vantage points to give the film a home-movie quality. In this manner Howe developed a comfortable realism which served to draw the film audience into the fight arena.*

1. George Morris, *John Garfield* (New York: Jove Publications, Inc., 1977), 25.
2. Bob Thomas, *Golden Boy: The Untold Story of William Holden* (New York: St. Martin's Press, 1983), 25.
3. Morris, *John Garfield*, 33.
4. *Ibid.*, 118.
5. Bosley Crowther, "'Body and Soul,' Exciting Story of Prizefighting, Starring John Garfield, at Globe — Two British Films Also Open," Review of *Body and Soul* (Enterprise Studios movie), *New York Times*, 10 November 1947.
6. Review of *Body and Soul* (Enterprise Studios movie), *Time*, 20 October 1947.
7. "Ex-jockey, Ex-pug Canada Lee Is an Actor by Accident," Warner Bros. Studio Publicity.
8. Chris Anderson, Sharon McGehee, and Jake La Motta, *Raging Bull II: Continuing the Story of Jake La Motta*, (Secaucus, N.J.: Lyle Stuart Inc., 1986), 16–18.
9. Jake La Motta, Joseph, Carter, and Peter Savage, *Raging Bull, My Story* (Englewood Cliffs, N.J., 1971), 162.
10. "Old Fight Films Coached Garfield," Warner Bros. Studio Publicity.
11. "Duplex System in First Film Use," Warner Bros. Studio Publicity.
12. Sarah Gonley, Review of *Body and Soul* (Enterprise Studios movie), *Daily Worker*, 28 August 1947.

Howe's work in Body and Soul *is representative of his talents. Photographing several more boxing films, he would go on to win an Academy Award for his work in* On the Waterfront.

Body and Soul (1981)

The Cannon Group, Inc., Drama, Color, 100 minutes

Producer: Menahem Golan, Yoram Globus. *Director*: George Bowers. *Screenplay*: Leon Isaac Kennedy, suggested by the original screenplay by Abraham Polonsky. *Film Editor*: Samuel D. Pollard, Skip Schoolnik. *Director of Photography*: James Forrest. *Music*: Webster Lewis.

Leon Issac Kennedy (Leon Johnson), Jayne Kennedy (Julie Winters), Peter Lawford (Big Man), Michael V. Gazzo (Frankie), Perry Lang (Charles Golphin), Kim Hamilton (Mrs. Johnson), Gilbert Lewis (Tony), Muhammad Ali (Himself), Nikki Swasey (Kelly), Danny Wells (Sports Announcer #1), Johnny Brown (Sports Announcer #2), Azizi Johari ( ), Rosanne Katon (Melody), Chris Wallace (Dr. Bachman).

Remakes of classic films rarely succeed. It is not enough that the new interpretation stand on its own merit, but it must also overcome skepticism, sentimental prejudice and a critical comparison to the original's high standard. To his credit, if not his wisdom, a young actor/producer named Leon Issac Kennedy attempted to defy the unsettling odds against capturing lightning in a bottle twice. He did this by resurrecting Robert Rossen's boxing classic *Body and Soul*.

Kennedy proceeded as if possessing complete conviction in his vision. Not only did he cast himself in the lead role of the prizefighter,* but he selected his real-life wife Jayne Kennedy as his leading lady. Jayne, a former Miss Ohio beauty queen, was nationally known as the host of two National TV talk shows; *NFL Today*, and *Speak Up, America*.[1]

Kennedy revised *Body and Soul* by making its protagonist an African-American, and by placing the action in a contemporary setting. A young sister who suffers from sickle-cell disease was also written into the script to strengthen the ethnic bent and to add a new element of sentiment for the fighter who boxes to pay for her medical treatment.

Updated alterations notwithstanding, the new production retained the central elements of Robert Rossen's original story. Leon Johnson (Kennedy) boxes his way to the championship, but alienates his mother by choosing boxing over a more reputable profession. His relationships with his best friend and girlfriend (J. Kennedy) are also tainted by his newfound success. The fighter is confronted with the ultimate question as to whether or not he will forfeit his soul to his manipulative promoter (Lawford); he passes the test and emerges both spiritually and professionally triumphant.

Bob Roberts, the associate producer of the original version of *Body and Soul*, attempted to keep the Kennedy version out of theaters by seeking a permanent injunction against the exhibition of the film. Roberts claimed that he continued to maintain the rights to the screenplay and the literary material upon which the new film was allegedly based. Kennedy's faction, Cannon Group, acquired the rights to the film from Paramount, which Roberts contended never possessed the remake rights to transfer.[2]

While the suit may have had bona fide financial implications for Roberts, any fear of artistic piracy was unfounded, as a viewing of a few moments of the remake would quickly reveal.

The film begins with "a slow, sloven start and has a string of trite and unnecessary expressions," wrote Marie Moore of the *New York Amsterdam News*.[3] The film's triteness was in fact endemic, and the pic-

---

*Just prior to *Body and Soul*, Kennedy had some success playing the lead in another film with some boxing sequences entitled *Penitentiary*. Two sequels would follow.

ture could not claim to be a success by any interpretation. Kennedy had the gumption to step up to the table and roll the dice, but they had bounced back with two ominous snake-eyes.

Ed Naha of the *New York Post* correctly observed that *Body and Soul* was "taking it on the chin from a lot of critics," but the Kennedys' ridicule was actually twofold.[4] Jayne's recent appearance in *Playboy*, which featured pictures of her from the movie, was simultaneously maligned by the press.[5]

While *Body and Soul* was neither an artistic or critical success, at least the picture was refreshing. As white faces continued to unrealistically dominate the boxing rings of Hollywood, the film undertook the long overdue racial overhaul, by featuring an African-American starring as the fictional lead in a film. Kennedy also produced the picture himself, raising over $2 million for his project. "I'm one of the few Black producers even doing anything," Kennedy explained. "I put 30 other Black people to work in front of and behind the cameras, including a Black crew and a Black director," the entrepreneur noted.[6]

For the boxing fan, appeasement came in the form of Muhammad Ali, who appeared as himself in a minor role. True to life, Ali steals the show as the champ marches towards his ringside seat to the familiar chant of "Ali, Ali, Ali." Admittedly, watching Ali beseech Kennedy to employ the "rope-a-dope" from a ringside seat does not have much of an authentic air about it, but Ali fans enjoyed it. At one point in the film Ali tells Kennedy's character that he looks like a mosquito, and later, when they enter the ring to spar together, the barb proves prophetic. Members of the fistic fraternity joining Ali in the film are junior middleweight Robbie Epps and welterweight Andy Price who portrayed boxers, referee Richard Steele who acts as the third man in the ring, and then WBA light-heavyweight champion and current trainer Eddie Mustafa Muhammad, who has a brief cameo appearance.

The influences of Muhammad Ali and former four-division world champion Sugar Ray Leonard on the picture are clearly evident. The character of Leon Johnson periodically lapses into a mimic of Ali's verbal *shtick*, both in and out of the ring. Kennedy, who bears a resemblance to Leonard, also adopts his fleet-footed, jabbing boxing style. As a cinematic fighter, Kennedy displays a fast pair of hands and feet, but he throws looping punches in his attempt to imitate Leonard, who was actually a textbook puncher even while showboating.

There are several fight scenes in the picture and the final match is unusually lengthy. The ring action is engaging enough, but quite often the film goes too far. An opponent named "The Iceman" fights bloodied and with both eyes closed to the point of criminality on the part of the referee before the match is finally stopped. Additionally, the final bout is an incredible foul fest, which not only defies every rule laid down by the Marquess of Queensberry, but also makes Fritzie Zivic and Mike Tyson look like a pair of poster boys for clean sportsmanship.

Undoubtedly, Kennedy's final opponent, Richardo "Madman" Santiago, was inspired by Robert Duran, who had just completed two matches with Leonard a year earlier. If there is any question that the ferocious Latino with the mop of bouncing black locks was inspired by Duran, it is dispelled at the film's conclusion when he grabs his crotch and gestures to the press row as Roberto did after the first Leonard fight in Montreal!

1. Robert E. Johnson, "Leon and Jayne Answer Critics about Their Sizzling Photos," *Jet*, 20 August 1981, 58.
2. "Bob Roberts Sues over 'Body and Soul'," *Variety*, 13 May 1981, 12.
3. Marie Moore, "Divorce-Bound Kennedy Still Tied 'Body and Soul'," *New York Amsterdam News*, 28 November 1981, 30.
4. Ed Naha, "You Can't Divorce This Body from This Soul," *New York Post*, 24 November 1981, 21.
5. Johnson, "Sizzling Photos," 58.
6. *Ibid.*, 60.

Body and Soul (1998)

Metro-Goldwyn Mayer, Drama, Color, 91 minutes

Producer: Peter Mcalevey. *Director*: Sam Henry Kass. *Screenplay*. *Film Editor*: Mitchell Danton. *Cinematography*: Arturo Smith.

Jordan Ancel (Valet), Jennifer Beals (Gina), Michael Chiklis (Tiny), Angelo Dimascio (Perky), Ray "Boom Boom" Mancini (Charlie "Kid" Davis), Joe Mantegna (Alex Dumas), Rod Steiger (John Ticotin), Tahnee Welch (Felice).

After the spirited but less than satisfying remake of Robert Rossen's acclaimed *Body and Soul* by producer/actor Leon Issac Kennedy, it would take an individual of particular courage to attempt a second revival. Enter former WBA lightweight champion Ray "Boom Boom" Mancini, who possessed the trait in spades.

After a successful ring career, Mancini began to apply the no-nonsense, head-on approach that he utilized in boxing to establish an acting career. "Boom Boom" was quick to realize the parallels between the fight game and the film industry. "I'm coming from a world where you control your own destiny," he explained, and in movies "the only way to work on a consistent basis was to own my own properties." "I'm producing to act," noted Mancini, who started his own production company to obtain the projects he wished to appear in. Mancini admitted that he "wasn't interested in doing Shakespeare" but noted that he could "play a tough guy," and specifically set his sights on *Body and Soul*. "I'd never do a fight movie unless it was '*Body and Soul*,'" Mancini explained. "To me, it's the best boxing movie ever made."[1] To develop his own interpretation of the Rossen story, the origin of lead character Charlie Davis was moved from New York's lower East Side to Beaver Falls, Pennsylvania, and the fight venues shifted from New York to Reno, Nevada. However, the story of the fighter's struggle with worldly temptations and their subsequent strain on human relationships was adopted in principal.

Mancini had acted in an off-off Broadway play entitled *Siddown*, written by Sam Henry Kass, and he hired Kass to fashion his screenplay.[2] The script possesses plenty of street vernacular, locker-room talk and witty dialogue. Some of the lines are clichéd, but the majority of the script is entertaining, providing a realistic insights into the masculine, often crude and cut-throat world of the fight business.

Mancini engineered some very astute casting moves. A quality line-up was assembled, including the incomparable Rod Steiger as his fight trainer, Joe Mantegna as his self-interested promoter and Michael Chiklis as his pal from Beaver Falls. What Steiger brings to the film is incalculable, and the making of the film is justifiable based upon Steiger's performance alone. His interpretation of the fight manager is multi-textured, offering an instantaneous believability and displaying a rainbow of emotions. Steiger develops his character with his first few lines as only a consummate professional can do. Despite the limitations of his character's development by the script, one is hard-pressed to find an actor who has portrayed a fight trainer in such a convincing manner.

Mantegna has a barrage of witty lines, and he brings to life the self-absorbed character who is simultaneously forward and unpersonable. He gives an excellent characterization of a sleazy promoter. Chiklis's character Tiny is most apt to run afoul of realism, but if accepted as "over-the-top" from the onset can be enjoyed for what he has to say.

The boxing vignettes are spread consistently throughout the film, and thankfully a measured amount of time is spent on training glorifying sequences. Mancini's Charlie Davis is Mancini, with his ever-pressing, whirlwind style featuring plenty of body punches and left hooks. The fight scenes are artistically standard, but Mancini legitimizes Charlie Davis in the ring. "I may not be a great actor yet," Mancini said in comparing himself to John Garfield, the original Charlie Davis, "but he's not the fighter I was."[3]

In truth, Mancini is dwarfed by the acting talent which surrounds him, as the struggle of Charlie Davis seems secondary to Steiger's magnetism, Mantegna's presence and Chiklis's clowning. It is no surprise that Mancini was unable to create another classic boxing story, but like his style in the ring, there was no failure of effort expended or entertainment spared.

1. Robert Dominguez, "Mancini Tackles Heavyweight Role with *Body & Soul* Remake," In Focus, New York Vue, *New York Daily News*, 8.
2. *Ibid.*
3. *Ibid.*

Born to Fight (1938)

Conn Pictures Corp., Drama, B & W, 64 minutes

Producer: Maurice Conn — Conn Production. *Director*: Charles Hutchinson. *Screenplay*: adapted by S. Baranley from Peter B. Kyne story.

Frankie Darro ("Baby Face"), Kane Richmond ("Bomber"), Jack La Rue ("Smoothy"), Frances Grant (Nan), Stella Manors (Ada), Monty Collins (Gloomy Gus), Eddie Phillips (Duffy), Fred "Snowflake" Toones (Snowflake), Philo Mccullough (Goodall), Hal Price (Heckler), Donald Kerr (Broadcaster), Gino Corado (Matire de Hotel), Charles Mcmurphy (Cop), Bob Perry (Referee), Olin Francis (Hobo), Harry Harvey (Reporter).

Having already portrayed a prizefighter as the lead in the 1930 serial *The Leather Pushers*, Kane Richmond returned to the squared circle in *Born to Fight*, a garden-variety dueler co-starring the diminutive Frankie Darro. In *Born to Fight*, "Bomber Brown" (Richmond) is a contending light-heavyweight boxer who assaults a gambler known as Smoothy (LaRue) and flees New York to avoid prosecution. Following a brawl in a hobo camp, Bomber makes the acquaintance of Baby Face Madison (Darro) and the pair move on to Chicago. Bomber adopts the alias Tom Hayes and begins to manage Baby Face's ring career. The fighter trains at Morgan's Gym and becomes enamored with its owner, a young woman named Nan (Grant).

While the police search for Bomber, the ex-fighter and Baby Face endure the typical trials and tribulations of fighter and manager with Baby Face eventually receiving a shot at the featherweight champion. Risking arrest, Bomber appears at Madison Square Garden, providing Baby Face with the necessary encouragement to win the championship. After the bout, Bomber is taken into custody. However, when Smoothy, the complaining witness, is killed by gamblers for welching on his bet against Madison, Bomber is freed to pursue a romance with Nan.

The critics' reviews of *Born to Fight* were less than complimentary. Regina Crewe of *The Journal-American* equated the film to a "run-of-cargo production," while *Variety* found "nothing approaching originality in any part of this film's formula or execution."[1] The reviewer for the *New York Post* managed to muster a backhanded compliment: " In spite of crude production and not even estimable photography, there's enough good humor and fast action in 'Born to Fight' to earn a fair report."[2] Frankie Darro, the film's co-star, fared no better with the critics. Comparing his role as a pug to his recent portrayal of a jockey, the critic for the *New York Daily News* quipped, "I'd advise him to stick to the horses."³

Some 60 years after its release *Born to Fight* both amuses and amazes on several unintended levels. One can only marvel at the writers' shameful reworking of "Brown Bomber," the moniker of then heavyweight champion Joe Louis to create the name "Bomber Brown." This transgression might be overlooked, but for the painfully obvious fact that Madison's nickname "Baby Face," was stolen from another of the era's great fighters, Jimmy McLarnin.

The fight scenes are ample, lengthy and at least passable in their effort to create acceptable ring decorum. However, one particular sparring session between Baby Face and a heavier spar mate is unintentionally comedic in its utter lack of realism. Equally amusing is the gushing admiration and knowing glances regularly exchanged between Bomber and Baby Face. One begins to get the impression that the real romance lies between the two fighters rather than Bomber and Nan, who appear to have a platonic relationship — until they finally kiss at the curtain's close.

Snowflake, Baby Face's black trainer, was added to provide comic relief, but the character now stands as a shocking case study on film's contribution to a virulent racist society. If one can turn a blind eye to this degrading and offensive exhibition for a few seconds, they can still appreciate the lyrics to one of Snowflake's songs: "... Why Maxie Baer says a prayer when I climbs in the ring, 'Da Preem' Carnera swings with terror, 'cause when I hit Carnera Sings ..."⁴

Soon after *Born to Fight*, Darro's pugilistic services were in demand at Monogram Studios, another "B" film factory of the era. In his second boxing lead, Darro starred for that studio in *Tough Kid*, along with Dick Purcel, another actor familiar to "B" audiences. At best, the picture was supporting material for a double feature. Barn of *Variety* appropriately noted that *Tough Kid* is "just a pic for the action houses, and strictly a ho-hummer."⁵

1. Regina Crewe, "Darro Star of Fight Film," Review of *Born to Fight* (Conn Pictures Corp. movie), *New York Journal-American*, 5 March 1938; Review of *Born to Fight* (Conn Pictures Corp. movie), *Variety*, 25 May 1938.
2. Review of *Born to Fight* (Conn Pictures Corp. movie), *New York Post*, 21 May 1938.
3. Review of *Born to Fight* (Conn Pictures Corp. movie), *New York Daily News*, 21 May 1938.
4. *Born to Fight*, produced by Conn Productions, directed by Charles Hutchinson, 64 minutes, 1938.
5. Barn, Review of *Born to Fight* (Conn Pictures Corp. movie), *Variety*, 11 January 1939.

Bowery Blitzkrieg (1941)

Monogram Pictures, Comedy, B & W, 62 minutes

Producer: Sam Katzman for Banner Pictures Corp. *Director*: Wallace Fox. *Screenplay*: Sam Robins, based upon a story by Brendan Wood and Don Donmullahy. *Film Editor*: Robert Golden. *Photography*: Marcel Le Picard. *Musical Directors*: Lange & Porter, A.S.C.A.P.

Leo Gorcey (Muggs McGinnis), Bobby Jordan (Danny Breslin), Huntz Hall (Limpy), Sunshine Sammy Morrison (Scruno), Donald Haines (Skinny), David Gorcey (Pee Wee), Warren Hull (Tom Brady), Charlotte Henry (Mary Breslin), Keye Luke (Clancy), Bobby Stone (Monk Martin), Dennis Moore, Martha Wentworth (Mrs. Brady), Jack Mulhall (Officer).

Whether cast as the Dead End Kids, the East Side Kids, or the Bowery Boys, the clowning and general slapstick of Leo

Gorcey, Huntz Hall and friends remains for many an indelible childhood memory. Beginning in the late 1930s in the Broadway production *Dead End* and later in the film of the same name starring Humphrey Bogart, the trio of Gorcey, Hall and Bobby Jordan appeared in numerous films as New York's lovable juvenile delinquents. The crew's impending middle age brought the series to a conclusion in 1958 with *In the Money*.

As the Dead End Kids, the boys initiated their film career in major motion pictures with dramatic themes, which were produced for Warner Brothers. Appearing in such films as *Dead End*, *Angels with Dirty Faces*, and the boxing yarn *They Made Me a Criminal*, the group provided comedic support for major stars like Humphrey Bogart, James Cagney and Claude Rains. After establishing their own reputations, Monogram Pictures beckoned; thus as the East Side Kids or the Bowery Boys, the ensemble was given an opportunity to star in their own low-budget features, several of which utilized boxing as a central theme.

By 1941, Gorcey and Jordan had already made a number of films as the East Side Kids. Huntz Hall would rejoin the group acting under their new banner in a boxing flick entitled *Bowery Blitzkrieg* (1941). In *Bowery Blitzkrieg*, a teenage hoodlum intentionally undermines the friendship of a wiry youth portrayed by Jordan, and his wise-cracking pal played by Gorcey. When Jordan's character is shot in a botched robbery, Gorcey provides him with a needed blood transfusion, reestablishing their friendship moments before he enters the ring to win a boxing match.

Bowery Blitzkrieg suffered the critical backlash of its "B" pedigree. Howard Barnes of the *New York Herald-Tribune* found the boys "at their least engaging and their least significant," while William Boehnel of the *New York World-Telegram* criticized the film as "too weak to spank, too nondescript to praise — even faintly."[1] Perhaps the most complimentary critic was J.D.B. of *The Christian Science Monitor* who said, "Though story and direction are routine, Leo Gorcey and Bobby Jordan supply vitality and win sympathy."[2] Notwithstanding the film's less than auspicious reviews, beyond the inherent foibles of low-budget, black-and-white films, *Bowery Blitzkrieg* is still good for a few chuckles.

The boxing story line in *Bowery Blitzkrieg* was merely a vehicle to advance its morality message. Consequently, fight fans must subsist on gratuitous glimpses of Gorcey working out on the rowing machine or shadow boxing, until the anticipated championship fight is finally staged to wrap up the story. No doubt boxing fans were less than satiated with the film's limited fistic action, but perhaps none were more disappointed than those fight fans attending the Rialto Theater in New York. Rialto patrons expecting to see a replay of the recent Joe Louis-Lou Nova heavyweight championship match were thrown Gorcey's Golden Glove tiff as a last-minute substitute![3]

As evidenced in his performance in *Bowey Blitzkrieg*, Leo Gorcey rates only fair as a pugilist. While he was the group's cinematic leader, Gorcey was not the best boxer in his troupe, as would soon be proven in a later entry in the series entitled *Kid Dynamite* (1943), a light-hearted World War II propaganda piece in which Bobby Jordan laces on the gloves. Not only does Jordan have a better physique than Gorcey, but he also possesses the better boxing technique. Odds are that Jordan rather than Gorcey was the real champ of the Bowery.

Several years after making *Kid Dynamite*, Gorcey, Hall and company returned to the squared circle with their ubiquitous hats tilted back in *Mr. Hex* (1946), a fight farce with a mystic twist. Gorcey learns to hypnotize Hall with a small metallic coin called "the Genie." Under the coin's hypnotic power, Hall becomes a pugilist *nonpareil*. Commenting on the film, Brog of *Variety* stated that it furnished "plenty of the antics liked by those who follow the doings of the rough and ready gang."[4]

Unlike other films in which the Bowery Boys traversed the canvas, *Mr. Hex* uses the action inside the roped square to create comedy. In *Mr. Hex*, the ring scenes are played strictly for laughs. To maximize the humor, boxing chores were given to Hall for the first time in the series. The producer's engagement of frequent fight film adviser John Indrisano must have been perfunctory, as no duplication of conventional boxing technique is intended. In his role as Satch, Hall fights throughout the film wearing his trademark baseball cap in the ring. The final match is lengthy, and gives Hall ample opportunity to use his gangly body and varied facial expressions to effect humor in a climactic scene in which the frenzied silliness spills out onto the ring apron and into the audience. While Hall does not approach the comedic ring antics of Buster Keaton, or even Danny Kaye, he proves pleasantly amusing at pugilistic slapstick.

Leo Gorcey was drawing laughs from film audiences with his East Side vernacular and rapid-fire mutilation of the English language long before Carroll O'Connor established his own brand of tortured elocution as television's Archie Bunker on *All in the Family*. In *Newshounds* (1947), the boys' next boxing feature, Gorcey gives a classic display of the comic technique, spewing a tirade of nonsensical phrases in his portrayal of an aspiring sportswriter who works with Hall, an enthusiastic shutter bug, to free the fight game from racketeers.

Brog of *Variety* critiqued that "*Newshounds* adds up to one of the best of Monogram's Bowery Boys series."[5] While the picture contains no ring action, *Newshounds* is a boxing film on a more benign level. During the 1940s and 50s gangsters such as Frankie Carbo and Blinky Palermo controlled the careers of outstanding pugilists such as Ike Williams and Sonny Liston, and maintained a vise-like grip on the championships for which they vied. Nobody received a shot at the title without permission from "the boys." *Newshounds*, while light-hearted in its approach to the influence of organized crime in boxing, begins to poke at one of the sport's raw nerves, foreshadowing the more serious examination of the subject that was soon to come in such films as *Body and Soul, On the Waterfront,* and *The Harder They Fall*.

A more mature gang worked the periphery of the ring to assist a troubled neighborhood family in *Fighting Fools* (1949). Gilb of *Variety* observed that "although there are liberal fight scenes, these sequences for the most part are pegs on which to hang the crusty humor of the Bowery Boys."[6] Notwithstanding its comedic veneer, *Fighting Fools* was still Monogram's most sincere attempt to utilize the Bowery Boys to fashion a legitimate fight yarn. Generous time is devoted to ring scenes which are equal or superior to most found in "B" films. Frankie Darro, a veteran of several boxing movies including *Tough Kid* and *Born to Fight*, knows his way around the ring better than most of his contemporary actors, and lends the film a dose of credibility. Commenting on his ring chores Darro noted, "I've fought some amateur fights that were rough, but they weren't as hard on me as the bouts I had in *Fighting Fools*. I had to use all the pugilistic tactics I knew to make the bouts look real, but at the same time I had to avoid being hit, so I wouldn't get bruised and spoil my later scenes."[7]

1. Howard Barnes, Review of *Bowery Blitzkrieg* (Monogram Pictures movie), *New York Herald-Tribune*, 1 October 1941; William Boehnel, "Rialto Shows Bowery Blitzkrieg," Review of *Bowery Blitzkrieg* (Monogram Pictures movie), *New York World-Telegram*, 1 October 1941.
2. J.D.B., Review of *Bowery Blitzkrieg* (Monogram Pictures movie), *Christian Science Monitor*, October 1941.
3. Rose Pelswick, "*Bowery Blitzkrieg* Screened at Rialto," Review of *Bowery Blitzkrieg* (Monogram Pictures movie), *New York Journal-American*, 1 October 1941.
4. Brog, Review of *Bowery Blitzkrieg* (Monogram Pictures movie), *Variety*, 11 December 1946.
5. Brog, Review of *Newshounds* (Monogram Pictures movie), *Variety*, 25 June 1947.
6. Gilb, Review of *Fighting Fools* (Monogram Pictures movie), *Variety*, 27 April 1949.
7. Studio Publicity for *Fighting Fools*.

Cain and Mabel (1936)

Warner Bros., Musical-Comedy, B&W, 89 minutes

Producer: Cosmopolitan. *Director*: Lloyd Bacon. *Screenplay*: Laird Doyle based on a story by H.C. Witwer, *Film Editor*: William Holmes. *Photography*: George Barnes. *Music and Lyrics*: Harry Warren, Al Dublin.

Marion Davies (Mabel O'Dare), Clark Gable (Larry Cain), Roscoe Karns (Reilly), David Carlyle (Ronny Cauldwell), Walter Catlett (Jake Sherman), Hobart Cavanaugh (Milo), William Collier, Sr. (Pop Walters), Allen Jenkins (Dodo), Ruth Donnelley (Aunt Mimi), E.E. Clive (Charles Fendwick), Pert Kelton (Toddy), Eily Malyon (The Old Maid), Robert Middlemass (Café Proprietor), Allen Pomery (Joe Reed), Joseph Crehan (Reed's Manager), Sammy White (Specialty Numbers).

William Randolph Hearst was an enigma. Outwardly he was shy like Joe Louis, modest like Rocky Marciano, with the high-pitched voice of Mike Tyson, and the retiring disposition of Ezzard Charles. Inwardly, he combined the sober confidence of James J. Corbett, the haughty attitude of Gene Tunney, and the ruthlessness of Sonny Liston, topped off with the megalomania of Muhammad Ali. This was the composite of the man who reigned supreme as the king of the American print media for the first half of the twentieth century.[1]

Hearst manipulated the masses through the dozens of newspapers he controlled to bring about events of national and international importance. In the process, he created media stars, presidents, and even war.[2] When the U.S.S. *Maine* was sunk in 1898, Hearst papers accused Spain and rabidly campaigned for its expulsion from the Western Hemisphere. To emphasize the press mogul's sentiment that the United States would easily overwhelm Spain in a conflict, Hearst's *New York Journal* went so far as to suggest the formation of "a regiment of giant athletes" including heavyweight champions Bob Fitzsimmons and James J. Corbett, both of whom had purportedly agreed to join the proposed outfit. "They would overawe any Spanish regiment by their mere appearance," the *Journal* exclaimed condescendingly.[3]

Hearst's zone of operation knew no boundaries. His early enemies included President McKinley, Joseph Pulitzer and France.[4] Later, he would add boxing to his list, once again using his *Journal* to apply unrelenting pressure to help bring about a ban on boxing in New York state from 1917 to 1920.[5]

While he advocated boxing's ban in the teens, Hearst saw no hypocrisy in his attendance at the first Dempsey-Tunney bout in Philadelphia in 1926.[6] He even made an unsuccessful attempt to purchase the broadcasting rights for the second Dempsey-Tunney fight held in Chicago the following year.[7]

But not all of Hearst's power was used in an acrimonious fashion. Some was reserved simply for self-interest. When the aging newspaper kingpin became smitten with a lovely actress named Marion Davies, he fired up his presses to advance her career. Davies, who had left a convent to become a dancing girl, made her way into film in 1918 in Pathe's *Runaway Romany*.[8] Hearst peddled his influence to prompt Metro to star Davies in expensive pictures before she had earned the requisite box-office clout.

By the Depression, Davies was a screen veteran. In 1936, she was cast opposite Clark Gable, one of MGM's biggest stars, in the musical-comedy *Cain and Mabel*. The picture received financial backing from Hearst. Despite the fact that Hearst and Louie B. Mayer were not on good terms, MGM's Irving Thalberg fulfilled a prior commitment to have Gable star in the Davies vehicle.[9]

In *Cain and Mabel*, Larry Cain (Gable) is the heavyweight champion of the world.

Mabel O'Dare (Davies) is a waitress turned Broadway dancer. In an effort to provide the pair with publicity, their respective management teams steer the press to link the pair romantically. In reality, the two had a distaste for one another. Later, the predictable romance blooms.

Cain and Mabel was a critical failure. Howard Barnes of the *New York Herald-Tribune* panned the film, writing that it possessed "a listless romance" and "some ridiculously ornate production numbers, trivial songs and the kind of talk that baffles even resourceful character actors."[10] Kate Cameron, writing for the *New York Daily News*, added that "the quips lack punch and the production numbers are overly tedious."[11]

Davies herself also received unfavorable reviews. Eileen Creelman of the *New York Sun* wrote that Davies "has not yet learned to read lines," adding that "she permits the comedy to fall completely flat."[12]

To mitigate the harsh commentary of the objective press, Hearst papers spread Davies' propaganda. Rose Pelswick of the *New York Evening Journal* represented the biased sentiments of the Hearst press when she pegged the film as "outstanding entertainment," noting that "Miss Davies gives a gorgeous performance."[13]

The numerous disparities found in a comparison of the Hearst papers' assessment of Miss Davies' acting ability, and those opinions offered by the print media on the same subject, eventually developed into its own topic of discussion. Taking a subtle jibe at Hearst regarding the glaring inconsistency of the critics' evaluation of his paramour's talent, a writer for the *New York Post* wrote that "such uniform divergence of opinion may make you wonder."[14] Hannen Swaffer of *World Film News* was more direct, writing that Davies "can't dance or sing too well," and that "her acting is all right, but she ought to thank heaven for Clark Gable—and the Hearst newspapers, which always say how marvelous she is."[15]

As for Gable, his performance in *Cain and Mabel* was respectable. The critic for the *New York World-Telegram* summed it up best when he wrote that "Mr. Gable is amusingly brash as the pugilistic champion."[16] But the role did little to enhance his reputation. As pointed out by J.T.M. of *The New York Times*, "Mr. Gable's roles are becoming routine matters. He needs another *Mutiny on the Bounty*."[17]

In the ring, Gable is seen in one vignette at the end of the picture. He is enough of a physical specimen to look the part of a prizefighter and he is passable as a purveyor of the sweet science. As could be predicted, Hearst's *New York Journal* was highly complimentary of the fight scene, describing it as "a thrillingly realistic prize fight sequence."[18] The critic for *Variety* found it to be "a spirited punch fest."[19]

In the end, Hearst lost money on *Cain and Mabel*. However, all was not lost. A wonderful carousel used in the film was salvaged from the set by Hearst, and taken back to his castle at San Simeon, California, to provide entertainment for many of Hearst and Davies' party guests.[20]

1. W.A. Swanberg, *Citizen Hearst* (New York: Charles Scribner's Sons, 1961), 101.
2. *Ibid.*, 130.
3. *New York Journal* as quoted in W.A. Swanberg, *Citizen Hearst* (New York: Charles Scribner's Sons, 1961), 143.
4. Swanberg, *Citizen Hearst*, 131.
5. Mel Heimer, *The Long Count* (New York: Atheneum, 1969), 110.
6. *Ibid.*, 115.
7. Swanberg, *Citizen Hearst*, 395.
8. Joe Franklin, *Classics of the Silent Screen: A Pictorial Treasury* (New York: The Citadel Press, 1959), 155.
9. Jane Ellen Wayne, *Clark Gable: Portrait of a Misfit* (New York: St. Martin's Press, 1993), 146.
10. Howard Barnes, Review of *Cain and Mabel* (MGM movie), *New York Herald-Tribune*, 19 October 1936.
11. Kate Cameron, Review of *Cain and Mabel* (MGM movie), *New York Daily News*, 19 October 1936.
12. Eileen Creelman, " 'Cain and Mabel,' a Feeble and Expensive Musical Comedy Starring Marion Davies," Review of *Cain and Mabel* (MGM movie), *New York Sun*, 10 October 1936.

13. Rose Pelswick, "'Cain and Mabel'—Marion Davies, Clark Gable Co-Star in Gay and Sparkling Comedy," Review of *Cain and Mabel* (MGM movie), *New York Evening Journal*, 19 October 1936.
14. Review of *Cain and Mabel* (MGM movie), *New York Post*, 27 October 1936.
15. Hannen Swaffer, *World Film News*, March 1937, 27.
16. Review of *Cain and Mabel* (MGM movie), *New York World-Telegram*, 19 October 1936.
17. J.T.M. Review of *Cain and Mabel* (MGM movie), *New York Times*, 19 October 1936.
18. Pelswick, "Gay and Sparkling Comedy."
19. Review of *Cain and Mabel* (MGM movie), *Variety*, 21 October 1936.
20. Lyn Tornabene, *Long Live the King: A Biography of Clark Gable* (New York: G.P. Putnam Sons, New York, 1976), 208.

The Champ (1931)

Metro-Goldwyn Mayer, Drama, B & W, 87 minutes

Producer: A King Vidor Production. *Director*: King Vidor. *Dialog*: Leonard Praskins, from Frances Marion's original story, with additional dialogue by Wanda Tuchock. *Film Editor*: Hugh Wynn. *Photography*: Gordon Avil.

Wallace Beery (Champ—Andy Patell), Jackie Cooper (Dink), Irene Rich (Linda), Roscoe Ates (Sponge), Edward Brophy (Tim), Hale Hamilton (Tony), Jesse Scott (Jonah), Marcia May Jones (Mary Lou).

Despite the minimal expectations of Metro-Goldwyn Mayer, and a lukewarm reception by film critics, movie-goers were smitten with *The Champ*. A sleeper in the true sense of the word, the King Vidor Production sent theater turnstiles spinning on its way to becoming a viewer favorite. Not until the release of *Rocky* in 1976 would another unheralded boxing film be so embraced by the public.

Similar to *Rocky*, which cast Burgess Meredith and Talia Shire fresh off Academy Award nominations, *The Champ* also featured two hot properties who were recently recognized by Oscar nominations. The film's lead, the gravelly-voiced Wallace Beery, had been nominated the year prior for best actor for his role in *The Big House*. His co-star Jackie Cooper, the pouting-faced, yellow-haired child actor best known from the Hal Roach *Our Gang* serials, was also a 1930 Academy nominee for his role in *Skippy*.

Devoid of plot complications or lofty underlying messages, *The Champ* is a simple love story between father and son. The Champ (Beery), once heavyweight champion, has since fallen prey to alcohol and gambling. Despite the Champ's frequent intoxication, gambling and general inability to support his son Dink (Cooper), he is idolized by the boy.

While the disheveled ex-pug adores the boy with a similar passion, his vices have spawned a role reversal. Dink monitors his father's drinking and gambling, undresses his father for bed when he is too intoxicated to do so himself and even assumes the responsibility of driving their jalopy. A horse that the Champ buys for Dink from gambling money, which he periodically loses and wins back, is symbolic of the Champ's good intentions but poor fathering.

When the Champ's estranged ex-wife, a socialite named Linda (Rich) resurfaces with her well-bred husband (Hamilton), the Champ initially resists their proposal to raise the boy in splendor. Later, when another stint in jail awakens him to the reality that he is an unfit provider, he reconsiders. Without Dink, the Champ's spirit is broken. However, the boy runs away and reunites with his dad, inspiring him to train for a match against the Mexican heavyweight champion. The Champ is hopeful that the large purse will provide Dink with money for a proper education and a home, and secure once and for all the return of

Dink's beloved horse. During the Champ's fight, he receives a brutal beating. Dink wants to throw in the towel, but the Champ refuses, and comes back to win the bout. After the match, the Champ suffers a heart attack and dies in the arms of a disbelieving and non-accepting Dink.

The superlative chemistry between Beery and Cooper — both of whom gave top-notch performances — infused the simple narrative with character and emotion, earning screenwriter Frances Marion an Academy Award and the film an Oscar nomination for best picture. King Vidor was also nominated for best director, but lost to Frank Borzage's *Bad Girl*.

Beery's performance as the lax but softhearted prizefighter yielded his first and only Oscar for best actor, establishing him as a top box-office draw for several years to follow. Richard Watts of the *Herald-Tribune* felt Beery was "at his best," hailing his performance as "robust" and "shyly tender."[1] Thornton Delehanty of the *Evening Post* opined that Beery had "never given a more warm and affecting performance."[2]

Beery may never have obtained the coveted statuette but for the slight of hand of MGM boss Louis B. Mayer. When the Oscar for best actor for 1931–32 was presented to Paramount's Fredric March (*Dr. Jekyll and Mr. Hyde*), Mayer rushed backstage to find out why Beery had not won the award. Incredibly, upon learning that Beery was a mere one ballot shy of March in the voting, Mayer coaxed Academy executives into issuing a second Oscar to Beery, who he rationalized was equally deserving.[3]*

Cooper's performance, as the child who unconditionally loves his father, left no eye dry and no hanky unwet. "Not in the history of talkies was weeping so profuse and enjoyable," exclaimed Irene Thirer of the *New York Daily News*.[4] Delaney concurred, stating "never was there such a wet night at any theater."[5]

The critics loved Cooper's performance. Richard Watts hailed it as "one of the finest and most knowingly sensitive portrayals of the recent cinema."[6] Julie Shaw was even more profuse in her praise stating that Cooper was "unquestionably the most talented child actor" she had ever observed.[7]

Perhaps the charismatic youth deserved an Oscar of his own, particularly in light of his true sentiment toward Beery. Years later in his autobiography, Cooper would confess "I really disliked him. It began the very first day on *The Champ*. There was to me then no warmth to the man. He always made me feel uncomfortable."[8]

While Thirer found the fight scenes "gripping," and Shaw believed the final bout to be "the most realistic pugilistic encounter ever staged for the cameras," the dated ring action has aged poorly.[9] The action is brisk, but perhaps too much so. One is convinced that the speed of the film was turned up by the filmmakers to increase the pace of fighting. As a boxer, Beery sports a middle-aged paunch, and is unacceptably soft by today's standards. However, while one can criticize other flaws it is best to enjoy the movie for its emotional impact.

In 1938, *The Champ* was reissued. A few years later, Wallace Beery recreated his role in a pair of Lux Radio performances on the radio, the second of which was broadcast on June 29, 1942.[10] In 1953, the film's fight theme was converted to a circus setting, with Red Skelton portraying the lead in a variation entitled *The Clown*. Finally, in 1979, MGM remade the Frances Marion story casting Jon Voight and Ricky Schroder in the lead.

1. Richard Watts, Jr., Review of *The Champ* (MGM movie), *New York Herald-Tribune*.
2. Thornton Delehanty, Review of *The Champ* (MGM movie), *New York Evening Post*.

Another source indicates that the issuance of the Oscar was made under less dramatic circumstances. The American Film Institute Catalog, *referencing an issue of the* Hollywood Reporter, *states that a recently instituted AMPAS rule deemed any candidate within two votes of the leading tally would share the award.*

3. James Robert Parish and Gregory Mank, *The Best of MGM: The Golden Years, 1928–1959* (Westport, Ct.: Arlington House, 1981), 47.
4. Irene Thirer, Review of *The Champ* (MGM movie), *New York Daily News*.
5. Delehanty.
6. Watts, Jr.
7. Julie Shaw.
8. Jackie Cooper with Dick Kleiner, *Please Don't Shoot My Dog: The Autobiography of Jackie Cooper* (New York: William Morrison & Company, Inc., 1981), 54.
9. Thirer; Shaw.
10. Patricia King Hanson, *The American Film Institute Catalog of Motion Pictures Produced in the United States, Volume F3, Feature Films, 1931–1940* (Berkeley: University of California Press, 1993), Film Entries A-L, 313.

The Champ (1979)

Metro-Goldwyn Mayer, Drama, Color, 121 minutes

Producer: Dyson Lovell. *Director*: Franco Zeffirelli. *Screenplay*: Walter Newman, based upon a story by Frances Marion. *Film Editor*: Michael J. Sheridan. *Director of Photography*: Fred J. Koenekamp. *Music*: David Grusin.

Jon Voight (Billy), Faye Dunaway (Annie), Ricky Schroder (T. J.), Jack Warden (Jackie), Arthur Hill (Mike), Strother Martin (Riley), Joan Blondell (Dolly Kenyon), Mary Jo Catlett (Josie), Elisha Cook (Georgie), Stefan Gierasch (Charlie Goodman), Allan Miller (Whitey), Joe Tornatore (Hesh), Shirley Kong (Donna Mae), Dana Elcar (Hoffmaster), Randall Cobb (Bowers), Christoff St. John (Sonny), Gina Gallego (Cuban Girl), Jody Wilson (Mrs. Riley), Reginal M. Toussaint (Groom), Bob Gordon (TV Reporter), Gene Picchi (Dolly's Trainer), Anne Logan (Horse Owner), Bill Baldwin (Race Track Announcer), Dick Young (Referee), Sonny Shields (Boxing Handler #1), Larry Duran (Boxing Handler #2), Lars Hensen (Ring Doctor), Jeff Temkin (Ring Announcer), Ralph Gambina (Time Keeper), Eddie "El Animal" Lopez (Corner man).

When MGM brushed the dust off the Frances Marion classic *The Champ* and situated it in a contemporary setting, the studio undoubtedly braced itself for inevitable comparisons to the 1931 original. The first version featured Academy Award nominees Wallace Beery and Jackie Cooper, and it was apparent that the producers of the remake had no intention of being outdone by their predecessors.

The highly popular Ryan O'Neal was initially cast in the lead. However, he soon left the production citing "artistic differences." Some claim these amounted to nothing more than O'Neal's unwillingness to do the film without his 12-year-old son Griffith.[1]* Next MGM engaged Robert Redford. At the time Redford was a top box-office draw; however, the parties could not agree upon the script.[2]

In a late-round casting coup, Jon Voight, last seen in his Academy Award winning role in *Coming Home,* was drawn out of a film hiatus by MGM to fill Beery's shoes. Voight, who had also previously been nominated for his work in *Midnight Cowboy,* had already portrayed a boxer on the screen in *The All-American Boy*.† At six feet three inches tall and 190 pounds, Voight offered both ring experience and the appropriate physique to complement his ample screen presence.

For the female lead, MGM signed Faye Dunaway, one of the most accomplished actresses of the era. Dunaway, who was discovered by Elia Kazan in a college play, won Oscar nominations for her work in both *Bonnie and Clyde* and *Chinatown* before

---

*Still other reports indicate that O'Neal was peeved that the role could not be fitted for his daughter Tatum.
†The All-American Boy, *released in 1973, also starred E.J. Peaker, Ned Glass, Anne Archer and Carol Androsky.*

winning the Academy Award for best actress in Paddy Chayefsky's *Network*. Other veteran stars like Joan Blondell, Oscar-nominated for her role in *The Blue Veil*, and Jack Warden, a nominee for *Heaven Can Wait* and *Shampoo*, rounded out the superlative cast.[3]* The film's other Oscar-level talent included Joseph Biroc and Fred J. Koenekamp, who won Academy Awards for best cinematography for *Towering Inferno*, and David Grusin, who was nominated for his musical score on *Heaven Can Wait*.

With stars highlighting *The Champ* roster, MGM needed an accomplished child actor to their liking to play T.J., the picture's central character. A coast-to-coast casting search was launched with more than 5,000 candidates vying for the coveted role. Out of this vast pool, MGM selected Ricky Schroder, a second grader from Staten Island, New York. While never having appeared in a motion picture, Schroder was a veteran of numerous television commercials.[4] More importantly, the seven-year-old had a smile and a pout that could disarm even the most hardened critic. While Italian director Zeffirelli had advertised for a boy with dark hair and brown eyes, he gave the part to the sandy-haired, blue-eyed Schroder "because he has the look of total innocence coupled with incredible street smarts."[5]

The Champ was shot on the MGM sound stages, the Hialeah Park Race Track, and other locales in Southern California and Florida.[6] The film is the heart-warming story of a son who unconditionally loves his big-hearted father who is less than an ideal parent. Maintaining the structure of Vidor's original, Zeffirelli's version strengthens the conflict created by the Champ's estranged wife, who fights to bring their son back into her life. Ultimately, the retired Champ reenters the ring in an effort to prove his parental worth, but meets with tragedy.

Zeffirelli improves upon the original version's emotional finale, driven by the stunning performance of Ricky Schroder and the seamless work of Voight. The Champ's final moments lying on a trainer's table are captured by a sideways close-up of Voight's face; a grotesque mask of grayish skin with bloodstained teeth. Schroder meets the Champ's death with a tempered emotional outburst laced with subtlety and nuances. He poignantly conveys his heartbreak and disbelief.

Of the newer version of *The Champ*, King Vidor, the director of the original remarked, "It takes a lot of courage to remake a popular, successful movie. I think Zeffirelli succeeded marvelously."[7] Intimating that *The Champ* had recaptured some of the sentiment of the original, Liz Smith of the *New York Daily News* reported that "there wasn't a dry eye in Hollywood the other night after MGM premiered *The Champ*."[8] However, contrary to the spirit of the assessment offered by Smith, Vincent Canby of *The New York Times* tagged the film "an anthology of cheap, not especially moving or invigorating sentiments that exploit the sort of child-image that has now all but vanished."[9] The critic for *Chicago Magazine*, like that of *The New York Times*, also found misgivings with the film's continuity and concluded, "*The Champ* is an idea whose time has passed."[10]

Standing above the picture's weaknesses is Voight's impeccable performance. Exhibiting an expansive range, he is equally captivating whether gruff or angered by frustration, happily boyish, or touched by sentiment. As noted by Morna Murphy of *Shooting*, his portrayal "is hailed by many as another Academy-Award-winning display of talent by the versatile young actor."[11]

The many compliments of little Ricky Schroder were justified. As genuine a child actor as any to appear on screen, Schroder appeals to the audience's emotions early in the picture and hits them dead-on by film's end. Tony Schwartz of *Newsweek* credits Schroder with stealing "the show from both

---

*As a teen, Warden fought 13 fights as a welterweight under the ring alias Johnny Costello.

Voight and the formidable Faye Dunaway ... a considerable feat, especially for an 8-year old in his very first film."[12]

To cultivate the character of "Champ," Voight studied a number of boxers, both famous and unknown. Assisting Voight was veteran fight trainer of the stars, Jimmy Gambina. Gambina put Voight through the paces in a ring set up on the actor's front lawn in Miami when he wasn't on the set.[13] The fight scene, shot over five days, was staged at the Olympic Auditorium in Los Angeles in front of 2,000 movie extras.[14] Portraying Voight's opponent was a boxer named Randall "Tex" Cobb, a colorful character with a 7-0 professional record.[15] Cobb would later maul his way into heavyweight contention, earning the dubious or heralded distinction (depending on one's perspective) of retiring Howard Cosell from the fight game.* In the ring against Cobb, Voight moves adroitly, fights competently on the inside, and puts his punches together well. Long range shots of the fast-paced ring action are nicely utilized and the climactic knockout is top-notch.

1. *New York Daily News*, 17 February 1978, 5.
2. Aljeau Harmetz, *New York Times*, 29 April 1978.
3. "MGM Production Notes."
4. Tony Schwartz, "The Heartbreak Kid," *Newsweek*, 23 April 1979, 69.
5. *Variety*, 21 September 1977; Aljeau Harmetz, *New York Times*, 29 April 1978.
6. "MGM Production Notes."
7. Review of *The Champ* (MGM movie), *Women's Wear Daily*, 26 March 1979.
8. Liz Smith, "Tears in Ears," *New York Daily News*, 23 March 1979, 6.
9. Vincent Canby, "Child Stars Today Aren't Always Kids," Review of *The Champ* (MGM movie), *New York Times*, 8 April 1979, 19.
10. *Chicago Magazine*, June 1979.
11. *Shooting*, May 1979, 2.
12. Tony Schwartz, "The Heartbreak Kid," *Newsweek*, 23 April 1979, 69.
13. "MGM Production Notes."
14. "MGM Production Notes."
15. Herbert Goldman, ed., *1984 Record Book and Boxing Encyclopedia*, (New York: The Ring Publishing Corp., 1984), 541.

Champion (1949)

United Artists, Drama, B & W, 90 minutes

Producer: Stanley Kramer, for Screen Plays Corporation. *Director*: Mark Robson. *Screenplay*: Carl Foreman, based on a short story by Ring Lardner. *Photography*: Frank Planer. *Film Editor*: Harry Gerstad. *Music*: Dimitri Tiomkin, Goldie Goldmark.

Kirk Douglas (Midge Kelly), Marilyn Maxwell (Grace Diamond), Arthur Kennedy (Connie Kelly), Ruth Roman (Emma Bryce), Lola Albright (Mrs. Harris), Paul Stewart (Tommy Haley), Luis Van Rooten (Jerome Harris), John Day (Johnny Dunne), Harry Shannon (Lew Bryce), Ralph Sanford (Kansas City Promoter).

As a fledgling independent producer, Stanley Kramer lacked the reputation to obtain financing to bring Ring Lardner's boxing story *Champion* to the screen.† Needing leverage to secure funding for his project, Kramer gilded the lily. He characterized his thirty-day option to buy *Champion* from Lardner's estate as actual ownership and represented his intention to release the film through United Artists as a *fait accompli*.

---

*On November 26, 1982, Cobb took such a frightful beating from heavyweight champion Larry Holmes for 15 rounds that Cosell forever turned his back on the sport. The perpetually jovial Cobb, however, was not as perturbed by the spectacle. After the final gong sounded, ending the 15 round massacre, Cobb embraced Holmes and exclaimed, "Let's party!"

†*Champion* was one of two boxing stories appearing in Lardner's Round-Up written in 1929. The other was entitled A Frame-Up.

Maintaining a good poker face, Kramer successfully induced a loan.[1]

For his director Kramer drew an ace named Mark Robson. Robson had started as an uncredited film cutter for Orson Welles on *Citizen Kane*. His reputation was principally confined to a sector of RKO's internal hierarchy, who, recognizing his talent, had advanced him to film editor on several of their B pictures. More recently, Robson had been handed the directorial reins for several of the studio's movies, but these too were of a lesser quality. Despite the inherently limited material fed to Robson by RKO, Kramer discerned his ability and hired him.[2]*

For the lead of Midge Kelly in *Champion*, Kramer interviewed numerous actors, none of whom he found suitable. Finally a relative newcomer named Kirk Douglas entered his office. "Rawboned and lean, yet muscular," as the producer described him, Douglas was the appropriate physical type.[3] The actor had just been invited to join the elite trio of Ava Gardner, Gregory Peck and Ethel Barrymore to anchor MGM's top-shelf production of *The Great Sinner*. However, Douglas was so ignited by the opportunity to play Midge Kelly he ripped off his shirt and flaunted his muscles in the producer's office, pleading for the part. So impassioned was the actor that Kramer instinctively hired him without ever having seen him perform on the stage or screen.[4] For the opportunity to pilot Kramer's longshot, Douglas sidestepped the advice of his agents, rejecting the $50,000 contract offered by MGM.[5]

Paradoxically, Kramer made *Champion* because he "desperately hated the fight game."[6] Having experienced its sordid elements firsthand while growing up in New York's Hell's Kitchen, the producer could relate to Lardner's story and he bled it for all of the author's intended wrath. *Champion* lays bare the corrosive power of a prizefighter's unbridled ambition. All those who are drawn into Midge Kelly's orbit are left in the wake of his quest for recognition and obsession to achieve status through the middleweight championship. Loyal wife Emma (Roman) is abandoned by Kelly without regard to his marital obligations, and his paternal manager Tommy Haley (Stewart) is callously thrust aside after guiding him to the cusp of the championship.

Kelly's self-interest stings others with equal purpose. He coolly seduces Palmer (Albright), the young wife of his second manager Harris (Van Rooten), then abruptly dismisses her affections in favor of more pressing financial necessities. Even his crippled brother, Connie (Kennedy), is not beyond the purview of Kelly's psychological manipulation and physical intimidation. When Connie becomes openly contemptuous of his sibling's indifference, he too feels the Champion's scorn.

For the zealous Kelly, the mere specter of the championship inspired him to rationalize his selfish actions. The power of the championship itself spawned corruption: from whimsical revenge of "fat belly" cigar-smoking promoters and cynical blondes who unabashedly declared that they came with a price tag, to the heartless destruction of his abandoned wife and his brother, whose deepening affection he undermined solely for the sake of satiating his own ego.

Kelly is not alone in screenwriter Carl Foreman's pool of human degradation, but symbolically stands at the vortex of the moral degeneracy of a tempestuous fight crowd, where greedy big-time gamblers and two-bit promoters trample integrity in pursuit of blood money. Equally transparent are the pampered and perfumed women who sell sex and manipulate partners for the privilege of appending themselves to the most powerful and wealthy "men of the moment."

The producer had previously requested that Robson direct So This Is New York, *a film based upon another story by Ring Lardner. Robson, however, was unimpressed by the script and declined.* Champion *was the second attempt at a Kramer-Lardner-Robson combine and this time Robson agreed to direct the Lardner yarn for Kramer's film version.*

At the conclusion of *Champion*, Kelly suffers a post-fight cerebral hemorrhage. Withering under death's weight, he pleads his case for validation with his very last breath. "Those fat bellies with the big cigars aren't going to make a monkey out of me," Kelly defiantly states before slipping away.[7] Asked for a statement by the press, his brother Connie spares the public the stinging truth by perpetuating the myth of his brother as a true "Champion"— one who ironically is left with the legacy of a man beyond the reproach of the decadent fight game.

Champion's critics found the film's forceful elements its most seductive quality. Jimmy Fidler of the *Boston Daily Record* described *Champion* as "raw meat" and P.S.C. of *The Baltimore Sun* as "brutal stuff."[8] *Variety* found the film "a stark, realistic study of the boxing rackets and the degeneracy of a prizefighter."[9] The film, however, is not without its deficiencies, principal among them a less than original story line. Otis L. Guernsey, Jr. of the *New York Herald-Tribune* also found a certain unevenness writing, "*Champion* is something like a haymaker. It is clumsy and telegraphed, but it hits hard when it happens to land."[10]

Taking into consideration the film's budget of less than $600,000, and a production schedule of just twenty-four days, the picture's flaws are justifiably excused.[11] *The New York Times* appropriately credits the direction of Robson for compensating for some of the weaknesses in the story by creating scenes which are "strongly atmospheric and physically intense."[12]

The boxing content of the picture is high-caliber. The *New York Herald-Tribune* wrote that "Mark Robson has staged an effective montage of training and boxing sequences, in which the flavor of the gym and the arena is captured to the most exacting taste."[13] It was Kramer however, who covertly directed the film's major fight scenes, as well as one of the most original boxing training sequences ever filmed.[14] In that scene Douglas jumps rope, does jumping jacks, punches the heavy and speed bags, shadow boxes, spars and even flexes his mouthpiece, all with the delightful score of Dimitri Tiomkin punctuating Douglas's every move. After directing the sequence, Kramer acted as the post-production editor.[15]

Champion also features a unique vignette of a slow-motion knockout fashioned into a newsreel format reminiscent of the Pathe-Movie Tone reels of the day. Film editor Harry Gerstad masterfully paced the stylized fight sequences, which helped earn him the Oscar for best film editor. Without detracting from Gerstad's work, the uncredited contributions of former cutters Robson and Kramer, who both edited portions of the film, deserve recognition.[16]

Much of the film's intensity can be credited to Douglas's portrayal of Midge Kelly, which earned the actor his first of four Academy Award nominations. Douglas's interpretation of the emotionally vital prizefighter has Kelly brimming with arrogance on some occasions, and chillingly self-absorbed on others. Regardless of the particular disposition Douglas conveys at any given moment, he faithfully maintains Kelly's purposeful and conniving intent.

John Rosenfield of *The Dallas Morning News* critiqued, "The title part is a thespic knockout for 33-year-old Kirk Douglas."[17] *Time* wrote that Douglas "fills out every corner of Kelly's unattractive pug with bulging assurance and conviction." Stahl of *Variety* wrote that Douglas "makes the character live" and praised him for his "versatility," and *Cue* went so far as to dub Douglas's performance as "astonishing, a job of acting that surpasses anything he has ever done on the screen."[18] "My gut instincts told me to do *Champion*," Douglas would later write.[19]

Douglas prepared for the boxing portion of his role by training for several weeks under the tutelage of former junior welterweight champion Mushy Callahan. *The New Yorker* found the fight scenes developed by Callahan and enacted by Douglas to be "alarmingly authentic."[20] While in top physical condition, Douglas brings more to the part of the enraged prizefighter than his taut stomach and baseball-like biceps. Douglas shows great concentration in the ring. His intense focus on his opponent draws the viewer into the ring. Perhaps his best characteristic is his patented snarl and grimace. On occasion Douglas's ring countenance is ripe with anger and he leaves no doubt that Midge Kelly is a man on a mission.

The supporting cast made their own meaningful contributions to the production. Marilyn Maxwell is well-cast as the perfect condescending bitch, whose seductive qualities make men yearn for her. Arthur Kennedy is sensitive and sympathetic as Connie, and creates an emotional and moral contrast with Douglas's character. Paul Stewart is steady as the fight manager who is violated by the sport he loves, but is resigned to return for more of its abuse.

Champion was met with a last-minute obstacle. RKO commenced legal action against United Artists and Screenplays, Inc., seeking an injunction against the exhibition of the film claiming that it infringed on its previous release, *The Set-Up*. The parties, however, ultimately settled the suit, which stipulated that United Artists would cut 101 feet of film and a couple of words of dialogue from Kramer's production.[21]

Champion's success set the course for Kirk Douglas's film career for decades to follow. The picture also proved pivotal for both Robson and Kramer, bringing them critical acclaim for their work for the first time. Soon thereafter, Kramer became an important Hollywood player, producing the legendary *High Noon*.

1. Donald Spoto, *Stanley Kramer, Film Maker* (New York: G.P. Putnam's Sons, 1978), 36.
2. Herbert G. Luft, "Mark Robson Did Not Dally Long with Message Films," *Films in Review*, May 1968, 288–291.
3. Stanley Kramer with Thomas M. Coffey, *A Mad, Mad, Mad, Mad World: A Life in Hollywood* (San Diego: Harcourt Brace & Company, 1997), 23.
4. Kramer, *Mad, Mad World*, 24.
5. Kirk Douglas, *The Ragman's Son: An Autobiography* (New York: Simon and Schuster, 1988), 146.
6. Spoto, *Stanley Kramer, Film Maker*, 35.
7. *Champion*, produced by Stanley Kramer, directed by Mark Robson, 100 minutes, Artisan Home Entertainment, 2000, DVD.
8. Jimmy Filder, Review of *Champion* (United Artist Pictures movie), *Boston Daily Record*, 31 March 1949; P.S.C. Review of *Champion* (United Artist Pictures movie), *Baltimore Sun*.
9. Stahl, Review of *Champion* (United Artist Pictures movie), *Variety*, 16 March 1949.
10. Otis L. Guernsey Jr., "To Make Boxing Films, Follow the Formula," *New York Herald-Tribune*, 17 April 1949.
11. John Rosenfield, "This Prizefighter Film Has Heart and Head as Well as Rowdy Ring Sequences," Review of *Champion* (United Artist Pictures movie), *Dallas Morning News*, 3 June 1949, p. 20.
12. Bosley Crowther, "Kirk Douglas Plays the Hero in 'Champion,' Film of Ring Lardner's Fight Story," Review of *Champion* (United Artist Pictures movie), *New York Times*, 11 April 1949.
13. Guernsey, Jr., "Follow the Formula."
14. Spoto, *Stanley Kramer Film Maker*, 38.
15. *Ibid.*
16. Kramer, *Mad, Mad World*, 29.
17. Rosenfield, "This Prizefighter Film."
18. Stahl, Review of *Champion* (United Artist Pictures movie), *Cue*, 9 April 1949.
19. Douglas, *The Ragman's Son: An Autobiography*, 146.
20. Review of *Champion* (United Artist Pictures movie), *New Yorker*, 9 April 1949.
21. *New York Times*, 21 May 1949.

City for Conquest (1940)

Warner Bros., Drama, B & W, 101 minutes

Producer: Anatole Litvak. *Director*: Anatole Litvak. *Screenplay*: John Wexley, based upon the novel by Aben Kandel. *Film Editor*: William Holmes. *Cinematography*: James Wong Howe, Sol Polito. *Music*: Max Steiner.

James Cagney (Danny Kenny), Anne Sheridan (Peggy Nash), Frank Craven ("Old Timer"), Arthur Kennedy (Eddie Kenny), Donald Crisp (Scotty MacPherson), Frank Mchugh ("Mutt"), George Tobias ("Pinky"), Elia Kazan ("Googi"), Anthony Quinn (Murray Burns), Jerome Cowan ("Dutch"), Lee Patrick (Gladys), Blanche Yurks (Mrs. Nash), George Lloyd ("Goldie"), Joyce Compton (Lillie), Thurston Hall (Max Leonard), Ben Welden (Cobb), John Arledge (Salesman).

Although he grew up on the rough-and-tumble streets of Yorkville in New York City, James Cagney ironically put on his first pair of boxing gloves at summer camp in Stepney, Connecticut. When the lad returned to New York, he further cultivated his pugilistic proclivity, taking public boxing lessons at a local athletic field. "I can do *that*," Cagney would later exclaim while watching professional boxers train at a gym in Yorkville.[1]

Young Jimmy had aspirations of becoming a pro. In time, a family friend secured the youth a four-round bout at the Polo Grounds Athletic Club in what was to be his debut. Cagney arose early in the morning to do his roadwork, dreaming of the hefty ten-dollar purse, which would be increased by a fin if he was the winner. Then Jimmy's mother stumbled upon her son's ambition and the roadwork immediately ceased. "You'll have to lick me first," mother Cagney challenged, instantly nipping the boy's boxing career in the bud.[2]

Boxing's loss would soon prove to be Hollywood's gain. In just over a decade James Frances Cagney, Jr. went from an unknown stage player to the apex of his profession. *Public Enemy* (1931) brought the actor early public recognition, and further critical acclaim was earned in *Angels with Dirty Faces* (1938). *Yankee Doodle Dandy* (1942) would eventually elevate him to the status of entertainer *nonpareil*. On his way to film stardom Cagney portrayed a prizefighter on several occasions. The first, *Winner Take All* (1932), was a standard fight film marked by the actor's strong personality and surprising ring acumen. *The Irish in Us* (1935) followed — a simple comedy tenuously held together by the celtic camaraderie of Cagney and his off-screen pals Pat O'Brien and Frank McHugh.

City for Conquest, a film based upon the Aben Kandel novel of the same name, was to be the last in a trio of Cagney's boxing movies. The actor had read the book, a best-selling entry of the 1936 literary season, and was "thrilled" when several years later Warner Brothers purchased the screen rights and cast him in the lead.[3] New York playwright John Wexel was chosen by the studio to adapt Kandel's multi-plot novel for the screen, a challenge which demanded heavy pruning of the lengthy story to fit the film's 100-minute format.

City for Conquest is the story of the individual desires and struggles which comprise the mosaic of New York; a city which is unforgiving yet hopeful. Ambition, the picture's central theme, manifests itself in several different forms. Danny Kenny (Cagney) is a truck-driver who seeks to secure love through the prize-ring, while his girlfriend Peggy Nash (Sheridan) exploits her dancing ability to court fame. Boyhood chum Googi (Kazan) turns to a life of crime to achieve respect and Danny's brother Eddie (Kennedy) seeks self-realization through his music.

Peggy's and Danny's careers take a parallel path. Each sky rockets and then fizzles, with Danny eventually blinded in the ring through foul play. Along the way their relationship is shattered. Their friend Googi meets an untimely end while attempting to avenge Danny's loss of sight. Only Eddie emerges triumphant, to champion their collective desires through his "Symphony of New York," a musical piece which is enthusiastically embraced by the very citizens who are the inspiration for his composition.

Critics reacted with different perspectives of the film. Bosley Crowther of *The New York Times* wrote, "To folks who vision New York in strictly tabloid terms, we can heartily recommend this compendium of life's little tragedies."[4] Conversely, M.M. of *The Daily Worker* found the picture to be an unwelcome rehash of familiar film themes. "The slum kids, the gangster, the prizefighter, the dancer, the musician, the truck driver, all hamburged by Warner's grinding cameras in the past, have here been mixed into a sticky paste and labeled 'The Symphony of a Great City,' New York."[5] William Boehnel of *New York World-Telegram* looked past the picture's many frills to find the plain wrapper beneath. "For all its salty flavor, bright lights, smell of resin, crisp and pungent dialogue," he wrote, "*City for Conquest* is only middling-fair fun."[6]

Cagney had high expectations for the picture, but they never quite materialized. The film was originally to be directed by his friend Raoul Walsh, but Anatole Litvak, whom he detested, was ultimately given the post. Cagney, and his brother William, an associate producer on the picture, were also unhappy with Wexler's adaptation and had it rewritten with the assistance of Robert Rossen, the writer who would later pen the screen version of *Body and Soul*. Still, the results were not what they had envisioned.[7] Many years later Cagney would tell Hedda Hopper that the picture "was alright, but it didn't represent the effort we all made."[8]

Despite mixed reviews and Cagney's unfulfilled expectations, *City for Conquest* still plays as an enjoyable piece of entertainment. The on-screen performance of Cagney justifies his personal efforts and the making of the picture itself. Archer Winsten of the *New York Post* wrote that Cagney gave a "stunning performance."[9] "One of his greatest contributions to the screen," noted Kate Cameron of *The New York Daily News*.[10] William Boehnel of *The New York World-Telegram* was in agreement dubbing Cagney's portrayal "among the best" of the actor's distinguished career.[11] Strong supporting efforts by a star-studded cast also served to complement Cagney's superlative work.

To prepare for the picture's fight scenes Cagney engaged the services of Harvey Perry, who had also trained him and acted as his sparring partner for *Winner Take All* and *The Irish in Us*. The 43-year-old Cagney rose at 5:30 A.M., doing ten miles of road work as part of his training program. This included shadow-boxing, wrestling and a limited diet which all helped him to achieve the best physical condition of his life.[12] In his two previous boxing movies, *Winner Take All* and *The Irish in Us*, Cagney proved that he knew his way around the prize-ring. However, *City for Conquest* is the least appealing due to its average fight choreography, inferior to the boxing vignettes in the other films.

Nevertheless, *City for Conquest* did serve as a breeding ground for fight film figures. While the movie marked the end of Jimmy Cagney's fight picture run, it spawned several others. Elia Kazan, featured in one of his rare appearances in front of the cameras, would later go on to direct Marlon Brando as an ex-pug turned reluctant activist in *On the Waterfront*.

Fellow newcomers Arthur Kennedy and Anthony Quinn, who both showed great promise in *City for Conquest*, were cast the following year by Warner Brothers in *Knockout*, a "B" picture based upon the Rupert Hughes novel, *The Patent Leather Kid*. The story was first brought to the screen by First National Pictures during the silent era under its original name, with Richard Barthelmess in the starring role.

In *Knockout*, Kennedy portrays a fighter who jeopardizes the love of his wife for the excesses of ring success, while Quinn plays his conniving and self-interested manager. Kennedy, who is far from being a physical specimen, is just passable as a "B" film leather-pusher and is more believably cast outside the ring. As the fighter's sensitive brother in *City for Conquest* Kennedy shined. Later he would achieve an even greater success as Kirk Douglas's crippled sibling in *Champion*. Likewise, Anthony Quinn went on to more impressive boxing film roles. Depicting rogues in both *City for Conquest* and *Knockout*, he would later display his full range of acting talent, movingly portraying the slow-witted but sensitive character of Mountain Rivera in *Requiem for a Heavyweight*.

1. John McCabe, *Cagney* (New York: Albert A. Knopf, 1997), 28–9.
2. *Ibid.*, 30.
3. *Ibid.*, 191.
4. Bosley Crowther, Review of *City for Conquest* (Warner Bros. movie), *New York Times*, 28 September 1940.
5. M.M. "Tabloid View in Film 'City for Conquest,'" Review of *City for Conquest* (Warner Bros. movie), *Daily Worker*, 28 September 1940.
6. William Boehnel, "City for Conquest Presents Jimmy Cagney at His Best." Review of *City for Conquest* (Warner Bros. movie). *New York World-Telegram*, 28 September 1940.
7. McCabe, *Cagney*, 24–25.
8. Patrick McGilligan, *Cagney: The Actor As Auteur* (New York: Da Capo Press, Inc., 1975), 82.
9. Archer Winsten, "'City for Conquest' Opens at the Strand." Review of *City for Conquest* (Warner Bros. movie), *New York Post*, 28 September 1940.
10. Kate Cameron, "'City for Conquest' Has Dramatic Punch," Review of *City for Conquest* (Warner Bros. movie), *New York Daily News*, 28 September 1940.
11. Boehnel, "Jimmy Cagney at His Best."
12. McCabe, *Cagney*, 193.

City Lights (1931)

United Artists, Comedy, B & W, 81 minutes

Producer: Charles Chaplin (Unaccredited). *Director*: Charles Chaplin. *Screenplay*: Charles Chaplin (Unaccredited). *Film Editor*: Charles Chaplin (Unaccredited). *Cinematography*: Gordon Pollock, Roland Totheroh.

Virginia Cherrill (Blind Flower Girl), Florence Lee (Her Grandmother), Harry Myers (An Eccentric Millionaire), Allan Garcia (His Butler), Hank Mann (A Boxer), Charles Chaplin (A Tramp).

Much of the genius of Charlie Chaplin was his ability to perceive the comedic potential in all aspects of life. As early as 1914, Chaplin's first year of filmmaking, the pantomime artist had already identified boxing as a valuable vehicle for his artistic exploits, and the sport quickly became a theme for several of his short features.

In 1914, Chaplin directed and starred in a short entitled *Mabel's Married Life*. In the film Chaplin purchases a life-size boxing dummy to provide his wife with protection from a wolf. While drunk, Chaplin mistakes the dummy for a real person and attempts to fight it. In comic fashion, Chaplin loses the encounter.[1] That same year, Chaplin starred with Fatty Arbuckle in a Keystone production produced and directed by Mack Sennett, entitled *The Knockout*, which also featured a slapstick boxing sequence.[2] The following year, Chaplin directed himself in another boxing short entitled *The Champion*, in which Chaplin utilizes a horseshoe and later a dog to help fight his way to the title.[3]

By the late 1920s, Chaplin had established himself as one of America's premier feature-film comedians. In March of 1928 he began production on *City Lights*, a comedy romance in pantomime. A wave of talking motion pictures were released that year, and Chaplin, aware of the shifting public tastes, temporarily halted production of his silent film to consider the use of sound.[4] However, Chaplin had pledged that his "little tramp" character would never utter the spoken word. True to his promise, he completed the film in its original silent format despite the inherent financial and professional risks.[5] "To talk," Chaplin theorized regarding the consequences, "he would have to step off his pedestal, the pedestal of the silent film."[6]

City Lights is a simple film with a simple premise which expertly blends comedy and pathos. Chaplin, in the guise of his little tramp character, falls in love with a blind girl, who mistakenly believes that he is wealthy. He illegally obtains money to prevent her eviction and pay for an operation to cure her blindness, and winds up in prison. At the close of the picture, the little disheveled tramp, recently released from jail, returns to the girl who is no longer blind. In spite of her expectation of wealth and his actual lowly station in life, she lovingly welcomes the little tramp's return.

The film opened in New York on February 6, 1931, and although the "silents" had become passé, the film succeeded wonderfully.[7] In the review of the picture, at the time of its original release, the critic for *Time* magazine recognized the timeless nature of Chaplin, writing that he "will be doing business after talkies are traded in for television."[8] Indeed, decades after the film's release, it is still heralded as a film classic. After viewing the picture at a 1950 revival, critic Richard Watts Jr., writing for the *New York Post*, succinctly summarized the picture: "This film is a delight and a joy, no matter how you look at it. It is hilarious, it is imaginative, it is strangely touching, it has wonderful freshness and vitality, and the little fellow playing the lead role is nothing short of a comic genius."[9] In 1976, the critic for *1000 Eyes Magazine* stated that *City Lights* "is probably the most significant comedy ever made."[10]

Boxing takes center stage in *City Lights* when the little tramp enters the ring to earn money to pay the blind girl's rent. Chaplin's ring pantomime is a more developed version of sequences which he already used in *The Knockout* and *The Champion*. After viewing the film during one of its many re-releases in 1950, the critic for *Time* magazine complimented Chaplin's boxing vignette, writing that "in another sequence beautifully timed and sustained, he turns a prizefight into a uproarious ballet in which he and his murderous opponent dance briskly around a dancing referee."[11] In another memorable scene the little tramp somehow manages to get a rope attached to the ring bell caught around his neck. Rounds now begin and end with each dramatic move across the canvas.

Yet for all of Chaplin's gift for slapstick, some of the more priceless boxing-related humor occurs more subtly. In an intelligent bit which exploits role reversal, Chaplin is found carrying his own bucket into the ring and holding the ring ropes open for his handlers. In another scene set in the dressing room, the little tramp bats his eyes and girlishly shrugs his shoulders in an attempt to defuse his hardened opponent. His adversary becomes wary of his coyish expressions, and to be on the safe side ducks behind a curtain when he has to change into his fighting trunks. It is Chaplin's expansive range — from exaggerated falls to the canvas to the most subtle of glances from a ringside stool — which make his performance so captivating.

In Hollywood, Chaplin attended the opening of *City Lights* accompanied by Albert Einstein. "Oh, he seemed to enjoy it very much," Chaplin said, explaining his famous companion's reaction to his latest work. "He roared like a boy."[12] Apparently, the world renowned scientist was also a pretty astute film critic.

1. Harvey Marc Zucker and Lawrence J. Babich, *Sports Films: A Complete Reference* (Jefferson, N.C.: McFarland & Company, Inc., 1987), 110.
2. *Ibid.*, 103.
3. *Ibid.*, 70–71.
4. *1000 Eyes Magazine*, January 1976.
5. Richard Sarris, *Village Voice*, 5 December 1963, 16.
6. *Ibid.*
7. *1000 Eyes Magazine*, January 1976.
8. *Time*, 9 February 1931, as quoted in "Hardy Perennial," *Time*, 17 April 1950, 105.
9. Richard Watts, Jr., "Some Applause for Charlie Chaplin," *Sunday New York Post*, 30 April 1950, sec. M, p. 4.
10. *1000 Eyes Magazine*, January 1976.
11. "Hardy Perennial," *Time*, 17 April 1950, 105.
12. "Charlie Chaplin Comes to Town," *New York Sun*, April 1950.

City of Bad Men (1953)

Twentieth Century Fox, Western, Color, 82 minutes

Producer: Leonard Goldstein. *Director*: Harmon Jones. *Screenplay*: George W. George, George F. Slavin. *Film Editor*: George A. Gittens. *Photography*: Charles G. Clarke. *Music*: Lionel Newman.

Jeanne Crain (Linda Culligan), Dale Robertson (Brett Stanton), Richard Boone (John Ringo), Lloyd Bridges (Gar Stanton), Dale Robertson (Brett Stanton), Jean Crane (Linda), Carl Betz (Phil Ryan), Carole Mathews (Cynthia London), Whitfield Connor (Jim London), Hugh Sanders (Sheriff Gifford), Rodolfo Acosta (Mendoza), Pascual Garcia Penn (Pig), Harry Carter (Jack), Robert Adler (Barney), John Doucette (Cinch), Alan Dexter (Flint), Don Haggerty (Thrailkill), Leo V. Gordon (Russell), Gil Perkins (Bob Fitzsimmons), John Day (James Corbett), James Best (Gig), Richard Cutting (Mr. Davis), Douglas Evans (William Brady), Kit Carson (Deputy), Tom Mcdonough (Deputy Tex), Charles B. Smith (Henry), Harry Hines (Stewpot), Jane Easton (Singer in Saloon), Anthony Jochim (Blister), Leo Curley (Harry Wade), George Selk (Old Timer George Melford), Charles Tannen (Cashier), Gordon Nelson (Doctor).

In 1894, heavyweight champion James J. Corbett became motion pictures' first contractual actor performing before Thomas Edison's Kinescope machine in a boxing exhibition with fellow heavyweight Peter Courtney.[1] Several years later, top contender Bob Fitzsimmons made his own entry into the film industry when he boxed another contender named Peter Maher.

Edison was hired by promoter Dan Stuart to film the Fitzsimmons-Maher bout as well. Fitzsimmons, however, had inked his deal with Stuart prior to Edison's engagement and was miffed that the promoter had made the motion picture arrangements to his financial exclusion. Not to be outflanked by Stuart, "Ruby Rob" dispatched Maher in 95 seconds—before the Kinescope could get rolling—depriving Stuart of his monetary windfall![2]

Despite the Fitzsimmons-Maher fiasco, the Kinescope company maintained its interest in the fight game, as did Dan Stuart. Stuart offered $15,000 in purse money for the right to promote the long-awaited Fitzsimmons-Corbett bout. This time, Fitzsimmons, now more seasoned in affairs of business, secured a third of the fee provided by the Kinescope company as additional payment for his services.[3]

The James J. Corbett-Bob Fitzsimmons St. Patrick's Day clash of 1897 for the heavyweight championship of the world became the first boxing match in history to be preserved on film for public display. The bout was photographed by Enoch J. Rector on 38mm film, which was used in the Vertiscope, an innovative machine especially designed to shoot outdoors. All of the preliminaries as well as the 14 rounds in which Corbett and Fitzsimmons engaged one another were recorded.[4]

Over time, portions of the old nitrate

film disintegrated jeopardizing the film segment in which Fitzsimmons delivers his title-winning solar plexus blow to Corbett. The sequence has since been salvaged by reassembling bits of the fragmented frames, and luckily the famed blow is now preserved on video, albeit in a somewhat jerky form.

With Corbett and Fitzsimmons's fight a milestone of the budding film industry, it was fitting for Twentieth Century Fox to make a motion picture that centered around their match, although the chosen story vehicle is somewhat offbeat. *City of Bad Men* is a standard Western picture with the expected gunslinger and romantic rivalries, but with the unique setting of Carson City, Nevada, on the eve of a heavyweight championship bout.

In *City of Bad Men*, Ringo (Boone), Gar Stanton (Bridges), his brother Brett (Robertson), and Thrailkill (Haggerty), are a quartet of unsavory characters who converge upon Carson City. A rivalry between Ringo's faction and that of Thrailkill threatens the town's stability and the staging of the fight itself, forcing Sheriff Gifford (Sanders) to orchestrate a temporary truce with the help of Brett. Brett's assistance, however, is self-motivated. His goal is to allow the fight to proceed so that he can hijack the estimated $100,000 in gate receipts while the fight is in progress.

On the eve of the bout, Brett's ex-lover Linda (Crane) agrees to a reconciliation, prompting Brett to call off the robbery. Nevertheless, Ringo and Gar proceed with the heist, forcing Brett at gunpoint to facilitate entry to the box office. Ringo, Gar and company then flee to Fitzsimmons's (Perkins) training camp where Ringo betrays Gar by putting a bullet in his back.

Brett and a posse pursue Ringo. Brett ultimately wins a final shootout with Ringo, who lies dead on the training ring's canvas, as a bullet-riddled heavy bag swings in the foreground with sand pouring from its holes. Motivated by sibling rivalry, Gar, with his last breath, unsuccessfully tries to kill Brett. A rehabilitated Brett finally returns to Linda amid the celebration of Fitzsimmons's victory.

To recreate the arena at Carson City, Nevada, Twentieth Century Fox's research department relied on old newspaper etchings, historical society files, and photographs. A few men who actually attended the fight were also found to assist with recreating relevant detail. For example, the ring's unusual construction featured eight padded posts rather than the modern four unpadded corners.[5] While numerous details were carefully attended to in an effort to recreate the feel of the turn-of-the-century site, the keen boxing historian will note a number of inaccuracies, principal among them the fighters' ring attire. Both the fight film and still photographs show that Fitzsimmons and Corbett wore unusually short boxing trunks. In fact, Corbett's were so short that a large portion of his derrière was revealed. In the movie, however, both Fitzsimmons and Corbett wear more modest attire.

Details notwithstanding, the premise of the film itself is largely fictitious. As described by Bosley Crowther of *The New York Times*, the picture is "a slight reinforcement of sporting history, to be taken with a large-sized grain of salt."[6] Case in point is a scene featuring the Corbett-Fitzsimmons match in which a gang of pistol-packing *hombres* are shown swaggering throughout the arena. In reality, promoter Stuart hired the famed Bat Masterson and his cronies to collect all firearms and knives from the fight spectators, as was the common practice at early prizefights staged out West.[7]

The picture also detours from realism in fashioning its characters. Noting the readily visible element of caricature embedded in the film's principals, Bosley Crowther of *The New York Times* wrote, "Dale Robertson as the bandit is just a shade too immaculate and refined, and Lloyd Bridges as his wicked brother is just a trifle too sneaky and mean. Jeanne Crain as the hero's one-time sweetheart is just a whisper too noble and pure, and Richard Boone as another of the bandits is entirely too much of a cur."[8]

Two of the film's less stereotypical characters were the boxers. To portray James J. Corbett and Bob Fitzsimmons, the studio cast John Day, who had already portrayed a boxer in Stanley Kubrick's *Champion*, and Gil Perkins, a stuntman with a proclivity for a row. Perkins had previously staged the classic fisticuffs between John Wayne and Randolph Scott in *The Spoilers*.

Perkins's bald palette and lean but muscular physique helped make him an excellent "Ruby Rob." Day's build did not quite measure up to Corbett's, but his facial type was appropriate enough. To prepare for their roles, Day and Perkins trained for several months at the well-known Frankie Van's gym.[9] Both actors perform admirably in the ring, though the boxing scenes are fairly brief and limited to the championship bout itself. Otis Guernsey of the *New York Herald-Tribune* lamented that the picture did not possess more boxing scenes, writing, "The trouble is that you miss most of the heavyweight fight while the hero takes on the villains under the stands and across the countryside."[10] In fact, Fitzsimmons's knockout of Corbett is not even reenacted. After the film's Western showdown is completed, the scene cuts to a triumphant Fitzsimmons being carried off on the shoulders of his handlers.

As advertisement for the film the studio urged their distributing theaters to arrange for their local boxing club to establish a boxing tournament to award one or more "Fitzsimmons-Corbett Memorial Trophies" to the winners of the competition.[11] A treasured prize no doubt, at least for those with grandpas old enough to tell them the tale of Corbett and Fitzsimmons.

1. *The Heavyweights*, "The Stylists," Produced by Ross Greenburg, 57 minutes, HBO Sports in Association with Big Fights, Inc., 1990, videocassette.
2. Gilbert Odd, *The Fighting Blacksmith: The Story of Bob Fitzsimmons* (London: Pelham Books, 1976), 117.
3. *Ibid.*, 135.
4. *Ibid.*, 147.
5. "World Championship Fight Is Restaged For 'Bad Men,'" Twentieth Century-Fox Exhibitors Campaign Book.
6. Bosley Crowther, Review of *City of Bad Men* (Twentieth Century-Fox movie), *New York Times*, 21 October 1953.
7. Odd, *The Fighting Blacksmith*, 139.
8. Crowther.
9. Twentieth Century-Fox Exhibitors Campaign Book.
10. Otis Guernsey Jr., Review of *City of Bad Men* (Twentieth Century-Fox movie), *New York Herald-Tribune*, 21 October 1953.
11. Twentieth Century-Fox Exhibitors Campaign Book.

Conflict (1936)

Universal, Drama, B & W, 60 minutes

Producer: Trem Carr. *Director*: David Howard. *Screenplay*: Charles Logue and Walter Weems, based upon the story *The Abysmal Brute* by Jack London. *Editor*: Jack Ogilvie. *Cinematography*: A.J. Stout.

John Wayne (Pat), Jean Rogers (Maude), Tommy Bupp (Tommy), Eddie Borden (Spider), Frank Sheridan (Sam), Ward Bond (Carrigan), Margaret Mann (Ma Blake), Harry Wood (Kelly), Bryant Washburn (City Editor), Fran Hagney (Malone).

Best remembered for penning *The Call of the Wild*, Jack London and his diverse literary genius also spawned several boxing stories. "I would rather be Heavyweight Champion of the world ... than King of England, or President of the United States, or Kaiser of Germany," the writer proudly pronounced. London boxed nearly every day of his life. He also loved to spar, and did so on occasion with former heavyweight champion Bob Fitzsimmons, whom London met while "Ruby Rob" was on theatrical tour. London even wrote Fitzsimmons a one-act play about a boxer entitled *The Intruder* that was performed by the former champ under various titles in San Francisco, London and New York.[1]

In addition to Fitzsimmons's vaudevillian sketch, London penned two boxing short stories: *A Piece of Steak* and *The Mexican*,* along with two full length boxing novels: *The Game* and *The Abysmal Brute*. Heavyweight champion Gene Tunney would later cite *The Game* as a major influence in his decision to retire in 1928. "I was determined not to let 'The Game' beat me," Tunney said.[2] Many years later, Tunney advised Rocky Marciano to read the book, and he felt that it hastened Marciano's ring retirement as well.[3]

London's words had a broad social impact reaching far beyond the intimate circle of heavyweight champions. After Jack Johnson defeated Tommy Burns for the heavyweight championship in Australia, it was London who led the hue and cry for the white race to mobilize to regain the coveted heavyweight crown. Writing for the *New York Herald*, London pleaded with former heavyweight champion James J. Jeffries to come out of retirement. "But one thing now remains. Jim Jeffries must now emerge from his alfalfa farm and remove that golden smile from Jack Johnson's face. Jeff, it's up to you. The White man must be rescued."[4] The emotional impact of London's words acted as a verbal siren, setting in motion the Johnson-Jeffries encounter at Reno — one of the nation's most relevant social events of the early century.

In 1923, Universal Pictures released the silent film version of London's *The Abysmal Brute*, directed by Hobart Henley and starring Reginald Denny, Mabel Julienne Scott and Hayden Stevenson. Many of London's characters for the story where based upon real-life figures of the fight game including world champions Battling Nelson, Kid McCoy, and Philadelphia Jack O'Brien.[5]

In 1936, the studio revamped the London tale for John Wayne by placing the action in the great Northwest and changing the yarn's title to *Conflict*. At this juncture in his career, Wayne was nothing more than a prolific actor of the "B" Western. However, Wayne had recently been offered an eight picture contract with Universal to star in non-western action pictures, and he eagerly signed with the studio.[6] It would be another three years before Wayne catapulted himself to movie stardom in John Ford's classic *Stagecoach*.

Filmed against the background of the Sierra Mountains of California, 900 miles from Hollywood, *Conflict* is the story of a con man named Pat (Wayne) who travels from town to town with a group of tricksters.[7] The troupe's *modus operandi* is to fix prize-fights and then capitalize on their own side bets.

At a lumber camp in Cedar City, Pat serves as the advance man for the group's next fixed fight. He ingratiates himself with the locals and establishes a reputation as a stand-up citizen who is handy with his fists. After he builds a strong constituency who will back him with their dollars, a match is fabricated. The intention is for Pat to lose the bout, providing monetary gain for the swindlers, but causing the financial ruin of Pat's new supporters.

Before the match occurs, Pat befriends a young boy named Tommy (Bupp) whom

---

In 1952, Universal studios brought The Mexican *to the screen under the title of* The Fighter. *Richard Conte was cast in the lead as a boxer. The supporting cast also featured Lee J. Cobb, who had previously appeared in* Golden Boy, *and Frank Silvera, who would soon feature in Kubrick's fight story* Killer's Kiss. *H.H. of* The New York Times *wrote: "The Fighter, yesterday's United Artists release at the Mayfair, is one of those disturbing misfires, an altogether respectable film that seldom realizes its potentialities." Five years after* The Fighter *hit American movie theaters, Russia's Artkino Pictures released* The Mexican *in the United States, yet another film version of the Jack London story.*

he saves from drowning, and falls in love with a female reporter named Maude (Rodgers). Unable to betray Tommy, Maude, and his new friends, Pat attempts to withdraw from the match. However, when rumors persist that Pat is a phony, he decides to attempt to win the fight to prove himself worthy of Tommy and Maude's affections.

Aware of Pat's change of heart, his opponent Carrigan (Bond) enters the ring with loaded gloves. The match eventually goes off on the level, with Pat scoring a triumphant knockout. Redemption completed, Pat is reunited with Maude and Tommy.

Described as a "a simple little package of sentimentalism" by Dorothy Masters of the *New York Daily News*, *Conflict* exploited the usual melodramatic plot stratagems.[8] "One of the oldest of all the formulas," the critic for the *New York Post* wrote.[9] As with many of Wayne's other Universal collaborations with director Trem Carr, the picture was churned out in a 5-7 day shooting schedule.[10] Even with the London story as its foundation, *Conflict* was given "assembly line treatment."[11] Given these production circumstances it was not surprising that G.M.C. of the *Brooklyn Eagle* wrote that the "direction, acting and production place this in the "C" class."[12] Wayne himself expressed disappointment with Carr, who may have brought his "B" Western mentality to the set.[13] Nevertheless, Bland Johaneson of *The Daily Mirror* found several admirable aspects of the picture, writing that it is "packed with fights and action, is played by an able company, snappily directed, generously sprinkled with comedy relief."[14]

Wayne himself received mixed notices. *The Brooklyn Eagle* was not particularly impressed describing him as "manly and inarticulate as usual," but Dorothy Masters saw an appealing quality in the future star, rhetorically asking why "the movie cameras haven't been seeing more of John Wayne."[15]

Working with Wayne in the film was the great character actor Ward Bond, who would become a life long friend of the Duke. The rapport between the pair seemed to translate well in the film, prompting Edga of *Variety* to write that "the mugg slapping between Wayne and Ward Bond, who puts plenty of give into a subsidiary role, look like the McCoy."[16] There was more truth to Edga's comment than the critic may have realized. In one particular scene the script called for Bond to slug his pal. Six times the pair rehearsed the blow. Each time Bond connected, Wayne rolled with the punch. However, on the final take, Bond connected forcefully, dropping Wayne to his knees. Rising quickly the Duke reprimanded his friend. "Call your shots," Wayne said in his famous drawl.[17]

During the mid–1930s, Wayne still possessed the athletic physique he developed as a football star at U.S.C. He proves an acceptable pugilist and it is something of a treat to see him punching someone out without a cowboy hat on his head. The choreography of the fight sequences, however, leaves something to be desired. The bouts possess an amateurish element and some of the close-up action looks particularly fake, although Wayne is not to be faulted. One brief training sequence shows Wayne hitting the speed bag, and while those more rugged viewers may not want to admit it, Robert Taylor proved better at the task in *The Crowd Roars*.

Consistent with Wayne's macho image, the Duke could on occasion be spotted in the crowd at a major fight. In 1959, Wayne sat at ringside for the first Floyd Patterson-Ingemar Johannson contest. The sponsor of the event was Wayne's new film, *The Horse Soldiers*. Co-starring William Holden of *Golden Boy* fame, the United Artists movie was also the first motion picture to sponsor a championship boxing match. The accompanying radio broadcast of the fight ran advertisements for the John Ford picture during the respites of Les Kiner's blow-by-blow call.

In the third round Johannson hit Patterson with a thunderous right hand punch depositing the champion on the canvas. As recalled by Patterson many years later, coming out of a daze the champ found himself gazing into the eyes of none other than the Duke himself, who was sitting at the edge of the ring apron next to Howard Cosell. Just moments after he locked eyes with Wayne, the ten count was administered to Patterson, and on cue the radio broadcast eerily cut to a prerecorded message. "This is John Wayne," the voice began, "I'm glad you were with us on the biggest fight of the year. I'd just like to add that you'll find *The Horse Soldiers* charged with just as much excitement as this evening—be sure to see it, won't you?"[18]

1. Russ Kingman, introduction to *Jack London: Stories of Boxing*, edited by James Bankes (Dubuque, Iowa: Wm. C. Brown Publishers, 1992), p. 7–9.
2. *Ibid.* 7.
3. James Bankes, *Jack London: Stories of Boxing* (Dubuque, Iowa: Wm. C. Brown Publishers, 1992), 5.
4. Randy Roberts, *Papa Jack: Jack Johnson and the Era of White Hopes* (New York: The Free Press, 1983), 68.
5. Bankes, *Jack London: Stories of Boxing*, 38.
6. George Carpozi, Jr., *John Wayne Story* (Westport Ct.: Arlington House, 1979), 74.
7. "*Conflict* Opening." Current Publicity for *Conflict*.
8. Dorothy Masters, "Jack London Film Is Dated But Appealing," Review of *Conflict* (Universal Pictures movie), *New York Daily News*, 18 January 1937.
9. Review of *Conflict* (Universal Pictures movie), *New York Post*, 18 January 1937.
10. Donald Shepherd, Robert Slatzer with Dave Grayson, *Duke: The Life and Times of John Wayne* (Garden City, N.Y.: D-Day and Company, 1985), 131.
11. *Ibid.*
12. G.M.C. Review of *Conflict* (Universal Pictures movie), *Brooklyn Daily Eagle*, 5 or 8 February, 1937.
13. Shepherd, *The Life and Times*, 131.
14. Bland Johaneson, Review of *Conflict* (Universal Pictures movie), *The Daily Mirror*, 19 January 1937.
15. G.M.C.; Masters, "Jack London Film."
16. Edga, Review of *Conflict* (Universal Pictures movie), *Variety*, 27 January 1937.
17. "Call Your Shots," Current Publicity for *Conflict*.
18. Original ABC Radio Broadcast of the Floyd Patterson-Ingemar Johannson heavyweight championship bout aired 26 June, 1959.

The Contender (1944)

PRC, Drama, B & W, 63 or 66 minutes

Producer: Bert Sternbauch. *Director*: Sam Newfield. *Screenplay*: George Sayre, Jay Doten, Raymond Schrock from the original by George Sayre and Jay Doten. *Film Editor*: Holbrook N. Todd. *Photography*: Robert Cline. *Music*: Albert Glasser. *Technical Fight Advisor*: Art Lasky.

Buster Crabbe (Gary Farrell), Arline Judge (Linda), Julie Gibson (Rita), Donald Mayo (Mickey Farrell), Glenn Strange (Biff), Milton Kibbee (Pop Turner), Roland Drew (Kip), Commandant (Sam Flint), Duke York (Bomber), George Turner (Sparky).

With the exception of the occasional professional baseball player or prizefighter, it was actually the amateur athlete who drew the admiration of the American public during film's formative years. A swimmer named Johnny Weismuller, for example, garnered five gold medals at the 1928 Olympic games at Amsterdam and then parlayed them into a successful movie career.[1]

Indeed, Weismuller was not the only product of the Amsterdam games to later make his mark on Hollywood. A six foot, three inch all-American football star from Washington University named Herman Brix won the shot-put championship at the very same competition and soon found himself on the screen as well.[2] Still another aquatic star named Buster Crabbe also competed at Amsterdam. He later won a gold medal at the 1932 games at Los Angeles in the 400 meter freestyle event to help solidify a motion picture career of his own.[3] Together, these three Olympians helped pioneer the phenomenon of athlete-turning-thespian that is still in existence today.

Principally due to their sculptured physiques, the trio of actors found themselves in direct competition for the same role. When MGM's Irving Thalberg obtained exclusive film rights to Edgar Rice Burroughs's *Tarzan the Apeman*, Douglas Fairbanks, Sr. suggested to director W.S. Van Dyke that Brix be cast in the title role. Brix, however, thwarted the possibility when he broke his shoulder while shooting *Touchdown*. Johnny Weismuller was taking up lodging in the same hotel as Cyril Hume, the scenarist for *Tarzan the Apeman*.[4] As a result, Weismuller tested for the role, winning the part over Buster Crabbe, who also auditioned.[5] Intimating that MGM had miscast the part, Crabbe made his film debut as "Lionman" in *King of the Jungle*, a competing Paramount production which was *Tarzan*-inspired.[6]

Undaunted by the shoulder injury, several years later, the virile form of Herman Brix found its way to a "B" boxing film entitled *Flying Fists* (1937). While Johnny Weismuller refrained from trading in his leopard-spotted loincloth for a Taylor foul proof cup, Buster Crabbe followed the lead of fellow Olympian Brix, entering the squared circle in a "B" boxing film of his own entitled *The Contender*.

In *The Contender*, Crabbe portrays Gary, a truck driver who enters a boxing tournament to earn money to pay his adoring son's (Mayo) military school tuition. Fight manager Kip Morgan (Drew), observes Gary winning the tourney and signs him to a contract. Kip's woman, a man-eater named Rita (Gibson), also thinks Gary is an attractive find, though on a more personal level. A newspaper woman named Linda Martin finds the heavyweight equally engaging, and Gary reciprocates her interest.

Linda uses her paper's publicity to advance Gary's career, eventually securing him a shot against a contender. Rita competes with Linda for Gary's affections, with Rita's seductive ways initially winning out over Linda's genuine nature.

Gary becomes a contender, but his increasingly cavalier and self-indulging attitude leads to the neglect of his son. The fighter is subsequently suspended for a mounting alcohol problem and frustration leads him to strike his boy. Deeply remorseful, the boxer attempts to make amends by going on the road and fighting under an alias to raise money to keep Mickey in school. The fighter, now washed-up, is ultimately rescued by Mickey and Morgan, who offer their forgiveness, and Linda who offers her hand in marriage.

Variety's movie critic described the film as "a homily built around the threadbare theme of a rising pug" and a "rehash of most pugilistic fables," which while "not a contender," was "O.K. for duels."[7]

The Contender is replete with fight sequences and training scenes and makes a solid effort to maintain its "fight picture" status. Technical assistance for the fight vignettes was provided by Art Lasky, a heavyweight contender who is best remembered for losing a fifteen round decision to James J. Braddock just two months prior to Braddock upsetting Max Baer for the heavyweight crown in 1935. Unfortunately, low production values do nothing to enhance the realism of the fight scenes, and the critic for *Variety* accurately observed that "clips from actual fights" were "awkwardly inserted into the continuity" of the picture.[8]

Dorothy Masters of the *New York Daily News* rated Crabbe as "creditable" in the role, and the critic for *Variety* found him "O.K. as the vacillating pug," but his performance, at least in the ring, is partially assailable.[9] While the six foot, one inch, 188 pound actor utilized his barrel chest and muscular legs to exhibit enough natural athleticism to impersonate the amateur boxer found at the beginning of the film and the fighter in decline scripted for film's end, he is not so convincing when asked to reproduce the ring finesse of a contender for the heavyweight crown.

While *The Contender* has long since been forgotten by all but the film historian, many continue to hold fond childhood memories of Crabbe's enduring portrayals of Flash Gordon and Buck Rogers.

1. Thomas G. Aylesworth and John S. Bowman, *The World Almanac Who's Who of Film* (New York: Bison Books Corporation, 1987), 106.
2. Gabe Essoe, *Tarzan of the Movies: A Pictorial History of More than Fifty Years of Edgar Rice-Burroughs' Legendary Hero* (New York: The Citadel Press, 1968) 67.
3. Aylesworth and Bowman, *Who's Who of Film*, 106.
4. Essoe, *Tarzan of the Movies*, 67.
5. Ibid., 87.
6. Ibid., 78.
7. Review of *The Contender* (PRC movie), *Variety*, 19 July 1944.
8. Review of *The Contender* (PRC movie), *Variety*, 19 July 1944.
9. Dorothy Masters, "Boxing and Western Films for New York," Review of *The Contender* (PRC movie), *New York Daily News*, 12 July 1944.

The Crowd Roars (1938)

Metro-Goldwyn Mayer, Drama, B & W, 92 minutes

Producer: Sam Zimbalist. *Director*: Richard Thorpe. *Screenplay*: from a screenplay by Thomas Lennon, George Bruce and George Oppenheimer, based on a story by George Bruce. *Film Editor*: Conrad A Nervic. *Photography*: John Seitz. *Music*: Edward Ward.

Robert Taylor (Tommy McCoy), Edward Arnold (Carson, alias Jim Cain), Frank Morgan (Brian McCoy), Maureen O'Sullivan (Sheila Carson), William Gargan (Johnny Martin), Lionel Stander ("Happy" Lane), Jane Wyman (Vivian), Nat Pendelton ("Pug" Walsh), Charles D. Brown (Bill Thorne), Gene Reynolds (Tommy McCoy — as a boy), Donald Barry (Pete Mariola), Donald Douglas (Murry), Isabel Jewel (Mrs. Martin), J. Farrell McDonald (Father Ryan).

One of the few leading men of his era to rival Clark Gable in his appeal to the opposite sex, Robert Taylor forged a film reputation as a romantic lead. Desiring to expand Taylor's horizons and strengthen his draw with male movie-goers, MGM tested Taylor in his first rugged part in *A Yank at Oxford*.[1] While the movie fared well, Taylor's film audiences were still conditioned to his exclusively romantic persona.

MGM, however, was pleased with Taylor in his first robust role and as a follow-up, they daringly cast him as a boxer in *The Crowd Roars*. The picture presented Taylor with a dual challenge. Not only would he have to transform his body into that of a prizefighter, but he would also have to convince movie-goers to accept his usually suave temperament and extraordinarily handsome visage as pugnacious.

The Crowd Roars was loosely based upon the real-life friendship of Joe Salas and Jackie Fields, two schoolmates from Los Angeles who fought their way onto the 1924 United States Olympic boxing team as the country's featherweight representatives. After each won five consecutive matches at the Games, the pals were matched against one another in the finals, with Fields winning the World's Olympic Championship.[2]

In *The Crowd Roars*, Tommy McCoy (portrayed by Reynolds as a boy) is the son of a lazy ex-vaudevillian (Morgan). He is discovered by the light-heavyweight champion Tommy Martin (Gargan) and taken on tour, where he sings and learns to box. Later McCoy (Taylor) becomes a contender and is forced to box his friend to make money to cover his father's gambling debts.

When the pair meet, McCoy scores a knockout and Martin tragically dies. Tommy, who is dubbed "Killer McCoy" by the press, becomes depressed and leaves the fight game. However, he is seduced back by a promoter named Cain (Arnold). Cain endeavors to protect his daughter Sheila (O'Sullivan) from the sordid fight world, but she nevertheless embarks on a secret romance with McCoy.

Gamblers detain Sheila and McCoy's father as insurance that McCoy will throw his title opportunity. The elder McCoy momentarily turns the tables on his captors, and Sheila escapes. Sheila's freedom allows McCoy to fight in earnest and win the title. The new champion then takes Sheila as his bride, but Mr. McCoy, who was killed by the kidnappers, only attends the nuptials in spirit.

The Crowd Roars embraces some of the most over-used plot stratagems in the boxing film genre. The fighter's dad drinks and is irresponsible. There is a clandestine romance to avoid the woman's disapproving father, and there are gangsters, gambling and the fixed fight. Despite the reliance on these predictable vehicles, the film is pleasant and the acting keeps the story interesting. MGM strikes a fine balance in their top-flight cast. Supporting Taylor are Edward Arnold and Frank Morgan, two accomplished veterans; sure-fire character players like Lionel Stander; and Maureen O'Sullivan and Jane Wyman, two budding ingenues.

While Taylor could boast of a three-year friendship with former heavyweight champion Max Baer, his only previous fighting experience was, according to the star, as a kid in Nebraska who got "his face rubbed in the dirt regularly."[3] To improve on his less than auspicious fistic origins, Taylor converted his personal ranch into a boxing training camp, erecting a ring near his horse stables. Under the keen eye of fight choreographer and former boxer John Indrisano, Taylor began his training with a two-week mini-camp where he labored six or seven hours a day.[4]

Typical workouts included a five-mile run, rope skipping and workouts on the light and heavy bags. To learn actual ring technique, Taylor boxed in the squared circle with two seasoned professionals, Patsy Perroni and Jock McVoy.[5] The film's star, who only weighed between 155 and 160 pounds prior to the movie, also embarked on a vigorous weight training program, which concentrated on arm and chest development. By production, Taylor was a light heavyweight, carrying 174 pounds on his six-foot frame.[6]

As the pugilist, Taylor is nimble on his feet and offers a nice facsimile of Gene Tunney's backpedaling ability. Taylor also displays a pair of fast hands and unlike most actors who try to box, he hold his hands up high, a skill which he no doubt learned from practicing on the speed bag. In the ring, Taylor delivers a climactic knockout in the blistering final round of the picture's final fight. Outside of the ring, Taylor carries himself with the confidence of a prize athlete.

Most critics bought the Taylor transformation. Critic Jack Pearl felt Taylor successfully emerged from Indrisano's cocoon, writing "his role as a boxer is played to perfection."[7] Flin of *Variety* found his portrayal a "convincing portrait of a young fighter."[8] Eileen Creelman of *The New York Sun* and Bland Johaneson of the *New York Daily Mirror* were also persuaded, respectively writing that Taylor "carries off his role well," and that his performance is "very good."[9]

Despite ample evidence of the actor's metamorphosis, at least one critic still found Taylor trapped by his previous moonlight kisses. Chiding the movie's star, B.R.C. of *The New York Times* wrote, "If you can visualize Robert Taylor as a prize-fighter known as Killer McCoy, you won't find it hard to accept the other fictional premises of *The Crowd Roars*."[10] Howard Barnes of the *New York Herald-Tribune* recognized Taylor's new brand of masculinity, but did not believe it translated into good boxing cinema. "If you are keenly interested in just how virile he can be, you will be intrigued. If you are looking for a genuinely entertaining prizefight picture, you are likely to be disappointed."[11]

Commenting on his role in *The Crowd Roars* many years later, Taylor said, "I only wish I had made it a year or so before I did. Then when I played romantic stuff, they would have remembered my flying fists and there'd have been less nonsense in the press."[12]

In the match against Johnny Martin, more than 20,000 square feet of floor space was utilized to create one of the largest sound stages ever. To view the shoot of the scene, such boxing notables as Abe "Newsboy" Brown, Abdullah Abbis and Larry Williams attended.[13]

In the film's final bout, in which Taylor engages a character portrayed by Patsy Perroni, a former Joe Louis opponent, over 800 extras were utilized on the set, which simulated New York's Madison Square Garden.* Brief footage of the Garden itself is edited into the picture to add flavor. During the shoot of round seven of the fight, the timekeeper neglected to ring the bell, resulting in Taylor receiving an additional two minutes of leather from Perroni.[14]

Former world champions Maxie Rosenbloom and Jimmy McLarnin make the briefest of cameo appearances in a gym. The film also captures a rare visual of famed radio broadcaster Clem McCarthy, who announced many of boxing greatest fights, including the first Joe Louis — Max Schmeling bout in which "Herr Max" pulled off a monumental upset, handing Louis his first professional loss. Howard Barnes of the *New York Herald-Tribune* wrote that McCarthy, who provided the blow-by-blow description for three matches in the film, "adds enormous conviction and excitement to the climax" of the film's final bout.[15]

Only nine years later MGM remade *The Crowd Roars*, retitling it *Killer McCoy*. The picture was directed by Roy Rowland and starred Mickey Rooney, one of the studio's biggest box office draws of the 1940s, who was starring in his first adult role. Stalwart heavy Brian Donlevy drew the role of scheming Jim Cain, James Dunn portrayed the fighter's boozing father, and Sam Levene played Rooney's trainer.

Although Frederick Hazlitt Brennan fashioned a new screenplay, *Killer McCoy* is a near duplication of *The Crowd Roars* in both plot and dialogue. Most critics were pleased with the remade film, which also did well at the box-office, grossing over $2 million domestically.[16]

Of the film's star, Tom Pryor of *The New York Times* wrote, "Mickey Rooney is in there punching now ... and whatever one may think of him as a prizefighter, he is a wonderful little actor."[17] Predisposition might lead one to dismiss Rooney in the role of a pug, but he actually does fairly well. True, Rooney is particularly small, but one only needs to believe that he is 135 pounds.

In the ring, Rooney has a tendency to paw a bit with the jab and only poke with his left hook, but when the script calls for him to fight aggressively, as in the last round of the final match, the actor is more than adequate in creating a whirlwind attack. Rooney's fine acting also assists him in emoting a cocky, no nonsense attitude, adding to his credibility as a fighter. Early in the film Rooney does a soft-shoe dance to *Swanee River* with James Dunn. It is a shame that the picture did not integrate more of Rooney's natural nimbleness and spectacular footwork into his boxing role.

1. Patricia King Hanson, *The American Film Institute Catalog of Motion Pictures Produced in the United States, Volume F3, Feature Films, 1931–1940* (Berkeley: University of California Press, 1993), Film Entries A-L, 432.

2. John V. Grombach, *The Saga of the Fist* (Cranbury, N.J.: A.S. Barnes and Company, 1977), 144–145.

3. Lawrence J. Quirk, *The Films of Robert Taylor* (Secaucus: Citadel Press, 1975), 69; "Too Skinny When He Made His 1st Screen Test, Taylor Now

---

Perroni lost a ten round decision to Joe Louis on January 4, 1935, in Detroit in Louis's thirteenth professional match.

Tips Scales at 174!" Exhibitor's Service Sheet for *The Crowd Roars*.

4. *Ibid*.

5. "Taylor Battles with Three Experts in Too Tough Role." Exhibitor's Service Sheet for *The Crowd Roars*.

6. "Too Skinny When He Made His 1st Screen Test," Exhibitor's Service Sheet for *The Crowd Roars*.

7. Jack Pearl, Review of *The Crowd Roars* (MGM movie).

8. Flin, Review of *The Crowd Roars* (MGM movie), *Variety*, 3 August 1938.

9. Eileen Creelman, Review of *The Crowd Roars* (MGM movie), *New York Sun*, 5 August 1938; Bland Johaneson, Review of *The Crowd Roars* (MGM movie), *New York Daily Mirror*, 5 August 1938.

10. B.R.C. Review of *The Crowd Roars* (MGM movie), *New York Times*, 5 August 1938.

11. Howard Barnes, Review of *The Crowd Roars* (MGM movie), *New York Herald-Tribune*, 5 August 1938.

12. Quirk, *The Films of Robert Taylor*, 69.

13. Regina Crewe, *New York-American*, 7 August 1938.

14. "Robert Taylor Gets a Two-Minute Beating That Wasn't in the Script." Exhibitor's Service Sheet for *The Crowd Roars*.

15. Barnes, Review of *The Crowd Roars*.

16. Arthur Marx, *The Nine Lives of Mickey Rooney* (New York: Stein and Day, 1986), 149.

17. Tom Pryor, *New York Times*, as quoted in Arthur Marx, *The Nine Lives of Mickey Rooney*, 149.

Dempsey (1983)

Made for television, Bio-Drama, Color, 150 minutes

Producer: Lawrence Turman, Martin Ritt. *Director*: Gus Trikonis. *Screenplay*: Edward Dilorenzo. *Cinematography*: Sol Negrin, Ric Waite. *Music*: Billy Goldenberg.

Treat Williams (Jack Dempsey), Sam Waterston ("Doc" Kearns), Sally Kellerman (Maxine Kates), Victoria Tennant (Estelle Taylor), Peter Mark Richman ("Tex" Rickard), Jesse Vint (Bernie Dempsey), Robert Harper (Damon Runyon), John Mcliam (Hyrum Dempsey), Bonnie Bartlett (Celia Dempsey), James Noble (Gavin McNab).

A product of the "Golden Age of Sport," along with Babe Ruth, Red Grange, Bobby Jones, and Bill Tilden, Jack Dempsey was one of modern America's first sports heroes. The only athlete of his era to rival Babe Ruth in both popularity and historical significance, he was voted by the Sports Writers of America as the greatest athlete of the first-half of the twentieth-century.

Several heavyweight champions preceding Dempsey, including John L. Sullivan, James J. Corbett, Bob Fitzsimmons and Jack Johnson, had used the title as a springboard to the entertainment world and stage acting. The "Manassa Mauler" was another in a continuing tradition.

Dempsey distinguished himself among boxer-thespian's by becoming the very first heavyweight champion to regularly feature in motion pictures. Soon after winning the title in 1919, his services were secured by Fred C. Quimby of Pathe in New York. Pathe contracted to pay Dempsey $50,000 down and 50 percent of the gross to appear in a 15-episode series entitled *DareDevil Jack*. In the serial, Dempsey portrayed a sports star, who used his fists to assist the story's heroine played by Josie Sedwick.[1]

However, before the serial was completed, Dempsey was accused in the press of being a war slacker, and the serial was shelved. On February 27, 1920, the champ was indicted by a federal grand jury for "unlawfully, willfully, knowingly, and feloniously evading and attempting to evade the draft." The highly publicized "Slacker Trial" concluded on June 15, 1920, with a verdict of "not guilty."[2] With the ruin of the champion's film career having been averted, the serial was completed and released for public screening. Dempsey went on to appear in several feature length films including *All*

Good Marines, which also featured James J. Corbett, and *The Prizefighter and the Lady*.

Dempsey's station in the pantheon of American sport almost guaranteed that his own story would reach the screen. During the 1930s, filmmakers had a brush with the Dempsey legend, but only in the form of short subjects. In 1932, an 18 minute independent production entitled *Dempsey Returns* was released, outlining Dempsey's career from his title winning effort against Willard to his pair of losses to Gene Tunney. Four years later, a 22 minute documentary called *The Idol of Millions* was produced, surveying the champ up until the opening of his famous Broadway restaurant.[3] Despite the fact that Dempsey's life was the embodiment of a Horatio Alger tale, it was an incredible one-half century after his retirement before the entertainment industry finally dedicated a feature length film to his life. The belated tribute to the hero of the Roaring Twenties, simply entitled *Dempsey*, was a made-for-television film, originally aired by CBS.

Dempsey traces the champ's life from his humble beginnings as a Colorado farm boy and his stint in the coal mines and hobo camps of the great West, to his mega fights at the Polo Grounds, and his entree into the fashionable circles of New York and Hollywood.

Woven into Dempsey's rise to fame is the exploration of several of his important personal relationships. Considerable examination is made of his anguished marriage to Maxine who is finely portrayed by Sally Kellerman. Dempsey's later nuptials with silent movie star Estelle Taylor provide the romantic focus in the latter part of the picture.

The story also delves into the champ's roller coaster partnership with his flamboyant manager Jack "Doc" Kearns. Kearns served as Dempsey's surrogate father and the driving force behind his fistic ascension, but was also the source of much of the fighter's personal and professional discontent. These depictions are fairly accurate and hold closely to the Dempsey autobiography upon which the film is based.

Dempsey's "Slacker Trial" is offered appropriate attention and the film also addresses Dempsey's metamorphosis in public perception from rogue to hero. However, the Dempsey-Carpentier match, which featured the real-life French World War I hero against the "draft-dodger" champion, was a natural vehicle to develop the film's recurrent theme concerning the public's dislike of Dempsey. Its omission was a large oversight. The screenwriters also make an unforgivable blunder. During the famous "Battle of the Long Count," Gene Tunney recovers from the storied seventh round knockdown to eventually knock Dempsey down. The film, however, depicts Jack Dempsey going down in the legendary seventh, when in fact, he hit the canvas in the following round.

Dempsey's survey of the champ's ring career includes his second round knockout of Gunboat Smith, the title winning massacre of Jess Willard, his "pier-six brawl" with Luis Angel Firpo, and his two matches with Gene Tunney. The recreation of the Willard match deserves compliment for its strict attention to detail. The fans are decked out in the straw hats and caps of the day. The ring announcer wields a bull horn to introduce the fighters who sport closely cropped haircuts. True to life, while the fighters rest in their corners, they are protected from the blazing Fourth of July sun by giant umbrellas held by their handlers.

To prepare for the role of the Manassa Mauler, Treat Williams worked out for a period of two months. The actor began his training at the 14th Street Gym in New York City under the tutelage of former light-heavyweight champion Jose Torres, and then moved on to Los Angeles where he trained under the eye of fabled trainer Al Silvani, who also had a cameo in *Dempsey* as one of Tunney's corner men. The actor also spent hours studying film footage of Dempsey in action.[4]

Williams, who appeared in such musicals as *Grease* and *The Pirates of Penzance*, was a former Broadway dancer. He felt that his dance background helped him with his boxing footwork, but he admitted there was much more to learn for the part. "I had to learn Dempsey's style, his crouch, the way he tucked his head into his shoulder and how he used his powerful left hook," the actor explained.[5] The final product was a good imitation of Dempsey's bobbing and weaving style.

Production for the Dempsey-Willard fight took two days, and the bouts with Gene Tunney required a total of four. In one of the fight sequences, Williams did not hear the bell to begin fighting; however, his opponent did, knocking the film's star cold. "It was an unpleasant sensation," Williams would later note.[6]

Critic Judy Flanders of the *New York Daily News* hit Williams just as hard, reviewing his portrayal of Dempsey as "a flat performance that doesn't give a clue to the inner man."[7] This criticism is unjustifiably harsh, though in truth one does walk away from the film knowing Maxine and "Doc" Kearns better than then they do the champ. Flanders also wrote that "the movie is stylishly put together, but it's sluggish and empty."[8] With similar irreverence Tom Jory of the *New York Post* opined that "for all of its gloved heroics, *Dempsey* ... is a curiously punchless drama."[9]

Admittedly, *Dempsey* delivers neither drama, nor an insightful study of his psyche. It does, however, provide an entertaining chronicle of his remarkable life, along with a vivid reenactment of his ring exploits, both of which should draw favorable reviews from fight fans.

1. *Dempsey*, produced by Lawrence Turman, directed by Gus Trikonis, 150 minutes.
2. Jack Dempsey and Barbara Piatelli Dempsey, *Dempsey* (New York: Harper and Row Publishers, 1977), 116–119, 122.
3. *Ibid*.
4. Harvey Marc Zucker and Lawrence J. Babich, *Sports Films: A Complete Reference* (Jefferson, NC: McFarland and Company, Inc., Publishers, 1987), 263.
5. Kay Gardella, "A Dempsey Treat," Review of *Dempsey* (CBS television movie), *New York Daily News*, 23 September 1983, 74.
6. *Ibid*.
7. Judy Flanders, "TV Choices," Review of *Dempsey* (CBS television movie), *New York Daily News*, 28 September 1983, 61.
8. *Ibid*.
9. Tom Jory, "Dempsey Film Doesn't Pack Enough Punch," Review of *Dempsey* (CBS Television movie), *New York Post*, 28 September 1983, 82.

Diggstown (1992)

Metro-Goldwyn Mayer, Drama, Color, 97 Minutes

Producer: Robert Schaffel. *Director*: Michael Ritchie. *Screenplay*: Steven Mckay, based on the novel *The Diggstown Ringers* by Leonard Wise. *Film Editor*: Don Zimmerman. *Director Of Photography*: Gerry Fisher. *Music*: James Newton Howard.

James Woods (Gabe Caine), Louis Gossett Jr. ("Honey" Roy Palmer), Bruce Dern (John Gillon), Oliver Platt (Fitz), Heather Graham (Emily Forrester), Randall "Tex" Cobb (Wolf Forrester), Thomas Wilson Brown (Robby Gillon), Duane Davis (Hambone Busby), Willie Green (Hammerhead Hagen), Orestes Matacena (Victor Corsini), Kim Robillard (Sheriff Stennis), John Short (Corney "Buster" Robbins), Michael Mcgrady (Frank Mangrum), Roger Hewlett (Sam Lester), Rocky Pepeli (Buck Holland), Jeff Benson (Tank Miller), James Caviezel (Billy Hargrove), Frank Collison (Prison Guard), Marshall Bell (Warden Bates), Raymond Turner (Slim Busby), Wilhelm Von Homburg (Charles Macum Diggs), George D. Wallace (Bob Ferris), John Walter Davis (Chet Willis), Alex Garcia (Minoso Torres), Cyndi James Gossett (Mary Palmer), Kenneth White (Ben Culver),

David Fresco (Fish), Benny Urquidez (Referee), Jeremy Roberts (Sonny), Michael Delorenzo (Paulo), Troy A. Smith, Larry Ham (Betting Guards), David Candreva (Coach), Jose Alcala, Victor Kollacos (Boxing Kids), Nelly Bly (Emily's Friend), Laura Mae Tate (Marcy), Kevin La Rosa (Helicopter Pilot).

MGM studios was taking something of a risk in casting the 55-year-old Louis Gossett Jr. in the role of a prizefighter. Unquestionably, the native of Brooklyn sported a fine acting dossier. Gossett had proven his ability to engage in his Emmy-award-winning performance as "Fiddler" in *Roots*, and displayed an unequal command in his Oscar-winning role in *An Officer and a Gentleman*. Now, *Diggstown* would test less subtle physical abilities. To portray the lead of "Honey Boy" Roy Palmer, not only would Gossett be required to box, but he would also have to be credible as a man with extraordinary stamina, as the script required that he engage as many as ten men in the ring in a single evening.*

More problematic for the six foot, four inch actor, was the fact that he had recently ballooned to 242 pounds for his recent film *The Punisher*. "I did a Robert De Niro," Gossett commented comparing his weight change to De Niro's portrayal of Jake La Motta in *Raging Bull*.[1] De Niro, however, underwent his enormous weight fluctuation by gaining weight after having already played his fight scenes in fighting trim. Gossett faced the reverse, and perhaps more difficult challenge, which required that he lose his excess weight added for *The Punisher*, and then further refine his physique to reach the condition of a boxer. To achieve his goal, Gossett ate five to seven small meals a day, until he melted off between 35-40 pounds. Supplementing his diet was a vigorous four-month, six-day-a-week training program, including boxing workouts which ultimately reached 15 rounds per day of ring work.[2]

Diggstown is boxing's version of *The Sting*. James Woods (Kane) is a con man who uses his connection to a fighter (Randall "Tex" Cobb) to set in motion a multi-million dollar ring scam. Kane agitates Diggstown's fight promoter and most influential figure, John Gillon (Dern) into betting a substantial sum that Kane's boxer "Honey Boy" Roy Palmer (Gossett, Jr.) cannot last three rounds each with any ten Diggstown boxers of Gillon's choosing. The challenge for Kane is that the bet is made without having secured the services of Palmer. Despite harboring prior feelings of discontent, Palmer can not resist rejoining his old partner, and the contest proceeds. Gillon, who also fancies himself a hustler, goes head to head with Kane in an attempt to gain any possible advantage, including many outside the rules. The opposing brain trusts play a game of one-upmanship where a clever dupe is often outdone by a more devious double-cross. Kane proves the better duper and with the assistance of Honey Boy's gutty ring performance, the pair win their bet and bankrupt Gillon.

While *Variety* reported that the picture, with its $17 million production and advertising budget, was one of the biggest financial disasters during the regime of studio head Alan Ladd, the picture itself stood on firmer critical ground.[3] The *Daily News* wrote that "*Diggstown* may not arrive at local bijous with 'Summer Blockbuster' stamped all over it, but it's a lot more fun than many that have."[4] Audrey Farolino of the *New York Post* observed the film as "Gritty yet breezy ... If not exactly new, [it] is surprisingly fun and appealing."[5] "It's one sucker punch after another," wrote David Ansen of *Newsweek*, "but you'd have to be a rock not to fall for it."[6]

A great deal of the dialogue was improvised amongst the cast members, the leading players receiving recognition for

---

The concept behind Diggstown *has a bona fide precedent. On April 26, 1975, ex-heavyweight champion George Foreman consecutively engaged five professional boxers in three round exhibitions. The final three opponents only lasted two rounds apiece. Foreman's opponents were, in order, Charlie Polite, Boone Kirkman, Terry Daniels, Jerry Judge, and Alonzo Johnson.*

their fine work. Vincent Canby of *The New York Times* wrote that the film was "acted with immense style."[7] "As Gossett supplies the film's heart, Woods and Dern provide the flash and dazzle." The *Los Angeles Times* credited Woods for his "live-wire gall," Gossett for his "burning equanimity," and Dern for his "edgy intensity."[8]

Because there are an unusual number of fight scenes in the picture, director Michael Ritchie strove for diversity to keep the plot lively. "Some of the fights are fixed, some are counter fixed, so each fight had a way of appearing different to the audience," noted Ritchie. "Some are played for comedy, some for ballet, some are downright slugfests."[9] To create his potpourri of fight scenes, Ritchie utilized the talents of Bobby Bass and James Nickerson, who fashioned the memorable boxing vignettes in *Raging Bull*. Adding to the realism fostered by the pair of choreographers was the casting of several professional boxers, including one-time contender Alex Garcia, former Dallas Cowboy defensive end turned fighter, Ed "Too Tall" Jones, and Rocky Pepeli and Randall "Tex" Cobb, both of whom boxed Larry Holmes. Michael Wilmington of the *Los Angeles Times* credited "the big fight" for being "the movie's raison d'être."[10] *Variety* accurately summed up the boxing content of the film reporting that "the boxing scenes are compelling," noting that "Gossett convincingly comes across as an aging brawler with a potent right cross."[11]

1. Martin Borden, "Gossett's Film a Real Workout," Review of *Diggstown* (MGM movie) *New York Post*, 12 August 1992.
2. *Ibid*.
3. *Variety*, 31 August 1992, p.99.
4. "Phantom of the Movies," Review of *Diggstown* (MGM movie), *New York Daily News*, 14 August 1992.
5. Audrey Farolino, Review of *Diggstown* (MGM movie), *New York Post*, 14 August 1992, 29.
6. David Ansen, Review of *Diggstown* (MGM movie), *Newsweek*, 17 August 1992, 52.
7. Vincent Canby, Review of *Diggstown* (MGM movie), *New York Times*, 14 August 1992.
8. Michael Wilmington, Review of *Diggstown* (MGM movie), *Los Angeles Times*, 14 August 1992, 10.
9. Bob Thomas, *New York Daily News*, 16 August 1992.
10. Wilmington, 10.
11. Bob Lowry, Review of *Diggstown* (MGM movie), *Variety*, 3 August 1992.

Don King: Only in America (1997)

Television Movie (HBO), Bio-Drama, Color, 112 minutes

Executive Producer: Thomas Carter. *Producer*: David Blocker. *Director*: John Herzfeld. *Screenplay*: Kario Salem, based upon the book by Jack Newfield. *Film Editor*: Steven Cohen, A.C.E. *Director of Photography*: Bill Butler, A.S.C. *Music*: Anthony Marinelli.

Ving Rhames (Don King), Vondie Curtis Hall (Lloyd Price), Jeremy Piven (Hank Schwartz), Darius Mccrary (Muhammad Ali), Keith David (Herbert Muhammad), Gabriel Casseus (Jeremiah Shabazz), Loretta Devine (Connie Harper), Brent Jennings (Dick Sadler), Lahmard Tate (Carl King), Danny Johnson (Larry Holmes), Bernie Mac (Bundini Brown), Donzaleigh Abernathy (Henrietta King), Lou Rawls (Harold Logan), Teddy Atlas (Ritchie Giachetti), Jarrod Bunch (George Foreman), Ron Leibman (Harry Shondor), Don Elbaum (Himself), Sarah Scott Davis (Diane Holmes), Michael Gilio (Tony Panzarella), Ken Lerner (Bob Arum), Simon Templeman (Keith Bradshaw), Jennifer Griffin (Notary Public), Brad Garrett (Assassin), Fofo Lukata (Mobutu), Kurt Andon (Lou), Ntare Mwine (Emissary), Loni-Kaye Harkless (Mrs. Jackson), David Kirkwood (Mr. Jackson), Robby Robinson (Sam Garrett), Tanisher Sornson (Fetisher), James Black (Ernie Shavers), Detective Bob Tonne (Himself), K.J. Penthouse (Charles Wepner), Jim A. Douglas (Autograph Seeker), Michael Bowen (Boxing Spectator), Michael

Blanks (Buster Douglas), Israel Cole (Joe Frazier), Clifford Couser (Mike Tyson), Everton Davis (Evander Holyfield), King Ikpitan (Tony Tucker), Kevin Grevioux (Leon Spinks), Carlos Monroe (James "Bonecrusher" Smith), Denorvell "Dee" Collier (Pinklon Thomas), Alan Woolf (Scram), Jack Newfield (Reporter in Zaire).

Detractors have looked upon Don King as greedy, manipulative and disingenuous to the core. Meanwhile, his supporters have labeled him a self-made man and resonant voice for the advancement of African-Americans. If King's persona were a portrait it would be the *Mona Lisa*, so sharply contrasting are the interpretations it elicits. Street-urchin and corporate executive alike have learned that King's bombast and preacher-like rhetoric masks an excessively bright and shrewd adversary. *Don King: Only in America* is an exploration of the flamboyant and glib product of the ghetto who waltzed out of prison and two-stepped his way into the world of pin-striped suits and Harvard lawyers en route to becoming the world's foremost boxing promoter.

Author Jack Newfield, who penned the promoter's well-documented but unauthorized biography of the same name, provides the basis for the film offering a subjective and critical version of King's life. The countervailing argument is provided by the film's screenwriters on King's behalf.

Don King: Only in America cleverly expresses the two irreconcilable perspectives by using the traditional chronological narrative form to tell Newfield's tale, then periodically cutting away to scenes of King's proponent, Ving Rhames, vigorously refuting Newfield's version from the center of a boxing ring. Rhames, in a black tuxedo and clasping a cigar within his broad grin, alternatively beseeches and admonishes his unseen audience to see his version of the truth.

Parts of the screen adaptation that are rooted in Newfield's biography depict King as a self-interested manipulator who transfers his immoral code formulated on the streets of Cleveland to the offices of corporate America. In contrast, King's periodic rebuttals from ring center adopt the posture formulated and embraced by King in real life: King is portrayed as a victim of white oppression and poverty, who nevertheless transcends persecution to be counted among the country's greatest patriots.

Through the film's Jekyll and Hyde-like presentation, the often sordid events of King's life are parceled to the audience, who are left with the challenge of separating fact from fiction. As a loan shark, King is shown stomping and pistol-whipping a customer half his size to death. "Self-defense," King exclaims.[1] King's alleged connections with the Cleveland Mafia and its role in the promotion of the Ali-Wepner fight are also depicted, but summarily dismissed by King, who refuses to dignify the allegations with a response.

King is portrayed as playing the race card to court favor with the likes of Ali, Foreman, and Shavers, only to abruptly abandon each of them after they have served his financial needs. The promoter is also shown catering to Christian, Jew, and Islamic alike — but only when doing so offers personal reward. "I made everyone money," King says, rationalizing his uniformly consistent mistreatment of his counterparts.[2]

Don King: Only in America is a thoughtfully packaged and entertainingly played biography of, perhaps, the greatest showman the world has produced since P.T. Barnum. Casting Ving Rhames to portray King proved nothing short of genius. He is "competent and convincing" and "a dead ringer for King in his garrulous glory," wrote James C. Harris of the *New York Amsterdam News*.[3]

To prepare for his role, Rhames spent three days at King's mansion, went to a number of King's fights, and interviewed dozens of individuals.[4] The actor swallowed King's street-smarts, endowed himself with the promoter's boundless energy and desire, and utilized a few choice malapropisms to create a grotesquely charming and compelling character of multiple dimensions. Like an emotional hurricane, Rhames's promoter pours with defiance, howls in justification, and whistles with humor. Critics found Rhames's portrayal and the film's colorful and witty script to be the picture's most endearing qualities. "The story, as portrayed by Ving Rhames, is a marvelous verisumultsousness simulation of the real thing ... [it] hits all the high points," wrote Marvin Kitman of *Newsday*.[5]

Kitman also accurately observed that "the script is filled with pearls."[6] In one scene, King is found sitting at a Parisian café thanking his waitress in French. "Merceybou-cou," King says, before giving her the once over and turning to the camera to add, "and a nice booty, too." In another scene King meets with members of the Nation of Islam. "Salaham-Alakeem," they greet one another. "Salami and Bacon" the promoter adds, so as not to be excluded. "HBO, I made you mother-fuckers a fortune," King bellows at the film's conclusion, "you ain't making no movie about Bob Arum, now are you?"[7]

The boxing sequences in the film are sparingly used with effect to help enhance the character study of the film's subject. Still, they are in and of themselves acceptably choreographed. Marvin Kitman wrote, "The film has great fight scenes, which look real, but must have been electronically enhanced."[8] Ray Richmond of *Variety* found them to be of "Rocky-esque" variety, "with every punch appearing to carry knockout power."[9]

Despite the film's unique construct to provide an opportunity to present an even-handed portrayal of the promotional impresario, the movie nevertheless sets a prosecutorial tone. Don King claimed that HBO made the picture in retaliation. He had severed ties with the network and moved to Showtime after unsuccessfully demanding to have Larry Merchant removed from announcing matches that he promoted.

King denounced the script as "full of blasphemy and lies," bemoaning that Hollywood was trying to crucify him.[10] Producer John Herzfeld, however, met with Ali, Foreman, and Holmes in an attempt to maintain accuracy. Herzfeld also claimed that King himself contributed detail to the opening scene of the film.[11] When HBO aired the film in the same time slot as Showtime's replay of King's promotion of the Evander Holyfield-Michael Moorer bout, King bellowed to his spokesman Mike Marley, "I'm competing against myself! Only in America."[12]

1. *Don King: Only in America*, produced by David Blocker, directed by John Herzfeld, 112 minutes, 1997.
2. *Ibid.*
3. James C. Harris, *New York Amsterdam News*, 4 December 1997, 52.
4. Scott Williams, "Ving — Rhames with ring and 'King,'" *New York Daily News*, 12 January 1997, 74.
5. Marvin Kitman, "King of Big Words and Hair Is Subject of HBO Bio-pic," Review of *Don King: Only in America* (HBO Television movie). *Newsday*, 12 November 1997, sec. B, p. 31.
6. *Ibid.*
7. *Don King: Only in America*, produced by David Blocker, directed by John Herzfeld, 112 minutes, 1997.
8. Williams, "Ving," 31.
9. Ray Richmond, Review of *Don King: Only in America* (HBO television movie), *Variety*, 10–16 1997.
10. Richard Sandomir, "HBO's Movie on King has Promoter Jabbing," *New York Times*, 14 November 1997, sec. C, 5.
11. Marcus Baram, "He Spars No Effort," *New York Daily News*, 12 November 1997, 14.
12. Sandomir, "King Has Promoter Jabbing," 5.

Eastside, Westside (1927)

Fox Film Corp., Drama, B & W, Silent, 8,144 feet.

Director: Allan Dwan. Based on the novel of Felix Riesenberg. *Photography*: George Webber.

George O'Brien (John Breen), Virginia Valli (Becka), Farrell Macdonald (Pug Malone), Holmes Herbert (Gilbert Van Horn), John Miltern (Gerrit Rantoul), June Collyer (Josephine), Frank Allsworth (Flash).

George O'Brien was groomed for the ring from an early age. As a child, his father tied a pair of boxing gloves around George's wrists and advised, "Don't be afraid to fight if you have to." As a young man, O'Brien followed his father's advice, joining the submarine division of the Pacific Fleet, where he served during World War I, boxing twice a week, and winning the fleet's light-heavyweight championship.[1]

After the war, O'Brien bypassed a career in medicine, and was brought into the Hollywood fold by cowboy Tom Mix. He began at Fox Studios, at $15 per week, where he used his unusual strength to tote around heavy camera equipment. Soon, he was exploiting his roping and riding techniques on the screen as an extra, later graduating to more diverse small roles.[2]

The era of the slim and refined "sheik" actor was on the wane, and the highly muscular and athletic O'Brien was ideally suited for the new lead roles being offered. His breakthrough opportunity was provided by the incomparable John Ford, who cast him in *The Iron Horse*, in a role that required both his athleticism and fighting acumen. Boxing films soon followed.

In 1924, O'Brien starred in a William Fox Production entitled *The Roughneck*. In the film, he portrays a boxer who fears he has killed an opponent in the ring. In an improbable scenario, he flees to an island, where he is reunited with his estranged mother, and meets a love interest portrayed by Billie Dove.[3] The following year, O'Brien was again cast by Fox, this time in John Ford's boxing flick *The Fighting Heart*, which also starred former boxer and future Academy Award winner Victor McLaglen. McLaglen portrays the heavy who whips O'Brien in the ring, but receives his comeuppance from O'Brien in a long street fight. The latter scene may have been the impetus for Ford's revered countryside brawl featured many years later in *The Quiet Man*, which also starred McLaglen.[4] Regarding O'Brien's ring performance in *Fighting Heart*, one critic noted that "his remarkable physique and boxing ability show to great advantage."[5]

Fox again combined the talents of Ford and O'Brien in 1926, in *The Blue Eagle*, the film version of Gerald Beaumont's fine tale, *The Lord's Referee*, also starring Janet Gaynor. No leap of faith was necessary to accept O'Brien's portrayal of George Darcy, a sailor during World War I, who fights the enemy at sea, dope smugglers on land, and his romantic rival with the gloves. Of the climactic fight scene, *Chicago Post* critic Genevieve Harris wrote that it "is one of the fiercest I've ever seen filmed. If you are a fight fan, therefore, I'd advise you to see it."[6]

O'Brien the movie star was becoming synonymous with the squared circle, and he next starred as a fighter in the 1927 comedy "*Is Zat So?*" Former heavyweight champion Jack Dempsey dropped by the Fox set to observe the filming of the picture. After watching O'Brien go several rounds in front of the camera, he told the actor, "Any time you want some excitement, there's a wad of money waiting for you if you climb over the ropes. You sure pack a wallop."[7]

That same year, O'Brien also starred in director Allan Dwan's ambitious project, *Eastside, Westside*, in which a poor Irish boy from an East Side Jewish ghetto in New

York City uses the ring to elevate his position in life. Entering the upper-class world of Park Avenue and the West Side, he becomes an engineer and participates in the building of the great city, ultimately returning to his Jewish girl on the East Side.

O'Brien, who was perpetually fit, was trained for the picture's boxing scenes by former middleweight contender Leo Houck. He utilized the gym at Fox Studios, where he did pulley work, punched the bag, and boxed. Like Dempsey, Houck was impressed with O'Brien's skills and stated, "If George cared to adopt the ring for a profession he'd be champion. He has got everything. He is game as the proverbial pebble.... Fans nowadays demand the real thing in films and some of the fights that O'Brien has in the various pictures he appears in are more grueling than you see in the ring."[8] Heavyweight contender King Solomon also appeared in the film, complementing O'Brien's talents.

While in New York filming *Eastside, Westside*, O'Brien had the opportunity to attend the Vince Dundee-Pete Latzo welterweight championship fight. A true boxing fan, he also offered his own prognostication on the future of Jack Dempsey, who in just two months was to lose his bid for Gene Tunney's title in the famous Battle of the Long Count. "Jack Dempsey is a great friend of mine," noted O'Brien. "He's a smart fellow, but I don't think he will fight again. He's got all the world's goods he wants and he doesn't want to make a mug of himself by not being right when he steps into the ring again against fellows he could have whipped with one hand when he was at the top of his game."[9]

In 1934, O'Brien was boxing in the talkies, and starred opposite May Brian in *Ever Since Eve*.

But the silent film era had already begun to fade, and soon so would George O'Brien, boxing cinema's first body beautiful.

1. George O'Brien, "I Might Have Been an M.D., But—" 8.
2. *Ibid.*
3. Margaret Reid, "George—As He Is," *Picture Play*, May 1929, 112.
4. Harvey Marc Zucker and Lawrence J. Babich, *Sports Films: A Complete Reference* (Jefferson, N.C.: McFarland & Company, Inc., 1987), 128.
5. "Victoria Film 'Fighting Heart,'" Review of *Fighting Heart* (Fox Film Corp. movie).
6. Genevieve Harris, "These Marines Also Knew How To Fight." Review of *The Blue Eagle* (Fox Film Corp. movie), *Chicago Post*, 29 September 1926.
7. "George 'Sure Packs Wallop' Says Jack," *Newark Star Eagle*, 3 June 1927.
8. Barney Levy, "George O'Brien of Screen Might Have Been Star Had He Entered Ring," *New York Enquirer*, 5 June 1927.
9. *Ibid.*

Ex-Champ (1939)

Universal, Drama, B & W, 72 minutes

Producer: Burt Kelly. *Director*: Phil Rosen. *Screenplay*: Adapted by Alex Gottlieb and Edmund L. Hartmann from original by Gordon Kahn. *Film Editor*: Bernard Burton. *Photography*: Elwood Bredell. *Music*: Hans J. Salter, Frank Skinner.

Victor Mclaglen (Gunner Grey), Tom Brown (Bob Hill), Nan Grey (Joan Grey), William Frawley (Mushy Harrington), Constance Moore (Doris Courtney), Donald Briggs (Jeff Grey), Samuel S. Hinds (The Commissioner), Marc Lawrence (Biss Crosley), Thurston Hall (Mr. Courtney), Charles Halton (Tribly).

Choosing Victor McLaglen to portray the ex-champ in its film of the same name was a sound casting decision on the part of Universal Studios. With the vestiges of a once strapping physique, and a square jaw set off by a flattened nose, McLaglen looked the part. Indeed, the winner of the Best Actor Oscar for his performance in *The Informer* was also a former professional boxer. In fact, McLaglen achieved a place in ring lore on March 10, 1909, by boxing the scheduled distance of six rounds against heavyweight champion Jack Johnson.

In *Ex-Champ*, McLaglen portrays Gunner Grey, a former titleholder of the fictional "Tri-State Heavyweight Championship." Gunner trudges through his post-retirement days as a doorman. The ex-fighter has an upwardly mobile son Jeff (Briggs) who is ashamed of his father's blue-collar pedigree. Jeff conceals the existence of his family from his socialite fiancée Doris (Moore) and excludes Gunner from his wedding.

Returning to the fight game, Gunner guides a heavyweight prospect named Bob Hill to championship contention, while Jeff becomes entangled in a speculative and shady stock transaction. Gunner provides cash to cover his son's outstanding stock losses and the gesture serves to mend their relationship. However, to raise the necessary money, Gunner fixes Hill's fight for the welterweight championship and bets against his own charge. Believing that he has executed his plan, which includes putting Hill to sleep with a non-lethal drug, Gunner is filled with remorse. However, through a comedy of errors, Gunner's money is placed on Hill, who unharmed, goes on to win both Gunner's bet and the title.

While the critic for *Variety* found *Ex-Champ* to be "an agreeable and pleasing piece of light entertainment,"[1] Eileen Creelman of *The New York Sun* panned the picture as "a dull, little class C trifle."[2] Admittedly, the film will never be confused with a top-notch ring feature or comedy classic, but today's viewer may find that *Ex-Champ* possesses some simple charms.

William Frawley's portrayal of Gunner's pal Mushy, a tightwad and friendly freeloader, is comfortably reminiscent of the Fred Mertz character he later immortalized in television's *I Love Lucy*. *Variety* recognized Frawley as "effective in a comedy part," as did T.M.P. of *The New York Times* for "striving earnestly to inject a note of comedy into the banal dialogue."[3] No stranger to the boxing scene himself, Frawley was secretary to fight promoter Jack Hurley during 1915 while Hurley was in El Paso promoting the Jack Johnson — Jess Willard heavyweight championship bout. Frawley was also a close friend of former heavyweight champion Jim Corbett, whom he first met as a child in Burlington.[4]

For the dedicated movie fan, McLaglen's signature Cheshire cat-like grin and howling laughter are welcome additions to the film. Clearly McLaglen possessed personality and what Dorothy Masters of the *Daily News* called his "amphibian genius for being as much at ease in sentimental waters as he is on virile ground."[5] However, Universal failed to capitalize on his physical potential, limiting McLaglen's fisticuffs in *Ex-Champ* to a comedic poke to the nose of a drunken barfly.

Although McLaglen's fighting days were long over by the time of the production of *Ex-Champ*, he was still capable of appearing in a boxing ring. The actor continued to work out with the assistance of his personal trainer Abdullah Abbis. The actor met Abbis during World War I, while serving as the Assistant Provost Marshall of Bagdad. Abbiss was not only an ex-boxer, but a skilled physical instructor, expert masseur, and the regular sparring partner of the actor as well.[6] Years later, John Ford utilized the aged but still fit McLaglen in a donnybrook with John Wayne to create arguably the greatest fist fight outside of a ring in film history in *The Quiet Man*.

Far from Ford's masterful work, the fight scenes in *Ex-Champ* are standard fare. The boxing sequences were staged at Hollywood's American Legion Stadium. In addition to the film's star, other ex-boxers appearing included Joe Glick, Art Lasky, Al Bayne, Frankie Dolan, Frank Grandetta, High Loman, and Kid Chissel, former welterweight boxing champ of the 3rd Division of the Pacific Fleet.[7]

While Universal may have been dead-on with McLaglen and his supporting cast of pugnacious extras, some critics lambasted the choice of 26-year-old Tom Brown as the lead prizefighter. "If you can think of anything more ludicrous than Mr. Brown in the role of a pug you are more gifted than Universal's fight experts," quipped the critic for *The New York Times*.[8] *The New York Sun* was equally disdainful: "Tom Brown, looking as soft as only a young Hollywood actor can look, tries to play a welterweight champion. The results are forlorn."[9]*

1. Review of *Ex-Champ* (Universal Pictures movie), *Variety*, 17 May 1939.
2. Eileen Creelman, Review of *Ex-Champ* (Universal Pictures movie), *New York Sun*, 12 May 1939.
3. Review of *Ex-Champ* (Universal Pictures movie), *Variety*, 17 May 1939; T.M.P. "At the Palace," Review of *Ex-Champ* (Universal Pictures movie), *New York Times*, 12 May 1939.
4. "Personal Friend of Corbett," Exhibitors Advertising and Press Campaign for *Gentleman Jim*.
5. Dorothy Masters, "'Ex-Champ' Brings McLaglen to Screen,' " Review of *Ex-Champ* (Universal Pictures movie), *New York Daily News*, 12 May 1939.
6. "Arab Trains McLaglen for Screen Work," Universal Pictures "Publicity" material for *Ex-Champ*.
7. Universal Pictures "Publicity" material for *Ex-Champ*.
8. T.M.P.
9. Creelman.

Fat City (1972)

Columbia Pictures, Drama, Color, 100 minutes

Producer: Ray Stark. *Director*: John Huston. *Screenplay*: Leonard Gardner, adapted from his own novel. *Film Editor*: Walter Thompson. *Photography*: Conrad Hall, A.S.C. *Music Supevision*: Marvin Hamlisch.

Stacy Keach (Tully), Jeff Bridges (Ernie), Susan Tyrrell (Oma), Candy Clark (Faye), Nicholas Colasanto (Ruben), Curtis Cokes (Earl), Art Aragon (Babe), Sixto Rodriguez (Lucero), Billy Walke (Wes), Wayne Mahan (Buford), Ruben Navarro (Fuentes).

Lincoln Heights High School in Los Angeles, California, was an unusually ripe spawning ground for talented boxers. Its most esteemed alumni, Jackie Fields and Fidel LaBarbara, distinguished themselves as world champions, the former in the welterweight division, the latter in the flyweight class. While at Lincoln Heights, a schoolmate of the two future champions named John Huston pursued his own fistic ambitions, which included the middleweight championship.[1]

Huston fought as an amateur at the various fight clubs around the city, occasionally sporting a fictitious name or falsified weight to meet the promoters' needs. "When I put on the gloves, I felt easy and I hit straight," Huston would later recall. "I was so damned skinny I'd feel a beating for several days."[2] Huston's boxing career was brief, but the excitement, camaraderie, and seedy atmosphere of the boxing world made a lasting impression.

As the son of actor Walter Huston it

---

*Perhaps believing that the stinging reviews received by Brown in Born to Fight had faded over time, Republic Pictures cast Tom Brown in another boxing film entitled Duke of Chicago (1949). Released during the same year as such boxing classics as Champion and The Set-Up, Duke of Chicago was a "B" fight picture ripe for being passed on. "It'll give no competition to other prize ring stories now going into release," wrote Brog of Variety. As for Brown's fistic comeback, Variety pegged it as "adequate."

was little surprise that John went on to cultivate an interest in cinema. He eventually embraced fame as the director of such film classics as *The Maltese Falcon* and *The African Queen*. Later, the critically acclaimed *The Misfits* was followed by a decade of unheralded films made during the 1960s — a period in which Huston's genius appeared to be in decline.

Fat City, a novel by Leonard Gardner, surfaced as a rich palette upon which the director would reestablish his mastery. The film's title, which is a jazzman's slang for "having it made" or "being on easy street," is pure irony.[3] Exceedingly stark and gritty, the story is, on the surface, a window into the machinations of small-time boxing. But at its heart, it is a gripping and sometimes painful look at the hapless and hopeless drifters and dreamers trapped within its orbit.

In *Fat City*, Huston depicts the inglorious human condition with all of its decaying hope, fatalistic trappings and numbing realities. The center of the film contrasts dual protagonists. Tully (Keach) is an emotional shell whose near flat-line boxing career is a metaphor for his liquor-driven and degenerating personal life. Munger (Bridges), new to the fight game, possesses youthful vigor and wide-eyed hope and is the reincarnation of Tully's past. Munger's dreams hold palpable expectations of fulfillment, and although Tully's do not, the former's desire acts as a catalyst for the latter to attempt revival of his fading goals. In their parallel pursuit of career success and human intimacy they embody the struggle for survival of the downtrodden and alcoholic. They mirror the search for life's meaning by those confined within the dim bars, dank gyms and soup kitchens of Stockton. By the film's end, Munger's life begins to bear some of the markings of Tully's, and this foreboding of the demise of the film's most promising character drives home Huston's sobering message.

Fat City was a critical success. Following the picture's initial screening at the 1972 Cannes Film Festival, Huston was given one of the press's rare standing ovations.[4] "It's that kind of picture, a classic of its kind, that will defy the passing of years and styles," wrote Archer Winsten of the *New York Post*.[5] "One of those late films by the old masters that looks effortless because they are effortless," observed John Russell Taylor in *Sight and Sound*.[6] "*Fat City* is a moving and compassionate film, not because it pities the losers — it doesn't — but because it hears them," noted Vincent Canby, for *The Sunday New York Times*.[7]

Huston's original choice to portray Billy Tully was Marlon Brando. Brando was undecided about taking the role, so the director opted for Stacy Keach, whom he had seen in *The Traveling Executioner* and felt was "a wonderful talent."[8] Keach portrays Huston's alter ego, emoting a mixture of smoldering desire, burning frustration and wearied acceptance in a provocative performance. Co-star Jeff Bridges was brought into the fold after Huston sized up the young actor while guiding him around the Prado Museum, where the director lectured on art but never mentioned the film.[9] David Leach of *Films in Review* said that Bridges "is better as Keach's boxing buddy than he was last year in Peter Bogdanovich's instant classic *The Last Picture Show*, for which he was supporting actor Oscar-nominated."[10]

Huston held a private screening of *Fat City* for Muhammad Ali, who, according to the director, loved the film. In one scene, a young fighter talks about the need to want to "kick ass" to be successful, prompting Ali to scream aloud, "Hey that's me talking. Listen to me talking. You took that from me. That's my picture."[11] The film was, in fact, inspired by many faces and images from the boxing world. Huston cast many ex-fighters in the picture, some of whom were personal friends, including Curtis Cokes, a former welterweight champion, who believably portrays a non-boxer, and former lightweight contender Art Aragon who realistically plays a corner man.[12] Another ex-contender, Bert Colina, a ghost from Huston's Lincoln Heights days, also materialized.[13] Along with old-timer Bob Dixon and a few others, these former pugilists provided a genuineness that could only be conveyed through their real scar tissue, leathered skin and broken noses.[14]

However, it is Nicholas Colasanto's portrayal of a fight manager/trainer and the dead-on realism of the colloquial gym talk found in Leonard Gardner's script that sets a high mark for boxing film authenticity. In one memorable scene, a fighter's nose is broken and his trunks are splattered with blood. The trunks must be used by another amateur who is to fight the next bout. When the second boxer takes the crimson-stained shorts with an incredulous look, Colasanto blurts out half-reassuringly, "Don't worry about it, it's not your blood."[15]

Former light-heavyweight champion Jose Torres trained both Keach and Bridges for the picture.[16] Bridges proves a whiz on the speed-bag and he mixes in the ring with youthful exuberance and athleticism, notwithstanding a tendency to hold his guard a bit low. Keach emerges unusually natural in the ring. Bending his knees and feinting like a pro, he moves with polished ease. But it is Keach's face that wins the day: a doleful countenance with vacant eyes baring his already extinguished soul, which even victory in the ring cannot resuscitate.

Fat City offers some of the most authentic fight scenes ever put on film. "Huston's camera keeps a remote almost intellectual distance, avoiding *Rocky*-style amplification, and letting the punches land with a wan thud" noted Jim Farber of *Video Review*.[17] The untrained eye might be inclined to dismiss the ring vignettes as anticlimactic or banal, so expertly do they avoid sensationalism. In actuality, the scenes strike an exquisite blend of passive restraint, explosive aggression and uneven discourse. Collectively, these elements reflect the genuine pace and tempo found in the ring which is rarely duplicated on film.

1. Gerald Pratley, *The Cinema of John Huston*, (A.S. Barnes Co., Inc., 1977), 19.
2. *Ibid.*
3. Stuart Kaminsky, *John Huston: Maker of Magic* (New York: Houghton Mifflin, 1978), 190; Richard Natale, "Going Back to Huston," *Women's Wear Daily*, 27 July 1972, 12.
4. John Huston, *An Open Book* (New York: Da Capo Press, 1980), 339.
5. Archer Winsten, Review of *Fat City* (Columbia Pictures movie), *New York Post*, 27 July 1972.
6. John Russell Taylor, *Sight and Sound*.
7. Vincent Canby, "Huston Takes New Look at Life in 'Fat City.'" Review of *Fat City* (Columbia Pictures movie), *New York Times*, 27 July 1972.
8. Kaminsky, *John Huston: Maker of Magic*, 188.
9. Lawrence Grobel, *Taking the Fifth* (New York: Charles Scribner's Sons, 1989), 635.
10. David Leach, Review of *Fat City* (Columbia Pictures movie), *Films in Review*, October 1972, 507.
11. Natale, "Going Back to Huston," 12.
12. Kaminsky, *John Huston: Maker of Magic*, 188.
13. Natale, "Going Back to Huston," 12.
14. Axel Madsen, *John Huston: A Biography* (New York: Doubleday & Company, Inc., 1978), 236.
15. *Fat City*, produced by Ray Stark, directed by John Huston, 97 minutes, Columbia-TriStar Home Entertainment, 2002, videocassette.
16. Grobel, *Taking the Fifth*, 635.
17. Jim Farber, Review of *Fat City* (Columbia Pictures movie), *Video Review*, May 1988, 56.

The Fighter (1952)

United Artists, Drama, B & W, 78 minutes

Producer: Alex Gottlieb. *Director*: Herbert Kline. *Screenplay*: Aben Kandel and Herbert Kline, based upon Jack London's story, "The Mexican." *Film*

Editor: Edward Mann. *Photography*: James Wong Howe. *Music*: Vincente Gomez.

Richard Conte (Filipe Rivera), Vanessa Brown (Kathy), Lee J. Cobb (Durango), Roberta Haynes (Nevis), Frank Silvera (Paulino), Martin Garralaga (Luis), Hugh Sanders (Roberts), Rudolfo Hoyos, Jr. (Col. Alvarado), Claire Carleton (Stella), Argentina Brunetti (Maria), Margarita Padilla (Elba), Paul Fierro (Jose), Rico Alaniz (Carlos), Paul Marion (Rivas), Robert Wells (Tex).

Much too small to fuel a genre or even merit a film niche, the boxing/Western, for lack of a better descriptive term, is by definition an anomaly — a defect that slipped undetected through Hollywood's production line. It's movie miscegenation that only the most ardent fans of boxing or the Western can praise.

Perhaps the boxing film and the Western movie can be likened to ice cream and steak — individually each can be savored, but when consumed together they are bound to upset. As realistically assessed by Chic of *Variety* in his review of *The Fighting Champ*, an early entry of these peculiar products, "Boxing may not interest Western addicts, while ringside followers are apt to turn up their noses at cowboys, nobody being entirely satisfied."[1]

The Fighting Champ (1933) and *Rip Roarin' Buckaroo* (1936), both early offerings of hybrid celluloid, were sagebrush vehicles for Bob Steele and Tom Tyler respectively. One might fashion the argument that the impetus for making these pictures was that the sheer volume of "B" serials, in which each featured, simply drove their scenarists to experimentation. However, both proved to be misadventures, and it is not surprising that for many years thereafter, even the most daring of producers saw fit to leave the hide *on* the cow in one set of movies and as boxing gloves in totally separate offerings!

In 1950, Eagle-Lion, another "B" factory, resuscitated the punching cowboy, this time in glorious color, in a lame attempt to bring the Red Ryder comic strip to life in *The Cowboy and the Prize-Fighter*. Two years later, Universal finally breathed an air of legitimacy into the concept when they brought Jack London's story *The Mexican* to movie theaters, with the superior lens of James Wong Howe focusing on the talents of Richard Conte and Lee J. Cobb.

Based on Jack London's 1911 novel entitled *The Mexican*, *The Fighter* is the story of Mexican patriot Felipe Rivera (Conte). Rivera assists Mexican freedom fighters across the border in El Paso, Texas, who are working to free their imprisoned leader held in Mexico. Back in Mexico, Rivera harbors a rebel general named Durango (Cobb) and facilitates his escape. Rivera's father and fellow villagers become victims of the opposition forces, and Durango is captured. Rivera exacts revenge by freeing Durango, who is being held by his father's murderers. Durango then executes his captors for their prior savagery. Later, Durango makes a plea to Rivera for more weapons to fight the revolution, and Rivera enters the ring to secure the money necessary to purchase them. Motivated by the death of his loved ones and his dedication to the cause, Rivera wins his winner-take-all match and money for the guns needed to win the real fight.

The film was scripted in part by Aben Kandel, who also wrote the boxing novel *City for Conquest*, which was made into a major motion picture starring James Cagney. *The Fighter* was an ambitious attempt to lay down Jack London's tale in under 90 minutes. At times, one feels as if one is watching the Cliff's Notes version of London's saga. Nevertheless, a solid story and cast provide the film with a foundation. H.H.T. of *The New York Times* praised Conte, noting that he "performs with stolid authenticity," and O.L.G. of the *Herald-Tribune* found Lee J. Cobb to have given "a meaty performance."[2]

While Brog of *Variety* felt that the boxing match at the end of the picture "runs much too long," the ten minute sequence is well done and satiates the fight fans who are obliged to wait through the entire film to watch "The Fighter" in action.[3] The film's photographer, two-time Academy Award winner James Wong Howe, was already experienced at shooting fight scenes having filmed the creative vignettes in *Body and Soul* (1947). His unique style of utilizing selected shots of the action from a ringside vantage point, filming up through the ropes, and alternating close-ups and long shots, creates a pleasing cinematic experience for the viewer.

The *New York Herald-Tribune* found the fight scene to possess "a swift savagery," which was presented in "a raw impressionistic style with close-up cuts of punches, almost too fast to see."[4] *The New York Times* also praised the ring action, writing that it "adds up to one of the most graphically exciting screen bouts in years, with the opponents and Mr. Howe's camera ensnarled in a fragmentary masterpiece of which Mr. London would have been proud."[5] Richard Conte, as a boxer, possesses enough of the tough-guy look to carry the role in spite of his somewhat underdeveloped physique.

Maybe the secret to a good boxing/Western is to avoid a traditional Western story line or simply to offer a good underlying story like London's. Whatever the formula, Hollywood seemed to lose interest. The following year, after several decades and a paltry output of only a handful of films, the curious laboratory of quick draws and quick jabs was abruptly closed. The last of its kind was Twentieth Century-Fox's release of *City of Bad Men*, an inventive tale of bandits who attempt to steal the gate receipts of the James J. Corbett-Bob Fitzsimmons heavyweight championship contest.

1. Chic, Review of *The Fighting Champ* (Monogram Pictures movie), *Variety*, 21 March 1933.
2. H.H.T., Review of *The Fighter* (United Artists movie), *New York Times*, 31 May 1952; Otis L. Guerney, Review of *The Fighter* (United Artists movie), *New York Herald-Tribune*, 31 May 1952.
3. Brog, Review of *The Fighter* (United Artists movie), *Variety*, 7 May 1952.
4. Guerney.
5. H.H.T.

Flesh and Blood (1979)

Paramount Television, Drama, Color, 200 minutes

Executive Producer: Gerald W. Abrams. *Producer*: Herbert Hirschman. *Director*: Jud Taylor. *Screenplay*: Eric Bercovici, based on the novel *Flesh and Blood* by Peter Hamil. *Film Editor*: Gerald J. Wilson, A.C.E. *Director Of Photography*: Vilmos Zsigmond. *Music*: Bill Goldenberg.

Tom Berenger (Bobby Fallon), Mitchell Ryan (Jack Fallon), Suzanne Pleshette (Kate Fallon), John Cassavetes (Gus), Kristin Griffith (Michelle), Denzel Washington (Kirk), Bert Remsen (Jorgensen), Anthony Charnota (Freddie), Bob Minor (Walker Lewis), Peter Hobbs (Police Sergeant), Jack Rader (Charlie), Bill Elliott (Young), Sam Weisman (Stevens), Felix Shuman (Gloves Official), Patrick Billingsley (Man in Dressing Room), Eddy Donno (North Referee), Marques D. Houston (Raymond North), Nathan Davis (North Announcer), Ernest Robinson (North Corner), James Andelin (Harding), John Roselius (Solider Bartlett), Leo Ranieri (Bartlett Referee), Joe Rodgers (Reporter), Edward Grennen (Lewis Announcer), Stan Berg (Lewis Referee), Charles Warfield (Curly Anderson), Nathaniel Morgan (Anderson Referee), Al De Rose (Anderson Corner), Luca Josef Bercovici (Bellhop), Van Allen (Doctor), Bob Smith, Tony Quinn, Edwin Jahiel, Clarence Davidson (Ringside Reporters), Paul Napier (Television Producer), Pat Corley (Madison Square Garden Reporter), Mike Evans, Bill Henderson, Paul Tuerpe (Fight Reporters).

Peter Hamil, a notable sports journalist, once described boxing as "the great dark prince of sports ... which exuded the dangerous glamour of the urban night."[1] Hamil would attend fights at the "old" Madison

Square Garden to watch what he interpreted as "violence transformed into art."[2] Despite his predisposition to write what one might call "boxing *noir*," Hamil chose the incestuous relationship between a fighter and his mother as the underlying theme for his boxing novel entitled *Flesh and Blood*.

Several years later, Paramount Television translated *Flesh and Blood* into a lengthy movie that was aired by CBS. In *Flesh and Blood*, Bobby Fallon (Berenger) is a hot-tempered Chicago Irishman who serves time for assault. He does some boxing in prison and after his release he begins to train under a no-nonsense handler named Gus Caputo (Cassavetes).

While Caputo prepares Fallon for the Golden Gloves, Bobby's emotionally dependent relationship with his mother Kate (Pleshette) degenerates into forbidden love. His confusion and guilt manifest themselves in a Golden Gloves match in which he attacks the referee. Bobby is banned for life from the amateur game, so he turns professional.

Bobby briefly dates another woman but then dutifully follows Kate to Las Vegas. In Vegas, Bobby's estranged father surfaces. Fallon Sr. is a former boxer himself, and part of the management team of top contender Walker Lewis. Unsettled by his parents' rekindled relationship, Bobby agrees to box Lewis in exchange for his father's promise to leave Kate. Bobby is defeated by Lewis and Kate stays with Fallon Sr., despite dad's promise to their son. Despondent and lonely, Bobby returns to Gus to continue his boxing career.

Flesh and Blood's subject matter was controversial even for a theatrical release, but to translate the topic to television proved extraordinarily problematic. While Gerald Abrams, the film's executive producer, attempted to fit the oedipal material for the mass medium, the Reverend Donald Wildmon, a Methodist minister from Mississippi, was mobilizing his watchdog group, the National Federation for Decency. The group's members dispatched over 10,000 letters of protest to CBS prior to the film's debut.[3]

Worried network censors buckled in the wake of the mail blitz, and proceeded to edit ten critical seconds from the film. Deleted from the picture was footage showing the mother passionately kissing her son, while she begins to undress and lead him into the bedroom. Abrams felt that the censors had "robbed us of the chance to take viewers where television has never taken them."[4] Critics would later find the compromised version rather unsatisfactory, with Nicholas Yanni of *Cue* writing, "No one expected the movie to follow through on the incest theme, but after such long and careful titillation of the audience, the manner in which the whole issue is skirted/resolved is a real cop-out."[5]

Berenger's line "I love you, Ma," was also cut from the scene, which greatly perturbed author Pete Hamil. For Hamil, the line was instrumental in relating the pair's emotional dependency, which was central to their relationship. The final version used in the film shows a wanting Berenger standing in the doorframe of Pleshette's bedroom, as she sensually slips into the room. "It's all right. Everything is all right," she assures her son before the scene ends and cuts to a commercial.[6] Hamil found the conclusion "vulgar, cold, dirty, and devoid of emotion," but the edited version was still the film's signature piece.[7]

Judith Crist of *TV Guide* found the film to be "a peculiar mix of 'Oedipus Rex' and 'Rocky'."[8] On the lighter side, James Walcott of *The Village Voice* said, "With Suzanne Pleshette for a mother, who wouldn't be turned on?"[9] While the film received only fair reviews, it was nevertheless well acted by a talented cast. John J. O'Connor of *The New York Times* wrote, "Tom Berenger manages to drain from dumb, volatile Bobby a remarkable range of colors and nuances. Trapped in a number of impossible scenes, he emerges very impressively."[10] *The Village Voice* noted that "Pleshette pours such charm and care into her lines that the film briefly crackles with life."[11] John Cassavetes gives one of the most unaffected portrayals of a fight trainer and manager found in film. Peter Andrews of *Saturday Review* applauded Cassavetes, writing, "He works at it with the skill of the experienced craftsman he is, neatly pocketing the show with a performance that is tough, gritty, and touching."[12] Crist and O'Connor also praised newcomer Denzel Washington, respectively writing that he is "excellent" and "outstanding" in a supporting role.[13]

The work is also superbly filmed by one-time Academy Award winner Vilmos Zsigmond, shooting his first television movie.[14] With a 200 minute running time, *Flesh and Blood* had ample frames for both plot development and boxing vignettes. Consequently, the film serves a steady diet of training, sparring, fight montages and a couple of lengthy bouts. While Kay Gardella of the *New York Daily News* went somewhat overboard in writing that the fight scenes are "nothing less than remarkable,"[15] Judith Crist more accurately described the ring action as "exciting."[16]

Some of the better boxing sequences are early in the picture, with Berenger boxing in two well-choreographed sparring sessions that possess a realistic tempo and rhythm. Better than average as a pugilist within the roped square, Berenger also conveys his character's weaknesses and moments of trepidation outside the ring without compromising his credibility as a fighter.

1. Baxter, *Stanley Kubrick: A Biography* (New York: Carroll and Graf Publishers Inc., 1997), 35.
2. *Ibid.*, 36.
3. Harry F. Waters, "Does Incest Belong on TV?," *Newsweek*, 8 October 1979, 101.
4. *Ibid.*
5. Nicholas Yanni, Review of *Flesh and Blood* (Paramount Television movie), *Cue New York*, 26 October 1979, 25.
6. Waters, "Does Incest Belong on TV?," 101.
7. Marilyn Beck, "TV Traumas," *New York Daily News*, 13 August 1979, 8.
8. Judith Crist, *TV Guide*, 13 October 1979, A-7.
9. James Walcott, "M Is for the Many Things She Gave Me...," *Village Voice*, 15 October 1979.
10. John J. O'Connor, Review of *Flesh and Blood* (Paramount Television movie), *New York Times*, 12 October 1979, sec. c, p. 30.
11. Walcott, "M Is for the Many Things," 15.
12. Peter Andrews, "A Not-So-Prize Fight Story," Review of *Flesh and Blood* (Paramount Television movie), *Saturday Review*, 27 October 1979, 33.
13. Crist, A-7; O'Connor, sec. c, p. 30.
14. P. Gregory Springer, "Where Are All the People?," *Filmmakers Monthly*, August 1979.
15. Kay Gardella, "Intrique, Incest & Ideals," *New York Daily News*, 11 October 1979, 112.
16. Crist, A-7.

Gentleman Jim (1942)

Warner Bros., Bio-Drama, B & W, 104 minutes

Producer: Robert Buckner. *Director*: Raoul Walsh. *Screenplay*: Vincent Lawrence, Horace Mccoy, based upon the life of James J. Corbett. *Film Editor*: Jack Killifer. *Director of Photography*: Sid Hicox. *Music*: H. Roemheld.

Errol Flynn ("Gentleman Jim" Corbett), Alexis Smith (Victoria (Vicki) Ware), Jack Carson (Walter Lowrie), Alan Hale (Pat Corbett), Minor Watson (Buck Ware), Ward Bond (John L. Sullivan), Arthur Shields (Father Burke), John Loder (Carleton De Witt), Dorothy Vaughan (Ma Corbett), William Frawley (Delaney), Rhys Williams (Harry Watson), James Flavin (George Corbett), Pat Flaherty (Harry Corbett), Wallis Clark (Judge Geary), Marilyn Phillips (Mary Corbett), Art Foster (Jack Burke), Harry Crocker (Charles Crocker), Frank Mayo (Leland Stanford), Henry O'Hara (Huntington), Fred Kelsey (Sutro).

As the first heavyweight champion under the Marquess of Queensberry Rules, James J. Corbett secured a place as a legend of the early prize ring. His origins in the fledgling film industry however, remain curiously unheralded. James J. Corbett, in fact, achieved another famous first as the very first movie actor to sign a performance contract. In 1894, Thomas Edison's revolutionary Kinescope machine filmed "Gentleman Jim" during a six-round boxing exhibition with Peter Courtney. The famed inventor paid the champion boxer-turned-actor the sum of $4,700 for his services.[1]

Gentleman Jim smoothly made the transition from "film acting" to successful stage acting during the gay '90s, appearing in a number of plays including the biographical *Gentleman Jack*.[2] Commenting on the boxer's acting ability, the peerless thespian Lionel Barrymore once stated, "Corbett was one fighter who could and did get by in the theater on something more than the glamour of the heavyweight crown. 'Gentleman Jim' had ability and a great personality."[3]

In 1942, Warner Brothers Studios, well known for its production of film biographies including a recent pair of life stories of Thomas Edison,* directed attention to Corbett, the one-time Edison subject. Edison had once filmed Corbett and now Jack Warner was paying cinematic homage to both the inventor and the boxer.

A handsome face and Irish ancestry were prerequisites for the portrayal of the ex-bank clerk turned pugilist and the studio's resident swashbuckler Errol Flynn was the irrefutable choice. Flynn not only possessed Corbett's paradoxical blend of foppishness and ferocity, but he was apparently predisposed to the allure of the heavyweight championship. Upon arriving in New York City years earlier, Flynn's short list of sights to visit included the Broadway restaurant of Jack Dempsey, one of Corbett's successors to the throne.[4]

Production of the Corbett bio, titled *Gentleman Jim* after the fighter's well-known moniker, began on May 20, 1942, under the direction of Raoul Walsh.[5] Flynn's pending rape trial had helped his last picture, *Desperate Journey*, at the box-office, but fearing that the eventual results of the trial might prove unfavorable, the studio rushed *Gentleman Jim* to the screen.[6]

Loosely based on Corbett's biography, the film fully exploits artistic license, falling comfortably short of creating a historical chronicle. Corbett's family members are produced from a stereotypical mold bordering on caricature, and the fighter's romantic life is given an extra coat of Hollywood gloss. Notwithstanding this, and perhaps due in part to it, the picture captures the spirit and personality of the late nineteenth-century champion, while offering an engaging blend of comedy, romance and action in the process.

Unabashedly, the biography strays towards fictionalization to enhance its entertainment value. The whimsical elements of Corbett's love life are palatable in light of Hollywood's mandated romantic subtext, but the film's depiction of James J. as a friend of his predecessor John L. Sullivan borders on fantasy. In reality, the pair's mutual dislike lasted for nearly twenty years before their supposed reconciliation occurred under the banner of white unity and in the form of support of James J. Jeffries in his match against Jack Johnson. In sharp contrast, Warner's film version of their relationship, which offers a contrite Sullivan presenting his championship belt to a still idolizing Corbett with *Auld Lang Syne* playing in the background, is too contrived for the true boxing aficionado.

Yet this and other less pointed transgressions are quickly forgiven amid the rest of the hoopla. *The New York Times* accurately pegged the film as "primarily a fight fan's delight" adding that the picture "has Errol Flynn in the title role and enough other good qualities as an entertainment to

---

In 1940 Warner Brothers released Young Thomas Edison *starring Mickey Rooney and a sequel,* Edison, the Man, *starring Spencer Tracy.*

make it a satisfying show for anybody's money."[7]

Corbett was something of a "Fancy Dan" in the ring as well as out. T.M.P. of The *New York Times,* noting the actor's adaptation, wrote, "Errol Flynn is to the manner drawn as the impeccable Gentleman Jim."[8] In addition to being a dude, Corbett brimmed with a confidence which bordered on conceit. Flynn's performance also nicely captured these characteristics. To complement Flynn's ingratiating good looks and dynamic presence, the character was completed by making Corbett one of the most charming pranksters and opportunists to ever lace on a pair of gloves.

All the performances in the film were uniformly well received, and the movie's success owes as much to the ensemble cast as to Flynn's charm. *The Times* credited Alexis Smith for portraying her role "very entertainingly," also writing, "Ward Bond has the richest role of his long and serviceable career as the blustering Sullivan."[9] Joe Pihodna of the *Herald-Tribune* was another to laud Bond's performance pointing out, "Ward Bond deserves more than passing mention as Sullivan .... Mr. Bond, who heretofore has been cast in roles demanding no subtlety, turns in a magnificent performance."[10]

Scho of *Variety* wrote that Jack Carson "pretty nearly steals the picture in the comedy role," adding that "those scenes that Carson doesn't steal, Alan Hale cops." *Variety* also noted that veteran actor William Frawley is "himself an old hand at copping a bit."[11] Frawley, by small coincidence, was an intimate friend of the biographical subject.[12]

To recreate the Corbett-Choynski match, which occurred on a barge in San Franciscan waters, Warner Brothers utilized a giant water tank. The huge holding device was previously constructed and utilized for the studio's productions of *The Sea Wolf* and *Captain Blood,* the latter being one of Flynn's earlier projects. For *Gentleman Jim,* a barge and a pair of giant four-masted sailing ships were built and then placed in the tank. The specifically designed ships were replicas of the Alaska Packer Fleet, which sailed from San Francisco during the recreated period.[13]

To accurately duplicate fighting styles, settings, and ringside crowds of the era, Warner Brothers reviewed newsreel footage dating back prior to the turn of the century. Over 1,000 extras crammed on the ships and around the barge as director Raoul Walsh put five cameras in motion to capture the fighters and the roaring crowd around them. The filming of the final match between Corbett and Sullivan was an equally ambitious endeavor that took four days to film.[14] In fact, Flynn collapsed during the filming of the Sullivan bout, just weeks after he was turned down for duty with the armed forces for having "athlete's heart." A press release simply stated that the actor was suffering from "fatigue."[15]

The film's fight sequences are well-choreographed and capture the flavor of the transformative period in which the London Prize Ring Rules of bare knuckle fighting gave way to the mandatory use of gloves under the Marquess of Queensberry Rules. Samples of both types of fighting are offered and the picture's knockout sequences are particularly well done. Interestingly, director Raoul Walsh chose a number of professional wrestlers to portray boxers in the film, including Ed "Strangler" Lewis and Mike Mazurki.[16]

Flynn superbly portrays Corbett as a dancing master, who deftly confounds opponents with artful advances and retreats mixed with rapier-like left jabs. But Flynn was not the only one to have his hand in creating the Corbett illusion. The extreme close-ups of Corbett's footwork are the talent of light-heavyweight champion Billy Conn. Former middleweight champion Freddie Steele appears as the stand-in for Flynn in his barge fight against Choynski.[17]

Heavyweight contender Jack Roper also appeared in the picture and by Flynn's own admission, the boxer knocked him out three times in a single day, forcing Flynn to take a three-day sabbatical from filming. Despite the fact that Roper repeatedly knocked Flynn unconscious in the ring scene, the actor steadfastly held the film out as his favorite picture, one which continues to entertain the fight aficionado.

1. *The Heavyweights, 'The Stylists,'"* produced by Ross Grennburg, 57 minutes, HBO Sports in Association with Big Fights, Inc., 1990, videocassette.
2. James J. Corbett, *The Roar of the Crowd* (Garden City, New York: Garden City Publishing Company, 1925), 207.
3. Warner Bros. Exhibitor's Advertising and Press Campaign for *Gentleman Jim*.
4. Errol Flynn, *My Wicked, Wicked Ways* (Cutchogue, N.Y.: Buccaneer Books, 1976) 165.
5. Buster Wiles, *My Days with Errol Flynn: The Autobiography of Stuntman Buster Wiles* (Santa Monica, California: Roundtable Publishers, 1988), 123.
6. Tony Thomas, Rudy Behlmer, Clifford McCarty, *The Films of Errol Flynn* (Secaucus: Citadel Press, 1975), 117–118.
7. T.M.P. Review of *Gentleman Jim* (Warner Bros. movie), *New York Times*, 26 November 1942.
8. *Ibid.*
9. *Ibid.*
10. Joseph Pihodna, Review of *Gentleman Jim* (Warner Bros. movie), *New York Herald-Tribune*, 27 November 1942.
11. Scho, Review of *Gentleman Jim* (Warner Bros. movie), *Variety*, 4 November 1942
12. Warner Bros. Exhibitor's Advertising and Press Campaign.
13. *Ibid.*
14. *Ibid.*
15. Thomas, *The Films of Errol Flynn*, 117–118.
16. Wiles, *My Days With Errol Flynn*, 124.
17. Ray Mitchell, *Ray Mitchell's Boxing Quiz Book #1*, (Horwitz Publications, Inc., 1966), 47, 129; Wiles, *My Days with Errol Flynn*, 124.

Girlfight (2000)

Screen Gems, Drama, Color, 90 minutes

Producers: Sarah Green, Martha Griffin. *Director*: Karyn Kusama. *Screenplay*: Karyn Kusama. *Film Editor*: Plummy Tucker. *Cinematography*: Patrick Cady. *Music*: Coati Mundi.

Michelle Rodriguez (Diana Guzman), Jaime Tirelli (Hector), Paul Calderon (Sandro), Santiago Douglas (Adrian), Ray Santiago (Tiny), Victor Sierra (Ray), Elisa Bocanegra (Marisol), Shannon Walker Williams (Veronica), Louis Guss (Don), Herb Lovelle (Cal), Thomas Barbour (Ira), Graciella Ortiz (Female Student), John-Peter Linton (Mr. Price as J.P. Linton), Iris Little Thomas (Ms. Martinez), Dadi Pinero (Edward), Belqui Ortiz (Karina), Chuck Hickey (Gym Janitor), Anthony Ruiz (Tino), Jose Rabelo (Al), Jose Espinal (Ray's Friend), John Sayles (Science Teacher), Jack R. Marks (Pawnbroker), Yijo Guzman (Ray's Corner man), Diane Martella (Gym Coach), Michael Bentt (Fight Pro), Gus Santorella (Fight Pro Posse), Courtney Krause (Fight Pro Posse), Edgardo Claudio (Referee), Millie Tirelli (Candace), Allan Gropper (Referee), Alicia Ashley (Ricki Styles), Danny Gant (Referee), Josephine Pignataro (Wife), Sanford Redock (Announcer), Alice Woods Jr. (Janitor), Ricky Colon (Boxer), Andre Eason (Boxer), Jose Espinal (Boxer), Angel Hernandez (Boxer), Gabby Guzman (Boxer), Carlos Hernandez Jr. (Boxer), Carlos Hernandez Sr. (Boxer), Daniel Judah (Boxer), Christian Leyba (Boxer), Paul Maldonado (Boxer), Angel Osvaldo (Boxer), Ralphie Rivera (Boxer), Donnell Smith (Boxer), Angel Torres (Boxer), Angel Vega (Boxer).

Girlfight is a traditional Hollywood boxing story in that it depicts a youth who channels anger into the sport and consequently emerges with a new self-awareness and a better understanding of life. What undoubtedly distinguishes this film from the rest of its pedigree, however, is the fresh story perspective achieved by making the film's protagonist a woman.

The potential flaws of a story about a female boxer have always been obvious. Having an audience accept the requisite credibility of the premise is not any easy obstacle to overcome, and until several years ago, when women's boxing began to flourish, it would have been nearly impossible. However, because the material is handled by director Karyn Kusama with such a respect for her subject and the lead is portrayed by Michele Rodriguez with such an earnestness, *Girlfight* achieves what so many pictures about male boxers fail to do: it conveys a personal human struggle, not only universally recognizable, but universally felt as well.

In *Girlfight*, Diana Guzman (Rodriguez) is a tempestuous teenager growing up in the rough neighborhood of Red Hook, Brooklyn. Anti-social yet righteous, she lashes out at everyone and everything in the outside world, until the focus of her destructive energies begins to shift to the inside of a boxing ring. An underlying cause of the girl's angst is her bottled-up sorrow over the loss of her mother to suicide. Her inner conflict lies with her father, whom she blames for both her mother's death and her own feelings of inadequacy caused by his general non-supportiveness. It is through Guzman's physical toughness developed through boxing that she is ultimately able to confront both her own feelings and her father.

Kusama's story line could have allowed Guzman to compete against women only, as the actual rules of amateur boxing dictate. But in order to heighten the intensity of her struggle, and in order to legitimize her vindication vis-a-vis the male world, the rules of the sport are altered to allow mixed-gender competition in the same weight class — and the climactic finals tournament bout against her own boyfriend. When Guzman defeats her love interest in competition, the victory lies not in the win, but in the respect she receives from her man, who gives his all against her in the match.

Girlfight won the best-directing award and the grand jury prize at the Sundance Film Festival, and was also a hit at Cannes, Toronto and Deauville.[1] Rodriguez, who is of Dominican and Puerto Rican descent, attended an open casting call and her obvious magnetism won her the film's lead. "The entire dramatic interest of the movie lies in the moment-by-moment expression of pride and desire as it plays across her features," David Denby of *The New Yorker* would later write.[2]

The critics were somewhat mesmerized by the newcomer's performance, and likened Rodriguez to Marlon Brando. "If her performance doesn't remind you of Marlon Brando's smoldering power, you've probably never seen Brando perform," wrote Joe Morgenstern of *The Wall Street Journal*.[3] "The movie belongs to Ms. Rodriguez," wrote A.O. Scott, of *The New York Times*. "With her slightly crooked nose and her glum, sensual mouth, she looks like Marlon Brando in his smoldering prime, and she has some of his slow, intense physicality."[4] "This is a face made to smolder — the young Brando womanized," wrote Richard Corliss of *Newsweek*.[5]

The boxing gym, as used in *Girlfight*, serves as a cauldron in which Guzman's brewing anger simmers down into the controlled violence found in the ring. The picture nicely avoids the typical trite gym training sequences, because the focus in *Girlfight* is often on the physiological, and the interaction between Guzman and her trainer is able to strike just the right tone. "Jamie Tirelli — as her gruff, kindly trainer, Hector — has the loose good humor that this role, hardly the freshest in the fight-picture repertory, requires," wrote A.O. Scott.[6] Rather then showing all the grunts and groans at the gym, the film smartly shifts the venue in one scene to Guzman's gym class, in a light bit where she outshines her classmates in a physical-fitness program.

In the ring, Rodriguez offers the intensity and the determination one might expect of a boxer. Yet, in the depiction of her fighters, Kusama never loses sight of the fact that these are kids trying to fulfill their dreams, not polished fighters. As noted by *The New York Times* critic, "Diana and her young male sparring partners and opponents look good, but not too good: they flail with the energy of the youthful amateurs they're meant to be."[7] And like the picture itself, the boxing vignettes are uniquely Kusama's, even down to the fighters' verbal banter during a clinch, in which Guzman tells her boyfriend that she loves him. "The boxing scenes are staged and shot expertly," wrote the critic for *The Wall Street Journal*, "but even they reveal a distinctive style — a woman's style."[8]

1. Jonathan Foreman, "'Girl Fight Is a KO,'" Review of *Girlfight* (Screen Gems movie), *New York Post*, 29 September 2000.
2. David Denby, "Rough Stuff," *New Yorker*, 2 October 2000, 148.
3. Joe Morgenstern, "Notable New Movies," Review of *Girlfight* (Screen Gems movie), *Wall Street Journal*.
4. A.O. Scott, "Floating Like a Butterfly, Sting Like a Bee," Review of *Girlfight* (Screen Gems movie), *New York Times*, 29 September 2000.
5. Richard Corliss, "An Indie Knockout," *Newsweek*, 2 October 2000.
6. Scott, "Floating Like a Butterfly."
7. *Ibid.*
8. Morgenstern, "Notable New Movies."

Golden Boy (1939)

Columbia Pictures, Drama, B & W, 98 minutes

Producer: William Perlberg. *Director*: Rouben Mamoulian. *Screenplay*: Lewis Meltzer, Daniel Taradash, Sarah Y. Mason, Victor Heerman, based upon a story by Clifford Odets. *Film Editor*: Otto Meyer, *Photography*: Nick Musuraca, Karl Freund, *Music*: M.W. Stoloff.

Barbara Stanwyck (Lorna Moon), Adolphe Menjou (Tom Moody), William Holden (Joe Bonaparte), Lee J. Cobb (Mr. Bonaparte), Joseph Calleia (Eddie Fuseli), Sam Levene (Siggie), Edward S. Brophy (Roxy Lewis), Beatrice Blinn (Anna), Mr. Carp (William H. Strauss), Don Beddoe (Borneo).

Clifford Odets' "Golden Boy" first came to life as a successful play performed on the New York stage. In 1938, Columbia Studios' indomitable czar Harry Cohn purchased the film rights to the story for $100,000.[1] Director Rouben Mamoulian was interested in sitting at the helm for the screen version, but Cohn had other plans. Mamoulian, however, owned a short story which Cohn desired. Slyly refusing to sell Cohn the story, Mamoulian swapped it instead for the right to direct *Golden Boy*. The deal proved Cohn a fox as well, as his new acquisition soon became the basis for the timeless *Mr. Smith Goes to Washington*.[2]

Odets's European honeymoon left him unavailable for the adaptation of his own work for the screen, so Mamoulian hired a pair of young New York writers in his stead. Daniel Taradash, a Harvard law graduate, and Lewis Meltzer, a fledgling playwright, were shipped westward to a secluded locale in the Mojave Desert. Here, they fashioned a screenplay in just five weeks for a fee of only $2,000.[3]

The abundantly talented John Garfield, who had recently made the bi-coastal leap from stage to screen, had been lauded by the critics for his captivating stage performance as the brother-in-law of prizefighter Joe Bonaparte. Cohn was aware that Odetts had originally scripted the Bonaparte character for Garfield himself, and he sought the actor for the lead role. Garfield, however, was under contract with Warner Brothers and Cohn's equally domineering rival Jack Warner denied his request for a loan-out. Cohn also had designs on Tyrone Power, but Darryl Zanuck of Twentieth-Century Fox was similarly resistant to sharing his studio's key performer.[4]

Without a leading man, at the suggestion of producer William Perlberg, a campaign was launched by Columbia's publicity department to find "The Golden Boy." The search, which included the screen test of 65 individuals, concluded with the successful preview of 20-year-old Bill Beedle Jr. Acting under the more mature name of William Holden, Beedle had some stage experience as a member of the Pasadena Players, and could boast a contract with Paramount Studios, albeit for a paltry $50 per week. Holden, however, was completely devoid of film acting experience—a key factor in facilitating Cohn's purchase of half of the novice's seemingly valueless contract for Columbia Studios.[5]

Under the jaundiced eye of Cohn and his crew of experienced actors, Holden nervously produced work on the set which was subpar, and gossips whispered that Cohn's dismissal of his new find was in the offing. When the rumor reached the door of Holden's co-star Barbara Stanwyck, the established Hollywood veteran confronted Cohn and Perlberg, and persuaded them to keep the youth in place. Coaching Holden each night after filming, Stanwyck's tutelage not only salvaged Holden's film debut, but also provided him with his opportunity to become a Hollywood star.[6]

In *Golden Boy*, Joe Bonaparte (Holden) is faced with the dilemma of choosing between a career as a violinist or the life of a prizefighter. The violin provides Joe with a means of expression and represents a father's (Cobb) ambition for his son. Boxing, on the other hand, stands for power and money—a vehicle for Bonaparte to fulfill his own desires.

Bonaparte is caught between two forces. The fight mob led by his manager Moody (Menjou) pushes for the fistic career, while Bonaparte's father and his own love for music pull him toward the violin. Tipping the scale in the favor of the ring is Moody's gal Lorna (Stanwyck), whom Joe is in love with. Bonaparte eventually decides to use boxing to prove his worth to Lorna and win her affections, abandoning the violin and forsaking his father in the process.

Bonaparte becomes an established fighter and he and Lorna fall in love. For Bonaparte to reach the championship, he must defy his manager and submit to the control of a transparent gangster named Fuseli (Calleia). Lorna urges Bonaparte to quit boxing and find solace with the violin rather than become immersed in the depths of Fuseli's fight racket. However, Bonaparte fails to heed Lorna's advice, and quickly degenerates into a cheap copy of the shallow and greedy Fuseli.

The boxer wins the right to fight for the championship, but fatally injures his opponent in the ring. The incident awakens Bonaparte to his own spiritual "death" and disdain for his adopted lifestyle. Bonaparte is distraught, but with the help of Lorna he realizes that he can re-train his hands and heart to fulfill their intended musical purpose. Lorna then returns the prodigal son to his father.

Variety viewed *Golden Boy* as "displaying [a] fine blend of drama, action, romance and human appeal." The film follows the stage version closely, but then takes an abrupt detour from Odets' vision by eliminating Bonaparte's tragic death. William Boehnel felt that the film was not up to par with the theater version, writing that the picture "chiefly ... lacks the strife and the torment, the sympathy and the understanding which Mr. Odets brought not only to his theme but to each of his characters."[7] No criticism, however, could be found with the film's music, which was nominated for an Academy Award for best original score.

In preparation for the picture, Holden learned to bow the violin from concert artist Julian Brodetsky, had his hair curled and dyed black to appear Italian and learned to box from Cannonball Green.[8] Holden, who was making his film debut, was perceived by some critics as something of a diamond in the rough. Howard Barnes of the *New York Herald-Tribune* observed that the hand-picked "Golden Boy" "demonstrates unquestioned ability," but felt that he was "not felicitously cast" and "rarely achieves the hysterical intensity which the high, emotional moments of production demand."[9] Frank Nugent of the *New York Times* found his portrayal a "good interpretation of an unusual role," but also found the actor "guilty, in scattered scenes, of the exaggerated recoils, lip-bitings and hand-clenchings one associates with the old-time dramatic school."[10]

Still other critics were rather impressed with the newcomer. Kate Cameron of the *New York Daily News* wrote that he "enacts the title role admirably" and "he manages to convey to the audience, with conviction, the terrific struggle that takes place in the boy's dual nature."[11] *Variety* found Holden to be "capable and personable," handling his part "with impressiveness and ability." "He looks like a solid and lasting juvenile find," the critic noted.[12]

Critic Archer Winsten was rightfully complimentary about the entire cast. Winsten found Lee J. Cobb to offer "the best character rendition," and noted that Adolphe Menjou "plays the part of the manager perfectly." He also credited Sam Levene for "good work," but not the equal to Garfield's "brilliant" portrayal on the stage.[13]

The film's lone fight sequence of note, staged towards the film's end, was shot on location in Madison Square Garden. Photographers Nick Musuraca and Karl Freund shot the action through the ropes, from an overhead angle, and at both medium and close range, capturing the sustained action which included both a nicely choreographed knockdown and a knockout. Holden, who learned his lessons well from Green, alternates his punches between the body and head, adopting the style of a slashing boxer-puncher. While the ring action is somewhat limited, it is professionally stylized and stands among the best film offerings from its era.

1. Patricia King Hanson, *The American Film Institute Catalog of Motion Pictures Produced in the United States, Volume F3, Feature Films, 1931–1940* (Berkeley: University of California Press, 1993), Film Entries A-L, 796.
2. Bob Thomas, *King Cohn: The Life and Times of Hollywood Mogul Harry Cohn* (New York: McGraw-Hill Publishing Co., 1990), 154–155.
3. *Ibid.*, 155; Bob Thomas, *Golden Boy: The Untold Story of William Holden* (New York: St. Martin's Press, 1983), 25.
4. Thomas, *Golden Boy*, 22–23, 26–29; Thomas, *King Cohn*, 156.
5. Bob Thomas, *Golden Boy*, 29–31.
6. *Ibid.*
7. Review of *Golden Boy* (Columbia Pictures movie), *Variety*, 16 August 1939, William Boehnel, Review of *Golden Boy* (Columbia Pictures movie).
8. Thomas, *Golden Boy*, 28.
9. Harold Barnes, *New York Herald-Tribune*, quoted in Bob Thomas, *Golden Boy*, 32.
10. Frank Nugent, *New York Times*, quoted in Bob Thomas, *Golden Boy*, 32.
11. Kate Cameron, Review of *Golden Boy* (Columbia Pictures movie), *New York Daily News*, 8 September 1939.
12. *Variety*.
13. Archer Winsten, Review of *Golden Boy* (Columbia Pictures movie), *New York Post*.

The Golden Gloves Story (1950)

First National Pictures, an Eagle-Lion Release, Drama, B & W, 76 minutes

Producer: Carl Krueger. *Director*: Felix Feist. *Screenplay*: Joe Ansen, Felix Fiest, based upon a story by D.D. Beauchamp and William F. Sellers. *Supervising Film Editor*: William F. Clayton. *Photography*: John L. Russell Jr. *Fight Sequences*: Frankie Van.

James Dunn (Joe Reilly), Dewy Martin (Nick Martel), Kay Westfall (Patti Reilly), Kevin O'Morrison (Bob Gilmore), Gregg Sherwood (Iris), Arch Ward (Himself), Tony Zale (Himself), Izzy Klein (Himself), Jack Brickhouse (Himself).

Primarily a player in "B" pictures, veteran actor James Dunn reached the apex of his film career in 1945, winning the Academy Award for best supporting actor for his portrayal of the tender yet troubled alcoholic father in *A Tree Grows in Brooklyn*. Dunn appeared in five boxing films during his career, and similar to his Oscar-winning role, a paternal element was central to his character.

In his first fight flick, Dunn portrays a young man who enters the ring to support his wife and baby in *Bad Girl* (1931), a Fox production directed by Frank Borzage. The film was nominated for an Oscar, and Borzage won the Academy Award for best director. Soon afterwards, Dunn was cast in Fox's *Society Girl* (1932), as a boxer who pursues a society dame at the expense of his ring career.

Several years later, Dunn again appeared as a prizefighter in Columbia's *Two-Fisted Gentleman* (1936). Produced by Beau Pivar and directed by Gordon Wiles, the story, which also starred June Clayworth, was accurately pegged by *Variety* as an "ordinary" film. Although Dunn was admonished for "playing the same role in the same old way," he did receive some credit for his boxing in the fight scenes.[1]

After his stellar performance in *A Tree Grows in Brooklyn*, Dunn was cast in MGM's *Killer McCoy* (1947), where he gave a nice performance, this time as the alcoholic father of a boxer, depicted by Mickey Rooney. Brog of *Variety* wrote, "Dunn hokes up [the] assignment as the drunken actor-father with just the right amount of overplaying to stress 'ham' character."[2]

For his fight film finale, Dunn reverted to the familiar "B," starring in *The Golden Gloves Story*, produced by First National Pictures and released by Eagle-Lion. In *The Golden Gloves Story*, Dunn re-enters the ring, this time in the role of an amateur boxing referee. Dewy Martin, who had recently made his film debut in Nicholas Ray's *Knock on Any Door*, was cast as a boxer who swaps punches with another Golden Glover portrayed by Kevin O'Morrison.

The Golden Gloves Story pays homage to the sport of amateur boxing and its officials who are dedicated to the advancement of good sportsmanship and preservation of the safety of the fighter. In the film, Joe Reilly (Dunn) is a veteran Golden Gloves referee who lives with his daughter Patti (Westfall). Patti has a steady boyfriend named Bob Gilmore (O'Morrison), and another suitor named Nick Martel (Martin), who is alternately charming and insulting.

A romantic competition for Patti's affections ensues, and the rivalry spreads to the squared circle when both men face one another in the 160 pound open class of the Chicago Golden Gloves. Joe, who was appointed referee, awards the fight to Bob on a technical knockout. Because of Joe's rancor towards Nick, both the fighter and Patti call Joe's impartiality into question.

The following year, Bob recaptures the Chicago Golden Gloves Championship. Nick, who has relocated to New York, captures the New York Golden Gloves title, and the pair meet in the annual inter-city tournament. Joe is again assigned as referee. However, this time he withdraws in the interest of fairness to Nick. While Nick loses the bout, Joe's action teaches Nick the true value of sportsmanship. Mending his relationships with the Reillys and Bob, Nick emerges as a suitable mate for Patti.

Golden Gloves amateur boxing was born on March 11, 1927, the inspired vision of Paul Gallico, writer for the *New York Daily News*. The first show was held at the Ascension Parish House Gymnasium in New York City. The tournament quickly spread to over 200 cities nationwide and still endures today as a breeding ground for America's Olympic boxing hopefuls.[3] Esteemed alumni of the Golden Gloves include professional world champions Solly Krieger, who won the gloves in 1928; Billy Conn, who won the 160 pound championship in 1934; and Melio Bettina, who garnered 175 pound honors that same year.[4] More recent winners include eventual professional heavyweight champions Floyd Patterson and Riddick Bowe.

The Chicago Golden Gloves, which is sponsored by the Chicago Tribune Charities, Inc., was an offshoot of the New York tournament and is still one of the largest and most respected tourneys in the nation. Among its most notable participants are Barney Ross, a 1929 winner, who later reached the professional boxing hall of fame, and fellow pro hall of famer Tony Zale, who advanced to the final match of the 1932 edition of the tournament in the welterweight division.[5]

Zale, who had recently retired following his loss of the world's middleweight championship to Frenchman Marcel Cerdan, makes a welcome cameo appearance in *The Golden Gloves Story*. Fight historians will also appreciate the cameo of one-time contender Izzy Klein. The film, shot in its entirety on location in Chicago, also offers a brief glimpse of the neon sign of the old Chicago Stadium, the site of such famous ring encounters as Marciano-Walcott II and Robinson-Basilio II. Such ancillary sights and brief appearances by the aforementioned boxers are what make *The Golden Gloves Story* worth a look, in spite of the fight choreography's routine action and the tendency to rely heavily on montages and clips.

1. Char, Review of *Two-Fisted Gentleman* (Columbia Pictures movie), *Variety*, 2 September 1936.
2. Brog, Review of *Two-Fisted Gentleman* (Columbia Pictures movie), *Variety*, 29 October 1947.
3. "Hollywood Commemorates "Golden Gloves" in New Screen Thriller." Studio Publicity for *Golden Gloves*.
4. Nat Loubet and John Ort, comps., *The 1979 Ring Boxing Encyclopedia and Record Book* (New York: The Ring Book Shop, 1979).
5. *Ibid.*, 282, 254.

The Great John L. (1945)

United Artists, Bio-Drama, B & W, 96 minutes

Producers: James Edward Grant, Frank R. Mastroly, presented by Bing Crosby Productions. *Director*: Frank Tuttle. *Screenplay*: James Edward Grant. *Editor*: Theodore Bellinger. *Photography*: James Van Trees. *Musical Director*: Victor Young. *Fight Choreographer*: John Indrisano.

Greg McClure (John L. Sullivan), Linda Darnell (Anne Livingstone), Barbara Britton (Kathy Harkness), Lee Sullivan (Mickey), Otto Kruger (Richard Martin), Wallace Ford (McManus), George Matthews (John Flood), Robert Barrat (Billy Muldoon), J.M.Kerrigan (Father O'Malley), Joel Friedkin (Michael Sullivan), Hope Landin (Maura Sullivan), Harry Crocker (Arthur Brisbane), Simon Semenoff (La Savate Champion Monsieur Claire), Fritz Feld (Claire's Manager).

In the late 19th century, Vanderbilt, Rockefeller and Carnegie were America's undisputed captains of industry, Alexander Graham Bell and Thomas Edison its inventors extraordinaire, and John L. Sullivan its first national sporting hero. Sullivan, who was known to greet fellow tavern patrons by bellowing, "I can lick any son of a bitch in the house," spent most of his young adult life living up to his boast. The last of the bare-knuckle heavyweight champions, "The Great John L." reflected what his times demanded: a combination of excessive confidence, unbridled swagger and matchless talent.

Sullivan was one of the very first boxers to use his ring career as an entree to the entertainment world. During his championship days, Sullivan starred in a play entitled *Honest Hearts and Willing Hands*.[1] Predictably, the villain in the story gets his comeuppance in the ring at the hands of the Great John L. Other members of the Sullivan family, including nephew Billy, followed John L. into show business. Billy Sullivan starred in the 1925 Rayart Picture boxing film entitled *The Fear Fighter*, and also appeared in several episodes of the silent fight serial entitled *The New Leather Pushers*.

At the end of World War II, Bing Crosby, the famed crooner and actor, was branching out into movie production and he selected Sullivan's story as the subject of his first behind-the-camera foray. Crosby opted to tell a romanticized version of Sullivan's life and he cast the lead accordingly. At six feet and 185 pounds, the broad-shouldered and handsome Greg McClure fit Crosby's bill. McClure, a bit player in Hollywood, was signed on his appearance alone. He never even made a screen test.[2] Fittingly, Lee Sullivan, a distant relative on John L.'s father's side, was also cast in the picture as a singer.

The Great John L. is a fictionalized version of the life of the "Boston Strong Boy." Heavy emphasis is placed upon the champion's romantic interests, who included his childhood sweetheart Kathy and popular stage performer Anne Livingstone, portrayed by the similar looking and equally lovely Linda Darnell and Barbara Britton. Unfortunately, the film's focus on the love triangle provides a skewed lens into Sullivan's life. Fault lies principally with the script, which creates an entirely implausible camaraderie between the two female rivals.

Sullivan's battle with alcohol is the picture's other subplot, and this aspect of his life is more accurately treated, albeit equally sappy. It is an undisputed fact that Sullivan never let an upcoming fight stand in the way of his drinking, and, symbolically, he is depicted as training for his match with James J. Corbett on champagne and ale. Toward the end of the picture, a teary-eyed John L. throws his beer stein into the bar mirror, vowing never to drink again. Sullivan, in fact, did quit the bottle, becoming a teetotaler and temperance speaker.

The film takes a respectable stab at recreating John L. Sullivan's larger-than-life existence, taking full liberties to achieve its goal. In one of the picture's most memorable scenes, Sullivan has a bar fight with the French La Savate Champion Monsieur Claire, memorably portrayed by the great French ballet dancer Simon Semonoff. Claire kicks Sullivan around the bar while simultaneously sipping champagne and throwing flowers. Sullivan eventually retaliates by launching Claire with a punch, sending him crashing into a piano. In another bizarre but amusing scene, Sullivan is found drinking with Admiral Dot, one of P.T. Barnum's attractions portrayed by the 44-inch midget Jerry Maren, an ex-munchkin from *The Wizard of Oz*.[3]

Fight scenes in *The Great John L.* were staged by Hollywood's resident choreographer John Indrisano. The picture features one of Sullivan's early significant victories against Paddy Flood; his first bout against Charley Mitchell, which took place in France and ended in a 39-round draw; his 75-round marathon against Jake Kilrain; and the passing of the crown to Corbett. Sullivan's earlier title win against Paddy Ryan is treated summarily with a few frames of film capturing Sullivan's knockout blow.

To recreate the fight against Flood, which took place on a barge along New York's Hudson River, the studio's "General Service Tank" was fitted with a barge lit by kerosene lamps and the set was surrounded by a "sky cyclorama" and covered with canvas to simulate nighttime. The match required three days of shooting: the first for the long shots of the barge and the fans, the second for the fighters' boxing, and the final day to capture the boxers in close-ups.[4] The fight is enacted as a donnybrook which only Hollywood could script.

The knockouts of Flood and Sullivan are entertainingly fashioned, though not historically precise, and the rest of the picture's fight scenes are pedestrian. McClure looks the part of a young John L., with square shoulders which taper to a small waist, and his boxing technique is sufficient. A.W. of *The New York Times* wrote, "Greg McClure, a newcomer, plays the title role with surprising ease and conviction," but in truth McClure's acting does little to enhance the film.[5] After Ward Bond's fabulous rendition of Sullivan in Corbett's bio-pic *Gentleman Jim*, one can only draw the inescapable conclusion that the best John L. is not to be found in his own film biography.

1. Michael T. Isenberg, *John L. Sullivan and His America* (Urbana, Ill. and Chicago: University of Illinois Press, 1988), 287.
2. "Title Roleist Search Is One of Hollywood's Sagas." Studio Publicity for *The Great John L*.
3. "'Admiral Dot' Meets 'John L.'" Studio Publicity for *The Great John L*.
4. "It Took Hollywood Three Days to Film Sixteen Minute Bout." Studio Publicity for *The Great John L*.
5. A.W., "Crosby's Champ," Review of *The Great John L*. (United Artists Pictures movie), *New York Times* 9 July 1945.

The Great White Hope (1970)

Twentieth Century-Fox, Bio-Drama, Color, 101 minutes

Producer: Lawrence Turman. *Director*: Martin Ritt. *Screenplay*: Howard Sackler. *Film Editor*: William Reynolds, A.C.E. *Cinematograpy*: Burnett Guffey.

James Earl Jones (Jack Jefferson), Jane Alexander (Eleanor), Lou Gilbert (Goldie), Joel Fluellen (Tick), Chester Morris (Pop Weaver), Robert Webber (Dixon), Marlene Warfield (Clara), R.G. Armstrong (Cap'n Dan), Hal Holbrook (Cameron), Beah Richards (Mama Tiny), Moses Gunn (Scipio), Lloyd Gough (Smitty), Larry Pennell (Brady), Bill Walker (Deacon), Rodolfo Acosta (El Jefe), Rockne Tarkington (Rudy), Manuel Padilla, Jr. (Paco), George Ebeling (Fred), Roy E. Glenn, Sr. (Pastor), Marcel Dalio (French Promoter), Virginia Capers (Sister Pearl), Oscar Beregi (Ragosy), Karl Otto Alberty (Hans), Jim Beattie (The Kid).

Inspired by the life of Jack Johnson, the first African-American to fight for and win the heavyweight championship, playwright Howard Sackler's *Great White Hope* began as a smash hit on the stage. Initially made possible by a grant from the National Foundation of Arts, *The Great White Hope* took Broadway by storm during the 1968-69 theatrical season, winning the Pulitzer Prize, Drama Critic's and Antoinette Perry Awards for best play. James Earl Jones and Jane Alexander received Tony Awards for best actor and best supporting actress respectively, and Marlene Warfield received the Clarence Derwent Award as Broadway's best newcomer.[1]

Twentieth Century-Fox wasted no time bringing the story to film, with preparations beginning even before the Broadway run was completed. Lawrence Turman, who had purchased the screen rights to *The Great White Hope* long before Jones made it the centerpiece of a theatrical buzz, had recently completed his work on *The Graduate*. He would produce the film. Martin Ritt, the director of *Hud*, who years earlier featured in the Group Theater's *Golden Boy*, would direct. Sackler, an uncredited screenwriter for Stanley Kubrick's boxing noir *Killer's Kiss*, would reshape his stage version of *Hope* for the screen.[2] Casting for the film essentially duplicated the principal roles of the play. In addition to Jones, Alexander, and Warfield reprising their roles, George Ebling continued on as Brady's manager, as did Lou Gilbert in the part of Goldie.

The Great White Hope is the story of Jack Jefferson, a black fighter seeking to express his individuality and maintain his self-respect amid the racism of early twentieth century America. Prevailing white society disdains the boxer for committing two most egregious sins — winning the heavyweight championship of the world and loving a white woman — two activities reserved exclusively for white males. When law enforcement officials bring trumped up charges against the boxer he is exiled to Europe with his lover to complete his days as champion. Age finally robs the fighter of his skill and he makes a deal to defend his title against the latest White Hope in exchange for his re-entry into the country.

Filmed in Hollywood at Twentieth-Century Fox Studios and on location in Globe, Arizona, and Spain, *The Great White Hope* adheres to many aspects of Jack Johnson's real life story.[3] His pursuit of heavyweight champion Tommy Burns to Australia is alluded to and his defeat of James J. Jeffries in Reno is recreated. The U.S. Government's charges that Johnson violated the Mann Act,* his subsequent European boxing tour and his ultimate defeat by Jess Willard in Havana are also detailed. The anchor to the film's plot is Jefferson's tempestuous love affair with Eleanor, who closely reflects his white wife, and who, like the character in the film, is a victim of suicide.

Any discrepancies between Jack Johnson and Jack Jefferson should be automatically forgiven in light of Sackler's purpose, which was not to write a story that was "historically accurate," but rather to use "the story elements of Jack Johnson's career" to create "new characters, especially the girl."[4]

While the stage version dealt with the fight scenes as off-stage events left strictly to the audience's imagination, James Earl Jones was required to box in the film. At the time of the production of the movie, not only had Jones never boxed, but he had only seen one boxing match in his entire life; an event where he "found the spectators more interesting than the guys in the ring."[5] Former welterweight champion Mushy Callahan was enlisted to instill in Jones the fighter's mentality, teach him the fundamentals of the trade, and choreograph the three fight scenes in the film.[6] The first two vignettes are very brief and focus on Johnson's facial expressions and are carried by the force of personality. Jones, however, is required to do a significant amount of boxing in the final ring scene where he gives a credible performance.

While Jones was almost universally applauded by the critics, the reviews of the film as a whole lie across a broad spectrum. Joe Rosen of the *New York Morning Telegraph* found the film to be "far and away the best film of the year," while Richard Setlickel of *Life* dubbed it a "disappointment."[7] One recurring criticism seemed to be the film's inability to escape its theatrical roots. Pauline Kael of *The New Yorker* complained, "Although the play ... reads like a movie, the movie version, directed by Martin Ritt, clunks along like a disjointed play."[8]

James Earl Jones expressed a similar disappointment regarding the direction, which stressed the theatrical. Director Ritt requested that the actors reenact their stage performances which he then intended to "modulate." Jones felt that Ritt erred in his attempt to adapt stage performances which have a "frontal" orientation and require "projection," to create screen performances where the acting "must be subtle."[9] Such technical distinctions may have vexed the director and the actors, but they are hardly a concern for audiences of the film. Both Jones and Alexander were rightfully nominated for Academy Awards for their work. Andrew Sarris thought Jones's performance "powerful" and Jane Alexander's portrayal "scarcely less remarkable."[10] Jack Kroll of *Newsweek* wrote of Jones, "There is no better American actor than this tremendous presence, a presence in which physicality and intelligence spark galvanically in the gap between art and reality."[11]

Jones forcefully captures the entire

---

*The Mann Act prohibited the transportation of women across state lines for illegal or immoral purposes.

spectrum of human emotion in his character. Jack Jefferson exhibits an infectious sense of humor, unbridled joy, seething anger, smoldering shame and hollowed remorse. Jones's multifaceted portrayal of the flamboyant and controversial heavyweight champion is on par with Robert De Niro's depiction of Jake La Motta, as arguably the best screen performance ever to depict a prizefighter.

1. Clive Barnes, "Theater: 'White Hope,' Tale of Modern Othello, Opens in Capital." Review of *The Great White Hope* (Theater presentation by Arena Stage, Washington), *New York Times*, 14 December 1967, sec. L , p. 58; Wanda Hale, Review of *The Great White Hope* (Twentieth Century-Fox movie), *New York Sunday News*, 11 October 1970, sec. 7; James Denton, "Twentieth Century-Fox Production Information," 1 April 1970.

2. James Denton, "Twentieth Century-Fox Production Information," 1 April 1970.

3. *Ibid.*
4. James Earl Jones and Penelope Niven, *Voices and Silences* (New York: Charles Scribner's Sons, 1993).
5. *Ibid.*
6. Wanda Hale, Review of *The Great White Hope* (Twentieth Century-Fox movie), *New York Sunday News*, 11 October 1970, sec. 7.
7. Joe Rosen, Review of *The Great White Hope* (Twentieth Century-Fox movie), *New York Morning Telegraph*, 13 October 1970; Richard Setlickel, Review of *The Great White Hope* (Twentieth Century-Fox movie), *Life*, 6 November 1970.
8. Pauline Kael, Review of *The Great White Hope* (Twentieth Century-Fox movie), *New Yorker*, 17 October 1970.
9. Jones and Niven, *Voices and Silences*, 209–210.
10. Andrew Sarris, Review of *The Great White Hope* (Twentieth Century-Fox movie), *Village Voice*, 29 October 1970.
11. Jack Kroll, Review of *The Great White Hope* (Twentieth Century-Fox movie), *Newsweek*, 26 October 1970.

The Great White Hype (1996)

Twentieth Century-Fox, Comedy, Color, 90 minutes

Producers: Fred Berner, Joshua Donen. *Director*: Reginald Hudlin. *Screenplay*: Tony Hendra, Ron Shelton. *Film Editor*: Earl Watson, A.C.E. *Director of Photography*: Ron Garcia, A.S.C. *Music*: Marcus Miller.

Samuel L. Jackson (the Reverend Fred Sultan), Jeff Goldblum (Mitchell Kane), Damon Wayans (James "The Grim Reaper" Roper), Peter Berg (Terry Conklin), John Lovitz (Sol), Corbin Bersen (Peter Prince), Cheech Marin (Julio Escobar), Jamie Foxx (Hassan El Ruk'n), Salli Richardson (Bambi), John Rhys Davies (Johnny Windsor), Rocky Carroll (Artemus St. John Saint).

Back when vaudevillian-like pugilists boxed on stage, local toughs were coaxed from their seats to engage the traveling prizefighters. The chosen wagon driver or dockworker could earn a handsome cash prize if he lasted a prescribed number of rounds with the featured pug. On occasion the challenger would prove too vigorous, in which case he might be met with a whack on the head from behind the stage curtain to insure that the reward remained unpaid. If no one in the audience was game, a ringer who had already been planted in the crowd would eagerly step forward and take his pre-arranged lumps. On some unconscious level the paying customers were aware of the promoter's dupe, but participated in the ruse nonetheless.

In many ways, the multi-million dollar fights of today are no different then their carnivalesque counterparts of over a century ago. With somewhat illogical repetition, the modern boxing fan has dutifully followed promotional pied pipers such as Don King and Bob Arum. Like the mesmerized rodent led to its own demise, the boxing fan is drawn to the perpetual seduction of the promoter's hype. For the price of a pay-per-view ticket, the boxing fan rationalizes that he, too, can be part of the spectacle.

Satirizing the contemporary sale of boxing to the public, *The Great White Hype*, frames the come-on in the familiar packaging of racial prejudice. James "The Grim Reaper" Roper (Wayans) is the heavyweight champion of the world. Although another black man, Marvin Shabbaz, is the legitimate number-one contender, a promoter called "The Sultan" (Jackson) realizes that ticket sales rely on a lily-white opponent. When a legitimate white contender is not available, the Sultan resurrects a grunge rock singer and self-proclaimed pacifist named Terry Conklin (Berg), who defeated Roper in the amateurs, to become the centerpiece of his ballyhoo.

Conklin despises the racial overtones of the fight, but is nevertheless a walking billboard for "white" symbols, wearing a confederate flag emblazoned on his T-shirt in one scene and a Boston Celtics warm-up jacket in another. When he is dubbed "Irish" Terry, Conklin explains to his publicist Sol (Lovitz) that he is not Irish. "It's boxing, ... it just means you're white," Sol replies.[1] The effect of the publicity blitz on the public is a foregone conclusion. "Two bucks on the clean-cut white boy," an elderly woman tells the clerk as she places her bet at a casino.[2]

Little has changed since "The Great White Hope" era began in 1908 with the ascension of Jack Johnson to the heavyweight championship, although today, minorities placed in boxing's hierarchy are reaping their share of the rewards spawned by racial friction. *The Great White Hype*, however, goes beyond its jibes at America's psychological need to restore the heavyweight championship to a white boxer, attacking boxing's own ethnic and racial mosaic, and broadly characterizing its most notable personalities, rituals, and symbols.

No group is safe against the caustic pen of screenwriter Ron Shelton. Jews are depicted as publicity whores—prostituted conduits to the white public—who are pimped by an exploiting black promoter. Blacks are spoofed as inarticulate and gun toting and are saddled with innumerable ghetto stereotypes. The Irish bear the brunt of the film's backlash at white America's self-importance, with strains of *Danny Boy* still playing as Conklin lies prostrate on the canvas at the end of his match with Roper. Some might be offended by the humor, but Shelton, who also scripted *White Men Can't Jump*, has a knack for ethnic and racial comedy. Most will find, as Jack Mathews of *Newsday* did, that the film "plays like a good-natured farce, harmless fun."[3]

The sport of boxing is depicted, tongue-in-cheek, as a vulgar manifestation of American gullibility and shallowness. Members of the boxing fraternity are portrayed as self-serving and despicable to the last man. Unabashedly, the Sultan imitates Don King himself, with a turban in place of his puffed-up hair, disingenuously preaching brotherhood to those of all races, creeds and colors. Janet Maslin of *The New York Times* wrote that Jackson "makes a delightfully sly presence," and Mathews credited him for doing a "spirited parody of Don King."[4]

Julio Escobar (Marin), head of the WBI, is a carbon copy of WBC President Jose Sulliman, who has been accused of manipulating ratings and using other unethical favoritism for Don King's benefit. "Even I cannot rank a fighter who has not had a professional fight," Escobar exclaims to the Sultan, before being pressured into rating Conklin number eight in the world.[5]

Roper has the unmistakable lisp and quavering voice of Mike Tyson, who like the ex-heavyweight champion watches a martial-arts film before each fight. The champion's entourage is filled with gold chain-wearing "yes men" who epitomize all the negative aspects associated with the boxing entourage. Nothing more than hangers-on, they feed the champion's ego and then scavenge for his excess wealth.

The film is specifically aimed at fight fans, who should both enjoy and be amused by the picture, even if they do not find it hilarious. Noting that the film's skits are geared for a target group, Jamie Bernard of the *New York Daily News* wrote that "some work, some don't, but all of them pause for laughs that only select audiences will provide."[6]

Godfrey Chesire of *Variety* criticized that the film has "sporadic moments of dead-on satiric hilarity [which] only partly compensate for the general tepidness."[7] Stuart Klawans of *The Nation* opined that the gags are all "good," "or at least good tries, ... blithely ignoring the distinction."[8] However, boxing insiders might rightly question just how many of the boxing parodies these two critics picked up on. Janet Maslin of *The New York Times* seemed to best sum up the film, writing, "A lot of the film's gags are just throw aways, but its high spirits sustain a spiky comic style."[9]

Peter Berg, who starred in television's *Chicago Hope*, trained four hours a day for one month for his role as Conklin, working with boxing choreographer Rasho Khan and stunt coordinator Eddie Watkins. Berg also consulted with ex-lightweight champion Ray "Boom Boom" Mancini to improve his boxing technique. "I learned that if you catch a right in the nose, you get sick in the stomach, your eyes start tearing and you feel nauseous and angry all at once," Berg said, reflecting on the most elemental aspect of his boxing experience.[10]

Berg, who was placed on a high-protein, low-fat diet, gained 15 pounds for the film. However, his counterpart Damon Wayans, the star of *In Living Color*, who was scripted to be out of shape, did not need to aspire to physical fitness. "The champ has the same training regimen as George Foreman," Wayans joked. "You know, 20 burgers, a sit-up, and a cigarette." In fact, to make Roper appear overweight, Wayans was fitted with a prosthetic stomach, which took an hour to place on and 45 minutes to remove.[11] The boxing vignettes in the film are brief, and fairly well done, as is the actor's boxing, but it is all completely incidental to the satire beyond the roped square.

The picture was filmed in Los Angeles and Las Vegas. Ironically, the Vegas portion of the production was made just days before the Mike Tyson-Peter McNeeley fight was staged in that city. "Irish" Peter McNeeley, is the son of former heavyweight contender Tom McNeeley and Don King's latest White hype. Tyson dispatched McNeeley in one round, just as Roper did Conklin, further boosting the widely held theory that a "White Hope" will perform dismally — no matter what the circumstances.

As amusing as fight fans will find the Conklin-McNeeley connection, movie fans will enjoy the curious selection of set location by Twentieth Century-Fox. Filmed extensively at the MGM Grand Hotel, MGM's symbol of the lion appears throughout the film, providing free advertising for the rival studio.

1. *The Great White Hype*, produced by Fred Berner, Joshua Donen, directed by Reginald Hudlin, 90 minutes, 1996.
2. *Ibid.*
3. Jack Mathews, "A Racial Farce on the Ropes," *Newsday*, 3 May 1996, sec. B, p. 3.
4. Janet Maslin, Review of *The Great White Hype* (Twentieth Century-Fox movie), *New York Times*, 3 May 1996; Mathews, "Racial Farce."
5. *The Great White Hype*, produced by Fred Berner, Joshua Donen, directed by Reginald Hudlin, 90 minutes, 1996.
6. Jamie Bernard, Review of *The Great White Hype* (Twentieth Century-Fox movie), *New York Daily News*, 3 May 1996.
7. Godfrey Cheshire, Review of *The Great White Hype* (Twentieth Century-Fox movie), *Variety*, 6 May 1996.
8. Stuart Klawans, Review of *The Great White Hype* (Twentieth Century-Fox movie), *Nation*, 10 June 1936.
9. Maslin.
10. Production Notes for *The Great White Hype*.
11. *Ibid.*

The Greatest (1977)

Columbia Pictures, Bio-Drama, Color, 101 minutes

Producer: John Marshall. *Director*: Tom Gries. *Screenplay*: Ring Lardner, Jr., based upon the biography "The Greatest", by Muhammad Ali, Herbert Muhammad and Richard Durham. *Film Editor*: Byron Brandt. *Photography Director*: Harry Stradling, Jr. *Music*: Michael Masser.

Muhammad Ali (Himself), Ernest Borgnine (Angelo Dundee), John Marley (Dr. Ferdie Pacheco), Robert Duvall (Bill McDonald), James Earl Jones (Malcom X), Roger E. Mosley (Sonny Liston), Ben Johnson (Mullins), Paul Winfield (Draft Lawyer), Lloyd Haynes (Herbert Muhammad), Dina Merrill (Velvet Green), David Huddleston (Cruikshank), Malachi Throne (Payton Jory), Lucille Benson (Mrs. Fairlie), Theodore R. Wilson (John The Gardner), Richard Gullage (Commissioner), Arthur Adams (Cassius Clay, Sr.), Dorothy Meter (Odessa Clay), Rahaman Ali (Himself), Howard Bingham (Himself), Richard Venture (Colonel), Stack Pierce (Rahaman), W. Young Muhammad (Himself), Ben Medina (Ronnie), Paul Mantee (Carraha), Skip Hometer (Major), Lloyd Wells (Himself), David Clennon (Captain), George Garro (Mrs. Curtis), Ernie Wheelwright (Bossman Jones), Pat Patterson (Himself), George Cooper (Lawyer), James Gammon (Mr. Harry), Gene Kilroy (Himself), Toni Crabtree (Hooker), Sally Griers (Sponsor's Wife), Elizabeth Marshall (Sponsor's Wife), Don Dunphy (Himself), Fernado A. Lahrieu, Jr., (Grocer), Nai Boney (Suzie Gomez), Harold Conrad (Himself), Alberto Martin (Doctor), Ray Holland (Reporter).

A draft-dodging cur and villainous Black Muslim to some, a symbol of social conscience and righteous religious figure to others, the dichotomy of Muhammad Ali's public persona was surpassed only by the contradiction found in his personality. Paradoxically, the young Ali was both a distasteful combination of bombast and braggadocio and an ingratiating mixture of charm and wit.

Whether you loved him or despised him, by the late 1970s Muhammad Ali had become one of the most recognizable human beings on the face of the earth. Not surprisingly, this rising icon of the twentieth century became the first active American boxing champion to portray himself in a feature film. Columbia Pictures took the leap when it cast Ali to play himself in *The Greatest*, a bio-drama surveying the life of the three-time heavyweight champion.

Based upon the autobiography of the same name, *The Greatest* traces Ali from his pre-Muslim days as Cassius Clay, the "Louisville Lip" who captured the gold medal in the light-heavyweight division at the 1960 Rome Olympic Games. The film continues through to an arid evening in Kinshasa, Zaire, Africa, 14 years later, where as a prohibitive underdog, he stripped George Foreman of his cloak of invincibility by knocking out the then-undefeated world heavyweight champion.

In *The Greatest*, the story of Ali the boxer is really secondary to that of Ali the man. Considering that Ali is arguably the greatest heavyweight champion of all time, this speaks volumes to either his social significance or his ego—and most likely both.

While the film only summarily addresses the mayhem of the 1960s, it captures the essence of the era from the boxer's perspective. The champ's application for draft exemption was based upon the grounds that as a minister of the Nation of Islam he was forbidden to participate "in any war in which the lives of human beings are being taken."[1] However, Ali's conscientious objection extended beyond his religious beliefs and possessed a distinctly social flavor. To Ali's and the film's credit, no attempt is made to restrict Muhammad's stance on the Vietnam War to his legally vindicated religious convictions. "Black people should not be required to fight yellow people who never lynched us, raped us, or called us niggers," Ali tells military personnel in the film after refusing to be inducted into the U.S. armed forces.[2]

On more than one occasion, *The Greatest* uses racial epitaphs to thrust to the fore American racism in its most elemental form. In this manner, *The Greatest* is at least forthright, although not comprehensive in its attempt to pierce subject matter that many other films of the day timidly approached with polite, cursory or circuitous treatments.

In dealing with Ali's stance on the Vietnam War and the race issue, the film does strive for candor. However, despite these honest moments, further made credible by Ali's presence, the film's undeniably self-effacing framework also spawns the trite and self-indulgent. When Ali receives word that the Supreme Court has unanimously reversed his conviction for draft evasion, he is surrounded by a gaggle of cheering children to whom he exclaims his freedom. It is scenes such as this that surely prompted critic D.C. of *Cineaste* to describe the film as "a publicity puff-piece," and Richard Shickel of *Time* to bemoan the work as the "latest flurry in that blizzard-like snow job Ali has huffed and puffed to keep blowing for well over a decade."[3]

The Greatest is also guilty of the omission of certain portions of Ali's career and life, most notably the controversial second Liston bout and his relationship with Malcolm X. An insightful explanation of Ali's motivation behind his denunciation of Christianity in favor of the Islamic faith and Ali's feelings regarding the Muslim-Malcom X schism is also lacking.

True to Ali's ability to provoke controversy, the film spawned an array of opinions, although no one was effusive in their praise. Jack Kroll of *Newsweek* panned the film, calling it "a stumble bum," while *Time* labeled the film "artless and slightly flaky."[4] Clancy Segal of *The Spectator* found some merit, calling the picture "a Black Rocky," while Ernest LeoGrande of the *Daily News* complimented the film as "a smoothly crafted and entertaining testimonial."[5] Nelson George of the *New Amsterdam News* simply wrote, "Ali fans will love it."[6]

Ali's film debut as an actor was, with perhaps the exception of Max Baer, the most warmly received of any pugilist-turned-actor. While David Sterritt of *The Christian Science Monitor* wrote, "Ali the actor is so far an unskilled entity," Murf of *Variety* found Ali more promising, writing that "his charisma would lend much credibility to a variety of roles."[7] Archer Winsten of the *New York Post* noted that Ali "is not awed the slightest bit by the camera ... speaking his lines and poetry and anger without a trace of the amateur."[8]

At a minimum, *The Greatest* creates an historical document of Ali's skill and courage by the use of original fight film footage, particularly through clips from the Foreman bout. In his later years, Ali, who has steadfastly adhered to his faith, has suffered greatly from the nerve disorder Parkinson's Disease, which has disabled the champ's body, although not his mind. While the condition has buttoned the once irrepressible "Louisville Lip," and has physically reduced Ali to a figure who stands in stark contrast to the once great physical specimen, the champ's human spirit burns brighter than ever.

1. Muhammad Ali with Richard Durham, *Greatest: My Own Story* (New York: Random House, 1975).
2. *The Greatest*, produced by John Marshall, directed by Tom Gries, 101 minutes, 1977.
3. D.G., Review of *The Greatest* (Columbia Pictures movie), *Cineaste*, Fall 1977; Richard Shickel, Review of *The Greatest* (Columbia Pictures movie), *Time*, 6 June 1997.
4. Jack Kroll, Review of *The Greatest* (Columbia Pictures movie), *Newsweek*, 30 May 1977; Shickel.
5. Clancy Sigal, Review of *The Greatest* (Columbia Pictures movie), *Spectator*, 20 August 1977; Ernest LeoGrande, Review of *The Greatest* (Columbia Pictures movie), *New York Daily News*, 21 May 1977.
6. Nelson George, Review of *The Greatest* (Columbia Pictures movie), *New York Amsterdam News*, 28 May 1977.
7. David Sterritt, Review of *The Greatest* (Co-

lumbia Pictures movie), *Christian Science Monitor*; Murf, Review of *The Greatest* (Columbia Pictures movie), *Variety*, 25 May 1977.

8. Archer Winsten, Review of *The Greatest* (Columbia Pictures movie), *New York Post*, 21 May 1977.

Hard Times (1975)

Columbia Pictures, Drama, Color, 94 minutes

Producer: Lawrence Gordon. *Director*: Walter Hill. *Screenplay*: Walter Hill, Bryan Gindoff, Bruce Henstell. *Film Editor*: Roger Spottiswoode. *Director of Photography*: Philip Lathrop, A.S.C. *Music*: Barry Devorzon.

Charles Bronson (Chaney), James Coburn (Speed), Jill Ireland (Lucy Simpson), Martin Strother (Poe), Maggie Blye (Gayleen Schoonover), Michael McGuire (Gandil), Edward Walsh (Pettibon), Felice Orlandi (LeBeau), Bruce Glover (Doty), Robert Tessier (Jim Henry), Frank Mcrae (Hammerman), Nick Dimitri (Street).

Well-proportioned, with lean muscles and rippling abdominals, Charles Buchinsky was a young actor destined to play the role of a boxer. In 1954, Buchinsky would get the first of several opportunities to appear in a fight picture when he was cast as a scrapper named Sixty Jubel in the dramacomedy *Tennessee Champ*. Writer Art Cohn, who had already penned a fine adaptation of Joseph Moncure March's *The Set-Up* several years earlier, scripted the film's screenplay, based upon a Eustace Cocktrell story entitled *The Lord in His Corner*.[1]

Tennessee Champ starred Shelley Winters, who played opposite Keenan Wynn, an unscrupulous fight manager of a religious boxer portrayed by Dewey Martin. Martin uses spiritual fortitude in *Tennessee Champ* to persuade his manager to turn legit. The film, which also features Earl Holliman as one of its boxers, culminates with Martin boxing Buchinsky.

Buchinsky fared well as a prizefighter, and several years later, he was again cast as a boxer in an episode of the science-fiction television series *One Step Beyond*. Buchinsky portrayed "Yank" Dawson, an American scheduled to fight in the East End Arena during World War II. Many years earlier, a fighter named Paddy was killed in the Arena, and legend has it that his ghost visited other boxers before they met a similar fate in the same ring. The manager of Dawson's opponent exploits the ghost story to spook Dawson and hires an actor to portray Paddy. However, the real ghost appears to several of those remaining in the Arena after the fight, including Dawson, who are then killed in a bombing raid, fulfilling the haunting.[2]

One Step Beyond allowed the actor to further display his natural ring style and proficient boxing ability. Buchinsky, who had come to be known as Charles Bronson, was still playing supporting roles when he landed a part in Elvis Presley's fight vehicle entitled *Kid Galahad* (1962). Bronson was endowed with all the muscle and had the superior boxing technique, but Elvis was the star, so he got to wear the gloves while Bronson carried his towel and spit bucket.

As his career gained momentum, Bronson continued to use masculine roles, principally in action pictures, to become a bona fide movie star. By the early 1970s Bronson was middle-aged, but his fabulous physique had scarcely changed. With his face now somewhat aged and weathered, his composite physical characteristics were perfectly suited for the lead in *Hard Times*. *Hard Times* relates the story of Chaney, a stoic drifter with a fierce independent streak who survives for a spell as a bare-knuckle boxer in the underground fight culture of the Depression. Chaney is managed by a voracious gambler with a twinkle in his eye named Speed, memorably portrayed by James Coburn. Speed treats Chaney as chattel, causing a rift in their partnership, but Chaney ultimately returns to win a high-stakes match, saving Speed from his gangster creditors before disappearing back into his transient world.

The film relies heavily on atmosphere. As noted by Bronson, "The fight scenes are exciting, but in *Hard Times*, the story and style take precedence to the action."[3] Andrew Sarris of *The Village Voice* credited the screenwriter's sparing approach as "adroit enough to keep its dialogue to a minimum and let the baroque settings, portentous eye contacts, and rhapsodically edited violence do most of the talking."[4] Director Roy Hill even-handedly exploits the rich and diverse surroundings of New Orleans: the French Quarter, the Cornstalk Hotel, Magazine Street, the Irish Channel Area, the Chalmette railroad yards and St. Vincent DePaul Cemetery.[5]

Pauline Kael writing for *The New Yorker*, credited director Hill for "using Bronson with superb calculation" in a role which was well received by the critics.[6] "This star's granite presence is properly exploited for its resonant possibilities for the first time in *Hard Times*," wrote Frank Rich of the *New York Post*. "The tension hidden in the actor's body and the secrets locked beyond his cold sad eyes link Chaney to our most romantic image of the woeful hard-times hobo."[7]

The fight scenes in *Hard Times* are excellent entertainment. Despite the fact that the fights are not staged in a boxing ring under the Marquess of Queensberry rules, unlike most other "fist-fighting" movies, the matches in *Hard Times* are contested within finite physical perimeters. The rules of contest occasionally stray beyond those of traditional boxing, but the action is still in the spirit of the old London Prize Ring Rules of the bare-knuckle era.

Ship decks, open fields, and warehouse interiors serve as the combatants' makeshift rings, adding character and grit to the fight scenes. The boxing vignettes are also complemented by boisterous and roaring gamblers who encircle the fighters for all of the matches, save the finale, which intensifies dramatic tension through a near silent battle before a private audience. Bronson endows the fighting Chaney with an intense stare. Unperturbed and purposeful, he nimbly sidesteps blows and blocks and parries others, delivering his own crisp left-right combinations and whipping hooks with overwhelming hand speed. The bare-knuckle contests in *Hard Times* are a fine blend of boxing artistry and physical brutality, remaining one of Hollywood's more memorable contributions to fisticuffs.

1. Brog, Review of *Tennessee Champ* (MGM movie), *Variety*, 17 February 1954.
2. Television rebroadcast of episode of television series *One Step Beyond*.
3. "Charles Bronson," Columbia Pictures Studio Publicity.
4. Andrew Sarris, Review of *Hard Times* (Columbia Pictures movie), *Village Voice*, 3 November 1975.
5. "'Hard Times,' A Knockout '30s Drama," Columbia Pictures Studio Publicity.
6. Pauline Kael, Review of *Hard Times* (Columbia Pictures movie), *New Yorker*, 6 October 1975.
7. Frank Rich, Review of *Hard Times* (Columbia Pictures movie), *New York Post*, 9 October 1975.

The Harder They Fall (1956)

Columbia Pictures, Drama, B & W, 109 minutes

Producer: Philip Yordan. *Director*: Mark Robson. *Screenplay*: Philip Yordan, from the novel by Budd Schulberg. *Film Editor*: Jerome Thomas. *Photography*: Burnett Guffey. *Music*: Hugo Friedhofer.

Humphrey Bogart (Eddie Willis), Rod Steiger (Nick Benko), Jan Sterling (Beth Willis), Mike Lane (Toro Moreno), Max Baer (Buddy Brannen), Jersey Joe Walcott (George), Edward Andrews (Jim Weyerhause), Harold J. Stone (Art Leavitt), Carlos Montalban (Luis Agrandi), Nehemiah Persoff (Leo), Felice Orlandi (Vince Fawcett), Herbie Faye (Max), Rusty Lane (Danny McKeogh), Jack Albertson (Pop), Val Avery (Frank), Tommy Herman (Tommy), Vinnie Decarlo (Joey), Pat Comiskey (Gus Dundee), Matt Murphy (Sailor Rigazzo), Abel Fernandez (Chief Firebird), Marion Carr (Alice).

Having already struck the mother lode with *On the Waterfront* two years prior, Columbia Pictures returned to the Budd Schulberg mine to further tap the novelist's talents. While *Waterfront* had used a prizefighter as a central figure to reach outward into the world of social corruption, Schulberg's subsequent novel, *The Harder They Fall*, bored inward to the rank and squalor of the fight game itself.

Despite the mandatory disclaimers to the contrary, *The Harder They Fall* was, with minor adjustment, the tale of former heavyweight champion Primo Carnera. The film "might as well have been entitled 'The Carnera Story' for whatever difference it offered between fiction and fact," Carnera's biographer Frederic Mullally would later write.[1]

Carnera was an ex-circus strongman from Sequels, Italy, brought to the United States by manager Leon See at the start of the Depression to further advance his ring career.[2] The pair arrived in New York, and were immediately swallowed up by the corrupt fight racket of the day.

Carnera was soon within the tight grip of Owney Madden, a racketeer also known as "Owney the Killer." Madden owned interests in five world champions at one time or another, including Max Baer and Rocky Marciano, both of whom allegedly became his life-long friends.[3] Madden's partners in "team Carnera" were another notorious New York gangster Big Frenchy DeMange and Madden's old bootlegging pal "Big" Bill Duffy, who ostensibly managed the fighter.[4]

The Ambling Alp, as the boxer was known, was piloted to the heavyweight championship by his crooked management through a series of fixed fights, though in all probability Carnera was unaware of the extent of the shame. Many accounts claim that Madden and his gangster cronies were responsible for bilking Carnera out of millions in ring earnings. The role of See also remains suspect.[5]*

To portray the victimized fighter, producer Philip Yordan desired an unknown. Columbia embarked on a three-month worldwide search that spanned the United States, South America, Mexico, and Europe. The studio finally settled on a twenty-four year old named Mike Lane, who ironically was also an ex-circus strongman. At six feet, ten inches tall, 275 pounds, and a size 18-foot, Lane was figuratively and literally large enough to fill the shoes of the "Man Mountain," Primo Carnera.[6]

In *The Harder They Fall*, Primo Carnera is revisited, in the form of Toro Moreno (Lane), a gargantuan South American strongman imported to the United States by Nick Banco (Steiger), a shrewd and manipulative fight manager. Despite his imposing physique, the fighter has a powder puff punch and a glass jaw. To help sell his cha-

---

*The Mullally biography details the actions of See as being less than scrupulous.

rade to the public, Banco hires an inherently honest but disillusioned and financially needy newspaperman named Eddie Willis (Bogart) to ballyhoo the fighter. Toro and his equally naive manager Agrandi (Montalban) trust Eddie implicitly and buy into the half-truths and myths he creates, unaware that Toro is the centerpiece of a massive fraud.

Toro is guided into contention, but when an opponent (Comiskey) dies from an injury sustained during their bout, Toro's mother calls him home. After an attempt to appeal to the fighter's sense of loyalty fails, Nick threatens violence. Eddie is forced to reveal the entire scam to a deflated and disbelieving Toro in the hope that he will take the fight to earn a final payday. In the face of inevitable defeat, Toro's pride forces him to take a frightful beating before succumbing to a knockout.

The hospitalized boxer then sends Eddie to collect his purse. Standing behind his accountant (Persoff) and a mound of paperwork, Banco attempts to justify how the million-dollar gate has netted Toro $49.07. His self-respect resting in the balance, Eddie gives Toro his own share of the cut, $26,000, and puts him on a plane back to South America. Having already sold Toro's contract to another manager (Andrews), Banco holds Eddie accountable for exporting his merchandise. Defiant of Banco's threats, a resolute Eddie plants himself behind a typewriter and begins to pound out his tell-all exposé on Nick, and why he believes the sport of boxing should be banned.

The Harder They Fall is a deft and unsettling examination of the underbelly of boxing. If the sport of boxing was a stone resting on damp soil, then the film overturns the stone to reveal all that squirms beneath. A fighter who bungles a double-cross is knifed in his shower; piercing chicken wire is inserted into a fighter's mouthpiece to shred the inside of his lips; sly managers financially rape their fighters, who are at best treated as horses; and morally reprehensible promoters exploit human fatality to sell tickets. So critical of the fight game was the film that Schulberg, who possessed a deep affection for the sport, accused Robson of directing the film "with hate."[7] As a result, Schulberg disassociated himself from Robson, who in turn remained unforgiving of Schulberg for his reaction.[8]

Columbia had desired to shoot the fight scenes on location at a known fight venue. However, in reaction to the film's scathing indictment of the sport, boxing arenas across the nation, from New York to Chicago to Los Angeles, uniformly bristled at the studio's request to utilize their facilities.[9] The film's message might have jeopardized gate receipts, and the owners were unwilling to put their own necks in a financial noose.

The studio was forced to settle on building its own arena, which it did through the conversion of two sound stages. In the final match, over 500 extras were packed into the artificial venue to simulate the fight crowd.[10] To capture the ring action from every conceivable vantage point, director Mark Robson pushed a hand truck around the ring, while cameraman Burnett Guffey sat in the truck filming with his portable Aeroflex camera. Shooting lasted for an entire week.[11]

To simulate the progressive beating received by Toro, filming was periodically stopped to redo make-up. Everything from flesh-colored plastic skin to fake eyelids covered with thick pads of foam rubber was utilized to create the desired effect.[12] Bosley Crowther of *The New York Times* credited the work of screenwriter Yordan and director Robson, who fashioned "brutish and bruising fight scenes" that contributed to the establishment of "a stinging film."[13]

The Harder They Fall includes the most ironic cinematic fight ever filmed. As a contender for the heavyweight crown, Max Baer had given Ernie Schaaf a terrific beating, but powder puff puncher Primo Carnera was credited with "killing" Schaaf, when Schaaf died following a later match with

Carnera.* These factual circumstances were duplicated almost verbatim in the film. Max Baer, who portrays Buddy Brannen, injures Gus Dundee, played by Pat Comiskey, only to have the light-punching Toro credited with inflicting the damage, when Dundee dies at Toro's hands in a subsequent bout. In sum, the film revisits Baer's own real-life experience of severely injuring a ring foe along with Carnera's completion of the tragedy.†

In an effort to capture the appropriate shots within the ring, director Robson coached Baer, the erstwhile heavyweight champion. "Don't worry, I know all about cameras," Baer playfully assured. "When I was fighting, even when I was knocked down, I always faced the camera."[14] The jovial Baer acquitted himself nicely in the fight scenes, despite being 47 years old. Fellow heavyweight champion Jersey Joe Walcott was also in form, looking expectantly crafty in his sparring sessions with the Toro character. Gene of *Variety* noted that Jersey Joe Walcott "is surprisingly effective" as the "warm-hearted trainer."[15] Despite being a boxing novice, Mike Lane was physically appropriate for his part and gave an acceptable portrayal within the roped square.

Variety reported that Bogie's performance, in what was to prove his final film, was "competent as-per usual Bogart at work."[16] Rod Steiger, however, gives the best portrayal as Nick, turning in a commanding performance, which co-star Humphrey Bogart watched unfold with some jealousy. "You're going to kill me," Bogie would tell Steiger." "Bo, you got to get better parts," Steiger replied.[17] As artfully expressed by William K. Zinsser of the *Herald-Tribune*, "It is Steiger who gives the movie its veneer of cruelty and greed. He is a silky dictator who can juggle his fighters and his accounts with equal deceit."[18]

Zinsser also rightfully praised the film for depicting its generic content with "such brutal honesty and vivid detail," applauding Robson for "stripping" his characters "to their raw nature" and Yordan for his script which contains "talk in the hard, staccato way of people who come straight to the point."[19] While other aspects of the picture have become dated, the film's strong characters and pointed dialogue have endured, allowing *The Harder They Fall* to remain a highly entertaining and insightful study of the fight game.

1. Frederic Mullally, *Primo: The Story of "Man Mountain" Carnera* (London: Robson Books Ltd., 1991) 186.
2. *Ibid.*, 42.
3. Graham Nown, *The English Godfather Owney Madden* (London, Ward Lock Limited, 1987) 86–87.
4. Mullally, *"Man Mountain,"* 48.
5. *Ibid.*, 51.
6. "Six-Foot, Ten-Inch Mike Lane Plays 'Harder They Fall' Giant." Columbia Pictures Press Book for *The Harder They Fall*.
7. George Luft, "Mark Robson — Did Not Dally Long with Message Films," *Films in Review*, May 1968, 288.
8. *Ibid.*
9. "Bogart, Rod Steiger, Jan Sterling Star in Fight Film, 'Harder They Fall.'" Columbia Pictures Press Book for *The Harder They Fall*.
10. "Stage Arena Foils Fight-Mob Boycott," Columbia Pictures Press Book for *The Harder They Fall*.
11. "Film Fistic Fury in Boxing Expose," Columbia Pictures Press Book for *The Harder They Fall*.
12. "'The Harder They Fall' Title Bout Called Operation Slaughter!" Columbia Pictures Press Book for *The Harder They Fall*.
13. Bosley Crowther, Review of *The Harder They Fall* (Columbia Pictures movie), *New York Times*, 10 May 1956.
14. "Camera Conscious." Columbia Pictures Press Book for *The Harder They Fall*.
15. Gene, Review of *The Harder They Fall* (Columbia Pictures movie), *Variety*, 28 March 1956.
16. *Ibid.*

---

*Baer defeated Ernie Schaaf in 10 rounds in Chicago on August 31, 1932. Carnera KO'ed Schaaf in 13 rounds in New York City on February 10, 1933.

†Fact and fiction are further combined in the relationship of Baer and Comiskey. The two boxers had met prior to their staged confrontation as Brannen and Dundee in a professional boxing match held at Jersey City, New Jersey, September 26, 1940, in which Baer knocked out Comiskey in a single round.

17. A.M. Sperber, Eric Lax, *Bogart*, (New York: William Morrow and Company, Inc., 1997), 507.
18. William K. Zinsser, Review of *The Harder They Fall* (Columbia Pictures movie). *New York Herald-Tribune*, 10 May 1956.
19. Ibid.

Heart of a Champion: The Ray Mancini Story (1985)

CBS Made-for-Television Movie, Bio-Drama, Color, 100 minutes

Executive Producer: Sylvester Stallone. *Producer*: Rare Titles Production in association with Robert Papazian Productions, Inc. *Director*: Richard Michaels. *Writer*: Dennis Nemec. *Film Editor*: Peter E. Berger. *Director of Photography*: Jan De Bont. *Music*: Mike Post.

Robert Blake (Lenny Mancini), Doug Mckeon (Ray Mancini), Mariclare Costello (Ellen Mancini), Tony Burton (Grif), Ray Buktenica (Dave Wolf), James Callahan (Father O'Neil), Dick Bakalyan (Frank Jacobs), Curtis Conoway (Lenny), Luisa Leschin (Ellen, Jr.), Norman Alden (Ray Arcel), Ben Frank (Eddie Sullivan), Carl Steven (Ray, Age 10), Judith Penrod (Business Lady), James Arone (Freddy), Marty Denkin (Referee), Richard Doyle (Journalist #1), Steve Eastin (Male Reporter), Jimmy Gambina (Older Fan), Paul Jenkins (Steelworker), Marta Kober (Sandy), Jimmy Lennon, Jimmy Lennon, Jr. (Ring Announcers), Mario Machado (Broadcaster), Stephen Mendel (Eye Doctor), Duke Moosekian (Fan), Lycia Naff (Cynthi), Margery Nelson (Journalist #2), Dee Dee Rescher (Female Reporter), Scott St. James (Broadcaster), Steven Sotelo (Alexis Arguello).

The Greatest, *The Great White Hope*, and *Raging Bull* suggest that a prerequisite for a boxer's life to be memorialized in celluloid, as with Ali's, Jack Johnson's, or Jake La Motta's, is that the pugilist permeate the consciousness of the public at large. Measured by this standard, it is something of a surprise that the life of a courageous boxer of limited repute named Ray Mancini was brought to film. On the other hand, when there is an uncanny similarity between a fighter's life, such as Mancini's, and the bread-and-butter makings of a Hollywood melodrama, the story begs to be told.

Heart of a Champion is the story of Ray Mancini (McKeon), an Italian-American from a working class family in Youngstown, Ohio. Ray idolizes his father Lenny (Blake), who was once the number-one contender for Lew Jenkins's lightweight crown until his career was cut short by a wound sustained during World War II.* Mesmerized by his father's faded scrapbook, Ray is inspired to launch his own ring career and win the title for dad, who was robbed of his opportunity.

Ray endures all of the drudgery of training, the lonely nights on the road, and the tragic shooting death of his brother Len along the way to his shot at the crown. Just prior to his title opportunity against Alexis Arguello, Lenny has heart surgery, giving Ray even greater impetus to win the title. While Ray falls short in his effort against Arguello, he displays the true heart of a champion by winning the title in his second opportunity against Art Frias.

Conspicuously absent from *Heart of a Champion* is the tragic ring death of the fighter's Korean opponent Duk Koo Kim, which occurred shortly after Mancini won the championship against Art Frias. While the incident was clearly compelling drama, and would have offered greater insight into Mancini's personality and character, its inclusion would have taken the script beyond its storybook ending, a risk the producers

---

*Lew Jenkins won the lightweight championship with a third round knockout of Lou Ambers on May 10, 1940, in New York City.

were apparently unwilling to take. The choice to avoid the grave episode with Kim may have also been dictated by business considerations at CBS, which produced the made-for-television movie drama. Including a ring death amid calls for the ban of the sport could not have been considered prudent economics, particularly for a network that was still profiting from its regularly scheduled Saturday afternoon boxing contests.

Originally, Mancini was scheduled to portray himself; however, the film's shooting schedule conflicted with "Boom Boom's" previously arranged title defense of his WBA lightweight championship against Livingstone Bramble.* Mancini felt compelled to honor his contractual obligation to box Bramble and left the acting to Doug McKeon.[1]

To prepare for the role of Ray Mancini, McKeon trained at the Main Street Gym in downtown Los Angeles for two weeks with Jimmy Gambina.[2] Among others, Gambina tutored Jon Voight for *The Champ* and Sylvester Stallone for *Rocky*. Stallone, the executive producer of *Heart of a Champion*, and the modern dean of the staged ring encounter, drew upon his choreography talents honed in the *Rocky* films to fashion the exciting ring sequences for the Mancini biography.

The fight sequences are stylized in the slam-bam mold of the *Rocky* films, but Stallone was careful to maintain authenticity, recreating the action sequences while eliminating the lulls. Mancini fights are often "Rocky-esque," and that must have made Stallone's task that much simpler. Fights highlighted in the film include a pair of amateur bouts, Mancini's first professional contest, his breakthrough fight against Jose Luis Ramirez, and his championship contests against Alexis Arguello and Art Frias. McKeon finely reproduces the spectrum of Mancini's ring style, from his sometimes porous defensive to his lethal offensive arsenal spearheaded by his familiar combination of hooks to the body and head, delivered as part of his swarming style.

McKeon, who portrayed Jane Fonda's son in *On Golden Pond*, not only bears a facial resemblance to Mancini, but does an excellent job capturing the fighter's full physical persona, from his gait and voice intonation to his more subtle head bob and hand mannerisms. The actor also faithfully recreates Mancini's spunk, enthusiasm and spilling energy, which he exhibits both in and out of the ring. Jon Anderson of the *Chicago Tribune* wrote, "The evening's acting title goes to Doug McKeon. His 'Boom Boom' is energetic, thoughtful, [and] sentimental."[3] Daniel Ruth of the *Chicago Sun-Times* wrote that McKeon is "one of the major dramatic actors of the future" and that he "turns in a sensitive and gritty portrayal."[4]

Robert Blake also received praise for his role as the father whose dream is realized through his son. "In perhaps his best work since *In Cold Blood* 18 years ago, Robert Blake is first-rate as Lenny Mancini," wrote the *Chicago-Sun Times*.[5] While Mancini himself recognized that "Blake captured the emotion in our relationship," the boxer was very upset that the actor failed to grasp "the true essence" of his father, and criticized the actor for portraying him as a "stereotype of an old washed-up fighter," rather than a man of style and respect. "My father does not call other people bums, especially other fighters," a perturbed Mancini said, commenting on one of Blake's lines.[6]

Despite the fine reviews received by the picture's two principal players, the critics' response to *Heart of a Champion* was lukewarm at best. Laura Gross of the *New York Post* complimented the film, noting that it "has the look and feel of reality that high-gloss TV-movies usually don't have."[7] However, Daku of *Variety* seriously belittled the picture, calling it "an innocuous drama with all the punch of a powder puff."[8] Marvin Kitman of *Newsday* opined that the story

---

*Mancini would lose his WBA lightweight championship to Bramble via 15-round decision on June 1, 1984, in a classic slugfest.

was "curiously flat," finding that "the father and son bit ... pales after two hours."[9] Nevertheless, if one is willing to overlook the film's sentimental tone, *Heart of a Champion* can still be enjoyed for its quality acting and solid fight vignettes.

1. Kay Gardella, "'Boom Boom' Mancini Packs Punch as TV Project," *New York Daily News*, 26 February 1985, 68.
2. Tim Boxer, "'Boom Boom' Boos Blake," *New York Post*, 30 April 1985, 74.
3. Jon Anderson, "'Heart of a Champion' Plot Doesn't Have Knockout Punch," *Chicago Tribune*, 1 May 1985, sec. 2, p. 7.
4. Daniel Ruth, "Ray Mancini's Story Shows a Lot of 'Heart,'" Review of *Heart of a Champion: The Ray Mancini Story* (CBS Television movie), *Chicago-Sun Times*, 1 May 1985, 58.
5. Ibid.
6. Boxer, "Boom Boom Boos Blake," 74.
7. Laura Gross, "True-to-'Heart,'" Review of *Heart of a Champion: The Ray Mancini Story* (CBS Television movie), *New York Post*, 1 May 1985.
8. Daku, Review of *Heart of a Champion: The Ray Mancini Story* (CBS Television movie), *Variety*, 3 May 1985, 158.
9. Marvin Kitman, Review of *Heart of a Champion: The Ray Mancini Story* (CBS Television movie), *Newsday*, 1 May 1985, part 2, p. 68.

Heart Punch (1932)

Mayfair Pictures Corp., Drama, B & W, 66 minutes

Producer: Anchon Royer. *Director*: B. Reeves Eason. *Story*: Frank Howard Clark. *Adaptation and Dialogue*: John Thomas Neville. *Photography*: George Meehan.

Lloyd Hughes (The Cyclone Kid), Marion Shilling, George Lewis, Wheeler Oakman, Mae Busch, Walter Miller, Gordon De Main, Tammany Young, James Leong. Character names not available.

In 1915, Jess Willard, a big farm boy from Kansas, and latest of the "Great White Hopes," signed to fight Jack Johnson for the heavyweight championship of the world. In an effort to cash in on the free publicity already being generated by the sports press, Universal Studios offered to put the six-foot-six-inch, 245-pound contender in movies. For the fee of $1,000 and the pleasure of making a film with his fistic handlers Jack Hurley and Tom Jones, Willard signed with Universal.[1] The studio cast the "Potawamie Giant" in a boxing melodrama written for the screen by Stuart Paton entitled *Heart Punch*, co-starring Catherine Lee, Marie Wierman and Bobby Vernon. The title of the film was a metaphor for its plot: a fighter's boxing career strikes a blow to his love affair.

Years later, Frank Howard Clark borrowed the film's name, writing his own story and attributing a different significance to the title. In 1932, Mayfair Pictures adapted the Clark yarn and released its own version of *Heart Punch*. An early sound melodrama marked by its predictable story line, *Heart Punch* starred Lloyd Hughes, with a non-memorable supporting cast.

In *Heart Punch*, the "Cyclone Kid" (Hughes) is a promising boxer who kills his ex-navy pal Bobby Doyle in the ring with a blow to the heart. Inconsolable over his friend's death, the "Cyclone Kid" quits the fight game. Shortly afterwards, he begins the courtship of Doyle's sister Kitty, who is unaware of her new love's true identity. The couple plans to marry until Kitty learns that her fiancé was responsible for her brother's death. After they separate, Kitty is pursued by her boss Joe. She spurns his sexual advances and when a physical struggle ensues, Joe is shot dead by the girl, who is then charged with murder. The "Cyclone Kid" returns to the ring to earn money to pay for his estranged love's legal defense. Kitty, however, is initially unaware that the boxer is behind the noble deed. Ultimately acquitted, Kitty is released in time to watch her future husband wage a heroic "winner take all" ring battle to earn her outstanding legal fee.

Heart Punch offers the boxing fan a pair of lengthy ring encounters, one near the film's beginning, and the other at its close. Fight fans may consider these a reward for their indulgence of the telegraphed soap opera which lies in between. The character of Lefty Doyle was portrayed by George Lewis, the former light heavyweight boxing champion of the Pacific coast.[2] The critic for the *Motion Picture Herald* objectively wrote that "... the second of the two fighting sequences in the film does offer a bit of fast action ..." but the fight sequences in the film still require that the viewer overlook some unconvincing ring generalship.[3] Excluding Lewis's work, the actor's subpar boxing technique exposed by some of the close-up shots can make any trainer or true fight fan wince.

To distract one from the film's dated acting method, today's audiences would be advised to view this early Depression-era film through a historical lens. Unabashedly politically incorrect, *Heart Punch* maligns its sole minority group, a Chinese cook. "You know how Chinks are," and "I'll knock his yellow block off," the actors exclaim in an effort to cater to their Caucasian audiences.[4] Today's viewers may view with equal incredulity another scene in which the "Cyclone Kid" shows off his expensive suit he purchased for a whopping $32, or be amused by the lingo of an era in which people were "swell" and money was called "jack."

However, if one is not intrigued by these tidbits of social history, or is not a sentimental octogenarian, then the film is only for the boxing buff— one who can relate the cinematic death of Bobby Doyle to the actual ring fatality of Jimmy Doyle, who died at the hands of Sugar Ray Robinson.

1. Harvey Marc Zucker and Lawrence J. Babich, *Sports Films: A Complete Reference* (Jefferson, N.C.: McFarland & Company, Inc., 1987), 91.
2. "Publicity Promotes Paying Patrons." Movie Press Book for *Heart Punch* distributed by Mayfair Pictures Corporation, 4.
3. Review of *Heart Punch* (Mayfair Pictures movie), *Motion Picture Herald*, 29 October 1932.
4. *Heart Punch*, produced by Anchon Royer, directed by B. Reeves Eason, 62 minutes, 1932.

Here Comes Mr. Jordan (1941)

Columbia Pictures, Comedy-Fantasy, B & W, 94 minutes

Producer: Everett Riskin. *Director*: Alexander Hall. *Screenplay*: Sidney Buchman and Seton I. Miller from the play *Heaven Can Wait* by Harry Segall. *Editor*: Viola Lawrence. *Director of Photograpy*: Joseph Walker. *Musical Director*: M.W. Stoloff.

Robert Montgomery (Joe Pendleton), Evelyn Keyes (Bette Logan), Claude Rains (Mr. Jordan), Edward Everett Horton (Angel), James Gleason (Max Corkle), John Emery (Tony Abbott), Donald Mcbride (Inspector Williams), Don Costello (Lefty), Rita Johnson (Julia Farnsworth), Halliwell Hobbes (Sisk), Benny Rubin (Bugs).

Originally a vaudevillian in New York, James Gleason began in motion pictures in the early 1930s and eventually appeared in several hundred films. A playwright as well as an actor, Gleason was well acquainted with the fight game, having penned with Richard Taber the fistic stage comedy *Is Zat So?*[1] The story was later brought to the screen in 1927 by the Fox Film Corporation and subsequently remade as a sound film by Paramount under the title *Two-Fisted* (1935). Gleason acted in several boxing films as well, appearing in *Lady and Gent* (1932), which starred George Bancroft and a young

John Wayne, and Columbia Pictures' *Here Comes Mr. Jordan.**

Here Comes Mr. Jordan is an imaginative tale of a light-heavyweight boxing contender named Joe Pendleton (Montgomery), who is prematurely dispossessed of his body by an over zealous angel (Horton), and compelled to complete the balance of his earthly existence transplanted in other human forms.

While his body meets an untimely demise in a crematorium, Pendleton's spirit continues along an incredible journey to fulfill his earthly destiny. First he adopts the corpse of a recently deceased millionaire, and later the form of another prizefighter named K.O. Murdoch. Assisted by a heavenly figure named Mr. Jordan (Rains), and his own former fight manager (Gleason), the only other living person privy to his "reincarnations," Pendleton eventually ascends to his preordained position as light-heavyweight boxing champion of the world. Along his sojourn of substance over form, Pendleton discovers his soul mate, a young woman (Keyes) and proves that love is a bond of the spirit rather than a union of the flesh.

Well-received by audiences and critics alike, *Here Comes Mr. Jordan* was nominated for best picture of 1943. Robert Montgomery also received a nomination for best actor and Sidney Buchman and Seton I. Miller left the Academy Award ceremonies with Oscars for best screenplay.[2] Gleason also received fine reviews from the critics, including Walt of *Variety* who describes Gleason's portrayal as "a standout performance," comparing it to his earlier stage appearance in *Is Zat So?*[3]

Here Comes Mr. Jordan is fantasy rather than a fight story, and therefore the character of Pendleton could have plied any trade. Consequently, the film's boxing content is limited to a bit of sparring at the opening, and a few seconds of ring action near its conclusion, with a smattering of dialogue concerning the quest for the championship in between. Not surprisingly, the prizefight vehicle was dropped in favor of a gridiron backdrop when the film was remade as the Academy-Award-winning *Heaven Can Wait*.

1. Harvey Marc Zucker and Lawrence J. Babich, *Sports Films: A Complete Reference* (Jefferson, N.C.: McFarland & Company, Inc., 1987), 97.
2. Robert Osborne, *50 Years of Oscar: The Official History of the Academy of Motion Picture Arts and Sciences* (LaHabra, Ca.: ESE California, 1979).
3. Walt, Review of *Here Comes Mr. Jordan* (Columbia Pictures movie). *Variety*, 30 July 1941.

Honeyboy (1982)

Estrada Productions, Television Movie, Drama, 96 minutes

Executive Producers: Helen Azevedo, Irv Wilson. *Producer*: John Berry. *Director*: John Berry. *Screenplay*: John Berry, Lee Gold. *Music*: J.A.C. Redford.

Erik Estrada ("Honeyboy" Ramirez), Morgan Fairchild (Judy Wellman), Hector Elizondo (Emilio "The Flash" Ramirez), James Mceachin (Nate Walker), Robert Costanzo, Yvonne Wilder (Hortensia Ramirez), Phillip R. Allen (Jimmy Bowford), Robert Alan Browne (Ingalls), Jill Jaress (Arlene Ingalls), Bill Baldwin, Jem Echollas, Sugar Ray Robinson (Himself), Tom Huff, David Cadiente, Fahim Muhammud, David Darling, Peter Antico, Steve Hulin, Gene Scot Casey, Charles Picerni, Jr. (The Fighters), Davey Pearl (Referee), Marty Denkin (Referee), Chuck Hull (Ring Announcer).

---

*When Leon Errol, Joe Palooka's fight manager for the long-running Joe Palooka film series, passed away in 1951, another talented veteran actor was needed to portray Walsh. It was no surprise when Monogram filled the bill with James Gleason for its production of Joe Palooka in the Squared Circle.

Hollywood has long taken a passive interest in Latinos, limiting their screen opportunities. Ramon Novarro and Antonio Moreno represented the silent era, Lupe Velez and Maria Montez followed, and names such as Dolores Del Rio, Carmen Miranda and Fernando Lamas helped maintain a colorful, though sparse, Latin contingency. Many of the prominent Latino stars were featured in musicals and romance stories, with the boxing film assisting in advancing careers as well.

In 1943, Mexican singer and dancer Armida appeared in *The Girl from Monterrey*. Despite its misleading title, the picture is a legitimate fight film that also served as a vehicle to exhibit U.S. support for South America during World War II. The film, which ends with a spectacular knockout, depicts a Mexican fighter winning the championship from an American, prompting the critic for the *New York Daily News* to quip that the movie "carries the good-neighbor policy too far."[1]

A youthful and trim Ricardo Montalban is found in the ring in John Sturges' *Right Cross*, a 1950 MGM entry. In this picture with a social conscience, Montalban competes with Dick Powell for the affection of June Allyson while contending with Anglo bias. The film is now memorable for an early unaccredited appearance by Marilyn Monroe. *Variety* stated "The story is told with dialog that punches as hard as Montalban's fists," but T.M.P. of *The New York Times* lamented, "This is a picture with a lot of talk, cloyingly cute romantics and only a few rounds of fast, rough ring action."[2]

In 1952, Rita Moreno portrayed the teen-aged love interest of an aspiring Mexican-American prizefighter portrayed by obscure actor Lalo Rios in a little release entitled *The Ring*. Another film which brought Anglo-Latino friction to the fore, *The Ring* simultaneously tells a fight story while depicting the often sharp and biting class distinctions between Mexicans and whites in Los Angeles. Fight scenes are standard, but Moreno is especially appealing.

Enduring Latin star Caesar Romero, who often played the romantic lead, portrayed a suave fight promoter in Paramount's *The Leather Saint* (1957). The yarn focuses on a priest, depicted by John Derek, who clandestinely takes to the ring to earn money for a children's hospital. Throughout the film, Derek alternatively dodges his opponent's blows and the advances of Jody Lawrence who is unaware that he is a member of the cloth.

While such boxing stars as Manuel Ortiz, Lauro Salas, Eder Jofre, Ruben Olivares, and Alexis Arguello established an ever-growing Latino ring dominance from the 1950s through the 1970s, the motion picture industry took little notice.

Capitalizing on his success as the star of the weekly television series *Chips,* Erik Estrada finally took matters into his own hands, returning the Latino to the ring in his feature film debut entitled *Honeyboy*. The NBC made-for-television movie was produced under the banner of Estrada's own company.

Honeyboy is the story of Rico Ramirez, a handsome preliminary fighter from the South Bronx, who aspires to become the middleweight champion of the world. Holding closely to the tenets of the old Hollywood fight yarns, the film was updated for its contemporary audience by featuring a Latino in the lead and making Las Vegas the center of the fistic action.

Commenting on the film and its star, Judith Crist of *TV Guide* wrote, "It boasts moments of true contemporary grit, particularly from Erik Estrada."[3] John J. O'Connor of *The New York Times* was less impressed writing, "Mr. Estrada squeaks through," and noting that this type of film "has been seen a hundred times, but the concoction still manages to work reasonably well."[4] Whatever success Estrada had with television viewers, it failed to lead to any future interest on the part of MGM.

Honeyboy is filled with ample ring action, including several lengthy bouts, gym and training sequences, and the mandatory montage. The abundant fisticuffs are well-timed breaks in the predictable script. The fight scenes were created by stunt coordinator Ron Stein, who also worked on *Raging Bull* and *Rocky III*, and contain his trademark pinpoint punching, in which the fighters' heads and bodies move with their opponents' cleanly-landed blows.

Estrada worked on a daily basis to create the film's 17 fight sequences with the assistance of Stein and trainer Steve "Buck" Buckingham. One day, while a scene was in progress, Sylvester Stallone sauntered into the gym. Stallone, who had already made several of the *Rocky* films asked Stein whether he had given any of his secrets to Estrada and if the actor would like to box him for a couple of rounds. Stein responded in the negative on behalf of Estrada who would later comment, "I've often wondered who would have won that sparring match if I'd agreed to take him on."

Several members of the fistic fraternity appear in the film, including renowned West Coast referee Marty Denkin, Richard Steele, Nevada's controversial third man in the ring, and Chuck Hull, the premier ring announcer in Las Vegas, until Michael Buffer eclipsed him, as he did all ring announcers, with his trademark "Let's get ready to rumble."

Receiving third billing in the film was Sugar Ray Robinson, the all-time pound for pound champion, who is incorrectly introduced prior to the film's final fight as a former three-division champion. Robinson, in fact, had only held the welter and middleweight titles, although he owned the latter on five occasions. His appearance was only a cameo in which he wishes the fighters of the final bout good luck and then observes from ringside. Periodically, the camera would cut away from the ring and show Robinson, who remains expressionless amid the frantic action. These scenes take on an eerie tone when one considers that when filmed, Robinson may have already been victim of the debilitating effects of Alzheimer's disease, to which he would ultimately succumb.

1. Review of *The Girl from Monterrey* (PRC movie), *New York Daily News*, 29 December 1943.
2. Review of *The Girl from Monterrey* (PRC movie), *Variety*, 16 August 1950; T.M.P. Review of *The Girl from Monterrey* (PRC movie), *New York Times*, 16 November 1950.
3. Judith Crist, *TV Guide*, 16 October 1982, A-6.
4. John J. O'Connor, "3 Movies, Comedy on Cable Show," *New York Times*, 15 October 1982, sec. c, p. 26.

The Hurricane (1999)

United Artists, Drama, Color, 155 minutes

Producer: Armyan Bernstein. *Director*: Norman Jewison. *Screenplay*: Armyan Bernstein, Dan Gordon III. *Film Editing*: Stephen E. Rivin. *Cinematography*: Roger Deakins. *Music*: Christopher Young.

Denzel Washington (Rubin "Hurricane" Carter), Vicellous Reon Shannon (Lesra Martin), Deborah Kara Unger (Lisa Peters), Liev Schreiber (Sam Chiaton), John Hannah (Terry Swinton), Dan Hedaya (Police Sgt. Della Pesca), Debbi Morgan (Mae Thelma), Clancy Brown (Lt. Jimmy Williams), David Paymer (Myron Bedlock — Carter's Attorney), Harris Yulin (Leon Friedman — Carter's Attorney), Rod Steiger (Judge Sarokin), Badja Djola (Mobutu), Vincent Pastore (Alfred Bello), Al Waxman (Warden), David Lansbury (U.S. Court Prosecutor), Garland Whitt (John Artis), Chuck Cooper (Earl Martin, Lesra's father), Brenda Denmark (Alma Martin, Lesra's Mother, Brenda Thomas Denmark), Marcia Bennett (Jean Wahl), Beatrice Winde (Louise Cockersham), Mitchell

Taylor, Jr. (Young Rubin), Bill Raymond (Paterson Judge), Merwin Goldsmith (Judge Larner), John A. Mackay (Man at Falls), Donnique Privott (Boy at the Falls), Moynan King (Tina Barbieri), Gary Dewitt Marshall (Nite Spot Cabbie), John Christopher Jones (Reporter at the Bar), Gwendolyn Mulamba (Nite Spot Woman), Richard Davidson (Paterson Detective), George T. Odom (Big Ed as George Odom), Tony Patano (Woman at prison), Fulvio Cecere (Paterson Policeman), Phillip Jarrett (Solider #1 in U.S.O. Club), Rodney M. Jackson (Solider #2 in U.S.O. Club), Judi Embden (Woman in U.S.O. Club).

A ferocious puncher with a shaven head, dead serious eyes and unflappable scowl, Rubin "Hurricane" Carter intimidated his opponents. In the boxing ring, Carter carried a menace and anger fostered on the rough streets of urban New Jersey, and later in prison. Outside the ring, Carter was known to expound a righteous and liberal attitude. He assumed a posture considered dangerous for a black man, even one such as himself who had risen to the level of quasi-celebrity status.

On June 16, 1966, Carter's past transgressions and skin color would prove his undoing. On that evening, two armed black men entered the Lafayette Grill in Patterson, New Jersey. In an act tantamount to an execution, they opened fire. Moments later, two patrons, Hazel Tanis and Fred (Bob) Nauyoks, and bartender Jim Oliver lay dead on the barroom floor. Hours later, the police arrested Carter and 19-year-old John Artis for the murders.[1] The pair were eventually tried and convicted by an all white jury.[2] In what later proved to be less than a fair trial, each received a life sentence. Save the sideline of Carter's reputation as a boxer, which was sure to provide fodder for trivia buffs in years to come, the story of Rubin "Hurricane" Carter seemed to be at a close. In actuality, it was only the beginning of a truly unbelievable saga.

The resurrection of Carter began with social and political activists of the early 1970s who were drawn to potential injustices and took up Carter's cause. Soon an army of celebrities, including the likes of Muhammad Ali, Billy Bradley, Ed Koch, Jesse Jackson, Norman Mailer, Stevie Wonder and Bob Dylan, could be found leading rallies, barking at the media, or performing concerts in support of gaining Carter's independence. Dylan even recorded a popular ballad of Carter's unjust incarceration, entitled "Hurricane."[3]

Central to the convictions of Carter and Artis was the testimony of witness Alfredo Bello who claimed to have seen the duo fleeing the crime scene. A petty thief, Bello was given immunity regarding his own criminal activity for his testimony against Carter and Artis. The public recantation by Bello of his testimony provided the added impetuous necessary to force a new trial. However, by the time the second trial commenced, Bello, under police pressure, reverted to his original story. The murder of a black bar owner just six hours prior to the LaFayette murders was hyped by prosecutors to offer a motive and play on racial fears of the jury. Carter and Artis had been given the rare opportunity of a second trial but were again convicted.[4]

From any standpoint — legally, spiritually, or otherwise — Carter's fight for freedom had been delivered a death blow. In fact, for the first time since his imprisonment, Carter assumed the role of the defeated, cutting himself off from his family, his lawyers, and his supporters. Enter Lesara Martin, a black teenager living in Toronto. For twenty-five cents, Martin purchased a copy of Carter's autobiography, *The Sixteenth Round*.[5] The most improbable chapter of the Carter tale was about to unfold.

Reading Carter's story of injustice, Martin sent a simple letter to the boxer in prison expressing his empathy. Despite the hundreds of pieces of mail received by Carter that remained unopened, he read Martin's letter. Touched by the boy's words, the remaining spark in Carter was rekindled. The fighter replied to the youth and a correspondence ensued. Martin's concern soon spread to several adult members of the community home where Martin lived and was being tutored.[6]

The group of Canadians' recognition of an injustice soon mushroomed into an impassioned, almost single-minded dedication to securing Carter's release. Several of the group — Terry Swinton, Lisa Peters, and Sam Chaiton — eventually moved to New Jersey to champion Carter's cause full time. Martin, still involved, remained in Toronto to attend the University of Toronto. The perusal of box loads of trial transcripts, testimony, and other evidence led to discovery of new evidence and the improbable opportunity for Carter to regain access to the courts.[7] On November 7, 1985, Federal Justice Sarokin embraced new evidence presented on behalf of Carter. The judge freed the ex-boxer, noting that the prior convictions were "predicated upon an appeal to racism rather than reason, concealment rather than disclosure."[8] Carter's fight for freedom was waged all the way to the U.S. Supreme Court. On January 11, 1988, the U.S. Supreme Court denied the State of New Jersey's appeal and affirmed Judge Sarokin's decision, putting an end to Carter's incredible 22-year ordeal with the American justice system.[9]

Carter's story, rich with improbable details, was a filmmaker's dream come true. A bidding war for the opportunity to produce a film version of Carter's life ensued, with Armyan Bernstein and Beacon Communication emerging victorious.[10] *The Hurricane*, which is based upon two books, *The Sixteenth Round* and *Lazarus and the Hurricane,* is a prime example of Hollywood's depiction of biographical subjects that present the audience with a double-edged sword. At their best, they tap into our emotions providing us with the most promising means for vicarious participation, but they require that we subscribe to their factual looseness. As D.D. of *The New Yorker* observed, *The Hurricane* is "a very ... inspirational movie, factually untrustworthy."[11]

The fictional elements of *The Hurricane* are the film's Achilles' heel. They compromise its integrity and taint the public's historical perception of its subject. In the film, Rubin Carter is depicted strictly as victim and hero to create audience identification and empathy. Director Norman Jewison adorns Carter with a large white hat, its wide brim shading from our view Carter's less than noble deeds. In sanctifying Carter, the film portrays his title losing effort against Joey Giardello as another injustice perpetrated against him. In the film, the press and the champion's own hometown fans vehemently jeer the decision in favor of Giardello, creating the indelible illusion that Carter deserved the decision and the title. This contrivance goes beyond artistic license. Giardello has always been the accepted winner. Ironically, the film unabashedly alters undisputed fact to advance its own story of a man victimized by factual manipulation. As noted by Stephen Holden of *The New York Times*, "among its most egregious distortions ... [the film] inaccurately portrays the fight as lost by Carter solely because of the judges' racism."[12]

Another deficiency in the film is the downplaying or complete omission of Carter's prior criminal activity. Still, other depictions in the film serve to obscure reality, such as the disproportionate role given to Lesra Martin and the Canadian contingency in the legal struggle for Carter's release, while trivializing the role of his legal counsel. Additionally, during Carter's second trial, blacks sat on the jury, but this fact is all but misrepresented to the audience. As news writer and Carter proponent Selwyn Raab observed, the film "presents a false vision of the legal battles and personal struggles that led to his freedom."[13]

But as often as the film will irk the knowledgeable boxing fan and offend the amateur historian for its fast and loose wielding of the facts, it will move and inspire the viewer with its elements of hope, courage and humanity. Here, credit is due to director Jewison and screenwriters Armyan Bernstein and Dan Gordon III, who embraced sentimentality at all costs, ultimately delivering the desired human element to the picture. *The Hurricane* is, at its heart, a love story between Carter and Martin. It is a risky foundation to predicate the film on, but the filmmaker's vision is successfully realized in large part due to the gifted interpretation of Carter by Denzel Washington. Emanuel Levy of *Variety* observed, "Washington elevates the earnest, occasionally simplistic narrative to the level of a genuinely touching moral exposé."[14]

In one of the most satisfying roles of his career, Washington skillfully interweaves elements of the physical, emotional, and spiritual. He expertly uses his eyes and alters his voice to reveal Carter's intelligence and his complex nature, including a strong affinity with the philosophical. Jamie Bernard of the *New York Daily News* wrote that Washington gave a "rock-solid, towering performance."[15] Washington, who was nominated for an Academy Award for best actor and who won the Golden Globe Award in the same category, was rightfully deserving of the accolades bestowed upon him for his performance.

Washington molded his body into chiseled muscle, losing some 40 pounds to portray the middleweight boxer.[16] The fight scenes are artistically choreographed and filmed in crisp black and white film, providing a nice contrast with the rest of the film's color. The opening scene in the movie includes Carter's knockout victory over Emile Griffith, his match against Cooper, which graphically depicts a sensational knockout, and the last round of Carter's December 1964 match against middleweight champion Joey Giardello.

Despite the storybook ending of the film, which depicts a jubilant Carter basking in freedom's sunshine on the steps of a Federal Courthouse, the post-script to Carter's story reveals further challenges. Following his freedom, Carter joined the Canadians in Toronto and married supporter Lisa Peters. However, Carter battled a drinking problem he had developed from partaking of jailhouse moonshine.[17] His marriage to Peters did not endure. Carter has since become estranged from his Canadian liberators, a situation that has persisted despite the enormous success generated by the film.[18]

The film's release has also resurrected the controversy, prompting the vocal objections of relatives of those slain at the LaFayette Grill, who still dispute Carter's innocence. They petitioned Academy voters not to support the film or Denzel Washington. There is even a web-site entitled "Hurricane Carter: The Other Side of the Story"[19] that still embraces a guilty verdict. While some still continue to fan the fire of Carter's culpability, Carter himself appears to be a man at peace with himself, harboring no trace of anger or resentment. Commenting on his extraordinary journey, Carter recently said, "Everything that went before has made me what I am today ... I don't want to be anyone but who I am. I am perfect."[20]

1. James S. Hirsch, *Hurricane: The Miraculous Journey of Rubin Carter* (London: Fourth Estate Limited, 2000), 15–17.
2. Sam Chaiton and Terry Swinton, *Lazarus and the Hurricane: The Untold Story of the Freeing of Rubin "Hurricane" Carter* (New York: St. Martin's Griffin, 2000), 51.
3. Stephen Pearlstein, "Champion of the Innocents," *The Observer* (London), 9 January 2000, 17.
4. Hirsch, *Hurricane*, 42, 143–148, 156.
5. Chaiton, *Lazarus and the Hurricane*, 42.
6. *Ibid.*, 68–70.
7. *Ibid.*, 185–189.
8. Pearlstein, "Champion of the Innocents," 17.
9. Hirsch, *Hurricane*, 302.
10. "The Hurricane, Based on the Inspirational True Story of a Champion," 7.
11. D.D., *New Yorker*, 17 January 2000, 19.
12. Stephen Holden, "Fighting the Demons Within," *New York Times*, 29 December 1999, sec. E, p. 3.
13. Selwyn Raab, quoted in Kam Williams, "Hurricane Distorts," *New York Amsterdam News*, 6–12 January 2000.
14. Emanuel Levy, Review of *The Hurricane* (Universal Pictures movie), *Variety*, 20 December 1999, 56.
15. Jamie Bernard, Review of *The Hurricane* (Universal Pictures movie), *New York Daily News*, 29 December 1999.

16. Levy, 56.
17. Pearlstein, "Champion of the Innocents," 17.
18. *Ibid.*
19. Denene Millner, " 'Hurricane' Foes Fight Back," *New York Daily News*, 9 February 2000, 44.
20. Pearlstein, "Champion of the Innocents," 17.

The Irish in Us (1935)

Warner Bros., Comedy, B & W, 84 minutes

Producer: First National — Sam Bischoff. *Director*: Lloyd Bacon. *Screenplay*: Earl Baldwin, based on an idea by Frank Orsatti.

James Cagney (Danny O'Hara), Pat O'Brien (Pat O'Hara), Olivia De Havilland (Lucille Jackson), Frank Mchugh (Mike O'Hara), Allen Jenkins (Cagran), Mary Gordon (Ma O'Hara), J. Farell Macdonald (Captain Jackson), Thomas Jackson (Doc Mullins).

From the era of John L. Sullivan until the eve of World War II and the prominence of Billy Conn, Irish-Americans were a dominant force in the fight game. When social mobility proved to be the death-knell of their success, the sons of Erin symbolically passed their boxing gloves to those of Jewish, Italian, and African ancestry. Simultaneously, they shed the civil service uniforms and other indicia of the class they left behind.

Prior to elevating their station, Irish-Americans were fair game for a Hollywood that thrived on the stereotype. *The Irish in Us*, a simple comedy, is a prime example. The picture, which was the second of Jimmy Cagney's three boxing films, focuses on a trio of young Irish-American men in a patently stereotypical Irish-American family. Mother, who speaks with a brogue, is adored by her sons. Pat (O'Brien), the eldest, is a policeman who is courting his Irish captain's lovely daughter, Lucille (De Havilland). Mike (Jenkins) is a well-meaning but bumbling fireman who enjoys his liquor, and youngest brother Danny (Cagney) is an aspiring fight-trainer with a new fistic prospect, Cagran (Jenkins).

Familial strife arises when Danny meets Lucille and the pair become enamored with one another. In deference to his older brother, a guilt-stricken Danny moves from the family home. He still intends to pursue Lucille, but is deflated when their relationship proves casual.

Danny guides Cagran to a championship match. Moments before the fight, Mike attempts to cure Cagran's toothache with a bottle of gin. The pair become inebriated, forcing Danny to substitute for Cagran. Pat initially refuses to assist his brother in the corner; however, after Danny takes a shellacking for several rounds, he places their rivalry aside. As motivation, Pat reveals that Lucille has fallen in love with Danny and gives his blessing to their relationship. Fueled by the joyous news, Danny blazes his way to victory.

The ethnic comedy was filmed in a scant 18 days, with improvisation being the "B" film's *modus operandi*.[1] According to Allen Jenkins, "The script was a weak sister and the director said, 'Boys, anything you can think up, put it in.'"[2] Co-star Cagney, who admitted extensive use of ad-libs in his scenes with O'Brien and McHugh, explained, "There were times when we rehearsed scenes before the camera, and he [Bacon] would surreptitiously film and print those rehearsals."[3]

Bon of *Variety* wrote that the film was "built strictly for laughs," but was quick to point out that it was in "no danger of being included in the Academy Awards."[4] M.B. of *The New York Times* also qualified the film's comedic value, writing, "the occasional good laughs are jolting but salutary."[5] Winston Burdett of the *Brooklyn Daily Eagle* found that the film possessed both "laughs" and "sentiment."[6]

By today's standards the film is lacking in effective comedy. Its attempts to evoke laughter are repetitive, predictable, and generally flat. McHugh is good as a drunk trying to regain entrance to see his brother box, but most other characters fail to inspire mirth. As scripted, each time Cagran heard a noise that sounded like the ringing of a boxing bell, he would uncontrollably let his fists fly. The gag was not particularly funny, even on the first of many uses.

The film's strength is derived not from its plot or any intrinsic comedic quality, but from the presence and chemistry of its principal players: James Cagney, Pat O'Brien and Frank McHugh. On two previous occasions, these actors had been directed by Francis Bacon in *Here Comes the Navy* and *Devil Dogs of the Air*, and the trio proved worthy of a third outing in *The Irish in Us*.

Regina Crewe of *The New York-American* wrote, "The three musketeers of the sidewalks of New York, James, Pat and Frank, do nobly with fun factions allotted to them."[7] William Boehnel of the *New York World-Telegram* concurred, offering that the trio of players "are all actors good enough to make the average seem better than it actually is, and so, thanks to them."[8] Along the same lines, Kate Cameron, writing for the *Sunday New York Daily News*, said, "In spite of the many shortcomings of the production, ... [Cagney and O'Brien] manage to give you your money's worth of fun and fisticuffing."[9]

The Irish in Us also offers an early glimpse of Olivia de Havilland. De Havilland had been recently discovered by the prominent European producer and director Max Reinhardt.[10] While the *New York Herald-Tribune* found her performance "a little self-conscious," *The New York Sun* critic wrote, "Olivia de Havilland, one of Warner's newest newcomers, is a most acceptable heroine."[11] Bon of *Variety* was most adept at spotting the diamond in the rough writing that De Havilland "gives every indication of a gal who can be steered into lights. Classy looking, she also has warm personality and seems to know what it's about, even in the midst of boxing gloves and ad-lib slapstick."[12]

For the film's brief gym sequence, a number of ex-boxers were gathered by Warner Brothers including Jock Perry, who twice defeated former welter king Jack Britton, and also conquered Ted "Kid" Lewis, another crown holder in that division. The other usual suspects hired for the picture included Phil Bloom, who fought Benny Leonard, Johnny Dundee and Freddie Welsh; Joe Glick, who battled Jimmy McLarnin; Abe Goldstein and Sid Terris; and Sailor Vincent, who was a former "All Navy Champion." Mushy Callahan, who often acted as technical advisor for fight films, acted in this one as the referee.[13]

In preparation for his role, Cagney trained for three weeks and boxed 180 three minute rounds with former West Coast amateur boxing champion Harvey Perry, who also appears in the film as Cagney's opponent. While most movies employ pillow-like 10- or 12-ounce gloves, Cagney insisted that the near skintight 6-ounce versions be used for the film.[14] The lone fight scene, which was played straight, was filmed from a dozen different angles, took five days to complete and is the artistic highlight of the picture. Cagney, who had appeared as a boxer in an earlier film entitled *Winner Take All*, had already exhibited his ability in the ring. In *The Irish in Us*, he offers more of the same, parrying punches, catching blows in his gloves and displaying other ring techniques that you would expect from a real boxer. The final round in which Cagney rallies to victory is punctuated by a climactic knockout, and is particularly well done.

1. Patrick McGilligan, *Cagney: The Actor As Auteur* (New York: Da Capo Press, Inc., 1975), 58.
2. *Ibid.*

3. John McCabe, *Cagney* (New York: Albert A. Knopf, 1997), 138.
4. Bon, Review of *The Irish in Us* (Warner Bros. movie), *Variety*, 7 August 1935.
5. M.B. Review of *The Irish in Us* (Warner Bros. movie), *New York Times*, 1 August 1935.
6. Winston Burdett, Review of *The Irish in Us* (Warner Bros. movie), *Brooklyn Daily Eagle*, 2 August 1935.
7. Regina Crewe, "'Irish in Us' a Fast and Funny Comedy Offered at Strand," Review of *The Irish in Us* (Warner Bros. movie), *New York American*, 1 August 1935.
8. William Boehnel, "'The Irish in Us' Fun If You Like Slapstick," Review of *The Irish in Us* (Warner Bros. movie), *New York World-Telegram*, August 1 1935.
9. Kate Cameron, "Cagney Draws Applause for His Fist Work," Review of *The Irish in Us* (Warner Bros. movie), *Sunday New York Daily News*, 1 August 1935.
10. "Production Details, Biographies," Warner Bros. Studio Publicity.
11. Review of *The Irish in Us* (Warner Bros. movie), *New York Herald-Tribune*, 1 August 1935; Review of *The Irish in Us* (Warner Bros. movie), *New York Sun*, 1 August 1935.
12. Bon.
13. Francis Heacock, "Cagney Fights in Longest Boxing Bout in History," Warner Bros. Studio Publicity.
14. "Cagney Fights with Six Ounce Gloves," Warner Bros. Studio Publicity.

The Iron Man (1931)

Universal Pictures, Drama, B & W, 73 minutes

Director: Tod Browning. *Screenplay*: Adapted from the novel "Ironman" by W. R. Burnett.

Lew Ayres ("Kid" Mason), Jean Harlow (Rose), Robert Armstrong (Regan), John Miljan (Lewis), Eddie Dillon (Jeff), Mike Donlin (McNeil).

A stint as an assistant director to D.W. Griffith on *Intolerance* placed director Tod Browning at the foot of a path that he chose never to travel. Forgoing the spectaculars so closely associated with Griffith, Browning instead channeled his talents toward the examination of the bizarre. Embracing Lon Chaney, the king of the silent horror film, the director solidified his reputation as a maker of fright pictures, eventually carving himself a deep niche in the fantasy and horror film genre.

In 1931, Browning directed *Frankenstein*, and the following year he sat at the helm for *Freaks*; the former is still considered a horror classic, and the latter has achieved modern-day cult status. In between this pair of eerie and memorable pictures, Browning took a sabbatical from his favored genre to direct *The Iron Man*, Universal's boxing drama based upon the novel by W. R. Burnett. *The Iron Man* featured neither monster nor ghoul, but danger disguised in a shapely feminine form, lurking behind an unsuspecting prizefighter.

In *The Iron Man*, Kid Mason (Ayres) is a young fighter who is unable to successfully advance his prizefighting career. His wife Rose (Harlow), a showgirl and golddigger, has grown tired of waiting for her husband's financial success and deserts him. Mason then reunites with Regan (Armstrong), his manager, and revitalizes his career. Avoiding the shady elements of the fight game, he develops into a contender.

Learning of her husband's success, Rose fakes an illness to bring Mason back into the fold and smoothes her way back into his graces. Mason soon wins the championship, bringing Rose the wealth and luxury she desires. Rose, however, is unsatisfied, and begins an affair with a Hollywood producer named Lewis (Miljan). Regan is aware of the romantic dalliances of Rose, but is unable to convince Mason of her improprieties.

Eventually Mason is coaxed into taking on Lewis as his new manager. Regan releases Mason from his contract under the stipulation that Mason defend his title against O'Keefe, one of Regan's other boxers. Just before the match, Mason learns of his wife's affair, and moments later he loses his title. Without his wife or the championship, a tearful and contrite Mason is consoled by the unwaveringly loyal Regan.

The Iron Man liquefies womanhood into poison, with its protagonist swallowing the lethal dose. Heavily relying on its soap opera elements, the film keeps the ring action on the perimeter. A.D.S. of *The New York Times* correctly described the fight scenes as "sparse," assessing the picture as "good entertainment," which would have been that much better with more ring action.[1]

In fact, Mason's title-winning performance is not shown, with only the radio interview after the fight being depicted. The only fight of substance is rather brief, and most likely by design, considering that the gentle-looking Lew Ayres was portraying the prizefighter.

Although *The New York Times* was accepting of Ayres's fistic presence, finding that "he looks the part of a cold, intelligent young man of the Jimmy McLarnin type," the slender and delicately featured actor was not entirely believable as a pug.[2] "He does not ... contain enough iron in either his personality or his physique," wrote the *Motion Picture Herald*.[3] "Men will like [the film] if not entirely convinced with the impression of Ayres as a lightweight champ," Sid of *Variety* noted.[4] A year prior, co-star Robert Armstrong had portrayed an aspiring pugilist in *Be Yourself*, a Universal release that co-starred Fanny Brice. Perhaps Armstrong, and not Ayres, would have been more appropriately cast as W.R. Burnett's boxer. Nevertheless, Armstrong was fine as the fight manager. *The New York Times* wrote favorably of Armstrong for his "exhilarating performance," with the *Motion Picture Herald* observing that he "carries the heavy load in the picture and he steals it completely."[5] *Variety* found Jean Harlow's performance as Eve with the apple "woefully lacking in several spots," but predicted that men would nevertheless enjoy "her proverbial low cut and flimsy raiment."[6]

In 1937, screenwriter Lester Cole made another adaptation of the Burnett novel, with his version retitled *Some Blondes Are Dangerous*. Released by Universal Pictures, the drama was directed by Milton Carruth and featured Noah Beery, Jr., the nephew of Wallace Beery, in the role of prizefighter Bud Mason. Frequent boxing film actor William Gargan portrayed the pugilist's manager, with Dorothea Kent playing the fighter's vampish love interest. The remake proved unsuccessful. The critic for *Variety* succinctly dismissed the film as a "fight picture which hasn't much chance."[7]

In 1951, Universal resurrected the Burnett tale for one last time. Adapted by screenwriters George Zuckerman and Borden Chase, the third version bears the story's original title but takes a different bend. The remake of *Iron Man* starred Universal contract player Jeff Chandler and newcomer Rock Hudson, who portray two friends whose boxing careers are on a collision course. Hudson, at the time an unknown actor, was forced upon director Joseph Peveney by the film's producer Aaron Rosenberg. "He's a Southpaw," the exasperated director exclaimed upon learning that Hudson would play *Iron Man's* second principal boxer.[8]

Assigned to Universal trainer Frankie Van, the lefty actor had to be taught to fight as a right-hander, one part of his coach's challenge. "When he came in, he couldn't recognize a pair of boxing gloves," Van noted of Hudson.[9] Hudson's legs were naturally athletic, but he needed development in the forearms, deltoids and shoulders. After six weeks of training, Hudson was down from 202 pounds to a solid 191. "He was more like Gene Tunney than Gene Tunney," said Van, boasting of his finished product.[10] In the film, Hudson was athletically trim, displaying excellent footwork and a nice jab. He even took a punch realistically.

The handsome and now buff Hudson was soon to make a splash with women of all ages. His flesh-baring appearance in *Iron Man* coincided with a sudden increase in fan mail and no doubt contributed to his growing female fandom.[11] These fans would soon prompt his eventual casting in *Magnificent Obsession*, the film that made Rock Hudson a movie star.

1. A.D.S. "A Hapless Pugilist," Review of *The Iron Man* (Universal Pictures movie), *New York Times*, 18 April 1931.
2. *Ibid*.
3. Review of *The Iron Man*, (Universal Pictures movie), *Motion Picture Herald*, 28 March 1931.
4. Sid, Review of *The Iron Man*, (Universal Pictures movie), *Variety*, 22 April 1931.
5. A.D.S., "A Hapless Pugilist," Review of *The Iron Man*, (Universal Pictures movie), *Motion Picture Herald*, 28 March 1931.
6. Sid.
7. *Variety*, 10 November 1937.
8. Jerry Oppenheimer and Jack Vitek, *Idol, Rock Hudson: The True Story of an American Film Hero* (New York: Villard Books, 1986), 37.
9. *Ibid.*, 38.
10. *Ibid*.
11. *Ibid.*, 44.

Joe and Max (2000)

STARZ! Pictures, Bio-Drama, Color

Producer: Kelli Konop, Klaus Rettig. *Director*: Steve James. *Screenplay*: Jason Horwitch. *Film Editor*: Norman Buckley. *Director of Photography*: Bill Butler. *Music*: Jeff Beal.

Til Schweiger (Max Schmeling), Leonard Roberts (Joe Louis), Richard Roundtree (Jack Blackburn), Siena Goines (Marva), Bruce Weitz (Mike Jacobs), Paul Collins (Jim Farley), David Paymer (Joe Jacobs), Peta Wilson (Anny Ondra), Rolf Kaines, Wilfred Hochholdinger (Joseph Goebbels), August Zirner (David Lewin).

A good thing about television, from the boxing movie fan's perspective, is that a TV producer might make a boxing film that might not otherwise be produced by a Hollywood film studio. Consequently, the boxing buff has seen some unlikely but welcome stories in their homes. *Heart of a Champion: The Ray Mancini Story* is a good example that immediately comes to mind. Other more notable fighters such as Jack Dempsey, Rocky Marciano, and Muhammad Ali have also been portrayed on the small screen. However, taking into consideration that Ali is the only one of this trio of ring greats who has also been featured in a big screen production, it is all too clear that television provides the sport of boxing with a welcome supplementary film outlet.

Joe and Max, a production by STARZ! Pictures and aired on the STARZ! cable network, is television's latest contribution. Interestingly, it is the second motion picture produced for the small screen which delves into the lives and careers of heavyweight champions and ring rivals Joe Louis and Max Schmeling. The earlier television movie, *Ring of Passion*, produced in 1978, limited its focus to the period of the pair's two great matches (1936–1938). *Joe and Max* begins its examination during the same period, but attempts to place a greater emphasis on the duo's personal relationship, and then follows that relationship beyond their ring careers and into middle age.

The backdrop of the story of Joe Louis and Max Schmeling is a conflagration of political, social, racial and athletic drama that is so multi-faceted it defies even the most imaginative screenwriter's thirst for plot and conflict. In a nutshell, Schmeling, who wants to be nothing more than a sportsman, is pressured by Germany's Nazi regime, and even Hitler himself, to serve as one of their propaganda tools. Placed in conflict with his conscience, Schmeling is forced to walk the thin line between patriotism and loyalty to his Jewish friends and manager while trying to achieve his personal goal of winning the heavyweight championship. Louis, on the other hand, is seeking personal redemption against Schmeling who soundly thrashed him in their first encounter. He must also battle racial prejudice at home, while carrying the burden of being the hero of black America, as well as white America's instrument to vanquish German fascism.

Director Steve James's intent was to tell the tale of Max and Joe in parallel, to bring to the fore the similarities of two men's personas and experiences, despite their apparent differences. To a certain degree this goal was achieved. The film is adequate in developing Louis and the aforementioned challenges that he faces. James does a fine job of bringing forth Schmeling's dilemmas, chiefly through the help of a well-cast creepy Hitler and some equally distasteful Nazi henchmen. The picture also nicely uses the fighters' relationships with their respective wives and governments and their post-boxing hardships to further draw the parallel. However, lost somewhere in this incredible soap opera is the relationship of Joe and Max itself. For the first half of the film there is no connection between the two, and their contact is limited to Schmeling politely wishing Louis good luck at the weigh-in of their first bout.

After the midway point of the film, we see Louis visiting Schmeling in the hospital following their second bout in 1938. The scene is sentimental, and establishes the fact that neither fighter harbored personal malice for the other. Still, further development of their relationship is lacking, as we only see the pair together once more in the film, during the 1950s when Schmeling visits Louis in Chicago. Both scenes in which the duo interact convey a genuine warmth and empathy felt between the fighters, but the mutual respect and admiration displayed seems disproportionate to the limited nature and extent of their actual relationship.

Fight vignettes include brief knockout sequences of Louis stopping Paulino Uzcudun, and later Jimmy Braddock for the championship, as well as more lengthy vignettes of the two Louis-Schmeling bouts. Their first bout features solid action, and great attention was given to the recreation of the details surrounding the knockdown of Louis in the fourth round as evidenced by the accurate recreation of Louis vigorously shaking his head while lying on the canvas, and his grasping of the ring ropes. The second match accurately captures the brutality in which Louis disposes of Schmeling in less than one round.

Artistic license is abused when Schmeling's manager Joe Jacobs is heard bellowing his two signature comments, "I shoulda stood in bed" and "we wuz robbed," neither of which have any connection to the Louis-Schmeling encounters. The use of a lanky actor to portray the squat Rocky Marciano is quite simply an unacceptable casting gaff.

Notwithstanding some of its misgivings, *Joe and Max* is well acted and by-and-large an enjoyable foray into the world of Joe Louis and Max Schmeling. Boxing fans should welcome this small-screen offering, and any other serviceable fight pictures that may find their way into their living rooms.

The Joe Louis Story (1953)

United Artists, a Walter P. Chrysler Jr. presentation, Bio-Drama, B & W, 88 minutes

Producer: Stirling Silliphan. *Director:* Robert Gordon. *Screenplay:* Robert Sylvester. *Film Editor:* David Kummins. *Photography:* Joseph Braun.

Coley Wallace (Joe Louis), Paul Stewart (Tad McGeehan), Hilda Simms (Marva Louis), James Edwards ("Chappie" Blackburn), John Marley (Mannie Seamon), Dotts Johnson (Julian Black), P. J. Sidney (John Roxborough), Evelyn Ellis (Mrs. Barrow), Carl Rocky Latimer (Arthur Pine), John Mariott (Sam Langford), Buddy Thorpe (Max Schmeling), Issac Jones (Johnny Kingston), Royal Beal (Mike Jacobs), Ruby Goldstein (Himself).

Both a wonderfully gifted prizefighter and a born gentleman, the soft-spoken Joe Louis not only inspired an entire race of people, but he transcended established social norms as the first African-American athlete to be embraced by the American public at large. During his illustrious boxing career, Louis, also known as the "Brown Bomber," amassed a standing record of 25 successful defenses of his heavyweight championship over a still unsurpassed reign of 12 years. His peerless performance in the ring and his exemplary conduct outside of it enabled Louis to penetrate the color barrier, pioneering the efforts of Jackie Robinson that followed. When Robinson breached baseball's color line in 1947, Louis was already in his tenth year as the heavyweight champion. Both historically significant athletes would soon find their lives immortalized on the silver screen.

Louis's film biography, simply named *The Joe Louis Story*, traces the life of the all-time boxing great from his seminal fistic moment, in which he swapped his violin case for a pair of boxing gloves, until he was sadly vanquished by the next heavyweight great, Rocky Marciano. Director Robert Gordon, who was once an amateur boxer himself, faithfully depicts the legendary champion's ring career through the use of original film footage of his numerous fistic encounters, which are intermittently inserted throughout the film to punctuate Louis's eventful personal life.[1]

Flavor is added to the story by a smattering of many of the now-famous anecdotes that have become part and parcel of the Louis lore. A young Joe is shown catching a fly in his bare hand, *a la* Joe Gans, at the behest of Jack "Chappie" Blackburn, his beloved trainer. "Chappie" issues his warning that Negro fighters start with two strikes, to which Joe playfully responds that he will have fun with the third. The film revisits Louis's meeting with Franklin Delano Roosevelt, in which the President feels Joe's biceps and equates them with the muscle needed to defeat Germany. The Champ's historic "God's on our side" speech, in which Louis simply but poignantly explains why the Allies will win World War II, is also recreated.

Louis the spendthrift, the soft touch with the big heart, and his resulting tax problems with the United States Government are honestly, albeit summarily, reproduced by the writers. However, on the subject of his love life one finds notable omissions. The depiction of Louis's wolfish libido and his trysts with singer Lena Horne and ice-skater Sonja Henie, for example, are conspicuously absent from the film. While sex censorship in film was the fare of the day, and such controversial content was prohibited, their omission nevertheless detracted from the film's full development of Louis's persona. A.W. of *The New York Times* praised the film for "accentuat[ing] the memory and respect of a truly towering athlete" but acknowledged the picture's limitations, adding, "It rarely succeeds in developing Louis as a man."[2]

The film was released just a year prior

to the groundbreaking U.S. Supreme Court school desegregation case *Brown v. Board of Education*, and the issue of racial prejudice was also taboo. Hollywood had only recently begun to engage the topic in such films as *Pinky, Home of the Brave*, and *Intruders in the Dust*. Hift of *Variety*, who found *The Joe Louis Story* "sincere, touching and understanding," noted the picture's element of social awareness. The film "is headed for b.o. wallops among all kinds of audiences. But even more important is the fact that it shows the Negro on a level which Hollywood too often neglects."[3]

In an attempt to make a liberal representation of blacks, Louis's life story still presented its filmmakers with a "catch-22." How does one depict Louis raising race-consciousness, without delving into the nation's long-standing prejudices and Louis's sentiments regarding the same? To appease most black audiences on the race issue without offending the sensibilities of their white counterparts, the writers settled on inserting some carefully constructed dialogue, principally found in a single conversation between Louis and his mother. Perhaps progressive for the day, when judged against current standards, this treatment fails to do the subject justice.

Portraying the champ in *The Joe Louis Story* was Coley Wallace, a dead-ringer for the 'Brown Bomber' and a professional boxer himself. Wallace's most memorable ring achievement was a victory in the amateurs over Rocky Marciano. At the time of the filming of the movie, which was shot in part at the famed Grossinger's gym in the Catskills, Wallace was ranked sixth by *The Ring Magazine* with a record of 20-2. He had once even boxed on Louis's under-card, when the coming back champ fought Lee Savold.[4]

Of Wallace, A.W. of *The New York Times* wrote, "He is a close approximation of the expressionless, imperturbable Louis in deed if not in word," and Otis O. Guernsey, Jr. of the *Herald-Tribune* found the debuting actor to be "perfect as the young, taciturn Louis."[5] Guernsey also reported that James Edwards's portrayal of "Chappie" Blackburn was "a very strong performance" and "one of the film's greatest assets," crediting Edwards with creating a character with "an indomitable personality."[6]

Like most of the biographical pictures that rolled off the back lots during the Studio System era, *The Joe Louis Story* was sanitized and then wrapped in sentiment. The champ's fascinating life, which later included health problems and mental illness, is begging to be retold by modern filmmakers who are now afforded the free rein to fully explore the fascinating sojourn of this American hero.

1. Harold Rosenthal, "Cameras Ready to Roll on the Joe Louis Story," *New York Herald-Tribune*, Sunday, 8 May 1953.
2. A.W., "Coley Wallace the Fighter Is in Title Role of 'Joe Louis Story' at the Holiday," Review of *The Joe Louis Story* (United Artists movie), *The New York Times*, 4 November 1953.
3. Hift, "Bio of a Former Champ Done with Plenty of Heart and Carrying a Powerful B.O. Punch." Review of *The Joe Louis Story* (United Artists movie), *Variety*, 30 September 1953.
4. Harold Rosenthal, "Cameras Ready To Roll."
5. *New York Times*; Otis Guernsey, Jr., Review of the *Joe Louis Story* (United Artists movie), *The New York Herald-Tribune*, 4 November 1953.
6. Guernsey, Jr., Review of the *Joe Louis Story*.

Joe Palooka, Champ (1946)

Monogram Pictures, B & W, Comedy, 72 minutes

Producer: Hal E. Chester. *Director*: Reginald Le Borg. *Screenplay*: George Moskov and Albert De Pina, from an original story by Hal E. Chester.

Leon Errol (Knobby Walsh), Elyse Knox (Anne), Joe Kirkwood Jr. (Joe Palooka), Eduardo Cianelli (Florini), Joe Sawyer (Lefty), Elisha Cook Jr. (Eugene), Robert Kent (Brewster), Sarah Padden (Mom Palooka), Michael Mark (Pop Palooka), Lou Nova (Al Costa), Jimmy Mclarnin (Referee), Sam Mcdaniel (Smoky), Russ Vincent (Curly), Alexander Laslo (Aladar), Carole Dunne (Mrs. Oberlander), Betty Blythe (Mrs. Stafford), Phil Van Zandt (Freddie Wells).

From his modest origins as a fledgling comic strip character created in 1930 by Ham Fisher, Joe Palooka evolved into one of the most widely known fictional characters in America.[1] Born with the Depression, Palooka was not only a children's action hero in boxing trunks, but also a metaphor for a subdued nation: its unemployed, its empty-bellied, all of its Palookas striving to survive the lean times.

With the onset of World War II, the blonde and clean-cut pugilist would take on political dimensions that exceeded the larger-than-life character himself. As the first comic strip personality to enlist in the army, Palooka made fatigues look fashionable, prompting President Roosevelt to thank Ham Fisher during a White House press conference for helping to "put across the drafts."[2] Indeed, Palooka's fists had become ubiquitous, landing psychological blows against the Axis itself. Even Germany's Prime Minister of Propaganda, Hermann Goebels, was forced to confess that Palooka was highly effective anti-Nazi propaganda.[3]

At the end of the war, Palooka's tour of duty was over and at the time of his discharge the broad-shouldered hero was the most widely read comic strip in the nation, with a following of approximately 40 million.[4] Palooka, like the U.S., was ready to flex post-war muscle, and without a peer in comics, he would soon expand his sphere of influence into radio, movie shorts, feature length films and finally, television.

From the pages of newsprint, Palooka first punched his way onto the airwaves. Ham Fisher and Philip Gelb scripted 260 episodes of a duration of one-quarter of an hour, which were broadcast from 15 different radio stations. Palooka was brought to life through the voice of Norman Gottschalk, and Hal Lansing spoke for the irrepressible Knobby Walsh.[5]

A series of movie shorts followed, filmed at Vitaphone Studios in Brooklyn, New York, and sponsored by Sam Sax, the production chief at Warner's. Lloyd French directed the series of 20-minute vignettes, the first of which was entitled *For the Love of Pete*. Robert Norton portrayed Joe Palooka and Shemp Howard of *The Three Stooges* fame played Knobby.[6]

Despite his appearance in three media, a burgeoning Palooka audience remained unsatiated. In 1946, Monogram Studios released *Joe Palooka, Champ*, a movie based on an original story written by producer Hal Chester, and the first in a series of 11 feature films.

To bring the highly popular Ham Fisher comic strip to film, Monogram Pictures held a national contest for the casting of Joe Palooka. The contest culminated with the selection of a broad-shouldered, square-jawed professional golfer named Joe Kirkwood, Jr. Kirkwood had unwittingly entered the contest when his mother submitted photographs of her son.[7]

In *Joe Palooka, Champ*, boxing manager Knobby Walsh, portrayed by Leon Errol, seeks revenge against a syndicate boss named Florini, played by Eduardo Cianelli. Having already pirated Knobby's heavyweight fighter, Florini desires to exclude Knobby from the fight game altogether. Knobby is forced to go on the road, where he serendipitously discovers a new prospect named Joe Palooka. Palooka fulfills Knobby's aspiration by going on to win the heavyweight championship against Knobby's ex-charge.

A number of notable boxing champions of the day were given cameo appearances in *Joe Palooka, Champ*. Joe Louis, Henry Armstrong, Ceferino Garcia, and Manuel Ortiz are all afforded a few frames of film before Joe Palooka takes center ring.

Joining the quartet of champions in the film is former welterweight champion Jimmy McLarnin, who appears as a referee; former heavyweight contender and Joe Louis "victim" Lou Nova, who portrays Palooka's nemesis; Al Costa; and Meyers Grace, found wielding a microphone, who engaged eight world champions including Freddie Steele.[8]

On the set of *Joe Palooka, Champ,* the fight crowd was brought shoulder to shoulder with the movie colony. Director Reginald LeBorg could be found urging Ortiz to skip rope, a chore the former bantamweight champion disliked and which he indicated to the director was a waste of time. When not entangled with Leborg, Ortiz was advising comedian Leon Errol, sharing pointers which Errol later incorporated into his role as Knobby Walsh.[9]

Amid the ring talent on the set, Eduardo Cianelli, famous for his roles as the film "heavy," was found flashing an uncharacteristic smile. When his demeanor was questioned by co-star Elyse Knox, Cianelli glanced over to Armstrong, Louis, and company and queried tongue-in-cheek, "So you think any of my scowls or leers will frighten them or that this studio prop gun will give them goose pimples?" Indeed, the fictional aspect of the film was all too apparent to the real-life gladiators. During the shoot, when asked whether he preferred making pictures or fighting, heavyweight champion Joe Louis replied that movie making, unlike boxing, does not cause cauliflower ears.[10]

Reviews of *Joe Palooka, Champ* varied. While E.J.B of *The New York Times* warned that the film "follows the age-old formula of prizefight screen heroics — and not too well," Joe Pihodna of the *New York Herald-Tribune* credited the filmmakers for translating "an engaging comic strip character into a believable and beguiling film character."[11] Pihodna also applauded Leon Errol, who portrayed Joe Palooka's manager, finding him to be "excellent" in a semi-serious role and "absolutely right as a sentimental character touched by the heat of Jacob's beach."[12] The *New York Daily News* was similarly complimentary of Kirkwood, dubbing him "a promising newcomer."[13]

Monogram Pictures was quick to capitalize on homegrown boxing talent in the series opener in which five California-based fighters — Armstrong, McLarnin, Garcia, Ortiz, and Nova — were featured. In the second entry in the series, *Gentleman Joe Palooka* (1947), the studio continued the trend by casting other West Coast talent including heavyweight Jack Roper, who appears as a scrapper named Scranton. In real life, Roper was a competent mittsman, but had the dubious distinction of being knocked out by Joe Louis in one round in Los Angeles.[14] Also appearing in *Gentleman Joe Palooka* is Freddie Steele, another West Coast fighter who held the middleweight championship. Steele has a brief cameo in which he appears at Palooka's championship celebration. Ironically, Steele tells Kirkwood, "You were terrific tonight, and any time you get sick of the fight racket, I'll get you an agent who'll put you in the movies."[15]

Not to be outdone by earlier Palooka productions that featured the aforementioned boxing greats, a later entry, *Winner Takes All* (1948), featured one of the tallest fighters ever to lace on a pair of gloves. At a height of seven feet, one inch, Ben Moroz was the tallest professional boxer of his day, and according to Nat Fleisher's *Ring Record Book*, Moroz was the fifth tallest professional boxer in the history of the sport.[16]

Finally in 1951, with the release of *Triple Cross,* Joe Palooka's five-year run in films was brought to a conclusion. While the movies were only "B" programmers and not beyond the scorn of some critics, one could make the claim that the celluloid Palooka had benefited its newsprint version. Shortly before the release of the film *Joe Palooka, Champ,* the comic strip had a reading audience of approximately 40 million. During the half decade in which the films ran, newspaper circulation ballooned and just a few short years after *Triple Cross* was released, readership had risen to 70 million.[17]

By the time the film run had concluded in the early 1950s, only the new medium of television remained unexploited. In January of 1954, Guild Films released *The Joe Palooka Story*. The television series was comprised of 39 half-hour programs co-directed by Joe Kirkwood and Richard Bare. Kirkwood reprised his film role as Joe Palooka and his real-life wife Cathy Downs, featured in some of the films as Anne, continued in the television role. Former light-heavyweight champion turned actor, "Slapsie" Maxie Rosenbloom, assumed the role of Palooka's trainer.[18]

By the early 1950s, the *Palooka* strip, which had begun just a single generation prior, had evolved into a multi-media phenomenon and an early example of the merchandising mania so closely associated with today's marketing of movies. While there was no Burger King or McDonald's to tout the Palooka inventory, an array of Palooka paraphernalia was available to his admiring fans through distributors and print advertisement. Standard items included Palooka boxing gloves and a "bop bag," which was a freestanding punching bag with Joe's visage printed across the plastic outer covering. Items as diverse as Palooka baseball gloves, pipes, balloons and dolls were also available. Palooka also offered its own fashion line including polo shirts, sweat shirts, and sweaters. Wholesalers purchased Joe Palooka comics at 7.5¢ each, championship belt buckles at $7.50 per dozen, and then resold them to the public with a slight mark-up. Palooka lunch box tins were available to the wholesaler for 64¢ each and included as part of the price a one pound, six-ounce package of assorted wrapped candies.[19]

1. Monogram Studio publicity.
2. Fred Rodell, "Everybody Reads the Comics," *Esquire*, March 1945, vol. XXXIII, no. 3.
3. *Ibid*.
4. *Ibid*.
5. Monogram Studio publicity.
6. *Ibid*.
7. *Ibid*.
8. Studio publicity for *Joe Palooka, Champ*.
9. *Ibid*.
10. *Ibid*.
11. E.J.B., Review of *Joe Palooka, Champ*, (Monogram Pictures movie), *New York Times*, 6 April 1946; Joe Pihodna, Review of *Joe Palooka, Champ* (Monogram Pictures movie), *New York Herald-Tribune*, 6 April 1946.
12. *Ibid*.
13. *New York Daily News*.
14. Nat Loubet and John Ort, eds. *The 1979 Ring Boxing Encyclopedia and Record Book*. (New York: The Ring Book Shop, 1979).
15. Studio publicity for *Gentleman Joe Palooka*.
16. Loubet and Ort, *The 1979 Ring Boxing Encyclopedia*.
17. *Variety*, 9 December 1953.
18. *Ibid*.
19. Monogram Studio publicity.

Keep Punching (1939)

M.C. Pictures, Drama, B&W, 81 minutes

Producer and Director: John Clein. *Screenplay*: Marcy Klauber. *Story*: J. Rosamond Johnson. *Film Editor*: Al Harburger. *Photography*: J. Burgi Contner, Jay Rescher. *Music*: Lee Norman.

Henry Armstrong (Henry Jackson), Willie Bryant (Frank Harrison), Mae Johnson (Jerry), Hamtree Harrington ("Windy" Butler), Francine Everett (Fanny Singleton), Canada Lee (Speedy), Lionel Managas (Ed Watson), Arthur Dooley Wilson (Baron Skinner), Hilda Offley (Mrs. Jackson), Walter Robinson (Mr. Jackson), J. Rosamond Johnson (The Minister), George Wiltshire (Hemingway), Lee Norman's Orchestra.

When Al Jolson, wearing blackface, wowed audiences in *The Jazz Singer*, the era of sound film was officially underway. Like many entertainers of his day, Jolson followed the sport of boxing and was one of the Hollywood set to have the good fortune of seeing prospect Henry Armstrong in the ring. Sensing that Armstrong possessed special talents, Jolson backed his friend, Eddie Mead, a fight manager from Cleveland, with the money necessary to purchase his contract. The initial asking price for the contract was $5,000. However, the deal almost went awry when owner Wirt Ross held out for an additional five grand. Another Hollywood star, George Raft, became Jolson's silent partner, and unbeknownst to Armstrong, ponied up the other half of the purchase price.[1]

Under his new management team, Armstrong entered the big-time. In quick succession he copped the featherweight title from Pete Sarron, the welterweight crown from Barney Ross, and lightweight laurels from Lou Ambers, becoming the first and only man to hold three titles simultaneously. Armstrong's mother, who once had a vision of her son riding a white charger over a bridge wearing three crowns, proved to be prophetic.[2]

Riding the crest of Armstrong's unparalleled ring achievement, Mead produced a fictionalized version of Armstrong's life entitled *Keep Punching*. In the film, Armstrong's character bears his Christian birth name, Jackson. The soft-spoken and polite small-town boy is tempted by the allure of the big city, and placed in harm's way of its hustlers and loose women, but emerges as a clean-cut champion of the welterweight division.

The film, which features an all-black cast, premiered at the Apollo in Harlem on December 5, 1939. Cast members Mae Johnson, comedian Hamtree Harrington, and Harlemite William Bryant were all popular with black moviegoers of the day. For a novice, Armstrong is a fair thespian, and certainly stands head and shoulders above Joe Louis who, just two years prior, appeared in his own all–black biographical vehicle, *The Spirit of Youth*. "For a gent whose business is clubbing other fellows in the prize ring, Armstrong does not do so badly before the cameras," noted the critic for the *Hollywood Reporter*.[3]

The fight scenes in the picture are brief. Armstrong is seen sparring in the ring for a few moments and then boxing in the picture's finale. The fight vignette mixes shots made specifically for the picture, with actual footage from Armstrong's title-winning effort against Ambers. From a production standpoint the result is unsatisfactory. With the world's greatest fighter in tow, more should have been done in the ring, particularly since the film's producer, Mead, was himself a fight manager.

Also appearing in *Keep Punching* is Canada Lee. Born Leonard L. Cagnegata or Canegaya, depending on the source, Lee was once a jockey. After outgrowing the saddle, he turned to boxing. He was christened Canada Lee by a ring announcer who was unable to pronounce his real name. Turning pro in 1927, Lee, a welterweight, fought four former and future world champions: Jack Britton, Tommy Freedman, Lou Brouillard, and Vince Dundee — against whom he earned a draw. An injury left Lee blind in one eye, prematurely ending his boxing career in 1933.[4]

After boxing, Lee made the transition to the entertainment world. He won a critic's drama award for his portrayal of Bigger in *Native Son*. Lee also expanded into radio, the screen, and finally television. In addition, he appeared in the classic boxing film *Body and Soul* and in the acclaimed wartime drama, *Lifeboat*.[5]

While Lee built up his acting resume, Armstrong concluded his ring career, fighting professionally, and touring with the George Raft Caravan, staging boxing exhibitions during the war.[6] He later became a preacher and organized the Henry Armstrong Youth Foundation. The foundation's advisory board read like a "who's who" of Hollywood and Cauliflower Alley. Armstrong, of course, was president, and former foe Barney Ross acted as vice-president. Other fighters on the board included Jack

Dempsey, Ray Robinson, Mickey Walker and Jimmy McLarnin. From the film industry, Joe E. Brown, Wallace Ford, and Phil Harris served.[7]

1. Henry Armstrong, *Gloves, Glory and God* (Westwood, N.J.: Fleming H. Revell Company, 1956), 177–178.
2. Henry Armstrong, preface to *20 Years of Poems, Moods and Meditations* (n.p., 1954).
3. *Hollywood Reporter*, 5 December 1939, 1.
4. "Ex-Jockey, Ex-Pug Canada Lee Is an Actor by Accident." Advertising for *Body and Soul*.
5. Ibid.
6. Armstrong, *Gloves, Glory and God*, 234.
7. Ibid., 255.

The Kid from Brooklyn (1946)

RKO Radio Pictures, Comedy-Musical, Color, 113 minutes

Producer: Samuel Goldwyn. *Director*: Norman Z. Mcleod. *Screenplay*: Groves Jones, Frank Butler, Richard Connell, from the play *Milky Way* by Lynn Root and Harry Clork. *Film Editor*: Daniel Mandell, *Photography*: Gregg Toland. *Music and Lyrics*: Jule Styne, Sammy Cahn. *Music*: Sylvia Fine, Max Liebman.

Danny Kaye (Burleigh Sullivan), Virginia Mayo (Polly Pringle), Vera-Ellen (Susie Sullivan), Steve Cochran (Speedy McFarlane), Eve Arden (Ann Westley), Walter Abel (Gabby Sloan), Lionel Stander (Spider Schultz), Fay Bainter (Mrs. E. Winthrope DeMoyne), Clarence Kolb (Mr. Austin), Victor Cutler (Photographer), Charles Cane (Willard), Jerome Cowan (Fight Announcer), Don Wilson (Radio Announcer), Knox Manning (Radio Announcer), Kay Thompson (Matron), Johnny Downs (Master of Ceremonies), The Goldwyn Girls (Themselves).

If one embraces the axiom that "necessity is the mother of invention," then it must be puzzling to consider Hollywood's unlikely construct, the boxing/musical. Spawned from the same embryo as sound film itself, the screen musical almost instantly obtained bona fide status when, in 1931, MGM's *The Broadway Melody* won the first ever best picture award presented for a sound film.

The boxing film claimed *para su pari* status with the musical when Wallace Beery garnered the best actor award at the same Academy ceremony for his portrayal of the Champ in King Vidor's film of the same name. While the two genres received equal and almost simultaneous credibility with critics and the public alike, even the most creative and whimsical mind was bound to assume that the two brands of entertainment would go down storied but very divergent paths.

For the most part, conventional wisdom has prevailed, with southpaws and sopranos and hookers and hoofers predictably keeping their bolo-punchers and ballets in separate corners of film's canvas. Accordingly, musical talents in the boxing film have generally been limited to fine cinematic scores, such as the highly popular soundtracks of Bill Conti, which provided the musical massage for Sylvester Stallone's first two *Rocky* films.

Nevertheless, whether through creative indulgence, the manifestation of the inevitable anomaly, or otherwise, the musical and the fight story, like the bantam and the heavy, have sparred on rare occasion, and often with curious results.

One of the early efforts of this subgenre was the 1936 Marion Davies vehicle entitled *Cain and Mabel* which pleased neither the fight crowd nor the Broadway crowd. In 1939, the legendary musical director Busby Berkeley found himself at the directorial helm of a fight picture entitled *They Made Me a Criminal*. However, the giant of musical celluloid thought better than to tarnish his artistic sensibilities, and fashioned the John Garfield vehicle as a straight dramatic story. A few years later Producers Releasing Corporation dabbled in the unholy combination of the two subgenres when they cast Armida in a 1943 picture set in New York entitled *The Girl from Monterrey*.

Perhaps it was appropriate that MGM, renowned as the king of the musicals, was the first to mix leather-covered jabs with taps and scales with some success. Banking on the musical talents of Jule Styne and Sammy Cahn, they brought Lynn Root and Harry Clorks' play, *The Milky Way*, to the screen in 1946. Renamed *The Kid from Brooklyn*, the musical-comedy provided a showcase for the rich comedic talents of Danny Kaye, exploited the vibrant dancing of vivacious hoofer Vera-Ellen and capitalized on the stylized vocals of the radiant Virginia Mayo. Larger than life and filmed in striking Technicolor, the leggy Goldwyn Girls were also utilized to round out the lavish musical effects.

With the exception of the musical backdrop, *The Kid from Brooklyn* is a close duplicate of the original 1936 film version entitled *The Milky Way*, which starred Harold Lloyd. [See *The Milky Way* for story synopsis]. The picture proved to be a pleasant blend of the clowning of Kaye and a fine utilization of the score of Styne and Cahn. Stal, writing for *Variety*, noted that the final product "emerges as a lush mixture of comedy, music, and gals, highlighted by beautiful Technicolor and ultra-rich production mountings."[1]

Critic Bosley Crowther of *The New York Times* was less impressed with the film's overall delivery and wrote that when Kaye was not on the screen the picture was infected with a "blithesome spirit" and its "pace perceptively drags."[2]

Kaye, however, is wonderful. Like water seeking its proper level, he naturally adjusts his degree of animation, finding the mark with small gestures as well as broad physical slapstick. Whether delivering a well-timed hiccup or prancing around the ring, Kaye establishes a flirtation with the camera lens through his careful sense of timing. "Mr. Kaye has the best opportunity that he has yet had upon the screen to show his superior talent for the broad beguiling burlesque," observed Crowther. "Not since Charlie Chaplin made his several turns in the ring has such a bewildered boxer been seen upon the screen — well, unless you include Harold Lloyd in 'The Milky Way'."[3]

1. Stal, Review of *A Kid from Brooklyn* (RKO Radio Pictures movie), *Variety*, 20 March 1946.
2. Bosley Crowther, "'Kid from Brooklyn,' in which Redoubtable Danny Kaye Has Chance at Pugilist Talents, Attraction at the Astor," Review of *A Kid from Brooklyn* (RKO Radio Pictures movie), *New York Times*, 19 April 1946.
3. *Ibid.*

The Kid from Kokomo (1939)

Warner Bros., Comedy, B & W, 92 minutes

Producer: Sam Bischoff. *Director*: Lewis Seiler. *Screenplay*: story Dalton Trumbo, adaptation Jerry Wald and Richard Macauley. *Film Editor*: Jack Killifer. *Photography*: Sid Hickox.

Pat O'Brien (Billy Murphy), Wayne Morris (Homer Baston), Joan Blondell (Doris Harvey), May Robson (Maggie Martin), Jane Wyman (Marian Bronson), Stanley Fields (Muscles), Maxie Rosenbloom (Curley Bender), Sidney Toler (Judge Bronson), Ed Brophy (Eddie Black), Winifred Harris (Mrs. Bronson), Morgan Conway (Louie), John Ridgely (Sam), Ward Bond (Klewicki).

At Warner Brothers Studios, a proven commodity was a usable commodity. Edward G. Robinson and Humphrey Bogart, for example, made names for themselves as gangsters in *Little Caesar* and *The Petrified Forest*, respectively, leading the studio to regularly cast them in similar tough-guy roles. Fellow Warner player Wayne Morris featured as a prizefighter with the two actors in *Kid Galahad*. He also starred in another successful boxing film entitled *The Kid Comes Back*. True to form, the success of Morris's two boxing flicks inspired the studio to send Morris back into the ring for the third time in less than two years, in a picture entitled *The Kid from Kokomo*.

In *The Kid from Kokomo*, fight manager "Honest Bill" Murphy (O'Brien) and his girl Doris (Blondell) seek to exploit Klewicki (Bond), Murphy's latest prospect. Although Murphy fancies Klewicki as having the footwork of Gene Tunney, the right hand of James J. Jeffries and the speed of Fidel LaBarbara, his boxer is pummeled by a farm boy from Kokomo named Homer Baston (Morris). Convincing Homer that fighting will provide the exposure necessary to locate his missing mother, the reluctant youth agrees to box for Murphy.

Eventually, Murphy rescues a drunken shoplifter (Robson) from jail and pawns her off as his fighter's long-lost mother. Murphy also fabricates the miraculous return of Homer's father (Fields). Homer fights his way to a championship bout with Curley (Rosenbloom) and on the way falls in love with a pretty college girl named Marian (Wyman).

To cancel out "mom's" gambling debt and satisfy her gangster-creditors, Homer plans to throw his championship match. When Curly insults Homer's "mom," chivalry compels Homer to knock out his opponent. Ultimately "dad" must lead the way in rescuing Homer and Murphy from the revenge-minded crooks. Homer and Marian and "Mom" and "Dad" are then wed in a double ceremony, with the old couple being "adopted" by the fighter.

The Kid from Kokomo is a simple little comedy that features an experienced collection of players from Warner Brothers whose talents exceeded the material allotted. Joan Blondell has an occasional barb that is worthwhile, but the film's only real comedic success was credited to May Robson. Howard Barnes of the *New York Herald-Tribune* wrote that Ms. Robson "gives a superbly broad and humorous characterization which makes the film continually delightful when she has a hand in the action."[1]

Morris's notices for his performance in *The Kid from Kokomo* were far less kind than those he had received in his previous two boxing films.* While Char of *Variety* felt that Morris "leaves nothing to be desired," fellow critic Rose Pelswick found his performance "incredibly ingenuous" and Howard Barnes called it "definitely on the wooden side."[2] Herbert Cohn of the *Brooklyn Daily Eagle* felt that the Morris boxing formula had lost all of its potency writing that the film was "in perilous straights" until May Robson "miraculously snatched Wayne's feature from the junk heap."[3]† The fight sequences in *The Kid from Kokomo* vary, with some rating only fair while others are above average. Archer Winsten of the *New York Post* found them "routine in their conception," but critic Bland Johaneson characterized them as "lively," crediting Max Rosenbloom for lending the ring action "color and authority."[4] The sequence where Morris propels his opponent through the

---

*Dalton Trumbo, who would later be blacklisted as a Communist [before resurfacing in spectacular form with the help of Kirk Douglas as the credited screenwriter for Spartacus] was also a target of the film's criticism. Frank Nugent of The New York Times wrote "Dalton Trumbo and his adapters ... have succeeded merely in writing a cheap and ugly farce which gives Wayne Morris the doubtful distinction of playing one of the most pathetic saps in the screen's history...."

†In 1948, Morris would make The Big Punch, his fourth and final boxing film for Warner Bros. Directed by Sherry Shourds, the picture co-starred Hobart Henley and radio/recording star Gordon MaCrae in his film debut. MaCrae was cast as the prizefighter and Morris as a potential ring star who forgoes boxing for the pulpit. Critiquing Morris in the role of the preacher, Brog of Variety wrote that the actor "... could have used a more experienced directorial hand ... but on the whole pleases as the minister...."

ring ropes *a la* Dempsey-Firpo is particularly well done.

The inclusion of former light heavyweight champion Max Rosenbloom makes a viewing of the film worth the boxing fan's time. "Slapsie Maxie" appears in numerous scenes and has several speaking roles. His crude voice, flattened features and cauliflower ears indicate how the stereotyped 'look' of the fighter developed. The picture even pokes fun at Rosenbloom's famed punching style of the open-glove slap. "Couldn't you hit harder if you closed your gloves?"[5] Morris's character chides Rosenbloom during a sparring session.

On the film's set, Rosenbloom was joined by former junior welterweight champion turned technical advisor, Mushy Callahan. With more than one "champ" about, confusion on the set soon ensued. "Look here, Mushy" Rosenbloom teased, "when anybody calls out 'Hey Champ' around here, I don't want anybody to look up except me."[6]

As a character actor who made numerous film appearances for Warner Brothers, Rosenbloom was no more insulated from the publicity grist mill than Edward G. Robinson and Humphrey Bogart. In connection with *The Kid from Kokomo*, the studio's latest fight yarn, Rosenbloom was exploited through the usual media channels, including radio and print. Publicists, however, pushed for further exposure by urging the film exhibitors to obtain interviews with Max's former opponents. With more than 250 foes in his professional career, Warner Brothers rationalized — with perhaps some justification — that a "Slapsie Maxie" opponent was as close as a theater near you.

1. Howard Barnes, Review of *The Kid from Kokomo* (Warner Bros. movie), *New York Herald-Tribune*, 20 May 1939.
2. Char, Review of *The Kid from Kokomo* (Warner Bros. movie), *Variety*, 24 May 1939; Rose Pelswick, "'The Kid from Kokomo' Bows in at Strand Burlesque of Mother-Love Drama," Review of *The Kid from Kokomo* (Warner Bros. movie), *New York Journal-American*, 20 May 1939; Barnes.
3. Herbert Cohn, "May Robson Rescues 'The Kid from Kokomo,'" Review of *The Kid from Kokomo* (Warner Bros. movie), *Brooklyn Daily Eagle*, 19 May 1939.
4. Archer Winsten, "'The Kid from Kokomo' at the Strand Theatre." Review of *The Kid from Kokomo* (Warner Bros. movie), *New York Post*, 20 May 1939; Bland Johaneson, "'The Kid from Kokomo' Mixes Fight Thrills with Comedy," Review of *The Kid from Kokomo* (Warner Bros. movie), *New York Daily Mirror*, 20 May 1939.
5. *The Kid from Kokomo*, produced by Sam Bischoff, directed by Lewis Seiler, 92 minutes, 1939.
6. "'Slapsie Maxie' Trains for Beauty, Not Bout," Warner Bros. Studio Publicity.

Kid Galahad (1937)

Warner Bros., Drama, B & W, 101 minutes

Producer: Hal B. Wallis. *Director*: Michael Curtiz. *Story*: Story adaptation by Seton I. Miller from Francis Wallace story. *Film Editor*: George Amy. *Cinematography*: Gaetano Gaudio. *Music*: M.K. Jerome, Jack Scholl.

Edward G. Robinson (Nick Donati), Bette Davis (Fluff), Humphrey Bogart (Turkey Morgan), Wayne Morris (Kid Galahad), Jane Bryan (Marie), Harry Carey (Silver Jackson), Veda Ann Borg (The Redhead), William Haade (Chuck McGraw), Soledad Jiminez (Mrs. Donati), Joe Cunningham (Joe Taylor), Ben Welden (Buzz Barret), Joseph Crehan (Brady), Harland Tucker (Gunman), Bob Nestell (O'Brien), George Blake (Referee), Bob Evans (Sam), Hank Hankison (Burke), Jack Kranz (Denbaugh).

Though Wayne Morris never quite rose above his "B" leading-man status, his modest success as a movie actor is by and large attributable to his appearance in boxing movies. Standing six feet, two inches, and weighing 190 pounds, the blonde-haired actor possessed a physique on par with his attractive face, and Warner Brothers quickly embarked upon grooming Morris as a leading man.[1] Since the youngster already had experience boxing in college, a fight picture vehicle was a natural.[2] For his first starring role, Morris was cast in *The Kid Comes Back*. Initially entitled *Don't Pull Your Punches*, the film was a standard "B" fight yarn.[3]

Warner Brothers executives, however, were quick to observe that Morris's potential exceeded that of the film itself, prompting the studio to hold up the picture's release. Jack Warner and his brothers also owned a more ambitious fight story, *Kid Galahad*. Morris was quickly inserted into this production, joining some of the studio's elite players: Edward G. Robinson, Bette Davis, and Humphrey Bogart.[4]

In *Kid Galahad*, Nick Donati (Robinson) is a freewheeling boxing manager, Fluff (Davis), his long-suffering but loyal companion, and Turkey Morgan (Bogart), a big-time gangster and Nick's arch rival. In defense of Fluff, a naïve but handsome bellhop named Goosenberry (Morris) punches out McGraw (Haade), Morgan's heavyweight contender. Fluff takes an amorous interest in Goosenberry, and despite sensing this, Nick follows his financial impulses and signs the bellboy to a fight contract.

Fluff dubs Goosenberry "Kid Galahad," and Nick begins guiding Galahad up the heavyweight ladder. While Fluff harbors a secret affection for the Kid, Galahad instead falls in love with Donati's sister Marie (Bryan). Nick balks at their relationship and, in retaliation, designs a losing fight plan for Galahad's match against McGraw. Nick then bets against Galahad, and advises Morgan to do so as well.

Fluff and Marie learn of Nick's scheme, and midway through the match beseech Nick to reverse course. Nick capitulates, changing Galahad's ring strategy which results in his victory. Double-crossed, Morgan seeks a showdown with Nick and the pair mortally wound one another in a post-fight shootout.

Morris's appeal as a mannered and polite "Kid Galahad" with boyish charm and looks liberated the actor from the back pages of American movie magazines. "There have been rumors that Warner Brothers thought that they had something in Wayne Morris," wrote Archer Winsten of the *New York Post*. "Let this be an unqualified confirmation of the rumors."[5] "The best find that the films have made since Tyrone Power took over leading roles," opined Howard Barnes of the *New York Herald-Tribune*.[6] He "is headed straight for electric lights" concurred *New York Sun's* Eileen Creelman.[7]

The picture may have acted as a wonder drug for Morris's career, but for co-star Bette Davis, who had already achieved Oscar status, it proved nothing more than a double dose of unrequited love. While Wayne Morris spurned the advances of Davis's character in the film, the actress, who maintained an unfilled yearning for her co-star off screen as well, was "overwhelmed by Wayne."[8]

The younger actor was unaware of Davis's feelings, but his potential loss was an apparent gain for the film. Jack Warner had once commented that Davis plays loves scenes best when she is really in love, and her crush on Wayne may have enhanced her performance.[9] William Boehnel of the *New York World-Telegram* observed Davis's silent suffering, writing, "Miss Davis plays the losing woman in the case with fine restraint."[10]

Bogart and Robinson, who were paired five times during their long and illustrious careers, were in sync as usual. "Robinson and Bogart, both grim guys, make their rivalry entirely plausible" observed *Variety*.[11] Robinson is perpetually animated while alternatively edgy and angered as the fight manager desirous of a champion. "Always one of the finest actors in Hollywood, Mr. Robinson gives a biting and pungent characterization," critiqued William Boehnel. As the hoodlum, Bogart injects his character with an underlying smugness and a streak of cruelty, prompting Boehnel to write, "Mr. Bogart is superb as the menace."[12]

Director Michael Curtiz was a stickler for authenticity and he carefully scrutinized the choreography of his fight scenes for *Kid Galahad*. Complimenting Curtiz's attention to detail, *Variety* wrote, "The ring battles are superb for it can be said that no film has revealed better glove throwing than is witnessed here."[13] By today's standards *Variety's* praise may be excessive, but the fight scenes still show as brisk entertainment, and Morris's sculptured physique and plausible fighting technique remain believable.

The credibility of one of the boxing vignettes was also enhanced by an unfortuitous event. During one take in which Wayne Morris was boxing William Haade, Morris sent his fellow actor crashing to the canvas. "Retake! Retake! Fake Fight!" the director bellowed in disapproval. Haade, however did not respond to his director's instructions, because he had been knocked out cold. The studio doctor was quickly summoned, while another scene in which Haade did not appear was prepared.[14]

Following *Kid Galahad*, Morris was cast in his second feature, *Submarine D-1*. Finally the studio released *The Kid Comes Back*, Morris's third film and the unofficial second of his four boxing movies. Having already wooed the critics with his performance in *Kid Galahad*, Morris waited for another round of favorable notices for *The Kid Comes Back*, which was nothing more than a standard "B" picture. Nevertheless, the critics toed the line. Rose Pelswick of the *New York Journal-American* noted that Morris "wallops 'em around again" in his follow up to *Kid Galahad*, and Bland Johaneson of the *New York Daily Mirror* described Morris as a "new youthful hero of the action melodramas."[15]

The film's boxing scenes also received favorable commentary. Herbert Cohn of the *Brooklyn Daily Eagle* wrote, "*The Kid Comes Back* will be remembered for a few well-photographed boxing sequences." Irene Thirer of the *New York Post* noted that the film contained "smart dialogue of the Madison Square vernacular," a style which was in all likelihood not unfamiliar to the ensemble of boxers amassed for the film.[16]

In fact, as many as 28 prize-fighters were featured including Jock Perry, who also coached James Cagney for several of his boxing films; and Abie Bain, Anthony Quinn's inspiration for the *Requiem for a Heavyweight* protagonist, Mountain Rivera. Others of the fistic fraternity to appear were former bantamweight champ Lou Salica, Frankie Garcia, Joe Glick, Sammy Shack, Joe Stanley, Joe Ritchie, Willie and Phil Bloom, Sonny Valdez, Young Freddie Welsh, and Baby-Faced Matthewson. The most famous of the boxing-actors appearing in *The Kid Comes Back* was light-heavyweight turned film comedian "Slapsie" Maxie Rosenbloom. Never having been knocked out in his career, Rosenbloom is called upon in the film to meet the canvas on two separate occasions. "Too darn realistic," the ex-champ observed describing his new experience.[17]

In 1962, a musical remake of *Kid Galahad* was released starring Elvis Presley, Gig Young, Lola Albright and Charles Bronson. Carefully tailored to allow Elvis to belt out as many songs as opponents, the King is featured singing six tunes including *This Is Living, Ride the Rainbow*, and *I Got Lucky*.[18] Tube of *Variety* observed that "Presley's acting resources are limited, but he has gradually established a character with which he does not have to strain too much for emotional nuance."[19]

Not all reviewers critiqued Presley with the same polite restraint. *Time* magazine wrote that "Since Kid Galahad is Elvis Presley, he has trouble lifting his eyelids, let alone his eight-ounce gloves."[20] However, when the cameras were not rolling, not even *Time* magazine could have questioned Elvis's spunk. Upon seeing Elizabeth Montgomery, the beautiful wife of co-star Gig Young, Presley quipped, "I've just bought a new Rolls Royce, I'll trade you for her."[21]

Years later, when the King's version of *Kid Galahad* reached television, the original was renamed *The Battling Bellhop* so that young audiences seeking Elvis's gyrations would be spared an unexpected dose of Edward G.'s cigar chomping.

1. "Wayne Morris Boxes His Way to Stardom," Warner Bros. Studio Publicity.
2. *Ibid.*
3. Kate Cameron, "'Kid Comes Back' on Strand Screen." Review of *The Kid Comes Back* (Warner Bros. movie), *New York Daily News*, 6 February 1938.
4. *Ibid.*
5. Archer Winsten, Review of *Kid Galahad* (Warner Bros. movie), *New York Post*, 27 May 1937.
6. Howard Barnes, "Fight Films and the Feminine Viewpoint," Review of *Kid Galahad* (Warner Bros. movie), *New York Herald-Tribune*, 30 May 1937.
7. Eileen Creelman, "Bette Davis and Mr. Robinson in a Prizefight Drama, 'Kid Galahad,'" Review of *Kid Galahad* (Warner Bros. movie), *New York Sun*, 27 May 1937.
8. Lawrence Quirk, *Fasten Your Seat Belts: The Passionate Life of Bette Davis* (New York: Signet, 1990), 148–149.
9. *Ibid.*
10. W.B. "'Galahad' Portrays Real Life," *New York World-Telegram*, 29 May 1937.
11. Land, Review of *Kid Galahad* (Warner Bros. movie), *Variety*, 2 June 1937.
12. William Boehnel, "Strand 'Kid Galahad' Packs a Wallop," Review of *Kid Galahad* (Warner Bros. movie), *New York World-Telegram*, 27 May 1937.
13. Land.
14. Whitney Stine, *Mother Goddam: The Story of the Career of Bette Davis* (New York: Berkeley Books, 1974), 94.
15. Rose Pelswick, "Morris a Knock-Out in 'The Kid Comes Back.'" Review of *Kid Galahad* (Warner Bros. movie), *New York Journal-American*, 7 February 1938; Bland Johaneson, "'Kid Comes Back,' Wayne Morris' First Starring Picture," Review of *Kid Galahad* (Warner Bros. movie), *New York Daily Mirror*, 2 February 1938.
16. Herbert Cohn, Review of *Kid Galahad* (Warner Bros. movie), *Brooklyn Daily Eagle*, 7 February 1938; Irene Thirer, "'The Kid Comes Back' to the Strand Theatre," Review of *Kid Galahad* (Warner Bros. movie), *New York Post*, 7 February 1938.
17. Studio Publicity for *Kid Galahad*.
18. *Kid Galahad*, produced by Hal B. Wallis, directed by Michael Curtiz, 101 minutes, 1937.
19. Tube, "Another Likely Presley Money-Maker; Elvis Cast as Boxer in Familiar Prizefight Story with Songs," Review of *Kid Galahad* (United Artists movie), *Variety*, 25 July 1962.
20. "Jelloweight," Review of *Kid Galahad* (United Artists movie), *Time*, 3 August 1962.
21. Rose Clayton and Dick Heard, eds., *Elvis Up Close: In the Words of Those Who Knew Him Best* (Atlanta: Turner Publishing, Inc., 1994), 188.

Kid Nightingale (1939)

Warner Bros., Comedy-Musical, B & W, 56 minutes

Producer: Warner Bros. *Director*: George Amy. *Screenplay*: Charles Belden, Raymond Schrock based on an original story by Lee Katz. *Film Editor*: Frederick Richards. *Photography*: Arthur Edeson. *Songs*: George Whiting, Bert Reisfeld.

John Payne (Steve Nelson), Jane Wyman (Judy Craig), Walter Catlett (Skip Davis), Ed Brophy (Mike Jordan), Charles D. Brown (Charles Paxton), Max Hoffman (Fitts), John Ridgely (Whitey), Harry Burns (Strangler Columbo & Rudolfo Terrassi), William Haade (Rocky), Helen Troy (Marge), Winifred Harris (Mrs. Reynolds), Lee Phelps (Announcer), Frankie Van (Trainer).

Mushy Callahan, the former junior welterweight champion of the world, had joined Warner Brothers as a member of the studio's property department in 1933. Callahan was engaged by Jack Warner himself, who had met the fighter on a June evening while taking in the fights at the American Legion Stadium in Hollywood. On that night, Callahan had conveyed to Warner his opinion regarding Hollywood's boxing scenes, which he found on the whole to be unrealistic, with an over-reliance on the roundhouse punch. If the cameras were moved in closer, Callahan reasoned, more authentic-looking in-fighting could be staged and then captured by the camera. The studio boss was in agreement with the ex-pug, and soon Callahan was implementing his ideas in Warner Brothers fight pictures.[1]

Callahan would act as a film technical advisor for many Warner boxing productions in the years to come, including a little musical comedy entitled *Kid Nightingale*. Serving under Callahan's tutelage in preparation for the role of the prizefighter in *Kid Nightingale* was John Payne, the picture's star. Early in his career, the handsome Payne appeared in light vehicles and was sometimes given an opportunity to sing. Warner's casting of Payne as a singer in *Kid Nightingale* is representative of his earlier roles. Later, Payne would star in numerous action and adventure films.

Payne's leading lady in the picture is Jane Wyman. At this juncture of her career, the erstwhile Sarah June Fulks was still a bit-part actress under contract to Warner Brothers. The previous year, she had appeared in the boxing film *The Crowd Roars*. Now best known as the one-time wife of former President Ronald Reagan, Wyman would distinguish herself later in her career with an Academy Award for best supporting actress in *Johnny Belinda* (1948).

Kid Nightingale is the lighthearted tale of an opera-singing waiter who finds himself in the prize ring. The "Kid"(Payne) believes his fights are on the level but they are actually fixed as part of a promotional gimmick. After the Kid scores each knockout, he sings to the accompaniment of a band. When Judy (Wyman) uncovers the ruse, the Kid is given an opportunity to make an earnest effort in the ring.

A.T. Schneible of the *New York Daily Mirror* dubbed the film "a fair comedy," and Herb of *Variety* thought the picture "so absolutely silly it's almost good."[2] In contrast, Wanda Hale of the *New York Daily News* was less than enthusiastic noting that the film "is bound to succeed in forcing a few laughs from a ready and willing audience. But the waiting for such rare occasions in this film grows pretty tiresome." Hale also wrote, "Payne, an engaging young actor, is alright, but the picture isn't. It's one of Warner Bros.' frequent mistakes in casting."[3]

The critic for the *New York Post* wrote with tongue in cheek, "The girls just dote on the good-looking fighter, and are simply thrilled by the way he bursts into song every time he knocks out an opponent."[4] Likewise, the *Brooklyn Daily Eagle* was not blind to the perils of mixing the artistic with the animalistic, finding that the film "has no more punch to it than does its fighting hero, a fellow who is frank enough to admit that his vocal chords, rather than a pair of flexed biceps, are his greatest asset."[5]

During rehearsal of the fight scenes, Mushy Callahan had advised John Payne to work on his rollaway move from the right hand of his ring opponent, ex-navy pug Bill Haade. "If you don't get that roll, Bill will knock your brains loose," Mushy warned.[6] It was Haade, however, who broke a finger while sparring with Payne. Payne did not feel the injurious blow, although he did admit to experiencing his own pain to the nose, jaw and midsection as a result of their spirited sparring sessions.[7] Other ex-fighters who appeared in the film alongside Haade were Eddie Hogan, Jack Roper, Art Lasky, Joe Glick and Jimmy Dolan.[8]

One of the sets, a recreation of New York's Madison Square Garden, became a "hot spot" on the Warner lot during the shooting of the fight scenes, attracting other Warner stars such as Errol Flynn, Donald Crisp, Frank McHugh, Humphrey Bogart, Maxie Rosenbloom and George Bancroft.[9]

1. "'Kid Nightingale' Boxing Scenes Are Real McCoy," Warner Bros. Studio Publicity.
2. A.T. Schneible, "'Kid Nightingale,' at the Palace," Review of *Kid Nightingale* (Warner Bros. movie), *New York Daily Mirror*, 8 December 1939;

Herb, Review of *Kid Nightingale* (Warner Bros. movie), *Variety*, 22 November 1939.
3. Wanda Hale, Review of *Kid Nightingale* (Warner Bros. movie), *New York Daily News*, 8 December 1939.
4. Review of *Kid Nightingale* (Warner Bros. movie), *New York Post*, 8 December 1939.
5. "Crooning Slugger," Review of *Kid Nightingale* (Warner Bros. movie), *Brooklyn Daily Eagle*, 8 December 1939.
6. "Kid Nightingale Bouts Authentic," Warner Bros. Studio Publicity.
7. "John Payne Has Busy Time as 'Kid Nightingale' Star," Warner Bros. Studio Publicity.
8. Warner Bros. Studio Publicity.
9. "Fight Scenes Lured Stars to 'Kid Nightingale' Sets," Warner Bros. Studio Publicity.

The Killers (1946)

Universal-International, Drama, B & W, 105 minutes

Producer: Mark Hellinger. *Director*: Robert Siodmak. *Screenplay*: Anthony Veiller, from a story by Ernest Hemingway. *Film Editor*: Arthur Hilton: *Director of Photography*: Woody Bredell, A.S.C. *Music*: Miklos Rozsa.

Burt Lancaster (Ole "Swede" Anderson a/k/a/ Pete Lunn), Ava Gardner (Kitty Collins), Edmond O'Brien (Jim Riordon), Albert Dekker ("Big" Jim Colfax), Sam Levene (Lieutenant Sam Lubinsky), Vince Barnett (Charleston), Virginia Christine (Lilly Lubinsky), Jack Lambert (Dum Dum), Charles D. Brown (Packy Robinson-Swede's Manager), Donald Mcbride (Ken), Charles Mcgraw (Al), William Conrad (Max).

Like a surprising number of men of letters such as Jack London and George Bernard Shaw, Ernest Hemingway was fascinated with the sport of boxing. The author kept close ties to the game, and on one occasion even acted as a fight reporter for *Esquire* magazine. Covering Joe Louis's encounter with former champion Max Baer, the writer, never shy to express his opinion, dubbed the match "the most disgusting spectacle" he had ever witnessed.[1]

"Papa" also held his own pointed assessments regarding the heavyweight champions of his era. Hemingway harbored an ongoing dislike for former champion Jack Dempsey, railed Baer, whose fear of Louis he found disconcertingly palpable, and lauded Louis as a great fighter.[2]

Boxing's influence on Hemingway took root early in his literary career. Hemingway was inspired by an important match held in June of 1922, between Benny Leonard, the lightweight king and Jack Britton, the ruler of the welterweights. In the thirteenth round of their match at the Hippodrome in New York, Leonard fouled his opponent, losing his bid for Britton's welter laurels. Experts raised the specter of a fixed match.

Several years later, the author expanded upon the events of that evening, in a short story entitled *Fifty Grand*. In *Fifty Grand*, Hemingway's fighter bets $50,000 against himself, but is on the verge of losing his wager when his opponent fouls him. The fighter survives the ordeal, fouling his adversary in return, forcing his own disqualification and insuring the collection of his bet.

Late in 1927, Schribner's published a collection of Hemingway's short stories that included *Fifty Grand* and another tale of a prizefighter entitled *The Killers*. *The Killers* was penned in its entirety on May 16, 1926, along with two more stories in what may be Hemingway's most prolific single day of writing.[3]

Not unexpectedly, Hemingway, who had an ever-growing collection of literary works, had become a prime target for Hollywood's raiders. The author had already sold the rights to *To Have and Have Not*, and in December of 1945, Mark Hellinger purchased those to *The Killers* for $37,500.⁴* For the film version, screenwriter Hellinger looked to boxing film veteran Wayne Morris to portray the Swede, Hemingway's heavyweight, but Warners' $75,000 fee for a loan-out priced Morris out of the role.⁵

Hal Wallis had signed a new prospect, Burt Lancaster, to a contract with options. After a copy of Lancaster's screen test in *Desert Fury* made its way to Hellinger, Lancaster found himself as the lead in Hemingway's story for $2,500 per week.⁶

In *The Killers*, Hemingway's pulp fiction is darkened by screenwriter Hellinger and director Robert Siodmak to create classic film noir. At the picture's opening, an ex-boxer known as the Swede (Lancaster) is confronted by assassins. Resigned to accept his fate, he waits to be gunned down by the hired killers in cold blood. Riordan (O'Brien), an excessively curious and dogged insurance investigator, assisted by the Swede's one-time friend Police Lt. Sam Lubinsky (Levene) and several others, recreate the events leading to the murder.†

An unsolved payroll heist made by the Swede and his co-conspirators is brought to the fore. The Swede's murder is traced to a double-cross spawned by a love triangle between the ex-boxer, a femme fatale named Kitty (Gardner), and the group's leader, Colfax (Dekker). Revenge for the Swede is achieved posthumously when Riordan exposes Kitty and Colfax and brings them to justice.

The Killers began production on April 29, 1946, and was wrapped up in just over eight weeks. Hemingway was enthusiastic about the film version, as was Hellinger. "I have never told you before that I have made a great motion picture," Hellinger wrote to Abe Green of *Variety*. "*The Killers* is a great motion picture."§ Hellinger was so pleased with Lancaster's work that upon seeing the rushes of the first scene played by the former circus performer, he exclaimed, "So help me may all my actors be acrobats."⁷

The film premiered to a record-setting crowd at the Winter Garden Theater in New York, August 29, and the public and the critics responded enthusiastically to the picture and its star.⁸ Otis L. Guernsey, Jr. of the *New York Herald-Tribune* found the film "a polished and tantalizing chase melodrama ... a deft combination of acting and mystery."⁹ "A taut and absorbing explanation of the Hemingway tale," observed Bosley Crowther of *The New York Times*.¹⁰ *Variety* credited Lancaster for doing "a strong job," and the *Herald-Tribune* noted that "he portrays a likable fall guy in a most promising screen debut."¹¹

The Killers features a lone fight vignette which relies on the close-up and the effective use of light, but calls for little boxing from Lancaster. While the film failed to use the ring to fully exploit the finely tuned athletic ability Lancaster had developed as an acrobat, Hemingway's boxer is given an opportunity to take form in a post-fight scene in the locker room. It is there that Hemingway's respect and compassion for fighters is conveyed through the Swede, who is drawn as courageous and proud, but emotionally worn by a fickle fight crowd.

A quarter of a century after making his film debut in *The Killers*, Lancaster found himself at Madison Square Garden contributing to the closed-circuit broadcast of the first Muhammad Ali–Joe Frazier fight. Prior to the bout, former light-heavyweight champion and fellow broadcaster Archie Moore instructed the actor upon the proper

---

*Another of Hemingway's boxing stories entitled The Battler *made its way to the television screen in 1955, with Paul Newman in the lead role.*

†Sam Levene was a regular player in boxing films, always assuming a non-boxer role. Prior to The Killers, *he appeared in* Golden Boy *and* Sunday Punch. *In 1948, he supported a cast led by Cameron Mitchell and Virginia Grey in a picture entitled* Leather Gloves.

§The film received Academy Award nominations for best director, screenplay, film editor, and musical scoring of a dramatic or comedy picture.

method of throwing a jab. "Out!" Moore shouts at the actor with dead seriousness as Lancaster shoots out a left jab and then attempts to recoil his fist to the proper defense posture. The priceless segment has been preserved in a documentary film about the historic boxing contest entitled *Ali the Fighter*.[12]

1. Michael Reynolds, *Hemingway: The 1930s* (New York: W.W. Norton & Company, 1997), 212.
2. *Ibid.*
3. James R. Mellow, *Hemingway: A Life Without Consequences* (New York: Houghton Mifflin, 1992), 330.
4. Kate Buford, *Burt Lancaster: An American Life* (New York: Alfred A. Knopf, 2000).
5. Minty Clinch, *Burt Lancaster* (New York: Stein and Day, 1984), 13.
6. Gary Fishgall, *Against Type: The Biography of Burt Lancaster* (New York: Simon & Schuster, Inc., 1995), 49.
7. *Ibid.*, 50–1.
8. *Ibid.*, 52.
9. *New York Herald-Tribune*, quoted in Gary Fishgall, *Against Type*, 53.
10. *New York Times*, quoted in Gary Fishgall, *Against Type*, 53.
11. *Variety*, quoted in Minty Clinch, *Burt Lancaster*, 15; *New York Herald-Tribune*, quoted in Minty Clinch, *Burt Lancaster*, 15.
12. *Ali the Man: Ali the Fighter*, produced by William Greaves, directed by Rick Baxter, William Greaves, 142 minutes, 1975.

Killer's Kiss (1955)

Minotaur Production, Drama, B & W, 67 Minutes

Producers: Stanley Kubrick and Morris Bousel. *Director*: Stanley Kubrick. *Screenplay*: Stanley Kubrick. *Film Editor*: Stanley Kubrick. *Photography*: Stanley Kubrick. *Music*: Gerald Fried.

Frank Silvera (Palmero), Jamie Smith (Gordon), Irene Kane (Gloria), Jerry Jarret (Albert The Fight Manager), Mike Dana (Gangster), Felice Orlandi (Gangster), David Vaughan, (Conventioneer), Alec Rubin (Conventioneer), Ralph Roberts (Gangster), Phil Stevenson (Gangster), Julius Adelman (Mannequin Factory Owner).

Although Stanley Kubrick directed only 13 feature-length films in a career that lasted nearly a half-century, he left an indelible mark on modern film.[1] Regardless of the genre in which he ventured, Kubrick proved not only to be its master, but also a redefining force in the presentation of its subject matter. Whether realized through the thought-provoking science fiction of *2001: A Space Odyssey* or advanced by social introspection stimulated by *Dr. Strangelove* and *A Clockwork Orange*, Kubrick's vision would nearly always challenge cinema's known parameters.

Beneath Kubrick's many groundbreaking artistic triumphs is a film origin that has its roots in the sport of boxing. In 1949, while an apprentice photographer for *Look* magazine, Kubrick produced a still picture story on middleweight Walter Cartier called *Prizefighter*. Kubrick soon followed with a second photographic essay of a boxer entitled *Rocky Graziano, He's a Good Boy Now*, which appeared in *Look* in 1950.[2]

Around this time, Kubrick viewed a film featuring heavyweight contender Roland LaStarza and was unimpressed by its production.[3] Learning the technical aspects of the film business from an equipment salesman, he wrote and then filmed his own 16-minute narrative entitled *Day of the Fight* (1950).[4] For his film short, Kubrick again examined Walter Cartier, focusing upon his preparation for a match against Bobby James. The culmination of *Day of the Fight* is the boxing contest itself, which was shot live at Laurel Gardens, in Newark, New Jersey, on April 17, 1950.[5]

Kubrick sold the distribution rights for the film for $4,000 to RKO for its *This Is America* series.[6] While this was the most RKO had ever paid for a short, Kubrick only turned a razor-thin profit of $100 dollars.[7] However, the film was responsible for the twenty-two-year-old Kubrick's love affair with filmmaking.[8]

After making a few shorts, and his first feature-length film entitled *Fear and Desire*, the budding talent revisited the squared circle in *Killer's Kiss*. A virtual one-man film crew, Kubrick produced, directed, wrote, photographed and edited the movie. Being a jack of all trades was actually an economic necessity for Kubrick, who was working within a $75,000 budget principally financed by family and friends. Without money to record the film's dialogue or sound effects on location, Kubrick was forced to post-sync all of the film's dialogue.[9] The picture was shot in just 12-14 weeks, but post-production took an excruciating 10 months.[10]

In *Killer's Kiss*, Kubrick juxtaposes the neon lights of Times Square against the stark edifices, barren rooftops, and grim back alleys of New York City to create the backdrop for suspenseful *film noir*. The story's protagonist is Davy Gordon (Smith), a fading welterweight contender. The fighter unexpectedly becomes embroiled in the aftermath of a soured relationship between an unfulfilled dance hall girl named Gloria (Kane) and Palmero (Silvera), her obsessed lover. When Gordon makes a successful bid for Gloria's affections, Palmero, a gangster, attempts to have him murdered. The scheme, however, goes awry and results in the death of Gordon's manager. Ironically, it is the fighter rather than the gangster who is pegged by the police as the murder suspect. Unluckily, Gloria witnesses the misdirected murder, and Palmero holds the girl hostage in the fear that his ex might incriminate him. The story concludes in suspenseful and dramatic fashion, with Gordon helping to liberate Gloria from Palmero and his henchmen, thus clearing his name and facilitating the resumption of his love affair with the girl.

Kubrick produced *Killer's Kiss* entirely outside of Hollywood. Its star, Jamie Smith, was an unknown. Still, Kubrick managed to get United Artists to handle the worldwide distribution of his picture. Billed as a second feature, the film nevertheless turned a profit for United Artists.[11] Of those critics who reviewed the lower-case feature, many were "dismissive" of the film.[12] Kubrick himself would later criticize the film as amateurish, perhaps an overly harsh self-assessment, particularly when applied to the boxing vignettes.[13]

Early in the picture, Kubrick exhibits his sound instincts for the creation of action within the ring in his realistic depiction of the film's lone boxing contest marked by its measured choreography and skilled hand at the editing table. Borrowing one of his shots used in *Day of the Fight*, Kubrick creates unique imagery by photographing one of the boxers through the legs of his opponent, while the pair sit in their respective corners between rounds.[14] He also successfully conveys the genuine texture of a fight gymnasium and the silent tension of a pre-fight dressing room in the brief glimpses he offers of those venues. Working within budgetary limitations Kubrick dodged the costs of hiring extras to portray fight fans by dubbing in recordings of real prizefight crowds, and darkening the set beyond the first few ringside rows to create the illusion that the near empty arena was packed with fans.[15]

Based upon the content of the first quarter of the film, Kubrick could have fashioned a legitimate boxing story, but he abruptly abandoned the fight motif in favor of his true objective: *film noir*. *Killer's Kiss* was the last time that Kubrick would have to finance his own film.[16] He would soon go on to make his first important picture, *The Killing*, on his way to forging a most memorable film legacy.

1. Stanley Kubrick Filmography, Internet Movie Data Base.

2. Vincent LoBrutto, *Stanley Kubrick: A Biography* (New York: Penguin Publishing Group, 1997), 58–9.
3. *Ibid.*, 59–60.
4. Gene D. Phillips, *Stanley Kubrick: A Film Odyssey* (New York: Popular Library Publishers, 1975), 13.
5. LoBrutto, *Stanley Kubrick: A Biography*, 62.
6. *Ibid.*
7. *Ibid.*, 64; Phillips, *Stanley Kubrick: A Film Odyssey*, 14.
8. Phillips, *Stanley Kubrick: A Film Odyssey*, 14.
9. *Ibid.*, 24.
10. LoBrutto, *Stanley Kubrick: A Biography*, 96.
11. Phillips, *Stanley Kubrick: A Film Odyssey*, 24.
12. John Baxter, *Stanley Kubrick: A Biography* (New York: Carroll & Graf Publishers, Inc., 1997), 69.
13. Phillips, *Stanley Kubrick: A Film Odyssey*, 24.
14. *Ibid.*, 14.
15. *Ibid.*, 24.
16. LoBrutto, *Stanley Kubrick: A Biography*, 102.

King for a Night (1933)

Universal Pictures, Drama, B & W, 78 minutes

Producer: Universal. *Director*: Kurt Neumann. *Screenplay*: W.A. McGuire, Jack O'Donnell, Scott Pembroke, based upon a story by W.A. McGuire. *Photography*: Charles Stumar.

Chester Morris (Bud "Kid" Gloves), Helen Twelvetrees (Lillian), Alice White (Evelyn), John Miljan (Douglas), Grant Mitchell (Reverend Gloves), George E. Stone (Hymie), John Meeker (John Gloves), Frank Albertson (Dick), Warren Hymer (Goofy), John Sheehan (Manny), Maxie Rosenbloom (Maxie).

As the fruit orchards of Hollywood gave way to the wooden facades of the early studio lots, thousands of screen hopefuls boarded their local trains and headed for the burgeoning movie colony to make their mark. While many of the stage actors from the New York theater still turned up their noses at the motion-picture industry, starstruck waitresses, adventurous clerks and egotistical high-school prom queens anxiously made the journey. And then there were the boxers.

"Slapsie" Maxie Rosenbloom gained universal recognition as the light-heavyweight champion on July 14, 1932, with a 15-round decision over Lou Scozza in Buffalo, New York. Shortly thereafter, he made his way to Hollywood and Vine. While still the light-heavyweight champion of the world, Rosenbloom landed a role as a prizefighter in Universal's *King for a Night*. As this was one of his earliest film roles, Maxie had only a small speaking part. Later, he would feature more prominently as the heavy or as a prizefighter in many films of the 1930s and early 1940s. Other boxing film credits "Slapsie" Maxie later added to his resume include *Kelly the Second*, *Mr. Moto's Gamble*, *The Crowd Roars*, *The Kid from Kokomo*, and *Ringside Maisie*.

In *King for a Night*, Rosenbloom exchanges blows and jibes with the picture's star, fellow New Yorker Chester Morris. Morris portrays Bud Gloves, a lad whose propensity for fighting leads to a brief stint in the ring. Initially, Bud's career is at a standstill and he is forced to work as a soda jerk. When his sister Lillian (Twelvetrees) follows Bud to the big city, his luck begins to turn.

Bud's new girlfriend Evelyn (White) gets Lillian a job as a showgirl. A fight manager at the club where the girls perform named Douglas (Miljan) shows an interest in Lillian, and he agrees to manage Bud. Douglas guides Bud to a title fight, but the boxer is unaware that his sister has become romantically involved with his manager.

Before the championship match, Bud's world begins to unravel. First he learns that Evelyn is having an affair. Then, Douglas's relationship with Lillian sours. When Douglas threatens to inform Bud of their romance, Lillian shoots and kills him. Bud goes on to win the championship, but to protect his sister he takes the rap for the murder. Lillian confesses to the crime, but to no avail. Although his father is a preacher, Bud is an atheist. Bud is escorted to the electric chair by his father, the only one praying for Bud's salvation.

King for a Night is the tale of how the trappings of big-city life can bring about the demise of a simple country family. Thornton Delehanty of the *New York Evening Post* dubbed the film "effective hokum."[1] Other critics were less accepting. John S. Cohen, Jr. of *The New York Sun* found the film to possess "that hurried, loose look of a swiftly made talkie," and William Boehnel of the *New York World-Telegram* thought the picture to be "a maundering film in which the writing, directing and acting never quite take the measure of its imaginative melodramatic theme."[2]

The New York Times found the Brooklyn-born Morris "active as the gallant pugilist," with Kate Cameron of the *Daily News* complimenting the star for giving "a fine performance through the film, in the lighter, as well as in the heavily dramatic scenes."[3] "Chester Morris plays with that natural *sang-froid* which is his special gift," wrote the critic for *The Los Angeles Times*.[4]

The film utilized the recently resurrected 'Phantom Stage' as one of the picture's sets. Constructed in 1925 as a complete theater for the silent classic *The Phantom of the Opera*, the stage was the first in Hollywood made entirely of steel.[5]

Despite Maxie Rosenbloom's ring appearances in the picture, the fight scenes rate no higher than average. There is a lot of brisk "milling" while the fighters are in the ring, and an assortment of camera angles are utilized, but as noted by Char of *Variety*, the fight sequences "are incidental to the main elements of the story."[6] On occasion Rosenbloom's ring savvy contrasted poorly with Morris's; Morris looks like a novice trying to swap blows with the champion, though for the most part the actor handles himself adequately. While no Willie Pep, Morris is fit and trim and gives off an intensity in the ring that adds to his credibility. Almost a lifetime later, in 1970, Morris would appear as a boxing promoter in the film version of *The Great White Hope*.

1. Thornton Delehanty, Review of *King for a Night* (Universal Pictures movie), *New York Evening Post*, 11 December 1933; Crewe.
2. John S. Cohen Jr., "The New Talkie," Review of *King for a Night* (Universal Pictures movie), *New York Sun*, 9 December 1933; William Boehnel, "Capable Cast Performs in 'King for a Night' Film," Review of *King for a Night* (Universal Pictures movie), *New York World-Telegram*, 11 December 1933.
3. Review of *King for a Night* (Universal Pictures movie), *New York Times*, 25 November 1933; Kate Cameron, Review of *King for a Night* (Universal Pictures movie), *New York Daily News*, 10 December 1933.
4. "Prize Fight Screen Play at Pantages," Review of *King for a Night* (Universal Pictures movie), *Los Angeles Times*, 25 November 1933.
5. "'King for a Night' Borrows 'Phantom' Stage," Universal Pictures, Exhibitors Campaign.
6. Char, Review of *King for a Night* (Universal Pictures movie), *Variety*, 12 December 1933.

The Leather Pushers (1940)

Universal, Comedy, B & W, 64 minutes

Producer: Ben Pivar. *Director*: John Rawlins. *Screenplay*: Larry Rhine, Ben Chapman, Maxwell Shane. *Film Editor*: Arthur Hilton. *Photography*: Stanley Cortes. *Music*: Hans J. Salter.

Richard Arlen (Dick), Andy Devine (Andy),

Astrid Allwyn (Pat), Douglas Fowley (Slick), Charles D. Brown (Stevens), Horace Macmahon (Slugger), Shemp Howard (Sailor), Charles Lane (Mitchell), Wade Boteler (Commissioner), George Lloyd (Joe), Eddie Gribbon (Pete), Frank Mitchell (Grogan's Manager), Reid Kilpatrick (Commentator), Ben Alexander (Announcer).

Prior to becoming the latest in a series of vehicles for Universal's comedic duo of Richard Arlen and Andy Devine, *The Leather Pushers* had established a distinct history of its own. Written by H.C. Witwer and published in 1920, *The Leather Pushers* originally appeared in book form, episodically detailing the adventures of prizefighter Kid Roberts. Universal Pictures quickly picked up the film rights to the pugilist's adventures, and between 1922 and 1924 the studio produced twenty-four two-reel episodes. The series was produced and directed by Carl Laemmle and starred Reginald Denny for all but six of its entries. These other chapters were stylized under the name *The New Leather Pushers* and starred Billy Sullivan, the nephew of heavyweight champion John L. Sullivan. Other notable actors featured were Hayden Stevenson, Norman Shearer and Horace McMahon.[1]

With the advent of sound, Universal revived the series. In 1930–1931, director Albert Kelly fashioned 10 episodes based upon screenplays written by Douglas Doty, Ralph Ceder and Harry Frazier. Kane Richmond played the lead in these vignettes, which sported generic names such as *The Comeback*, *The Champion* and *The Knockout*.[2]

In 1940, Universal released their feature-length sound film starring Arlen and Devine. Arlen, who was born Cornelius Van Mattimore, was a staple hero of the "B" picture and possessed the rugged and natural physique of a boxer. In the female lead, Universal cast the leggy blonde Astrid Allwyn. Shemp Howard, who would later gain cult fame as a member of *The Three Stooges*, and Devine were added for comic relief.

In *The Leather Pushers*, Dick (Arlen), and Andy (Devine) are inseparable pals looking to turn a buck. Dick proves his fighting talent and is signed by promoter Slick Connolly (Fowley) to fight as a light-heavyweight. Unbeknownst to the fighter, Connolly fixes Dick's fights and columnist Pat Danbury (Allwyn) reports the story. Later, Dick takes Pat on as his new manager, the pair agreeing to use their profits to sponsor a sports camp.

A local fight promoter named Stephens (Brown), who is in cahoots with Connolly, assists in framing Dick as a fight fixer, temporarily sidetracking their efforts. Andy attempts to restore Dick's reputation, but lands in the hospital, an assault victim of Connolly. Dick provides Andy with a needed blood transfusion moments before his ring return. While Andy remains in the hospital, his voice is patched into the loudspeaker at the arena and he encourages a groggy Dick on to victory.

The fight scenes in *The Leather Pushers* are true to the spirit of this light comedy. On three occasions during the final bout the lights go out, with each of the participants and the referee taking turns landing on the canvas. Arlen grunts and sweats his way through fights scenes which are repeatedly cut away from to bring the surrounding shenanigans into the fold. Herb of *Variety found* the film to be "entertaining and well-produced" considering the film's budget limitations, accurately noting that MacMahon and Howard "create some laughs," but that the "gags as a whole are pretty weak."[3]

To give the film appropriate atmosphere, no less than twenty ex-pugs appeared in the film, including Phil Bloom, Joe Glick, Abie Bain, Sailor Vincent, Johnny Kernan and Mickey Golden.[4]

Abie Bain, once a promising light-heavyweight, was just an extra in *The Leather Pushers*, and never played a major role in a boxing movie. However, Bain was directly responsible for influencing one of the great portrayals of a boxer on film.

Many years after *The Leather Pushers*, Bain appeared as an extra in *Requiem for a Heavyweight*. On the set, the film's star Anthony Quinn vainly struggled to capture the voice he desired for his portrayal of Mountain Rivera. On the day prior to the shooting of the first scene, Bain spoke to Quinn in his raspy but soft-spoken voice. Quinn was immediately struck by the diverse qualities of Bain's voice. Powerful, yet tender, it intimated both pain and uncertainty. The next day, Quinn's interpretation of Abie Bain became the voice of Mountain Rivera.[5]

1. Harvey Marc Zucker and Lawrence J. Babich, *Sports Films: A Complete Reference* (Jefferson, N.C.: McFarland, 1987), 107.
2. *Ibid.*
3. Herb, Review of *The Leather Pushers* (Universal Pictures movie), *Variety*, 20 November 1940.
4. Scrapbook for *Leather Pushers*.
5. Anthony Quinn with Daniel Paisner, *One Man Tango* (New York: HarperCollins, 1995) 303.

The Life of Jimmy Dolan (1933)

Warner Bros., Drama, B & W, 89 minutes

Producer: Hal B. Wallis (Uncredited). *Director*: Archie Mayo. *Screenplay*: Adapted by David Bohm and Erwin Gelsey from the play "The Sucker" by Bertram Milhauser and Beulah Marie Dix. *Film Editor*: Bert Levy. *Cinematography*: Arthur Edeson.

Douglas Fairbanks, Jr. (Jimmy), Loretta Young (Peggy), Guy Kibbee (Phlaxer), Fifi D'Orsay (Budgie), Aline Macmahon (The Aunt), Lyle Talbot (Doc Woods), Shirley Grey (Goldie), George Meeker (Maggie), Mickey Rooney (Freckles), John Wayne (Boxer), David Durand (George), Farina (Samuel), Dawn O'Day (Mary Lou), Arthur Hobl (Malvin).

The saying that the apple does not fall from the tree applies to the famous father-and-son acting duo of Douglas Fairbanks, Sr. and Jr. The father often portrayed the swashbuckler who also managed to get the girl, while son Doug, a variation of his dad, who was known to portray a suave ladies' man, could also handle himself in a fight.

Despite appearing in a relatively small cache of films, the young Fairbanks was featured in boxing films on three occasions. The first was Fox Film Corporation's 1927 screen adaptation of *Is Zat So?*, a comedy based on the play by James Gleason and Richard Taber. In this production, Fairbanks's sophistication was capitalized on by casting him in the part of the millionaire, with the boxing chores left to George O'Brien.

Several years later, Fairbanks, Jr. would have the opportunity to put on the gloves himself, in Archie Mayo's *The Life of Jimmy Dolan*. In *Jimmy Dolan* Fairbanks portrays a cynical fighter who ascends to the world championship. A murder is committed at a small victory celebration, and the champ, who was in an alcoholic haze at the time, is framed by his manager as the killer. When his manager dies in a fiery car crash while driving Dolan's car, Dolan is believed to be dead, creating an opportunity to avoid the murder rap by taking on a new identity.

Dolan lives as a hobo under the alias of Jack Doherty for a while before being nursed back to health by a young girl named Peggy (Young). Over time, Peggy manages to erode Dolan's cynicism and egocentricism as a romance develops between the pair.

Despite the risk of exposing his identity, the morally awakened Dolan decides to financially assist Peg and the orphaned children on her aunt's farm by boxing a touring fighter. Phlaxer (Kibbee), the detective on his trail, tracks Dolan to the fight, but rewards the boxer's good deed by forgoing his arrest and allowing him to begin anew with Peggy.

Casting someone as handsome and proper as Douglas Fairbanks, Jr. in the role of a pug presented an inherent credibility issue, but the young actor displayed enough fire and athleticism to carry off the part. "He may be a bit too fastidious in his speech for the tough egg he is supposed to represent, but his feeling for the fighter's temperament seemed authentic," wrote Marguerite Tazelaar of the *New York Herald-Tribune*.[1] Tazelaar also credited the actor for "giving the part contrast and shading," while Mordaunt Hall of *The New York Times* simply found Fairbanks's boxer to be "efficient," predicting that the film would "probably appeal to those who favor subjects in which the hero is a pugilist."[2]

The film features a supporting cast of young talent, that would later emerge as stars. The large-eyed Loretta Young is glowing as the lead character's girlfriend, and a young Mickey Rooney displays the engaging verbosity which would make him a star by decade's end. Although a veteran of "B" films, John Wayne was still an unknown. Loretta Young got a bit part for Wayne, who had lost his contract with Fox and was making Western pictures at the smaller studios.[3] His portrayal of a boxer with pre-fight jitters offers a rare glimpse of the early Duke sans his cowboy duds. Wayne's character is only seen in the dressing room; he would not appear in a boxing ring until three years later in *Conflict*.

The fight sequences in *The Life of Jimmy Dolan* are limited to the picture's finale, where Fairbanks engages a much larger foe and gives his pound of flesh. The action is rather rousing, and it is here that the son of the great silent swashbuckling star exhibits a bit of the family's natural athletic prowess.

Several years after the production of *The Life of Jimmy Dolan*, Fairbanks, Jr. would again display his physical abilities in the portrayal of a bare-knuckle prizefighter, in *The Amateur Gentleman* (1936). The film was produced by Criterion Films, Ltd., a Fairbanks-owned company, and distributed by United Artists. Based upon a novel by Jeffery Farnol, the British film is a period piece set during the late nineteenth century.[4]

As was soon to be illustrated in *Gunga Din*, Fairbanks had the ability to master roles which required the portrayal of an action hero who was also a romantic lead. Noting the duality of Fairbanks's screen presence in the *Amateur Gentleman*, Jolo of *Variety* wrote, "Young Fairbanks is possessed of the requisite lightness of touch that demands a composite of the last century gallantry coupled with sufficient virility to look physically equipped to win a heavyweight championship fight."[5]

Fairbanks's father, Douglas, Sr., was in fact a close friend of Jack Dempsey's. The pair met across from Fairbanks's studio, at the Brunton lot, where Dempsey was filming a picture. On the day they met, Dempsey was courting a pretty actress named Bebe Daniels, when a gawking Fairbanks irked the Champ. The boxer was inclined to slug the actor, until the affable and charming Fairbanks revealed his identity to the taken-aback prizefighter.[6]

Dempsey and Fairbanks went on to make a film together entitled *All Good Marines*, which also starred Charlie Chaplin and former heavyweight champion James J. Corbett. The pair also sparred in an exhibition for the Red Cross. Of their boxing engagement Fairbanks, Sr. told his actor/son that hitting Dempsey "was like hitting a tree trunk."[7]

1. Marguerite Tazelaar, Review of *The Life of Jimmy Dolan* (Warner Bros. movie), *New York Herald-Tribune*, 13 June 1933.
2. Ibid; Mordaunt Hall, Review of *The Life of Jimmy Dolan* (Warner Bros. movie), *New York Times*, 14 June 1933.
3. Joe Morella and Edward Z. Epstein, *Loretta Young: An Extraordinary Life* (New York: Delacorte Press, 1986), 60.
4. Douglas Fairbanks, Jr., *A Hell of a War* (New York: St. Martin's Press, 1993), 42.
5. Jolo, Review of *The Life of Jimmy Dolan* (Warner Bros. movie), *Variety*, 5 February 1936.
6. Jack Dempsey with Barbara Piattelli Dempsey, *Dempsey* (New York: Harper & Row, Publishers, 1997), 123–24.
7. *Ibid.* 137.

Madison Square Gardens (1932)

Paramount Pictures, Drama, B & W, 70 minutes.

Producer: Charles R. Rodgers. *Director:* Harry Joe Brown. *Screenplay:* Alan Rivkin, P.J. Wolfson. *Cinematographer:* Henry Sharp.

Jack Oakie (Eddie Burke), Marion Nixon (Bee), Thomas Meighan (Carloy), William Boyd (Sloane), Zasu Pitts (Florrie), Lew Cody (Roarke), William Collier, Sr. (Doc Williams), Robert Elliot (Miller), Warren Hymer (Brassy), Mushy Callahan (McClune), Lou Magnolia (Referee), Damon Runyon, Jack Lait, Grantland Rice, Edward W. Smith, Westbrook Pegler, Paul Gallico (The Sportswriters), Jack Kearns, Teddy Hayes, Jack Johnson, Tom Sharkey, Tommy Ryan, Mike Donlin, Billy Papke, Stanislaus Zbyszko (Themselves).

Several decades ago, when the Pope was introduced to Harry Markson, the driving force behind the fight game at Madison Square Garden boxing, the Pontiff's eyes lit up and he exclaimed, "Ah, Madison Square Garden ... boxing."[1] Indeed, the mere mention of the famed arena's name conjures up the Garden's storied history, from Walker and Greb, to Marciano and Louis, to Ali and Frazier.

By the onset of the Depression, the third incarnation of Madison Square Garden had already occurred. Now established in its new location in mid-town Manhattan, it quickly attracted Hollywood to the doors to exploit it as an ideal story backdrop for an early talkie feature.

In *Madison Square Garden*, Eddie Burke (Oakie) is an aspiring middleweight who comes to New York with his manager Doc Williams (Collier Sr.) to make a mark in the fight game. The racketeers attempt to move in on Burke, but meet fierce resistance from Williams, who goes to the press. When Williams later becomes a matchmaker for the Garden and is prohibited from acting as Burke's manager, his ex-fighter falls into the hands of the fight-fixers. Burke is eventually matched for the championship; however, he is double-crossed when his own management backs his opponent, who fights with gloves loaded with plaster of Paris. Burke fails to win the title, but the fix is exposed and Burke and the employees of the Garden, a group of ex-professional athletes, exact revenge by out-brawling the hoodlums.

Madison Square Garden attempts to create the feel of a real sports venue by integrating clips of actual Garden events including ice hockey, bicycle racing, and of course, boxing. However, the film is still indistinguishable from most of the boxing movies that pit the honest supporters of the sweet science against the manipulative characters of the underworld.

What does makes the film valuable to the boxing fan and sports historian alike, some 70 years later, is the appearance of many notable sporting heroes of the early part of the 20th century. Featured from the world of baseball is Mike Donlin, and former champion wrestler Stanislaus Zbyszko also appears. For the boxing fan, the film offers former middleweight champions Tommy Ryan and Billy Papke, heavyweight contender Tom Sharkey, and former heavyweight champion Jack Johnson.

Watching this collection of sporting legends battle it out with the film's villains in the picture's finale, Richard Watts, Jr. of the *New York Herald-Tribune* noted, "It is particularly edifying to see Jack Johnson with fire in his eyes, battling for the honesty of the ring, while his old-time pals rally around him."[2] Curiously, while Ryan, Papke and Sharkey are found liberally punching out their enemies, the film draws the color line against Johnson, who watches the battle from several feet away. Apparently, this was a safe enough distance between Johnson's black fists and the rest of the white men for the audiences of 1932 to accept.

Notwithstanding the film's great assemblage of fistic talent, the fighting in the ring was left to Jack Oakie. The *New Yorker* observed that the film's star was "amusing and ingenious as a fighter."[3] The critic for the *London Times* was in agreement on the issue of Oakie's disposition but not on his fighting acumen, writing, "Mr. Oakie may not be a boxer — the camera is at its most ingenious in disguising his shortcomings — but he is the possessor of a most winning and good-natured grin."[4] Despite Oakie's deficiencies in the ring, John S. Cohen of the *New York Sun* felt that the ring action was "a thrillingly photographed prize fight, ... thrilling, indeed, over and above the countless thrilling movie prizefights."[5] In reality, Oakie does more holding, rabbit punching and slapping, than fighting, and by today's standards both the fight scenes and Oakie's ring performance would be rated well below par.

The first Madison Square Garden, located at Twenty-sixth Street and Madison Avenue in New York City, was erected in 1879. In existence for only a decade or so, it was soon replaced by a new Garden, also located at Madison Square. Among the classic fights staged in Garden II (which is often erroneously referred to as the original Garden) was the first meeting between Hall-of-Famers Gene Tunney and Harry Greb in 1922. In that match, Greb handed Tunney his only professional loss.[6]

Boxing finished its tenure of a near half-century at Madison Square in 1925, with Sid Terris winning an unpopular verdict against former featherweight and junior lightweight champion Johnny Dundee. That same year, the fisticuffs moved uptown to a third Garden located at Eighth Avenue between Forty-ninth and Fiftieth Streets. Garden III served as the uncontested top boxing arena in the world from 1925 through 1968.

The first main event in the third Garden featured a battle in which Paul Berlenbach won the light-heavyweight championship from Jack Delaney, via a 15-round decision on December 11, 1925. Among the great battles held below its rafters was Henry Armstrong's defeat of Lou Ambers in 1938 for the lightweight crown, a contest that made Armstrong the only fighter in boxing history to hold three titles simultaneously. In 1968, Garden IV opened its doors at its new location between Seventh and Eighth avenues and Thirty-first and Thirty-third streets. The arena continues to feature high-profile boxing contests, recently staging Bernard Hopkins's victory over previously undefeated middleweight champion Felix Trinidad.[7]

1. Anecdote by boxing historian Bert Randolph Sugar.
2. Richard Watts Jr., Review of *Madison Square Garden* (Paramount Pictures movie), *New York Herald-Tribune*, 12 October 1932.
3. Review of *Madison Square Garden* (Paramount Pictures movie), *New Yorker*, 22 October 1932.
4. Review of *Madison Square Garden* (Paramount Pictures movie), *Times (London)*, 6 February 1933.
5. John S. Cohen Jr., Review of *Madison Square Garden* (Paramount Pictures movie), *New York Sun*, 12 October 1932.
6. "Boxing Stirs Special Memories in Garden Centennial Celebration," *Madison Square Garden Boxing*, 1979, vol. x, no. 1, 16, 40–42.
7. *Ibid.*, 40–42.

The Main Event (1979)

Warner Bros. Comedy, Color, 112 minutes

Producers: Jon Peters, Barbra Striesand. *Director*: Howard Zieff. *Screenplay*: Gail Parent, Andrew

Smith. *Film Editor*: Edward Warschilka. *Director of Photography*: Mario Tosi. *Music Editor*: William Saracino. *Music Score*: Michael Melvin. *Technical Consultants*: Hedgemon Lewis, Jose Torres.

Barbra Streisand (Hillary Kramer), Ryan O'Neal (Eddie "Kid Natural" Scalon), Paul Sand (David), Whitman Mayo (Percy), Patti D'arbanville (Donna), Richard Lawson (Hector Mantilla), James Gregory (Gough) Chu Chu Malave (Luis), Richard Lawson (Hector), Richard Altman (Tour Guide), Earl Boen (Nose-Kline), Roger Bowen (Owner, Sinthia Cosmetics), Sue Casey (Brenda), Alvin Childress (Man in the Gym), Kristine De Bell (Lucy), Rene Dijon (Nose-Moss), Shay Duffin (Fight Announcer), Murphy Dunne (Mario), Ernie Hudson (Killer), Dave Ketchum (Photographer), Roslyn Kind, Jimmy Lennon (Announcer), Eddie "Animal" Lopez (Boxer at Kid's Camp), Gilda Marx (Exercise Teacher), Brent Musburger (TV Show Host), Robert Nadder (Nose-Dean), Harvey Parry (Referee in Long Beach), John Reilly (Alan Crane), Tim Rossovich (Cannibal), Jack Somack (Murry), Darrel Zwerling.

On the evening of February 15, 1978, millions across the nation and around the world watched an 8-1 underdog named Leon Spinks upset Muhammad Ali to become the heavyweight champion of the world. Barbra Streisand was one of the fight's countless viewers. Around the fifth round it became apparent to the entertainer, as to most other observers, that the title was beginning to slip from Ali's grasp. Leaping to her feet, Streisand began exercising in front of her television screen. "I just can't sit and watch Muhammad Ali, who's always been a winner, lose," she exclaimed to her companions Jon Peters and director Howard Zieff.[1]

While both Ali and Streisand had ascended to the top of their respective vocations, Ali's star was in decline during the late 1970s while Streisand's was still at its apex. Having established herself as an unrivaled entertainment commodity as both a screen actress and popular singer, her aggressive personality was already exerting a strong influence upon the production of her artistic endeavors.

By 1978, Streisand had already notched ten motion picture credits including *Funny Girl* and *The Way We Were*. However, idle for the past year or so, she was anxious to return to the screen. With one film remaining on her contract with First Artists, the entertainer wanted to fulfill her commitment with a project that would still afford her an element of control. In part because production privileges would rest with herself and co-producer/boyfriend Jon Peters, Streisand ultimately selected *The Main Event*, a Warner Brothers comedy about a boxer and his manager.[2] No longer mere spectators, the trio of Streisand, Peters, and Zeiff were allotted a $7 million budget to create fisticuffs of their own.[3]*

The picture reunited the actress with her former lover Ryan O'Neal, with whom she had successfully teamed previously in *What's Up Doc*. A retooling of the old Tracy and Hepburn battle of the sexes *Pat and Mike*, *The Main Event* adds a twist by reversing the gender roles. The female lead would now play the meddling manager with the male co-star assuming the role of the beleaguered athletic counterpart.

In *The Main Event*, Hillary Kramer (Streisand), is a successful independent businesswoman who owns a fragrance company. When her business manager embezzles her assets and flees to South America, she is left with a single item of value in her portfolio — the contractual rights to a handsome and libidinal ex-boxer named Eddie "Kid Natural" Scalon (O'Neil). A relentless Kramer verbally and legally harasses Scalon until he resumes boxing.

Kramer enthusiastically fumbles through the foreign world of boxing, exchanging verbal jibes with her resentful and uneasy fighter. As Scalon ducks and dodges punches to fulfill his contract, Kramer sidesteps his

---

The film was actually the third boxing flick to bear the predictable boxing moniker The Main Event. *In 1927, Pathe Exchange and director William K. Howard starred Charles Delaney and Robert Armstrong as a pair of fighters vying for the love of nightclub singer Vera Reynolds, and in 1938 Danny Dare directed a Columbia Pictures feature in which Robert Paige portrays a detective seeking a kidnapped boxer.*

attempts to make her a sexual conquest. However, by the eve of his big fight with Hector Mantia, it is Kramer who has become more amorous.

After making love, Scalon seeks marriage but Kramer is indecisive. Upset, he vows to beat Mantia to settle both his debt and relationship with Kramer. Intent on keeping her man, Kramer disrupts Scalon's winning effort by throwing in the towel. This results in a disqualification but secures the continuation of their relationship.

The Main Event features plenty of physical comedy of the slapstick variety. Falls off chairs, trips over tables, head bumping, face slapping and punches to the pit of the stomach are all featured, but often fail to ring true. While Robert Asahina of *New Leader* found that "some of the scenes are truly funny," the film failed to tickle the funny bone of several of his colleagues.[4] David Chute of *The Boston Phoenix* wrote, "Most of the comedy is cloddishly overstated," and Morna Murphy of *Shooting* noted that "the laughs here are generally mirthless and the sight-gags invariably overdone."[5]

Some of the funnier gags of the film relate to its boxing theme. Pouring ice down the fighter's trunks is admittedly predictable, but other moments shine. Kramer tapes her own finger within Scalon's hand wraps, becomes impossibly entangled in the ring ropes, and struts around in high heels forgetting her lone responsibility of providing Scalon with a ring stool.

The chemistry between the pair is evident on occasion and a number of the verbal barbs are effective. In one scene Kramer thwarts Scalon's sexual advances. The next morning Scalon enters the ring for sparring wearing his foul protector over his shorts. "Gee, I'm sorry about last night. I guess I went too far," Kramer exclaims.[6]

Streisand's forceful personality lends itself to diverse opinions. Liz Smith found Streisand to be "lovable," expressing her belief that Streisand "wins us by making fun of her own stridency, her own real-life perfectionism, her own dynamic, insistent personality, and even her own nose."[7] On the other end of the spectrum, Vincent Canby of *The New York Times* failed to find any self-deprecating humor on the star's part, finding the romp "another out-sized Streisand ego trip." Several nice reviews, however, were directed towards Patti D'Arbanville, Scalon's resident bimbo. Canby wrote that she "makes her presence felt," crediting her for adding a "dimension of comic dignity" to the picture.[8]

O'Neal, who had recently lost the leads in two other boxing movies, *Flesh and Blood* and *The Champ*, finally got his opportunity to enter the ring in Streisand's vehicle. Liz Smith wrote that O'Neal, in his deferred ring debut was "charming, funny and sweet" as the henpecked prizefighter.[9]

O'Neal, who had a number of boxing matches as a child, under the auspices of the Catholic Youth Organization, was coached for the film by former light-heavyweight champion Jose Torres.* Torres had O'Neal box 150 rounds, which not only assisted the actor in developing his timing, but resulted in his shedding 40 pounds. The picture's gym scenes were filmed at the Main Street Gym in downtown Los Angeles.[10] In the ring, O'Neal does what the script calls for — the impersonation of a second rate pug who often fights with a sense of desperation. O'Neal's boxing is serious; it is the action between rounds and before and after the fight that are weighted for comic effect.

Trainer Jose Torres, who became a friend of the actor, lived for a spell at O'Neal's Malibu home. The pair even began managing a stable of fighters together. Their boxers are said to have dropped by the O'Neal residence on occasion to pick up advances on their $200 a week salary and a juicy steak dinner, compliments of the

---

Others of the boxing world to contribute to the film were heavyweight contender Eddie "The Animal" Lopez and veteran ring announcer Jimmy Lennon, Sr., both of whom appeared in the film.

host.[11] The boxing bug bit O'Neal hard, and the actor even expanded into color commentary, handling the chores for the Holmes-Weaver and Duran-Palomino bouts at Madison Square Garden.[12]

At the time of the production of *The Main Event*, there was a flurry of boxing films in release or production including *The Champ* starring Jon Voight, *Rocky II* starring Sylvester Stallone, and *Raging Bull* starring Robert De Niro. O'Neal had originally been considered for the lead in *The Champ*, a role which eventually went to Voight. A rivalry between the pair was perceived. O'Neal stated that promoter Don King was interested in matching the pair in a bout, but that he felt he "could handle Jon." "I saw him fight in *The Champ*, and I rate him right hand crazy," O'Neal said. Regarding competition with other fellow actor/boxers, Ryan stated, "Sly Stallone would be another matter. I'd be giving away a lot of weight," and that Robert De Niro "might be an interesting opponent," crediting him for being "fast and tricky."[13]

1. James Spada, *Streisand: Her Life* (New York: Crown Publishing, 1992), 395.
2. Liz Smith, *New York Daily News*, 11 July 1979.
3. *Ibid.*, 396.
4. Robert Asahina, "Summer Fun and Games," *New Leader*, 2 July 1979, 21.
5. David Chute, "Ko'd in the first round," Review of *The Main Event* (Warner Bros. movie), *Boston Phoenix*, 3 July 1979, sec. 3, p. 4.; Morna Murphy, Review of *The Main Event* (Warner Bros. movie), *Shooting*, July 1979.
6. *The Main Event*, produced by Jon Peters, directed by Howard Zieff, 105 minutes, Warner Home Video, videocassette.
7. Liz Smith, "What You Didn't Know—Till Now," *New York Daily News*, 20 June 1979, 8.
8. Vincent Canby, *New York Times*, 1 July 1979.
9. Smith, "What You Didn't Know," 8.
10. Tom Buckley, *New York Times*, 13 July 1979, sec. c, p. 10.
11. *Ibid.*
12. Stephen M. Silverman, "O'Neil and Streisand—A K.O. at the B.O.," *New York Post*, 9 July 1979, 30.
13. Buckley.

The Man from Down Under (1943)

Metro-Goldwyn Mayer, Drama, B & W, 103 minutes

Producer: ____ *Director*: Robert D. Leonard. *Screenplay*: Wells Root, Thomas Seller, based on a story by Bogart Rogers and Mark Kelly. *Film Editor*: George White. *Cinematography*: Sidney Wagner.

Charles Laughton (Jocko Wilson), Binnie Barnes (Aggie Dawlins), Richard Carlson (Nipper Wilson), Donna Reed (Mary Wilson), Christoper Severn (Nipper—As a Child), Clyde Cook (Ginger Gaffney), Horace Mcnally (Dusty Rhodes), Arthur Shields (Father Polycarp), Evelyn Falke (Mary—As a Child), Hobart Cavanaugh (Boots), Andre Charlot (Father Antoine).

Australia stood at the pinnacle of the sport of boxing when on December 26, 1908, it hosted the world heavyweight championship contest in which American Jack Johnson defeated Canadian Tommy Burns in eight rounds to capture the title. Although neither participant that day was an Australian, and Australia had yet to crown its first world champion, Aussies would eventually make their own contribution to the history of the sport.

Hall-of-Famer and three-division champion Jeff Fenech, who terrorized lighterweight fighters in the late 1980s, is the most recent of the fighters from "the land down under" who have left their mark. Other notables who preceded him included bantamweight champions Jimmy Carruthers and Lionel Rose, featherweight king Johnny Famechon, and the great Peter Jackson, who was denied a title shot due to his skin color. Dave Sands, Les Darcy, and Tom Heeney, "the hard rock from down under," were also contenders for world-championship laurels.

Traditionally, Hollywood had little use for Australia as a story backdrop, but during World War II, the Pacific-theater nation became a logical locale for certain war-related story lines. Fitting this niche was *The Man from Down Under*, released shortly after the Allies had turned the war in their favor. In the film, Jocko Wilson (Laughton) is an English soldier who adopts two Belgian orphans, Nipper (Severn) and Mary (Falke), at the close of World War I. It is believed that the children are brother and sister, but they are actually unrelated.

In Australia, Jocko, an ex-boxer and one-time contender in England, trains Nipper in the "sweet science." Nipper (Carlson) fights his way into contention for the British Empire championship. Mary (Reed), away for many years, eventually returns from school. When the pair fall in love, a confused Nipper quits the fight game despite having won the Empire light-heavyweight crown.

With the onset of World War II, Jocko is again in uniform. Nipper is also serving in the armed forces. One evening during a battle, Jocko comes upon Nipper, who is trapped beneath debris, and rescues him. Later, the Axis forces raid Mary's town, and Jocko and Nipper conveniently arrive to liberate her. Mary and the Nipper eventually learn that they are not related, clearing the way for their love.

The Man from Down Under was frowned upon by the critics. Eileen Creelman of the *New York Sun* was blunt in her summary of the picture when she wrote, "The film is a hodge-podge of emotions and incidents, mixing up prize-fighting, religion, two World Wars and a strange love affair."[1] Otis L. Guernsey, Jr. of the *New York Herald-Tribune* launched his own verbal assault on the film writing that the script is "rambling, tedious, and weakened by frequent use of coincidence."[2]

For Laughton, the picture represented another step backward in a recent cinematic retreat from the stellar performances given in such fine pictures as *The Private Life of Henry VIII*, *Mutiny on the Bounty*, and *Rembrandt*. "For once in his life Mr. Laughton is giving a performance that is simply ordinary," noted T.S. of *The New York Times*.[3]

Assailing Laughton for failing to live up to his reputation as a thespian, the critics also found his fighting technique subpar. "It is my painful duty to report that when it becomes his mummer's duty to throw a punch or so, to prove that he was good in the old days, he swings like my Aunt Emma," wrote John T. McManus of *P.M. Reviews*.[4]

Fortunately, the actual boxing in the ring was enacted by Richard Carlson, who proved to be a very good leather pusher. Carlson appears in a fight vignette that is one of the better put on film up to that time and one of this film's highlights. Comparing Carlson's technique to that of Laughton, McManus wrote, "Young Richard Carlson ... an Australian hopeful for Joe Louis's crown ... handles himself better, and puts on one pretty socko bout to prove it."[5] "Richard Carlson stars in a really exciting boxing bout, one of the best the movies have ever staged," added Jane Corby, critic for the *Brooklyn Daily Eagle*.[6]

In the ring, Carlson shows a fast pair of hands with a straight jab, an equally tight right cross, and some good hooks. The pace is quick. Carlson throws many combinations to the body, and neatly spins his opponent off the ropes. The fight vignette nicely mixes long-range fighting with infighting. Clinching is used to enhance the realistic nature of the action without unduly slowing it down. The fight is a pier-six brawl with plenty of knockdowns. "Terrific boxing match," wrote Wanda Hale of the *New York Daily News*."[7] Otis L. Guerney, Jr. concurred, concluding that "it is one of the best ring scenes in a long time."[8]

1. Eileen Creelman, Review of *The Man from Down Under* (MGM movie), *New York Sun*, 27 September 1943.

2. Otis L. Guernsey Jr., Review of *The Man from Down Under* (MGM movie), *New York Herald-Tribune*, 27 September 1943.
3. T.S., Review of *The Man from Down Under* (MGM movie), *New York Times*, 27 September 1943.
4. John T. McManus, Review of *The Man from Down Under* (MGM movie), *PM Reviews*, 26 September 1943.
5. *Ibid.*
6. Jane Corby, Review of *The Man from Down Under* (MGM movie), *Brooklyn Daily Eagle*, 2 November 1943.
7. Wanda Hale, "Globe Shows Laughton in 'From Down Under'," Review of *The Man from Down Under* (MGM movie), *New York Daily News*, 26 September 1943.
8. Guernsey Jr.

Marciano (1979)

CBS Television Movie, Bio-Drama, Color, 100 minutes

Producer: John G. Stephens. *Director*: Bernard L. Kowalski. *Writer*: Paul Savage. *Editor*: Gloryette Clark. *Director of Photography*: Michael P. Joyce. *Music*: Ernest Gold. *Fight Choreographer*: Jose Torres.

Tony Lo Bianco (Rocky Marciano), Belinda J. Montgomery (Barbara Marciano), Vincent Gardenia (Al Weil), Michael O'Hare (Allie Columbo), Richard Herd (John Furst), Dolph Sweet (Menchemann), Frank Ronzio (Pierno), Michael Pataki (Squeak Squalis), Simmy Bow (Charlie Goldman), Booth Colman (Dr. Stephens), Natasha Ryan (Mary Anne), Anthony Carbone (Dr. Collyer), Vanna Salviati (Lena), Philip Simms (Izzy), Don Dunphy (Himself), Bill Baldwin (Telethon Host), Lou Cutell (Cashier), Preston Hanson (1st Businessman), Richard Carlyle (2nd Businessman), Barbara Baldavin (Nurse), Susan Plumb (Peggy West), Shay Duffin (Ring Announcer), Carmen Filipi (Father Santini), Ed McCready (Truck Driver), Tony Di Milo (Ring Announcer), Jim Goodwin (Pool Attendant), Tony Davies (Desk Clerk), Peter Marciano (Corner man), Coley Wallace (Joe Louis), Joe Tornatore (Policeman), Gene Lebell (Ring Announcer), Kathleen O'Malley (Supervisor), Paul Picerni (Johnny Addie).

Unlike the stereotypical fighters so often depicted by the media and in film, Rocky Marciano was endowed with an innate shyness, genuine loyalty, and natural affability. Some might even describe his manner as genteel. *Marciano*, a CBS made-for-television movie, rings true in its re-creation of these endearing personality traits of boxing's only undefeated heavyweight champion. From its warm portrayal of Rocky's affection for his aged immigrant parents, to his enduring loyalty to his boyhood friend and corner man Allie Columbo, *Marciano* carefully reproduces the fighter's affinity for his family and close *paesan* of his inner circle.

Marciano the man, however, was a much more complex, compelling, and human subject than the film suggests. In this sense, the story is biographically deficient, for it fails to explore the full range and depth of Rocky's underlying emotions and the strengths and foibles which they manifested.

Marciano's father earned his meager wages and gave his lifeblood in anonymity in the recesses of a Brockton, Massachusetts, shoe factory. Rocky's repulsion of the smell of shoe leather and his fear of repeating his father's economic and spiritual confinement drove him to become one of the most hardworking and dedicated fighters in history. It also led to an obsession never to be without money. *Marciano*, however, fails to capture the boxer's unparalleled desire, unwavering drive and unyielding intensity, which not only enabled Rocky to become the only undefeated heavyweight champion in the history of boxing, but lifted him to financial security as well.

By examining Marciano's ambition through the triangular relationship between Rocky, his wife, and manager Al Weil, the filmmakers have diffused Marciano's unequaled obsessions, reducing them to a pedestrian conflict between work and family. While the film handsomely duplicates Weil's ruthlessness and domineering personality and clearly conveys his influence in advancing the fighter's career at the expense of family life, the opportunity to examine one of the most motivated athletes of our time is forsaken for a soap opera of familial strife.

Critics were not particularly kind to the television bio-pic. John J. O'Connor of *The New York Times* wrote, "In many ways, the film ... is as colorless as its subject. Marciano tended to be all fists."[1] Kay Gardella of the *Daily News* quipped, "Rocky may never have been kayoed in the ring but he has been by CBS. It's not a knockout of a film."[2] O'Connor, however, was more receptive of Lo Bianco's performance, crediting him with capturing "the intense drive of an essentially simple man."[3] Alvin H. Marill of *Films in Review* agreed, finding Lo Bianco "quite acceptable," although he was unable to keep from wincing at some of the lines given to him."[4]

Lo Bianco bears a facial resemblance to "The Rock" but is a bit undersized for a heavyweight, even one as small as Marciano. As a thirty-three-year-old fighter with thinning hair the actor fit the bill, but he was a little too weather-beaten to portray the twenty-three-year-old "Brockton Blockbuster" who appears at the film's beginning.

To Lo Bianco's credit he does a respectable job recreating the prototypical Marciano, pouring it on until his opponent succumbed, though lacking the speed and muscular intensity of Marciano. The film's boxing vignettes did not skirt detail, recreating accurate scenes such as the one-of-a-kind knockout of Jersey Joe Walcott in Philadelphia. Fight sequences included Marciano's pro debut against Lee Epperson, his narrow victory against LaStarza in their first encounter, his pivotal defeat of Joe Louis, the annexing of the crown against Walcott, and his slugfest finale against Archie Moore. A nice touch was the use of Boxing Hall of Fame broadcaster Don Dunphy to provide the ringside radio blow-by-blow call for the LaStarza, Louis and Moore affairs.* Also making a cameo in the film was WBC welterweight champion Carlos Palomino, appearing as a poolside waiter who approaches Marciano for his autograph.

Marciano, on the surface, is a pleasant and agreeable tribute to a boxing great, but for a deeper look at this stolid and sturdy icon of the 1950s, a read of *Rocky Marciano: Biography of a First Son* is a must.

1. John J. O'Connor, "Marciano's Story Joins Live 'Sportsworld' Bout," *New York Times*, 19 October 1979, C36.
2. Kay Gardella, "Marciano Gets Kayoed — by CBS," *New York Daily News*, 19 October 1979, 70.
3. O'Connor, "Marciano's Story," C36.
4. Alvin H. Marill, Review of *Marciano* (CBS Television Movie), *Films in Review*, January 1980.

Matilda (1978)

American International Pictures, Comedy, Color, 103 minutes

Producer: Albert S. Ruddy. *Director*: Daniel Mann. *Screenplay*: Albert S. Ruddy, Timothy Galfas from Paul Galico's novel. *Film Editor*: Allan Jacobs. *Cinematography*: Jack Woolf. *Music*: Jerrold Immel.

*The use of Dunphy was more representative than accurate. The Marciano-Moore radio blow-by-blow, for example, was given by Russ Hodges, famous New York Giants baseball broadcaster who was immortalized by his call of Bobby Thomson's home run off Ralph Branca in the 1951 National League pennant game.

Elliott Gould (Bernie Bonnelli), Clive Revill (Billy Baker), Harry Guardino (Uncle Nono), Roy Clark (Wild Bill Wildman), Karen Carlson (Kathleen Smith), Art Metrano (Gordon Baum), Lionel Stander (Pinky Schwab), Roberta Collins (Tanya Six), Larry Pennell (Lee Dockerty), Gary Morgan (Matilda), Robert Mitchum (Duke Parkhurst), Lenny Montana (Hood #1), Frank Avianca (Hood #2), Joe De Fish (Hood #3), Pat Henry (Hood #4), Matty Jordan (Hood #5), Shepherd Sanders (Hood #6), Don Dunphy (Ringside Announcer), George Latka (Referee #1), Fred Carney (Clay), Charlie Brill (Barker), David Clarke (Sheriff), John Cunningham (Dave Holter), Rex Everhart (ASPCA Attendant #1), Bob Hodges (ASPCA Attendant #2), Ted Hartley (Payne Smith), Harry Holcombe (Mr. Hardy), Elizabeth Kerr (Mrs. Hardy), James Jeter (ASPCA Attendant #3), James Lennon (Ring Announcer), Edwin Max (Matson), John Thomas (Referee #2), Bill Quinn (Donohue), Rita Karin (Spectator).

During the last decade of the nineteenth century, the new medium of film was a lightning rod for experimentation. At the time, virtually every facade of human discourse was being captured on celluloid. The strange, the unusual, and the bizarre were no exceptions. All were recorded for posterity. Included in this cavalcade of carnival-oriented cinema was a real-life kangaroo engaged in the sport of boxing. The 1896 British short, simply titled *Boxing Kangaroo*, is believed to be the first "boxing" movie ever made.[1]

Marsupials were unable to make a lasting impression in the fight game and likewise proved unimportant to the world of cinema, but one did resurface in 1978, in a comedy from American International Pictures entitled *Matilda*. In *Matilda*, Bonnelli (Gould) is an entertainment promoter who hooks up with an old-time fighter (Revill) to advance the career of a boxing kangaroo from Australia. When Matilda (Morgan) knocks out the heavyweight champion of the world in an exhibition bout, it enrages the champion's pilot, an underworld figure named Nono (Guardino).

Nevertheless, the roo's career continues, assisted with publicity from a *New York Post* sportswriter (Mitchum), who is crusading against organized crime. Nono desires revenge and attempts to run Matilda out of the sport. However, Matilda eventually gets a shot at the championship to prove her place in the fight game.

Matilda, based upon the Paul Gallico play, was a flop. It was intended as a fairy tale for adults, but was a disappointment to audiences of all ages. The film's publicity department scheduled its star Robert Mitchum to appear with the kangaroo at a Madison Square Garden event, and even arranged a boxing match in front of the Time-Life Building with female boxer Cathy "Cat" Davis to bolster its prospects.[2] Publicity stunts couldn't salvage the film. Critic Kathleen Carroll's opinion was not colored by the fact that one of the story's characters worked at her newspaper, the *New York Post*, when she wrote, "Sitting through this fly-by-night- production ... is enough to make anyone hopping mad."[3]

For a star of Robert Mitchum's caliber, even *Matilda* could not hurt his reputation, though one wonders what motivated him to make the film. "Mr. Mitchum sort of lazes his way through the movie, knowing he's bigger than it is," noted Vincent Canby of *The New York Times*."[4]

The ring sequences, save the finale, are brief, and perhaps intentionally so, as the costumed actor playing Matilda is not believable. Prior to film production, the use of both a real kangaroo and a double appearing in costume to handle the fight chores was contemplated. A kangaroo was even trained for two years to appear in the film for the scenes outside of the ring. Ultimately it was decided that the audience would not accept the cross-cutting between the two disparate versions of the kangaroo.[5] However, the film's lone use of the costumed kangaroo was a failure in that the audiences could not accept it as credible on any level. "A hard-eyed backer would have taken one look at the monkey-suit-effect in the early rushes and canceled the project in despair at achieving the necessary suspension of disbelief," explained Tom Allen of *The Village Voice*.[6]

Essential to the boxing-comedy is the utilization of the ring to add to the film's humor. But, *Matilda* fails to exploit the opportunity. For the most part, the film is played straight, and Matilda is seen doing roadwork, sparring and wearing headgear, but no creativity was exercised in figuring out how a boxing kangaroo could entertain an audience.

An attempt to appease the ring aficionado is made by featuring the hall-of-fame broadcaster Don Dunphy as the fight finale's blow-by-blow announcer. "Matilda is a fine defensive fighter," Dunphy bellows as the man in the ridiculous furry costume boxes.[7] Viewers may not be laughing, though one certainly feels like crying at the wrestling-like atmosphere.

1. Harvey Marc Zucker and Lawrence J. Babich, *Sports Films: A Complete Reference* (Jefferson, N.C.: McFarland, 1987), 67.
2. Robert B. Frederick, "Producer Ruddy Tour — Touts for His Boxing Kangaroo," *Variety*, 28 June 1978, 42.
3. Kathleen Carroll, Review of *Matilda* (American International Pictures movie), *New York Post*, 22 June 1978.
4. Vincent Canby, Review of *Matilda* (American International Pictures movie), *New York Times*, 22 June 1978.
5. Frederick, "Producer Ruddy," 42.
6. Tom Allen, Review of *Matilda* (American International Pictures movie), *Village Voice*, 10 July 1978.
7. *Matilda*, produced by Albert S. Ruddy, directed by Daniel Mann, 105 minutes, Vestron Video, videocassette.

The Milky Way (1936)

Paramount, Comedy, B & W, 89 or 83 minutes

Producer: E. Lloyd Sheldon. *Director*: Leo McCarey. *Screenplay*: Grover Jones, Frank Butler, Richard Connell, from the play by Lynn Root and Harry Clork. *Film Editing*: Leroy Stone. *Cinematography*: Alfred Gilks.

Harold Lloyd (Burleigh Sullivan), Adolphe Menjou (Gabby Sloan), Verree Teasdale (Ann Westley), Helen Mack (Mae Sullivan), William Gargan (Speed MacFarland), George Barbier (Wilbur Austin), Dorothy Wilson (Polly Pringle), Lionel Stander (Spider Schultz), Charles Lane (Willard), Marjorie Gateson (Mrs. Winthrop LeMoyne), Bull Anderson (Oblitsky), Jim Marples (O'Rourke), Larry Mcgrath (Referee).

Charlie Chaplin, Buster Keaton and Harold Lloyd were all silent film stars who at one time or another used the prize ring to exploit their comic genius. Chaplin starred in *City Lights*, as well as several silent boxing shorts, including *The Knockout*, *The Champion*, and *The Kid*, while Keaton headlined in a feature-length film entitled *The Battling Butler*, which was also pre-talkie slapstick.

Sadly, neither of Lloyd's two esteemed contemporaries had great success in sound films. Similarly, Lloyd never recaptured the notoriety he achieved in the silent era with his bespectacled "Lonesome Luke" character. Nonetheless, his "glasses" persona persisted in film, resurfacing in *The Milky Way*, the tale of a naive milkman who is thrust into a ring career.*

In *The Milky Way*, Lloyd portrays Burleigh, a well-meaning but bumbling milkman, who through a comedy of errors is credited with knocking out middleweight

---

*The Milky Way, which was originally a successful stage play, was the first picture in twelve years which Lloyd starred in and did not produce. Production of the film took seven months — brief work for Lloyd, who was known for his excruciatingly long projects.

champion Speedy McFarland (Gargan). When the incident moves beyond clarification, Gabby (Menjou), the champion's unnerved manager, decides to capitalize on the ballyhoo by promoting Burleigh in a series of set-up fights. Gabby's long-term goal is to match Burleigh with Speedy in a legitimate fight, and collect on a long-shot bet. Burleigh unwittingly fumbles his way to a series of victories, his self-assurance increasing proportionately with Gabby's hype. Burleigh eventually learns his talent is a sham, but a sleeping medicine, accidentally administered to the champ, clears his path to victory.

As a youngster, Lloyd learned to box at a gym while he lived in Denver. He was capable enough to reach the semi-final round of a Colorado State amateur boxing tournament, but was forced to withdraw from competition at the insistence of his parents.[1] However, boxing experience was actually unnecessary for the film, as the fight scenes were played strictly for their comedic effect. In fact, Lloyd can be seen wearing his signature eyeglasses even while boxing!

Some of Lloyd's funnier moments include a vignette in which he foils his sparring partner's attempt to put on gloves and another featuring Lloyd's rapid succession of entanglements with a boxer, an ice bucket and the ring ropes. Relying on his wealth of slapstick experience, Lloyd ducks, dodges, sidesteps, pedals and pirouettes through the film. Yet, one who knows Lloyd's skill may have an inkling that the script does not allow for his physical talents to be properly highlighted in the ring. The memory of Keaton's more clever use of the squared circle and related boxing paraphernalia in *The Battling Butler* seems to confirm that suspicion.

Winston Burdett of the *Brooklyn Daily Eagle* offered an accurate assessment of the film writing, "Despite Mr. Lloyd's ingenuity, the comedy trots along at a pretty dogged pace, frequently more labored than lively and more quaint than hilarious."[2] However, a majority of the critics were most generous to both Lloyd and the picture. Regina Crewe of the *New York-American* wrote that the film was "an excellent vehicle for Mr. Lloyd's undiminished talents," and Abel of *Variety* concurred commenting that the role of the milkman "is almost made to order for Lloyd and he plays it to the hilt."[3] *Liberty Magazine* was effusive in its praise, writing that "Harold Lloyd has turned out more than his share of good comedies, but none, that we can remember, any funnier than *The Milky Way*."[4] Rose Pelswick of the *New York Evening Journal* felt that "with an amusing idea, an elegant supporting cast and some of the season's funniest lines, the film emerges as one of Lloyd's best."[5]

A sequence in which a boxing lion appears was added to the stage version for the film. A lion was utilized when the studio was unable to secure the services of a kangaroo.[6] The scene serendipitously conjures up the memory of Battling Siki, the eccentric Senegalese light-heavyweight champion who was known to bound about post-war Paris with a pet lion.*

Another more ingenious and recognizable connection to the boxing world was the inclusion of a boxing match staged for a milk charity for babies. The socialite in the film who sponsors the event was undoubtedly modeled after the wife of publishing magnate William Randolph Hearst. On numerous occasions during the Depression, Mrs. Hearst raised money for a charity, *Free Milk Fund for Babies, Inc.*, by promoting high-profile boxing matches. Her sponsored events included the second Barney Ross–Tony Canzoneri fight, in which Ross successfully defended his lightweight championship at the Polo Grounds, and Ross's defeat of Jimmy McLarnin to win the wel-

---

*Battling Siki (Louis Phal) won the light-heavyweight championship of the world by scoring a six-round knockout of Georges Carpentier on Carpentier's home turf in Paris on September 24, 1922. Siki lost the championship to an Irishman, Mike McTigue, over 20 rounds on St. Patrick's Day, 1923, in Dublin, Ireland.

terweight championship at the Madison Square Bowl.⁷

Paramount's advertising department also capitalized on the milk theme by arranging a campaign in conjunction with the Borden Milk Company. The milk bottles of Borden and its subsidiaries were fitted with a cardboard cut out featuring Lloyd's likeness. The cut-out, which fit neatly over the bottle neck, had a message from the film's star: "Good morning folks, here's your Borden's Milk. The Milky Way to health. Come and see me in my new picture 'The Milky Way' at your favorite theater near you." Paramount also urged theaters to hold a contest for the oldest milk-horse in their city.⁸

Whether or not asking for such enthusiasm was overly optimistic, at least one individual overseas exhibited the proper spirit. At the Carlton Theater in London, England, Mr. T. Baxter, chairman of the Milk Marketing Board, opened the first cinematic milk bar in England. As patrons of *The Milky Way* at the Carlton waited on line to be served a cool, fresh glass of milk, a life-sized photo of Lloyd vainly attempting to juggle 30 bottles of milk entertained them.⁹

1. "Boxing Taught Lloyd to Duck," Paramount Press Book, Adolph Zucor Presents "Harold Lloyd in The Milky Way."
2. Winston Burdett, "Harold Lloyd's New Picture, 'The Milky Way,' Arrives at the N. Y. Paramount — 'Everybody's Old Man' at the Center," Review of *The Milky Way* (Paramount Pictures movie), *Brooklyn Daily Eagle*, 26 March 1936.
3. Regina Crewe, "Harold Lloyd Romps through 'Milky Way' in Hilarious Fashion," Review of *The Milky Way* (Paramount Pictures movie), *New York-American*, 26 March 1936; Abel, Review of *The Milky Way* (Paramount Pictures movie), *Variety*, 1 April 1936.
4. Review of *The Milky Way* (Paramount Pictures movie), *Liberty Magazine*, 7 March 1936.
5. Rose Pelswick, "Harold Lloyd Portrays Goofy Film Comedian," Review of *The Milky Way* (Paramount Pictures movie), *New York Evening Journal*, 26 March 1936.
6. Paramount Press Book, Adolph Zucor Presents "Harold Lloyd in The Milky Way."
7. Joseph C. Nichols, *New York Times*, 12 September 1933; James P. Dawson, *New York Times*, 28 May 1934.
8. "Select City's Oldest Milk Horse-Contest," Paramount Press Book, Adolph Zucor Presents "Harold Lloyd in The Milky Way."
9. Dixon Campbell, "Harold Lloyd at His Best," *Daily Observer (London)*, 4 March 1936.

The Miracle Kid (1942)

Producers Releasing Corporation (PRC), Drama-Comedy, B & W, 66 minutes

Producer: John T. Coyle. *Director*: William Beaudine, based upon an original story by Henry Sucher. *Screenplay*: Gerald Adams, Henry Sucher and John T. Coyle. *Film Editor*: Guy V. Thayer, Jr. *Director of Photography*: Arthur Martinelli. *Musical Director*: Clarence Wheeler.

Tom Neal (Jimmy Conley), Carol Hughes (Pat Hilton), Vicki Lester (Helen), Betty Blythe (Gloria), Ben Taggart (J. Hamilton Gibbs), Alex Callam (Al Bolger), Thorton Edwards (Pedro), Minta Durfee (Pheney), Gertrude Messenger (Marge), Adele Smith (Lorraine), Frank Otto (Shady Lane), Paul Bryar (Rocco), Pat Gleasch.

William Beaudine, one of Hollywood's all-time prolific directors, had a reputation for settling for his first take. This approach was not inconsistent with his dispassionate sentiments regarding his work. By his own admission, Beaudine cared little for many of the films he was assigned to direct. On one occasion, a Monogram Pictures executive is said to have rushed onto one of Beaudine's sets demanding to know when the film would be finished. "You mean there is someone out there *waiting* for this?" the director replied incredulously.¹

Beaudine ambivalently churned out

"B" picture after "B" picture for the smaller studios such as PRC and Monogram Pictures. This included several boxing-related films including *Mr. Hex* and *Newshounds*, both vehicles for the Bowery Boys. *The Miracle Kid* was just another lowercase picture in the long procession. Tom Neal, a steady leading man of the "Bs" during the 1940s, stars in the picture. The film also features Betty Blythe, a former silent-screen beauty.

In *The Miracle Kid,* J. Hamilton Gibbs (Taggart) is an unscrupulous publisher of a physical culture magazine. His main competitor is his ex-wife, an equally proficient spin-doctor named Gloria (Blythe). Secretly working as a publicity man for both is an opportunist named Al Bolger (Callam). Another employee of Gloria's named Pat Hilton (Hughes), is engaged to wed a light-heavyweight prizefighter named Jimmy Conley (Neal). As a publicity stunt for Gloria's magazine, Bolger devices a scheme to promote Jimmy's future bouts by claiming he has a "hex" power over his opponents. Jimmy, however, has promised his wife that he will retire from the ring to assist her in operating a sports camp for children.

To eliminate Pat as an obstacle to Jimmy's ring career, Bolger creates the perception that Jimmy is romancing Gibb's attractive niece (Lester). As planned, the ploy interferes with the couple's relationship and Jimmy returns to fighting. Bolger employs the services of Shady (Otto), an aptly named manager who provides Jimmy with enough patsies to make him and the "hex" a sure-fire success.

Pat learns that Jimmy's bouts, including his next against "Killer" Kane, are set-ups orchestrated by Bolger and Gloria, and to protect Jimmy's reputation she pays off Kane's manager to have Kane fight on the level. Although the manager fails to follow through, Kane's non-combativeness tips Jimmy off that the bout's a fake. Jimmy forces Kane to box on the level by threatening to go to the commission. Jimmy gallantly loses a legitimately fought match, and returns to Pat who eagerly accepts him. The pair then resume their plans to open a summer camp and marry.

Wood of *Variety* found the film to be "weakly written and enacted," "a hodgepodge of almost unrelated events."[2] The critic for the *New York Post* was more neutral, writing the "cast is adequate, and production is not big-time but presentable," the *New York Daily News* went so far as to say, "*The Miracle Kid*, though undistinguished, is an agreeable little comedy."[3]

Neal, who also boxed in college, brought a modicum of credibility to the role of the pugilist, though he spends most of the film limbering up. He is not seen in action until the final scene, in which he performs admirably — that is for a boxer from Harvard. The muscle-toned actor was, in fact, a Harvard Law School graduate. He had the unusual distinction of earning that degree and, years later, serving a prison sentence for the manslaughter of his wife, whom he shot and killed.[4]

1. Wheeler W. Dixon, *The "B" Directors: A Biographical Directory* (Metuchen, N.J.: The Scarecrow Press, Inc., 1985), 44.
2. Wood, Review of *Miracle Kid* (Producers Releasing Corporation movie), *Variety*, 21 January 1942.
3. Review of *Miracle Kid* (Producers Releasing Corporation movie), *New York Post*, 7 January 1942; Review of *Miracle Kid* (Producers Releasing Corporation movie), *New York Daily News*, 7 January 1942.
4. Thomas G. Aylesworth and John S. Bowman, *The World Almanac Who's Who of Film* (New York: Bison Books Corporation, 1987), 313–14.

Monkey on My Back (1957)

United Artists, Bio-Drama, B & W, 94 minutes

Producer: Edward Small. *Director*: Andre' De Toth. *Screenplay*: Paul Dudley, Anthony Veiller, based upon the book, *No Man Stands Alone* by Barney Ross and Martin Abramson. *Film Editor*: Grant Whytock. *Cinematography*: Maury Gertsman. *Music*: Paul Sawtell, Bert Shefter.

Cameron Mitchell (Barney Ross), Dianne Foster (Cathy), Jack Albertson (Sam Pian), Kathy Garver (Noreen), Lisa Golm (Barney's Mother), Barry Kelly (Big Ralph), Dayton Lummis (J. L. McAvoy), Lewis Charles (Lew Surati), Raymond Greenleaf (Dr. A. J. Latham), Richard Benedict (Art Winch), Brad Harris (Spike McAvoy), Robert Holton (Dr. Sullivan), Paul Richards (Rico).

The challenges faced and risks taken by Barney Ross in the boxing ring cannot metaphorically do justice to his personal struggles. Even Ross's ring finale against "Hammerin" Henry Armstrong, which stands as a testimony to his courage, is reduced to anecdotal status when juxtaposed against the balance of his life experience.

Barney Ross was fighting someone or something all of his life. While only a boy, Barney found his bleeding father half-conscious on the floor of the family grocery store. His dad would die from the wounds he sustained during a robbery.[1] The loss of his father was the first of many demons that haunted Ross.

Born Barnet David Rasofsky, Barney was raised in a Jewish ghetto in Chicago that abutted an equally poor Italian enclave. Gangsterism was rampant in the area and Ross took to gang fighting. So prevalent was the criminal element surrounding Barney that he personally knew all seven of the men murdered in the St. Valentine's Day Massacre.[2] Ross even worked as a messenger boy for Alphonse "Scarface" Capone, until Capone, recognizing the inherent goodness in Barney, demanded he "go back to school, or get a job."[3]

After a Hall-of-Fame boxing career that included the lightweight and welterweight championships, Ross went on to serve at Guadalcanal, becoming a decorated war hero winning the Silver Star for gallantry.[4] Tragically, he also developed a drug addiction that began while taking narcotics as part of medical treatment for his injuries. His drug habit later served as a panacea during the days in which the crowds no longer cheered for him.

The details of Ross's fabled ring career, heralded war service, and painful fight against drug addiction were brought to the screen in a United Artists production entitled *Monkey on My Back* (1957). Ross once characterized his injuries incurred from Armstrong, his shrapnel wounds, and bout with malaria at Guadalcanal as "child's play" when compared to his narcotics addiction. He hoped that the film could help others defeat or avoid the horrible effects of drugs. To that end, Ross served as a technical advisor for the film, appearing every day on the set.[5]

To portray Ross, United Artists cast Cameron Mitchell. Jack Albertson and Richard Benedict were given the roles of his fistic handlers Sam Pian and Art Winch. Brief ring action at the beginning of the picture, a sampling of Ross's other addictions — women and horses — and a taste of combat action are all used to set-up the balance of the story, which focuses on the harrowing experience of drug addiction.

The film attempts, with modest success, to convey the personal human degradation caused by drug addiction and the resulting destruction of family life and interpersonal relationships. Hope is later offered through the prospect of rehabilitation. Tame by today's standards, and sometimes unintentionally humorous, the picture offered movie audiences of its day an honest look into rarely depicted subject matter, albeit with "B" movie production sensibilities.

Drug use had a Dr. Jekyll and Mr. Hyde effect on Ross's persona creating a diverse character for film depiction. Critic Gene of *Variety* noted, "Cameron Mitchell handles the Ross part with commendable flexibility." He added, "*Monkey* is played with uniform conviction."[6] While the picture was something of a success, Ross was far from pleased with the packaging of the final product. On May 17, 1957, the ever-combatant Ross filed a $5 million lawsuit against the producers of *Monkey on My Back*. He alleged that the film's advertisements were misleading, conveying the notion that he was still addicted to drugs, despite the fact that he kicked the habit many years prior.[7]

1. Barney Ross and Martin Abramson, *No Man Stands Alone: The True Story of Barney Ross* (Philadelphia: J.B. Lippincott Company, 1957), 14.
2. *Ibid.*, 67.
3. *Ibid.*
4. Barney Ross, "Ross Gets off the Hook," *Toronto Daily Star*, 1 June 1957, 27.
5. *Ibid.*
6. Gene, Review of *Monkey on My Back* (United Artists movie), *Variety*, 15 May 1957.
7. "Barney Ross Files Suit," *New York Times*, 18 May 1957.

Muhammad Ali: King of the World (2000)

Television Movie, Drama, Color

Producer: George W. Perkins. *Director*: John Sacret Young. *Screenplay*: John Sacret Young based upon the book by David Remnick. *Cinematography*: Eric Van Haren Norman. *Music Arrangement*: James Jacobson.

Saint Adeogba (Betty X), Rodger Boyce (Bill McDonald), Darryl Cox (Howard Cosell), Vince Davis (Izzy Sharnik), Blue Deckert (Gorgeous George), Gary Dourdan (Malcom X), Steve Harris (Sonny Liston), Jerry Haynes (Jimmy Cannon), Terrence Dashon Howard (Cassius Clay), Chi Mcbride (Drew "Bundini" Brown), Steve Shearer (Jack Kilon), Brandon Smith (Bill Barnstable), John Ventimiglia (Angelo Dundee), Jason Winer (Robert Lypsite).

One of the benefits of the proliferation of feature film bio-pics on Muhammad Ali is that they are able to accomplish what no single Ali film can. Collectively, they cover the complex panorama of the numerous personal, political and social incidents and events that have comprised the life of the three-time world heavyweight champion. *Muhammad Ali: King of the World*, a 2000 TV movie aired by ABC Television, makes its own contribution to the Ali collage by interweaving some of the more colorful moments of the boxer's life with his rise as a young boxer named Cassius Clay during the early 1960s.

Entertaining anecdotes that now comprise the Ali legend include the 1961 sparring match where the youthful upstart outslicks former champ Johannson; Clay's meeting with Gorgeous George, the garish wrestler who inspired Ali to adopt a flamboyant style; and the incident in which Liston slaps Ali at a gambling casino. Other moments include Jackie Gleason's prediction of Clay's demise at the hands of Liston and Clay's sly duping of a *Life* magazine photographer to feature him in a photo layout.

The film, based upon David Remnick's acclaimed book of the same name and other accounts of Ali's life, stars Terrence Howard in the lead role. Howard fails to capture Ali's dynamic personality, his loquaciousness comes across as loud rather than charismatic. For example, when Howard delivers Ali's poem about Liston being stopped in eight rounds, there is not a sense that one is listening to Clay, and anyone who has seen the original delivery in old newsreels knows he has been cheated. However, Howard does nicely emulate the dead-serious moments of repose Ali would from time to time display, as well as his softer side revealed to close friends and family. The portrayal of Sonny Liston by Steve Harris is well done, a small role that includes the infamous baleful stare and doleful exterior of the heavyweight champion, along with simplistic honesty, anger and a deep underlying sadness that comprised Liston, the tragic figure. Portrayals of trainer Angelo Dundee and confidant Drew "Bundini" Brown are acceptable, save the fact that Bundi was not a giant of a man as he appears in the picture.

Ali's relationship with Malcolm X and the Muslim faith is touched upon but never fully developed. Since Clay and Malcolm are rarely on-screen together, Clay's interest in the Muslim faith seems detached. Racism is also addressed, but is merely illustrative. There is simply not enough time in these feature films to tackle sweeping social issues between the exchanges of punches, and *King of the World* suffers from this same malady.

Boxing segments in the picture include a sparring session with Johannson, some brief training moments featuring Clay and Liston, Clay's bouts with Sonny Banks and his title-winning effort against Liston at Miami Beach. The Clay-Liston match is marked by the use of close-ups and fast-paced editing with some slow-motion shots. It is an interpretation of the action rather than a re-creation, and though it displays certain artistic elements, viewers do not get the sense that they are really watching Clay and Liston, as they do in Michael Mann's depiction of the same scene in his big-budget biography *Ali*.

Muhammad Ali: King of the World is an entertaining movie for the Ali fanatic who just can't be disappointed or the Ali neophyte who might not know what he is missing, but like all other Ali films, it fails to satiate the Ali expert or historian.

Night and the City (1992)

Twentieth Century-Fox, Drama, Color, 103 minutes

Producers: Jane Rosenthal, Irwn Winkler, a Tribeca Production. *Director*: Irwin Winkler. *Screenplay*: Richard Price, based on the film by Jules Dassin, *Screenplay*: Jo Eisinger, from the novel by Gerald Kersh. *Film Editor*: David Brenner. *Director of Photography*: Tal Fujimoto.

Robert De Niro (Harry Fabian), Jessica Lange (Helen), Cliff Gorman (Phil), Alan King (Boom Boom), Jack Warden (Al Grossman), Eli Wallach (Peck), Barry Primus (Tommy Tessler), Gene Kirkwood (Resnick), Pedro Sanchez (Cuda Sanchez), Gerry Murphy (Steel Jaw #1), Clem Caserta (Steel Jaw # 2), Anthony Canarozzi (Emmet Gorgon), David W. Butler (Bonney), Byron Utley (Frisker), Margo Winkler (Judge), Maurice Shrog (Gym Manager), Regis Philbin (Himself), Joy Philbin (Herself), Richard Price (Doctor), Frank Jones (Dugan), Tommy A. Ford (Herman), Peter Bucossi (Attacker), Bert Randolph Sugar (Guy at Bar), Nathaniel E. Johnson (Kid Client), Brenda Denmark (Kid's Mom), Barry Squitieri (Marty Kaufman), Lisa Vidal (Carmen), Carol Woods (Secretary), Joseph D'Onofrio (Mike), Michael Badalucco (Elaine's Bartender), Deborah Watkins (Nun), Nandan Sage (Gupta), Harsh Nayyar (Faruz), Ben Lin (Duk Soo Kim), John Polce (Bouncer), Rosalind Malloff (Frieda), Kennan Scott (Kid on Phone), Henry Milligan (Cotton), Victor Machado (Santiago), Chuck Low (Freddy DiMario), Lou Polo (Jap Epstein), Louis Cantarini (Boxing Official), John Quinn (Bartender), Philip Carlo (Peck's Guy), Cameron Lane (Mugger #1), Sharrieff Pugh (Mugger #2), Mitchell Tex Low (Delivery Man), Mitch Cunningham (Kid at Disco), Dave Reilly (Cop #2), Leslie Bart (Boom Boom's

Secretary), Ann Devaney (Gorgon's Girl), Lorenzo Palminteri (Tommy Carver), Catherine Russell (Singer).

When one thinks of the aggressiveness of Jack Dempsey, thoughts turn to the craftiness of Tex Rickard. A discussion of Joe Louis's versatility inevitably leads to a recounting of Mike Jacobs' guile. Recollections of Rocky Marciano's power conjure up the image of the equally dominant James D. Norris.

Every serious promoter dreams of obtaining the status of being mentioned in the same breath as a great fighter, and as the fight game has proved time and again, ethics have rarely stood in the way of their vision. Small-time promoters may have less lofty ambitions, but as finely illustrated in *Night and the City*, the means of achieving them are often no less unsavory.

In *Night and the City*, attorney Harry Fabian (De Niro) is an unabashed ambulance chaser. Harry is also a philanderer, conducting a secretive affair with Helen (Lange). Helen is the hardened but still attractive wife of Phil (Gorman), an edgy but unsuspecting bartender at the Boxer's bar, which Harry frequents.

Another regular patron at the fight watering hole is "Boom Boom" Grossman (King), a leading boxing promoter whose status in fistic circles is only exceeded by his proclivity for engaging in strong-arm tactics. To the dismay of Grossman, Harry enters the boxing promotional game. Harry's ace in the hole is "Boom Boom's" brother Al (Warden), an aged but still robust ex-pug, whom he employs as a talent scout. Harry has now become the custodian of Al, and Harry's safety from "Boom Boom" depends upon Al's welfare.

Without cash to bankroll his first promotion, Harry recruits Helen, who tricks Phil into providing half the funds. As a condition of the favor, Helen demands that Harry illegally obtain her own valid liquor license so she can make a clean break from Phil. Harry gets a license and passes it on to Helen, but unbeknownst to her it is a forgery.

On the morning of the fight card, the show is put into jeopardy when several fighters fail the physical. Further complications arise when Phil uncovers his wife's infidelity and holds back the remainder of the promotional money, forcing Harry to go to his loan shark Peck (Wallach). Back at the arena, Al goes into a seizure and dies in the arms of a disbelieving Harry. In spite of the licensing gaff, Harry has Helen agree to go to California with him. But before he can leave town, he is tracked down and shot by "Boom Boom's" henchman. Ultimately, Harry is whisked away in an ambulance with Helen at his side, with still enough life and humor to query his decision to enter the fight game.

Night and the City is a well-written and well-acted examination of the unsavory business of fight promotion, and the element it attracts. The picture was directed by Irwin Winkler, the producer of *Rocky* and *Raging Bull*, and was the follow-up effort to his directorial debut in *Guilty by Suspicion*.

Regarding the film, David Denby of *New Yorker* magazine wrote, "I was carried along by it as I was by few American movies this year."[1] Winkler was also complimented by David Ansen of *Newsweek*, who wrote that the director "gets the juices flowing with his nervous style, playing dread off gallows humor."[2] Steve Jenkins of *Sight and Sound*, seemed to hit on the picture's underlying appeal when he wrote, "The film's main pleasure lies in the occasional gems found in Price's dialogue."[3]

Still, it is the solid acting which serves as the movie's anchor. Critic Ansen correctly noted that the cast "could milk tension from a bus schedule," and the talent assembled certainly lives up to their collective reputation.[4] De Niro's histrionics blended well with Lange's hopeful desperation. David Sterritt of the *Christian Science Monitor* found De Niro "close to his best" and Jessica Lange "daringly unglamorous."[5]

Jamie Bernard, critic for the *New York Post*, found Eli Wallach's execution of his small role to be "effortless," and both Bernard and Jack Mathews of *Newsday* applauded Jack Warden's contribution.[6] As the gruff ex-boxer, Warden was well-cast, exhibiting a gruff brand of old-school masculinity. Comic Alan King, a highly underrated dramatic actor, was masterful in offering glimpses of his character's power, which simmered just beneath the surface of his threats. Warranted praise was given to King by Mathews for his display of "chilling menace."[7] "He strikes just the right note of menace without going over the top," critic Bernard wrote.[8]

Boxing fans will enjoy the appearance of boxing historian Bert Randolph Sugar in the opening scene and those with a sharp eye may spot popular cruiserweight Al Cole in a bar scene late in the movie.

1. David Denby, Review of *Night and the City* (Twentieth Century-Fox movie), *New Yorker*, 26 October 1992, 82.
2. David Ansen, Review of *Night and the City* (Twentieth Century-Fox movie), *Newsweek*, 19 October 1992, 67.
3. Steve Jenkins, Review of *Night and the City* (Twentieth Century-Fox movie), *Sight And Sound*, February 1989, 52.
4. Ansen.
5. David Sterritt, Review of *Night and the City* (Twentieth Century-Fox movie), *Christian Science Monitor*, 27 October 1992, 11.
6. Jamie Bernard, Review of *Night and the City* (Twentieth Century-Fox movie), *New York Post*, 23.
7. Jack Mathews, Review of *Night and the City* (Twentieth Century-Fox movie), *Newsday*, 16 October 1992, Par II, 77.
8. Bernard, 23.

Off Limits (1953)

Paramount Pictures, Comedy, B & W, 87 minutes

Producer: Harry Tugend. *Director*: George Marshall. *Screenplay*: Hal Kanter, Jack Sher. *Film Editor*: Arthur Schmidt. *Photography*: J. Perverell Marley. *Music*: Van Cleave.

Bob Hope (Wally Hogan), Mickey Rooney (Herbert Tuttle), Marilyn Maxwell (Connie Curtis), Eddie Mayehoff (Karl Danzig), Stanley Clements (Bullet Bradley), Marvin Miller (Vic Breck), John Ridgely (Lieut. Comdr. Parnell), Norman Leavitt (Chowhound), Kim Spaulding (Seaman Harker), Jerry Hausner (Fishy), Mike Mahoney (M.P. Huggins), Joan Taylor (Helen), Carolyn Jones (Deborah), Mary Murphy (WAC), Jack Dempsey (Referee), Art Aragon (Boxer), Tom Harmon.

When a man is named Leslie, there is little doubt that he will be forced to do some fighting. Such was the lot cast to Leslie Hope, the son of English parents, who grew up on the rough streets of Cleveland during the World War I era.

Les, as the teen was better known, soon learned that it was more desirable to administer a beating then receive one. Joining a gang called the Fairmont Boys, he eventually developed confidence with his fists.[1] When Les's pal Whitey Jennings signed up for an Ohio state amateur boxing tournament with the moniker "Packy" West (in tribute to pro sensation "Packy" McFarland), the competitive Hope countered by entering the same tourney as "Packy East."[2]

"Packy East" drew a dim-witted first-round opponent who foolishly looked at his seconds for instructions instead of keeping his eyes on Hope's fists. Advancing to the semi-finals, Hope was matched against "Happy Walsh," a lad who had the peculiar habit of grinning at his opponent after absorbing each blow. However, Walsh's ring antics belied his fistic talent and Hope's dreams of ring glory ended with his limp body being picked up off the canvas.[3]

Later in life, when better known as

famed comedian Bob Hope, Leslie, tongue-in-cheek, would blame his fistic downfall on his weight. At 128 pounds he was two pounds over the featherweight limit and claimed it was inequitable that he was forced to fight against lightweight opponents who weighed as much as 135 pounds.[4]

By the 1950s, Hope had grown into a heavyweight, both on the scales and as a box-office attraction, and the erstwhile Leslie Hope would again be given the opportunity to explore the fight game in Paramount Picture's *Off Limits*. In the picture, Wally Hogan (Hope) is a fight manager who guides Bullet Bradley (Darro) to the championship. But when Bradley is drafted into the Army Hogan is pressed into the service by the racketeers who control Bradley to keep a watchful eye over their meal ticket. However, when Bradley is discharged as mentally unfit, Hogan is squeezed out of the money.

While in the Army, Hogan takes on a "wanna be" fighter named Tuttle (Rooney), but his real aspirations are to bed his fighter's attractive Aunt Connie (Maxwell). Tuttle turns out to be a prospect after all, and Hogan, despite military entanglements, is able to lead his charge to a championship victory over Bradley and win the affection of Connie.

In the main, it is Hope's patented rapid-fire one-liners that are the backbone of the film's comedy. Some are dead-on, others are simply dead, and most fall somewhere in between. While A.W. of *The New York Times* found the story to be "thinner than an undernourished flyweight," he admitted that Hope was "delightfully fouled up," as the rackish fight manager.[5] Otis L. Guernsey noted that Hope "is in top form here," and commended the film as a "slapstick act put on in style by real movie professionals."[6]

In addition to the comedic talent of Hope, the film offered film veterans Mickey Rooney and Marilyn Maxwell. The film was the third of four boxing films for Rooney, who was also in *The Life of Jimmy Dolan*, *Killer McCoy* and *Requiem for a Heavyweight*. One of Rooney's ring opponents is portrayed by Frankie Darro, who appeared in *Born To Fight* and *Bowery Blitzkreig*, two earlier "B" boxing movies. Another of Rooney's ring opponents is played by lightweight contender Art Aragon, who was featured in other boxing flicks including *World in My Corner*.

The film includes one of the more unusual boxing vignettes found in a boxing movie. One of the matches occurs in a ring set up on the deck of a battleship. As the ship sways back and forth, so the ring pitches to and fro. The effect is used in the comedic scenario that finds a seasick Hope attempting to second his boxer Rooney. Another interesting effect utilized is the simulation of Hope's double vision of the ring action, brought on by his illness.

Most of the boxing-related comedy comes from Hope's verbal jibes to the crowd while instructing his fighter from the ring apron. The fight scenes are, by and large, played straight. A scene in which Hope is found inside a heavy bag and another in which he is resuscitated by his boxer while sitting on the ring stool, also provide some amusement.

Former heavyweight champion Jack Dempsey appears in two ring sequences as a referee, a role which he adopted on a number of occasions both in real life and in the cinema. In the film's opening scene, an "inside" boxing joke is embedded in the script. As referee Dempsey is counting out Hogan's fighter's opponent, Hogan looks up at Dempsey and exclaims "faster – you ought to remember."[7] The line, an obvious reference to the historical "battle of the long count," in which Dempsey lost his real chance to recapture the title on a disputed count, was a wink from screenwriters Hal Kanter and Jack Sher to boxing fans in the audience.

1. Lawrence J. Quirk, *Bob Hope: The Road Well-Traveled* (New York: Applause Books, 1998), 13.
2. Ibid, 15.

3. *Ibid.*, 16.
4. *Ibid.*, 15.
5. A.W., Review of *Off Limits* (Paramount Pictures movie), *New York Times*, 30 March 1953.
6. Otis L. Guernsey, Review of *Off Limits* (Paramount Pictures movie), *New York Herald-Tribune*, 30 March 1953.
7. *Off Limits*, produced by Harry Tugend, directed by George Marshall, 87 minutes, 1953.

Palooka (1934)

United Artists, Comedy, B & W, 86 minutes

Producer: Astor Pictures Corporation. *Director*: Benjamin Stoloff. *Screenplay*: Gertrude Percell, Jack Jevne, Arthur Kober, with additional dialogue by Ben Ryan and Murray Roth, suggested by the comic strip by Ham Fisher. *Film Editor*: Grant Whytock. *Photography*: Arthur Edeson. *Musical Director*: C. Bakaleinikoff.

Jimmy Durante (Knobby Walsh), Stu Erwin (Joe Palooka), Lupe Velez (Nina Madero), Marjorie Rambeau (Mayme Palooka), Robert Armstrong (Pete Palooka), Mary Carlisle (Anne), William Cagney (Al McSwatt), Frank Ardell (Doc Wise), Louise Beavers (Crystal), Snowflake (Smokey), Tom Dugan (Whitey).

As a boy growing-up in a coal-mining region of Pennsylvania, Ham Fisher dreamed of becoming both a boxer and cartoonist.[1] While he never became a prizefighter, Fisher's artistic ambition did come to fruition. Not surprisingly, it also served to advance his interest in the fight game.

Fisher's career-defining opportunity came unexpectedly while he was a young salesman employed by the McNaught newspaper syndicate. One of the company's officials favored Fisher's cartoon drawings of a character in boxing trunks, and the concept soon blossomed into a comic strip.[2] Almost overnight "Joe Palooka" became one of the nation's most popular cartoon dailies. Palooka later expanded to radio, with motion pictures the next logical step for the pen-and-ink creation.

Jimmy Durante, fabled for his fabulous nose and comedic antics which he honed on stage with his partners Lou Clayton and Eddie Jackson, had recently starred with Lupe Velez on Broadway in *Strike Me Pink*. "The schnoz," as the actor was affectionately called, and his sultry Latin co-star were both signed to the film version of Fisher's creation entitled *Palooka*.

The somewhat unexpected choice to portray Joe Palooka was Stuart Erwin. Erwin received a law degree from USC, and looked every bit the attorney, but scarcely resembled a prizefighter.[3] Robert Armstrong, who recently appeared in the now classic *King Kong*, was more appropriately cast as Palooka's ex-pug father. Armstrong had already featured onstage in Milwaukee with James Gleason in his boxing comedy *Is Zat So?* and on the screen as a fighter in *Be Yourself* and a fight manager in Universal's *The Iron Man*.

In *Palooka*, Pete Palooka (Armstrong), is a boxing champion and his outspoken wife Mayme (Rambeau) a showgirl. Pete's womanizing results in their divorce. A score later, their son Joe begins his own career and knocks out the champion McSwatt (Cagney) who enters the ring intoxicated. McSwatt's disloyal girlfriend Madero (Velez) recognizes Joe as her new meal ticket and seduces the naive fighter, who becomes wrapped up in his newfound celebrity. Blinded by Madero's charms, Joe leaves his girlfriend Anne (Carlisle).

Joe's manager, Knobby (Durante), steers Joe through a series of arranged matches. Panicked over a proposed rematch between McSwatt and Palooka, Knobby reveals Joe's success as a combination of luck and fraud.

Although Palooka's doubts are quickly dispelled by his dad, who provides his services as trainer, Joe loses to McSwatt. Ultimately, Anne forgives Palooka and his Dad and Mom also reunite. Knobby, on the run from gangsters who bet on his fighter, sends the Palookas money to open a family inn.

Palooka fared well with the critics of its day. "On the whole ... it offers some of the liveliest fare that has come to the screen in a long, long time," wrote Thornton Delehanty of the *New York Evening Post*.[4] Regina Crewe of the *New York American* found the film "a laughter-studded fight farce, embroidered with gags and giggles," and William Boehnel of the *New York World-Telegram* dubbed it "jolly and satisfactory entertainment."[5]

Jimmy Durante was uniformly praised for his performance. "Palooka is pure Durante, Durante at its loudest, funniest and most coherent," wrote E.C. of the *New York Sun*.[6] "Mr. Durante sinks his teeth into a fat role and emerges with honors, leaving his audience limp with laughter," wrote James Scott of the *Los Angeles Times*.[7] "It's as plain as the schnozz on the Durante kisser that 'Palooka' is going to specialize in vigorous tickling of the risibilities," noted Bige of *Variety*.[8]

Palooka is filled with word play, Durantesque verbiage, a steady dose of sight gags, and most of all, countless nose jokes. While *Palooka* may have been "a series of howls" in 1934, as Bland Johaneson of the *New York Daily Mirror* critiqued, time has eroded the comedic value of the picture considerably.[9] In fact, in Jhan Robbins' 1991 biography of the comic, the author lists the film under a chapter entitled "Screen Disasters."[10] What does remain engaging about this picture is the curious charm that Durante provides. In one memorable scene a drunken Durante smashes a plate glass window of a storefront and sits down at a piano, where he strokes the ivories as he sings his signature piece *Ink-A-Dink-A-Doo* to a female mannequin. In another, Durante recycles one of his own phrases from radio, urging Palooka to "hit him in the *labonza*," in his readily identifiable hoarse voice. The picture concludes with Durante doubling as his own infant son with his ghoulish mug peering out from a baby's bonnet.

Palooka marked the film debut of James Cagney's brother William. Mordaunt Hall, the critic for *The New York Times*, wrote, "At present William is no rival of his brother, but he does what he is called on to do without getting into trouble."[11] William not only finished second to James as a thespian, but he also failed to live up to his brother's cinematic ring acumen which had recently been displayed in *Winner Take All*. Comparisons aside, William rates a fair pugilist. It is actually Stuart Erwin who is the "Palooka" of the film. Erwin looks soft and lacks fighting technique.

The fight scenes in the picture are generally played straight, with comedy reserved for the ring apron and between round activities. Erwin, however, receives no help from the picture's sub-par choreography, which attempts to legitimize the ring action by surrounding it with numerous stock footage shots of crowd scenes. However, criticism should be tempered lest one forget that it is Durante and not the boxing vignettes that is the picture's intended showpiece.

Durante was once the proprietor of *Club Durant*, a popular 1920s speakeasy that served the spectrum of society's elite including gangster Legs Diamond, producer Billy Rose, movie star John Barrymore and heavyweight champion Jack Dempsey. An important part of the comedy act of Clayton, Jackson and Durante at the club predictably revolved around Durante's proboscis. At one point in the act, Clayton invites the audience members to come up on stage to autograph Durante's nose, or "the eighth wonder of the world," as he describes it. The request, of course, was rhetorical—except on one occasion Jack Dempsey jumped onto the stage and began signing his name onto Durante's protruding appendage. Midway, the champ suddenly jumped back and exclaimed, "It's alive! Run for your lives!"¹²

1. Studio Publicity release for *Palooka*.
2. *Ibid*.
3. *Ibid*.
4. Thornton Delehanty, Review of *Palooka* (United Artists movie), *New York Evening Post*, 28 February 1934.
5. Regina Crewe, Review of *Palooka* (United Artists movie), *New York American*, 28 February 1934; William Boehnel, "Durante Hits Record High in Fun Film," Review of *Palooka* (United Artists movie), New York World-Telegram 28 February 1934.
6. E.C. Review of *Palooka* (United Artists movie), *New York Sun*, 28 February 1934.
7. James Scott, "'Palooka' Tale of Prize Ring," Review of *Palooka* (United Artists movie), *Los Angeles Times*, 15 March 1934.
8. Bige, Review of *Palooka* (United Artists movie), *Variety*, 6 March 1934.
9. Bland Johaneson, "'Palooka' a Lusty Drama," Review of *Palooka* (United Artists movie), *New York Daily Mirror*, 28 February 1934.
10. Jhan Robbins, *Inka Dinka Doo: The Life of Jimmy Durante* (New York: Paragon House, 1991), 100.
11. Mordaunt Hall, Review of *Palooka* (United Artists movie), *New York Times*, February 28, 1934.
12. Robbins, *Inka Dinka Doo*, 58, 68–69.

The Patent Leather Kid (1926)

First National Pictures, Drama, B & W, Silent, 11,955 feet

Producer: Alfred Santell. *Director*: Alfred Santell. *Film Editor*: Hugh Bennett. *Cinematography*: Arthur Edison.

Richard Barthelmess (The Patent Leather Kid), Molly O'Day (The Golden Dancer), Arthur Stone (Puffy), Lawford Davidson (Captain Breen), Matthew Betz (Jake Stuke), Lucien Prival (German Officer), Raymond Turner (Mobile Molasses), Hank Mann (Sergeant), Nigel De Brulier (French Doctor), Fred O'Beck, Cliff Salm, Henry Murdock, Charlie Sullivan, John Kolb, Al Alborn (The Tank Crew).

Like so many early film stars whose images flickered across the silent screen, Richard Barthelmess could trace opportunity and early success back to D.W. Griffith, the granddaddy of American cinema. Barthelmess, a virile hero, replaced the more sensitive Robert Harron of *Intolerance* fame as Griffith's number-one leading man, and established his star status through Griffith's *Way Down East* and *Broken Blossoms*.¹

Broken Blossoms, a 1919 film about a girl who is physically and mentally abused by her boxer father, was Barthelmess's first brush with the cinematic ring. He appeared with former world boxing champion Norman Shelley, better known as "Kid" McCoy.² Barthelmess, who possessed "an appearance which suggested both a gentleness and a masculine strength," was under contract with First National Pictures during the mid-1920s, when he was cast in Rupert Hughes' war-time epic *The Patent Leather Kid*.³

The Patent Leather Kid is the story of a young boxer who initially avoids the draft during World War I. Later, he displays cowardice on the field of battle. Though he eventually finds the courage and resolve to fight valiantly, he is paralyzed in combat. Ultimately, his prayers are answered and his paralysis is cured, allowing him to salute the American flag he once disdained.

The Patent Leather Kid and its leading man Richard Barthelmess received ample critical praise. Mordaunt Hall, writing for *The New York Times*, dubbed the picture "an emphatically human chronicle."⁴ "The picture is great entertainment," offered Rose Pelswick for *The New York Evening Journal*.⁵ "Barthelmess gives a striking performance," wrote the critic for the *Fort Wayne News Sentinel*, sounding an opinion shared by many of his colleagues.⁶

The war scenes in the movie were the picture's most memorable. "Mr. Santell can be said to have filmed his war effects with remarkable artistry," Mordaunt Hall wrote in praise of the director.[7] The film critic for the *San Francisco Chronicle* found the war scenes to be "magnificent," noting the use of "thousands of troops, lumbering tanks and circling planes over a huge territory to reproduce a section of the front."[8]

The fight vignettes also made a significant contribution to the movie. The film critic for the *Denver Post* found them to be "great in atmosphere and action" noting that "none of the principals step out of character for a minute."[9] Grace Cutler, writing for the *Brooklyn Daily Eagle*, opined that the film possesses "Scenes of ... boxing arenas and training quarters — all of them effective." However, Cutler found misuse of the parallel vocabulary of the ring and that of the army, feeling that they were "abused in a series of punning sub-titles." She was also of the opinion that the use of Barthelmess's fight handlers for comic relief was a bit overdone. "The first is a hard guy, the second stutters and the third is a comical Negro. Any one of them would have been sufficient."[10]

The picture, which was filmed during the transitional period between silent and "talkie" films, featured sub-titles but also included elements of voice audio. The new voice gimmick was greeted with mixed reactions. Critic Grace Cutler felt that "the talking movie machine adds to the realism of the boxing matches."[11] Colleague Mordaunt Hall disagreed. "Joseph Plunkett has contributed some telling effects in his presentation of this picture, but it would do just as well if he modulated some of the loud-speaking phonograph voices used to stir up excitement during the prize fight scenes," the critic wrote.[12]

Barthelmess trained for six weeks with professional boxers to prepare himself for the fight vignettes. After a sneak preview of the film, former heavyweight champion Jack Dempsey stated that the picture was "the best fight stuff" he'd ever seen on the screen. Dempsey also wrote Barthelmess the following note: "Dear Dick: Just a little note to thank you for letting me see 'The Patent Leather Kid.' It's a Wow! You handled yourself like an old-timer, Dick, and it was a genuine pleasure to see a real ring battle on the screen. Congratulations and lots of success to you and 'The Patent Leather Kid.'"[13]

1. Joe Franklin, *Classics of the Silent Screen: A Pictorial Treasury* (New York: The Citadel Press, 1959), 129.
2. Harvey Marc Zucker and Lawrence J. Babich, *Sports Films: A Complete Reference* (Jefferson, N.C.: McFarland, 1987), 67–68.
3. Franklin, *Classics of the Silent Screen*, 129.
4. Mordaunt Hall, Review of *The Patent Leather Kid* (First National Pictures movie), *New York Times*.
5. Rose Pelswick, Review of *The Patent Leather Kid* (First National Pictures movie), *New York Evening Journal*.
6. Review of *The Patent Leather Kid* (First National Pictures movie), *Fort Wayne News Sentinel*, 22 April 1928.
7. Hall.
8. Review of *The Patent Leather Kid* (First National Pictures movie), *San Francisco Chronicle*, 13 April 1928.
9. Review of *The Patent Leather Kid* (First National Pictures movie), *Denver Post*, 7 April 1928.
10. Grace Cutler, Review of *The Patent Leather Kid* (First National Pictures movie), *Brooklyn Daily Eagle*, 16 August 1927.
11. *Ibid.*
12. Hall.
13. *Worcester Telegram*, 28 August 1927.

Play It to the Bone (1999)

Touchstone Pictures, Drama, B & W, 124 minutes

Producer: Stephen Chin. *Director*: Ron Shelton. *Screenplay*: Ron Shelton. *Film Editor*: Patrick Flannery, Paul Seydor. *Cinematography*: Mark Vargo. *Music*: Alex Wurman, John Lee Hooker.

Antonio Banderas (Caesar Dominguez), Woody Harrelson (Vince Boudreau), Lolita Davidovich (Grace Pasic), Tom Sizemore (Joe Domino), Lucy Liu (Lia), Robert Wagner (Hank Goody), Richard Masur (Artie), Willie Garson (Cappie Caplan), Cylk Cozart (Rudy), Jack Carter (Dante Solomon), Jim Lampley, George Foreman, Larry Merchant, Darrell Foster, Steve Lawrence, Mitch Halpern, Chuck Hull, Buddy Greco, Kevin Costner, James Woods, Mike Tyson, Rod Stewart.

In 1965, the incomparable Sugar Ray Robinson was on the verge of completing a spectacular twenty-five year professional boxing career. One of the bouts on his "swan-song" tour that year was against Fred Hernandez at the Hacienda Hotel and Casino in Las Vegas. The affair was to be nothing more than a postscript to his résumé of two hundred plus fights. But the fight-card was in trouble. In an effort to fill the undercard with last-minute replacements, the promoter made a desperate call to a Los Angeles boxing gym. Soon after, two friends, Paolo Corona and Pulga Serrano, were making the four-hour trek across the Nevada desert to face each other in a Las Vegas ring.[1]

It was to be a night where the preliminary fighters would even outshine the great Ray Robinson. Bill Caplan, head of public relations for promoter Bob Arum, recalls the evening: "I mean these guys were pals; they could have agreed not to go at each other very hard. But they fought their heart out, and they got a standing ovation. To this day, the handful of people who were there say it was one of the greatest fights they've ever seen."[2]

Recognizing potential in the unlikely tale of friends instantly transformed into combatants, the veteran sports film writer and director Ron Shelton built upon its basic premise to fashion his latest sports story, *Play It to the Bone*. "In Hollywood, they're always saying things like 'boxing movies don't sell,'" observed Shelton. "Well, somebody must be buying because boxing films almost qualify as an entire genre."[3]

Shelton kept the boxing rivalry at the heart of his story. But to add significance to the match between buddies Vin (Harrelson) and Caesar (Banderas), the Sheldon script promises the winner a shot at the middleweight championship. Conflict and intrigue are further heightened during the duo's trip across the desert by the addition of two traveling companions, a mutual ex-girlfriend (Davidovich) and a sexy hitchhiker (Liu).

"The boxers themselves are compelling characters ... and they live in one of the last really authentic worlds," noted Shelton. "That's what I want to get on film, while it's still around."[4] Shelton covers a lot of ground in the picture, including religion and the fighters' sexuality — even touching upon Caesar's experimentation with homosexuality, a groundbreaking topic for boxing movies. But like all Shelton films it is the natural, witty dialogue and accurate, illuminating depiction of the sports world that are the picture's strength. "Sheldon has a solid grip on the endemic corruption of the boxing game, knows how fighters are exploited and seems to know who's to blame," pointed out John Anderson for *Newsday*. "Some of the suspects even get cameos in the film. The rest are lampooned."[5] Many fight-game notables do appear in the picture, but to be accurate, they happen to be the more reputable individuals associated with the sport including announcer Michael Buffer, commentators Al Bernstein, Jim

Lampley, Larry Merchant, and George Foreman, writers Tim Smith and Michael Katz, and trainer Teddy Atlas.

Harrelson and Banderas were trained for the fight scenes by Darrell Foster, who had the privilege of working in Sugar Ray Robinson's corner. "He took over our lives," commented Harrelson, whose regimen under Foster included roadwork, weights, diet, and instruction on how to both deliver and pull punches.[6] Harrelson and Banderas appear well conditioned, and are adequate in the fight scenes. The long fight finale, which includes innumerable knockdowns and ends in a draw, is fairly entertaining, though not appreciated by some of the critics. "The fight scenes are flat and poorly staged," wrote Lou Lemrick for the *New York Post*.[7]

Critic John Anderson quipped, "the final fight scene ... feels longer than the 75-round Sullivan-Kilrain bare-knuckle bout of 1889."[8]

1. Megan Turner, *New York Post*, 21 January 2000.
2. Allen Barra, *New York Times*, Sunday, 14 November 1999, sec. 2, p.13.
3. *Ibid.*
4. *Ibid.*
5. John Anderson, Review of *Play It to the Bone* (Touchstone Pictures movie), *Newsday*, 21 January 2000, B3.
6. Barra, sec. 2, p.13.
7. Lou Lemrick, Review of *Play It to the Bone* (Touchstone Pictures movie), *New York Post*, 21 January 2000.
8. Anderson, B3.

The Power of One (1992)

Warner Bros., Drama, Color, 111 minutes

Producer: Aron Milchan. *Director*: John D. Avildsen. *Screenplay*: Robert Mark Kamen, based upon a novel by Bryce Courtenay. *Film Editor*: John G. Avildsen. *Cinematography*: Dean Semler. *Music*: Hans Zimmer.

Guy Witcher (P.K. Age 7), Simon Fenton (P.K. Age 12), Stephen Dorff (P.K. Age 18), John Gielgud (Headmaster St. John), Armin Fay Masterson (Maria) Mueller-Stahl (Doc), Morgan Freeman (Geel Piet), Nomadlozi Kubheka (Nanny), Agatha Hurle (Midwife), Nigel Ivy (Newborn P.K.), Tracy Brooks Swope (Mother), Brendan Deary (P.K. Infant), Winston Mangwarara (Tonderai Infant), Tonderai Masenda (Tonderai), Cecil Zilla Mamanzi (Ranch Foreman), John Turner (Afrikaner Minister), Robbie Bulloch (Jaapie Botha), Gordon Arnell (Minister at Mother's Funeral), Jeremiah Mnisi (Dabula Manzi), Paul Tingay (Grandfather), Hywell Williams (Captain), Michael Brunner (Kommandant Van Zyl), Clive Russell (Sergeant Bormann), Gert Van Niekerk (Lieutenant Smit), Winston Ntshona (Mlungisi), Ed Beeten (Prison Commissioner), Dominic Walker (Morrie Guilbert), Robert Thomas Reed (School Gate Guard), Simon Shumba (Man Without Pass), Stan Leih, Rod Campbell (Van Cops), Adam Fogerty (Andreas Malan), Ian Roberts (Hoppie Gruenwald), Tony Denham (Boxing Partner), Marius Weyers (Professor Daniel Marais), Eric Nobbs, Edward Jordan (City Cops), Brian O'Shaughnessy (Colonel Bretyn), Daniel Craig (Sergeant Botha), Faith Edwards (Miriam Sisulu), Raymond Barreto (Indian Referee), Liz Ngwenya (Ngana Ancient Woman), Andrew Whaley (Ticket Taker), Dominic Makuwachuma (Joshua), Robin Annison (Anita), Christien Anholt (Dinner Date), Nigel Pegram (Guest), Jon Cartwright (Jacob), Rev. Peter Van Vuuren (Minister at Maria's Funeral), Marcia Coleman (Woman Guest), Banele Dala Moyo (Boy Who Reads).

The mix in South Africa of the indigenous Blacks (Kafirs), with both the early Dutch, German and French settlers (Afrikaners) and their rival English colonial rulers, spawned a perpetually contentious and often violent environment. Centuries of unrest left in their wake an historical record that reads along the lines of Kurosawa's *Rashomon*— for the history of South Africa is as subjective as the myriad perspectives upon which it can be based.

Therefore, it was to be expected that *The Power of One*, which probes into South Africa's political thicket, would have its historical detractors. Despite the clear divide between the hearts and minds of the English, the Afrikaners, and the Blacks, they shared a commonality based upon mutual dislike and distrust. Thus, the premise of *The Power of One*— that a white boy could be the unifying hero of black South Africa — was fundamentally flawed.

The Power of One, the screen version of the novel by Bryce Courtenay of the same name, traces the life of a white boy known as P.K. (Witcher, Fenton, Dorff). It spans his birth in 1930 to his early manhood in the late 1940s when the system of segregation known as Apartheid was established.

Heavily influenced as a young orphan child by the blacks of the Zulu tribe, P.K. does not carry the racial prejudice that has infected so many of his countrymen. However, because P.K. is of English parentage, he himself is victimized by white Afrikaners, who hold a deep contempt for their English rulers. Physically and mentally abused by his Afrikaner schoolmates, P.K. develops a sense of justice and unwavering righteousness, and a heartfelt empathy for his black countrymen.

His world view is further broadened by his grandfather's German friend Doc (Mueller-Stahl), who tutors P.K. while both are interned at a prison camp during World War II. At the camp, P.K. learns to defend himself through boxing from a Kafir named Geel Piet (Freedman). While at the camp, P.K. smuggles tobacco and writes letters for the oppressed Kafirs. Through the promoting of Piet, P.K. emerges as a symbol of hope for the Kafirs, who adopt him as the mythical savior known as the "Rainman." P.K. further perpetuates the myth by winning the inter-prison boxing championship in his weight division, and by uniting the rival Kafir tribes for the first time in song.

After the war, P.K. pursues his formal schooling, but remains a crusader for the cause of justice and unity. As the "Rainman," he continues to inspire in the ring, and, in violation of the law, to educate the Kafirs with the assistance of his girlfriend Maria (Masterson). P.K. intends to travel to England with Maria to attend Oxford, but she is killed while attempting to further their cause. Instead, he remains in the country with his Kafir comrades to fight the battle against Apartheid.

The Power of One is the story of a white boy who becomes the messiah of black South Africa despite the institutional prejudices, overt racism, and deep-seated distrust and hatred between the races. Some critics found the story's premise as hard to swallow as arsenic. P. French of *The Observer, London*, for example, wrote that the film was a " ... ludicrous gloss of South African history."[1] Still, other critics admitted that it was almost possible to overlook the film's lack of plausibility. As noted by Jerry Tallmer of the *New York Post*, ... "If you can sit through the high-powered hokum and not be manipulated into righteous fury, you're a stronger and more hardened cynic than I am."[2]

Perhaps only someone like Jon Avildsen (*Rocky, The Karate Kid*), who is known to skimp on realism while attempting to overdose his audience with emotion, could have even attempted to direct *The Power of One*. As noted by Kenneth Turan of the *Los Angeles Times*, "Seeing a movie that doesn't know the meaning of shameless, that refuses to worry about plausibility, that acts as if subtlety hasn't been invented yet, does have a very basic kind of intrinsically cinematic pull."[3]

If, in fact, Avildsen mystified his audiences, then several others are to share the credit for the magic. Photographer Dean Semler fully exploits the natural beauty of Zimbabwe, where the film was shot on location. Sweeping landscapes are accentuated by glowing suns or misty-veiled moons, which rest above glistening waters, majestic mountains and graceful animals. The film's soundtrack utilizes indigenous music sung by a choir to set the film's pace and mood, and is often moving and inspiring.

First-rate performances by well-cast actors never leave the audience wanting. Morgan Freeman gives a standout performance as the subservient but dignified Kafir who trains P.K., and John Gielgud is perfect in the brief role of the schoolmaster. Guy Witcher, Simon Fenton and Stephen Dorff, who each portray P.K. at a different age, are not only believable but also ingratiating.

Avildsen, who had already handled the directorial chores for *Rocky*, was up to the task of managing the six training and boxing vignettes. The training scenes are brief, but nicely portray the development of seven-year-old P.K., who pounds the pillow which Piet holds, to develop the combinations he uses to win matches by age 12. Creating realistic child boxers is not easy, but the filmmakers do an admirable job in developing the adolescent Fenton for the ring.

The three fight scenes are well choreographed and executed, though they are a bit over-stylized and precise for amateur boxing. Both Fenton and Dorff, however, execute their ring chores well. During the film, Avildsen often uses boxing as a metaphor for the struggle for justice, succumbing to the temptation several times. On one occasion, the Kafirs are found singing outside of the arena at one of P.K.'s "whites only" matches. In the picture's final bout P.K.'s hand is raised in victory by his black opponent, who jubilantly declares P.K. the mythical "Rainmaker." The boxing gym also doubles as society's safe harbor of racial equality and respect, despite the recognized inequalities that exist.

Avildsen is not afraid to inflame his audience to drive them to support his protagonists. Young P.K. is urinated on by his Afrikaner schoolmates, and Piet is forced to eat feces by a white oppressor. Later he is beaten to death. P.K.'s girlfriend is also struck dead and lies bloodied with her eyes wide open. While such scenes may support critic Turan's observation that the film possesses "a primordial watchability," his colleague, John Anderson of *Newsday*, had a different response, noting that the film contained "episodes of mindless violence."[4] Similarly, Amy Davis of *Variety* noted that the ending of the film possessed "simplistic string-pulling violence," which she felt compromised "a classy project."[5]

Whether or not the violence engages or repulses, Avildsen does manage to use it to help clearly delineate the "good guys" from the bad — with both found among all of the ethnic groups presented. At least for these balanced portrayals, Avildsen may be commended for giving an objective view of South Africa.

1. P. French, Review of *Power of One* (Warner Bros. movie), *Observer (London)*, 6 September 1992.
2. Jerry Tallmer, Review of *Power of One* (Warner Bros. movie), *New York Post*, 27 March 1992, 29.
3. Kenneth Turan, Review of *Power of One* (Warner Bros. movie), *Los Angeles Times*, 27 March 1992, calendar, 4.
4. *Ibid.*; John Anderson, Review of *Power of One* (Warner Bros. movie), *Newsday*, Part II, 64.
5. Amy Davies, Review of *Power of One* (Warner Bros. movie), *Variety*, 23 March 1992, 106.

The Prize Fighter (1979)

New World Pictures, Comedy, Color, 99 minutes

Producers: Wanda Dell, Lang Elliott. *Director*: Michael Preece. *Screenplay*: Tim Conway, John Myhers. *Film Editor*: Fabien D. Tordjmann. *Cinematography*: Jacques Haitkin. *Music*: Peter Matz.

Bill Ash (Towel Man), Joan Benedict (Dori), Merle G. Cain (Bumper), Cisse Cameron (Polly), Robin Clarke (Mike), Holly Conover (Judy), Tim Conway (Bags), Alfred E. Covington (Ring Announcer), Bill Crabb (Turk), Kenneth Daniel (Stubby), Mike Defabis (Referee #2), Joe Dorsey (Stranger), J. Don Ferguson (Referee #1), Dan Fitzgerald (Big John), Charles Franzen (Reporter #1), Les Hatfield (Champ), Ted Henning (Jimmy), Charles R. Honce Jr. (Dale), Edith Ivey (Tough Lady), Billy J. Johnson (Photo Man), Bryan Jones (Andy), May Keller (Lilly), Irwin Keyes (Flower), Don Knotts (Shake), Michael Laguardia (Butcher), John Myhers (Doyle), Danny Nelson (Guesser), George Nutting (Timmy), Scott Oliver (Barker), Mary Ellen O'Neill (Mama), Marc Pickard (Reporter #2), Johnny Popwell Sr. (Grader), Fred Saxton (Radio Announcer), Howard Stopeck (Cook), Roy Tatum (Nails), Lou Walker (Janitor), David Wayne (Pop Morgan), Geoff Webber (Butler), Timothy Webber (Bradshaw), Wallace K. Wilkinson (Flash), Willie J. Woods (Spider), Jimmy Cook (Boxer), Perry Quinn (Boxer), Jerry Campbell (Boxer), Clyde Jones (Boxer), Richard Haliburton (Boxer).

When asked to comment on his new film *The Prize Fighter*, co-starring Don Knotts, Tim Conway was almost euphoric. "*The Prize Fighter* is the most exciting film I've ever done," the actor explained. "I'm excited as I've ever been in my life. It came out beyond my expectations."[1] Perhaps Conway's comments were made in earnest, perhaps he made them cognizant of their publicity value. In any case, *The Prize Fighter*, one in a wave of boxing films released in 1979, failed to elicit the public and critical response that Conway had desired.

In *The Prize Fighter*, Bags (Conway) is an ex-boxer and Shake (Knotts), a fight manager. The naïve pair fall within the orbit of Mr. Mike (Clarke), a dapper gangster. Mr. Mike uses the duo as patsies in a betting scheme in which he builds up Bags's reputation in a series of fixed fights. Pop Morgan (Wayne), who runs a gym, joins Bags and Shake in their climb to the top. On the way, Bags develops into a hero and pseudo-father figure for Jimmy (Henning), Pop's grandson.

Mr. Mike wants to develop a convention center on the land where Pop's gym is situated, but the old-timer steadfastly refuses to sell, intending to leave the gym to Jimmy. Consequently, Mr. Mike uses a corrupt city official to deceive Pop into thinking he is to lose the gym due to back taxes. He then offers Pop a wager: $10,000 against his deed to the property, with Pop's hopes riding on Bags in his big match against Hans "The Butcher" Miller (LaGuardia). In the bout, Miller is instructed by Mr. Mike to dispose of the overmatched Bags in the third round, but it is Bags who emerges victorious to save Pop's gym.

The Prize Fighter spoofs Hollywood's depiction of the boxing world, movies of the Depression era, and their archetypical characters. The entire picture was shot in Georgia in just six weeks and the response to the film was mixed.[2] James K. Loutzenhiser of *Box Office* agreed with Conway's opinion of the film, writing, "Tim Conway and Don Knotts are teamed again, but this time they star in a comedy worthy of their talents."[3] Contrastingly, Har of *Variety* was not impressed with the material, writing, "What the pair needs here is a script, and the lame, predictable, hackneyed mess cooked up by Conway and John Myhers leaves them with nothing but *schtick* and aged sight gags."[4]

For those who find no value in the Vito Corleone-esque voice of Mr. Mike, his lush of a blonde-haired moll, and Pop's gravelly voice and appearance (strikingly reminiscent of Mickey of *Rocky* fame) there are still the talents of Conway and Knotts. As pointed out by the critic for *Box Office*, "Conway and Knotts are excellent comedians. Their facial expressions alone can precipitate a laugh."[5]

Knotts gives his usual fine characterization, mixing his nervous smile and jumpiness with a sense of befuddlement and distress. Knotts blends well with Conway, who is really the comedic star of this vehicle. Conway displays his mastery of facial expressions, which include a perplexed look and an uneasy wariness, all complemented by an apologetic air. His body language finely assists his countenance, often providing the exclamation point to the comedic moment.

In one of the film's funniest bits, we find Bags in the locker room warming up. He knocks the door off the locker, and then, encumbered by his boxing gloves, attempts to retrieve and place the door back into position. It is excellent physical comedy. Some of the ring comedy doesn't click, but there are moments, as when Conway is briefly tangled in the ropes, which are as good as any ring pantomime that has been captured by the camera. The picture also spoofs *Rocky*, with a training montage that includes a bit in which Conway is unable to drink down his breakfast of raw eggs. Finally, Shake throws them into a frying pan. "Do I have to eat them out of the glass?" Bags queries.[6]

1. *Millimeter*, April 1979.
2. *Ibid.*
3. James K. Loutzenhiser, Review of *The Prize Fighter* (TriStar Pictures movie), *Box Office*, 14 January 1980.
4. Har, Review of *The Prize Fighter* (TriStar Pictures movie), *Variety*, 5 December 1979, 22.
5. Loutzenhiser.
6. *The Prize Fighter*, produced by Lang Elliot and Wanda Dell, directed by Michael Preece, 99 minutes, Media Home Entertainment, Inc., 1982, videocassette.

The Prizefighter and the Lady (1933)

Metro-Goldwyn Mayer, Drama, B & W, 102 minutes

Producer: W. S. Van Dyke. *Director*: W. S. Van Dyke. *Screenplay*: John Lee Mahin, Jr., John Meehan from a story by Frances Marion. *Film Editor*: Robert J. Kern. *Photography*: Lester White. *Vaudeville Sketch*: Seymour Felix.

Myrna Loy (Belle), Max Baer (Steve), Otto Kruger (Willie Ryan), Walter Huston (Professor), Jack Dempsey (Promoter), Jess Willard (Himself), Primo Carnera (Carnera), James J. Jeffries (Himself), Vince Barnett (Bugsie), Robert Mcwade (Adopted Son), Muriel Evans (Linda), Jean Howard (Show Girl).

In 1933, fresh from his dramatic knockout of Max Schmeling, handsome and playful Max Baer had positioned himself as the number-one contender for the heavyweight championship of the world. Baer was a fistic rarity. He was not only good-looking and personable, but could also fight. This fact was not lost upon MGM executives. Correctly surmising that their new screen find possessed tremendous potential for box-office appeal with moviegoers of both sexes, they shrewdly signed the "Californian Adonis" to the lead role in a glossy fight picture entitled *The Prizefighter and the Lady*.

When "The Man Mountain" Primo Carnera annexed the world heavyweight championship from Jack Sharkey, even a novice casting director could see that the gargantuan and homely Carnera would be the ideal cinematic foil for Baer's melodramatic adventure. Even better, if Baer could secure a shot at the real heavyweight title against Carnera while the film was in release, box-office success would be guaranteed. Carnera's managers, Duffy and Soresi, balked at the original script, calling for their fighter to lose. To appease the champion, the climactic fight scene was rewritten to conclude in a draw, thus allowing Carnera to retain his fictional title. A salary increase was added as additional incentive, and the services of the first and only Italian heavyweight champion of the world were secured.[1]

While Carnera had bested Baer in regard to the performance fees anted by MGM, it was "The Fighting Playboy" who triumphed over Carnera on every other front. The oafish Carnera, the product of the remote village of Sesquels, Italy, was misplaced in Hollywood's opulence and ill at ease with its glamorous women. Conversely, Baer thrived amongst its beauties and fed off both their attention and that of the camera. To magnify the pair's already disparate experiences, the mischievous Baer engaged complicit MGM studio hands to assist in making Carnera the target of numerous pranks.[2]

Carnera was only the bull's-eye of Baer's broad target of humor. On another occasion, Baer had co-star Myrna Loy's chair electrically wired, shocking her during the filming of a fight scene in front of the crew and a large cast of extras. Maxie's brand of humor was infectious. Former heavyweight champion Jack Dempsey exhibited Baer's spirit by giving Loy an exploding cigarette which was lit by co-accomplice director W.S. Van Dyke. Loy eventually exacted revenge with the assistance of a toy mouse, which drove the rodent-phobic Baer into the protective arms of Carnera.[3]

In many respects, Max Baer portrayed himself in *The Prizefighter and the Lady*. Max, like his alter ego Steve Morgan, was handsome, carefree and amorous. His obligations ranked a distant second to his libidinous indulgences. In the film, Steve Morgan (Baer), is discovered in a bar fight by an alcoholic has-been fight manager known as "The Professor" (Huston). After Morgan rescues a lovely young lady named Belle (Loy) following a car accident, she expresses her gratitude by attending one of Morgan's fights, and a courtship begins. Belle is already romantically involved with a racketeer named Ryan (Kruger), but she eventually succumbs to Morgan. She leaves Ryan and marries the fighter, who is spared from his rival's retribution only because of the gangster's unwavering commitment to his lost love's happiness.

Putting the bottle aside, the Professor steers Morgan into contention, but the boxer's home life is marked by marital indiscretion. Morgan is contrite when his extramarital affairs are exposed, and Belle is unusually forgiving. Nevertheless, Morgan continues his infidelity until Belle leaves him. Having forsaken Morgan, Belle returns to Ryan, but the heartbroken girl still loves the fighter.

Morgan finally boxes Carnera for the championship. Now remorseful over his mistreatment of Belle, as well as that of the Professor, whom he fired, the boxer resigns himself to failure in the ring. Belle, however, convinces the Professor to return to Morgan's corner. Inspired by the support of the Professor and his love, Morgan rallies with several knockdowns, earning a draw and a happy reunion with Belle.

Studio heavyweight Louis B. Mayer was displeased with early advances of *The Prizefighter and the Lady*, and had instructed latecomer Van Dyke to improve the picture. Director Van Dyke reviewed the several cans of film shot by his predecessor and then discarded them all.[4] Beginning his picture from scratch, Van Dyke's final product was well received by the public and critics alike.

William Boehnel of the *New York World-Telegram* found the picture to possess "a fresh and crisp and entirely believable story; terse, natural, pungent dialogue; masterful direction and acting that is unbeatable."[5]

Baer's performance as Steve Morgan bowled over the critics, and still stands as the best performance of a boxer in a leading film role. Mordaunt Hall of *The New York Times* was surprised by Baer's "extraordinarily capable portrayal," and Richard J. Watts, Jr. of the *New York Herald-Tribune* praised Baer as "an enormously engaging performer who can handle comedy, drama and romantic appeal with distinguished dexterity."[6] "What Baer has," noted Bige of *Variety*, "is the physique of an Apollo, a very likable personality and an obvious ability to take direction on a picture stage."[7]

While other leading ladies such as Joan Crawford, Norma Shearer and Jean Harlow were considered to play opposite

Baer, Myrna Loy landed the role and proved herself worthy.[8] Critic Philip K. Schuerer wrote that Loy "continues to advance as an actress of revealing poise and distinction."[9] *Variety* found Loy "the perfect opposite for Mr. Baer" and John S. Cohen of the *New York Sun* saw her as "never more genuine."[10]

In a galvanized performance, Otto Kruger provided, in the words of William Boehnel, "a suave menace that is all the more effective and piercing because of the way he under-emphasizes his characterization."[11]

The Prizefighter and the Lady offers a priceless segment featuring Baer performing in a musical stage review. Accompanied by a bevy of beauties, Max does a soft-shoe while singing "Lucky Fella on the Make for Love," and continues to entertain while they perform in choreographed numbers of rope jumping, shadow boxing and gymnastic ring maneuvers.[12]

Joining Baer and Carnera in the ring for the finale are former champions Jack Dempsey, Joe Rivers, Jackie Fields, Billy Papke, Jess Willard and James J. Jeffries. A view of this assemblage is itself worth the price of admission. Prior to the commencement of the final bout, Dempsey, who portrays the referee, turns to Willard, the man he brutalized in Toledo, Ohio, to win the heavyweight title. "A little bit of a problem we had in Toledo that day, Jess," Dempsey tells Willard. "Well, I don't remember much about that day, Jack," Jess replies.[13]

The numerous rounds of sparring with the champion in making *The Prizefighter and the Lady* proved invaluable to Baer. It was during these sessions that Carnera's Achilles' heel was revealed. Primo was a sucker for Max's overhand right. On June 14, 1934, at the Long Island City Bowl, wearing the very same robe which he wore in the ring against Carnera in the film, Max Baer proceeded to knock down Primo eight times.[14] This time, unhampered by the meddling of the MGM's scenarists, Baer knocked out Carnera to win the heavyweight championship of the world, proving that filmmaking can be both an art that imitates life and an art that life is bound to imitate.

1. Nat Fleischer, *Max Baer, The Glamour Boy of the Ring* (New York: n.p., 1970), 28.
2. *Ibid.*
3. Robert C. Cannon, *Van Dyke and the Mythical City of Hollywood* (New York: Garland Publishing, 1977), 280–81.
4. *Ibid.*, 279.
5. William Boehnel, Review of *The Prizefighter and the Lady* (MGM movie), *New York World-Telegram*, 10 November 1933.
6. Mordaunt Hall, "Max Baer, Myrna Loy and Walter Huston in 'The Prizefighter and the Lady,'" Review of *The Prizefighter and the Lady* (MGM movie), *New York Times*, 11 November 1933; Richard Watts, Jr., Review of *The Prizefighter and the Lady* (MGM movie), *New York Herald-Tribune*, 11 November 1933.
7. Bige, Review of *The Prizefighter and the Lady* (MGM movie), *Variety*, 14 November 1933.
8. Edwin Schallert, *Los Angeles Times*, 7 July 1933.
9. Philip K. Schuerer, "'Ring Melodrama 'Clicks.'" —————-, 15 December 1933.
10. *Variety*; John S. Cohen Jr., "'The Prizefighter and the Lady,' Max Baer's Debut — 'College Coach.'" Review of *The Prizefighter and the Lady* (MGM movie), *New York Sun*, 11 November 1933.
11. William Boehnel, *New York World-Telegram*.
12. *The Prizefighter and the Lady*, produced by MGM, directed by W.S. Van Dyke, 90 minutes, 1933.
13. *Ibid.*
14. Original NBC Radio Broadcast of the Primo Carnera — Max Baer heavyweight championship fight, 14 June 1934.

Raging Bull (1980)

United Artists, Bio-drama, B & W with color sequences, 128 minutes

Producers: Irwin Winkler and Robert Chartoff. *Director*: Martin Scorsese. *Screenplay*: Paul Schrader and Martin Mardik, based upon the book Jake La Motta, by Jake La Motta with Joseph Carter and Peter Savage. *Film Editor*: Thelma Schoonmaker. *Director of Photography*: Michael Chapman. *Music*: Pietro Mascagni. *Boxing Technical Advisor*: Al Silvani. *Consultant*: Jake La Motta.

Robert De Niro (Jake La Motta), Cathy Moriarty (Vicki La Motta), Joe Pesci (Joey La Motta), Frank Vincent (Salvy), Nicholas Colasanto (Tommy Como), Mario Gallo (Mario), Bernie Allen (Comedian), Joseph Bono (Guido), Lori Anne Flax (Irma), Theresa Saldana (Lenore), Frank Adonis (Patsy), Bill Hanrahan (Eddie Egan), Don Dunphy (Himself), Frankie Topham (Toppy), Charles Scorese (Charlie — Man with Como), Rita Bennett (Emma — Miss 48's), James V. Christy (Dr. Pinto), Floyd Anderson (Jimmy Reeves), Johnny Barnes (Sugar Ray Robinson), Eddie Mustafa Muhammad (Billy Fox), Kevin Mahon (Tony Janiro), Louis Raftis (Marcel Cerdan), Johnny Turner (Laurent Dauthuille), Jimmy Lennon (Ring Announcer — 2nd Robinson and Dauthuille Fight), Marty Denkin (Referee — Tony Janiro Fight) Joe Louis (Coley Wallace).

A crude, violent and oftentimes antisocial boxer who ascended to the middleweight championship, Jake La Motta was the perfect mold from which filmmaker Martin Scorsese could sculpt a brilliant interpretation of human character. La Motta, who won the middleweight championship in 1949 when he wrestled it away from the talented Marcel Cerdan, surrendered it to the incomparable Sugar Ray Robinson in 1951. Known for his aggressive and unrelenting style in the ring, La Motta was nicknamed "The Raging Bull." The moniker was also applicable to his behavior outside of the ring, which was marked by domestic violence and abuse.

It is this darker side of La Motta's personal life that Scorsese forces his audience to confront in his biographical exposé of the boxer entitled *Raging Bull*. Scorsese's La Motta is neither heroic nor redemptive: he is a rare film protagonist who asks film audiences to unconditionally accept his humanity.

Raging Bull was forged through a series of personal connections. The film's associate producer, Peter Savage, whose real name is Pete Petrella, was an intimate friend of La Motta, and co-authored *Raging Bull*. Savage had also worked with Robert De Niro, casting him in two pictures.[1] De Niro read the biography and referred it to his former director Scorsese. The director's initial reaction was "A boxer? I don't like boxing."[2]

Scorsese, however, became intrigued with La Motta on a personal level. For Scorsese, the real story lies in the primal elements of La Motta's character. Once hooked, he acquired the film rights. He then sent the book to screenwriter Martin Mardik, who had collaborated with him and De Niro on *Mean Streets,* to fashion the initial screenplay.[3] Another former co-worker of the duo, Paul Schrader, who scripted *Taxi Driver*, was brought in to add further structure to the story.[4] To fill the crucial role of Jake's brother Joey, De Niro personally brought in Joe Pesci.[5] In turn, Pesci recommended unknown 19-year-old Cathy Moriarity, whom he discovered in a disco and who was a dead-ringer for a young Vicki La Motta.[6]

Perhaps more risky than the film's casting of two unknown players in major roles was its highly unorthodox cinematographical foundation. The picture would have to pass muster with revenue-conscious executives from United Artists and money-paying audiences, and Scorsese's choice to use black-and-white film was nothing short of daring. His decision to forgo the conventional use of color was driven by his knowledge of color film stock's tendency to fade.

Additionally, he desired to distinguish his movie from the other five boxing films already in release or production that year. He also felt that black and white better suited his artistic sensibilities.[7] Cinematographer Michael Chapman produced an uncompromised realization of Scorsese's vision which included the creation of a period piece, something akin to a tabloid, and reminiscent of Weegee photographs.[8] Chapman received an Academy Award nomination for what critic Jack Kroll described as "powerful, spectral black and white cinematography, a stupendous achievement in its own right."[9]

Raging Bull bears the unmistakable mark of Martin Scorsese and Robert De Niro. Not surprisingly, behind their unparalleled contributions as director and lead actor is their uncredited re-write of the final draft of the screenplay.[10] The native New Yorkers injected genuine street-wise dialogue into the script. Unsentimental in tone and direct in delivery, the humor is sharp and the drama unforgiving. The result was a film which is uniquely "New York." Joel Siegel of *WABC-TV* would later write that the picture was "one of the best New York films ever made."[11] Rich in its ethnicity, the film's setting springs from Scorsese's and De Niro's roots, the lower East Side of Manhattan, a once thriving Italian enclave where traditional values formed an unholy alliance with pragmatism. Robert Hatch, writing for *The Nation*, found Scorsese's interpretation of La Motta's Italian-American world to be "tenderly handled but implacably unsentimental." "It is warm, sustaining and authoritative, it is male-dominated and fiercely protective of women; it breaks the law but adheres to the code."[12]

The nine fight scenes in the film set the unrivaled benchmark in fight choreography. They also comprise the most compelling and artful cinematic exposition ever to be made of the sport. Scorsese was unrelenting in is his commitment to the fight scenes. Although running slightly less than 15 minutes, they were afforded ten weeks, almost half of the film's shooting time.[13] Each scene was storyboarded down to the last punch.[14] Scorsese's approach was to stay in the ring and avoid cut-aways to the audience. Most importantly, he desired to film the action from Jake's point of view, so as to allow the viewer to vicariously experience La Motta's emotions.[15] The final product, as noted by Richard Corliss of *Time*, was "as violent, controlled, repulsive and exhilarating as anything in the genre."[16]

Amazingly, the fight vignettes were all shot by cinematographer Michael Chapman with one camera.[17] It is through the thoughtful, varied, and unique use of slow motion, tracking shots, and close-ups, along with the near revolutionary over-cranking of the film's speed, that a one-of-a-kind experience is created.[18] Jack Kroll of *Newsweek* captured the essence of the viewers' experience when he wrote, "The camera muscles into the action, peering from above, from below, from the combatant's point of view, panning 360 degrees as a doomed fighter spins to the canvas. Smoke, sweat, flesh and blood become Jackson Pollack abstractions as they pound home the essential blood lust of these sweet sciences, prizefighting and moviemaking."[19] Joseph Gelmis of *Newsday* also recognized "the harrowing realism" of the graphic fight details, calling them "brilliant, grueling, punishing."[20]

In one scene shot in slow motion, a bloody sponge is wrung out on La Motta's neck, evoking images of a ceremonial anointment. In another, blood drips from the ring ropes — an eerie epitaph of defeat; in still another blood spurts from the nose, reminiscent of the carnage of an animal sacrifice. Flashbulbs from the oversized 1940s cameras flash and crackle ringside, punctuating each and every bone crunching blow and adding an electric frenzy to the scenes. Artfully selected moments without sound are deafening in their impact. So stylized and emotionally based are the fight scenes that Pauline Kael, writing for the *New Yorker*, opined that "these aren't fights, really; they're cropped, staccato ordeals."[21]

To portray La Motta, Robert De Niro underwent perhaps the most startling transformation in cinematic history by gaining 60 pounds to portray the middle-aged La Motta.[22] So committed were Scorsese and De Niro to the latter's physical metamorphosis, that the shooting of the film was strategically halted for several months to allow De Niro to gain the weight.[23] In actuality, this was De Niro's second body-altering effort, having already undertaken a grueling training regiment to portray the rock-hard middleweight version of La Motta earlier in the film. De Niro's final illusion of La Motta's physical deterioration created, as critic John Coleman of the *New Statesman* put it, "an awe-inspiring experience."[24]

Both De Niro and Joe Pesci trained with Jake La Motta and his brother Joey in the Gramercy Gym in New York.[25] Over the course of a year, De Niro and Jake sparred an incredible 1,000 rounds during which the former middleweight champion received a broken nose, a fractured rib, several black eyes, and broken upper teeth.[26] De Niro even fractured one of Joe Pesci's ribs during a scene.[27] Commenting on his pupil, La Motta noted, "Right now Bobby's a main event fighter ... I could easily make him into a champion, he's that good."[28]

De Niro's passion for the role extended to other aspects of the portrayal. De Niro followed La Motta around for over a year with a tape recorder in what La Motta himself would describe as an obsessive effort to learn about him.[29] The result is a tour de force characterization where De Niro exhibits his mastery of his subject's entire being: from his use of simple gestures, speaking patterns and overt physicality, to his non-verbal communication through gaze, posture and countenance. Regarding De Niro's odyssey through Jake La Motta's persona, Robert Edelman of *Films in Review* wrote that he "chews into his role, digests it, and spits it out across the screen ... he is Oscar bound."[30] De Niro did in fact receive the Academy Award for best actor in a role which was lauded by Jack Kroll, among others, as "his most stunning yet."[31] De Niro is chameleon-like in adopting La Motta's various physical forms, but he never wavers from the essence of his brutality. He exhibits La Motta's animalistic tendencies toward others with stark realism, powerfully bringing to life the disturbing effects of his inwardly directed anger, paranoia and jealousy.

While accolades were bestowed upon De Niro and Oscar-nominated Joe Pesci, among others, the picture was not without criticism. Like other Scorsese efforts, detractors attacked the continuity and narrative flow of the story. There was also a uniform criticism of the film's failure to provide the audience with the reasons behind La Motta's pervasive anti-social behavior. But it is Scorsese's resistance to adhere to what he describes as "the old clichéd psychological structure," the necessity to explain and justify, that allowed him to push the envelope of filmmaking.[32] As noted by Robert Asahina of *New Leader*, Scorsese's ... forceful, at times daring direction scores heavily in the vicinity of viewers' viscera."[33]

Recognizing the picture's true import at the time of its release, Jay Gould Boyum of *The Wall Street Journal* described it as "a film of extraordinary power and rare distinction."[34] The movie, which received eight Academy Award nominations including one for best picture, has only grown in reputation, and was recently ranked number 24 on the American Film Institute's top 100 films of all-time.[35]

Martin Scorsese had once commented that he did not like the sport of boxing. "I don't think it's a very sportive thing ... I think it's savage."[36] Thankfully, Scorsese also felt that he was not above the sport. He also found certain unpleasant things in Jake La Motta that he recognized in himself— and in all of us — and in doing so, gave us the most significant boxing film ever made.

1. "The Delicate Art of Creating a Brutal Film Hero," *Sunday New York Times*, 23 November 1980, sec. 2.

2. Hildy Johnson, "What's Black & White and Red All Over? Martin Scorsese," *In Cinema*, December 1980.

3. Mary Pat Kelly, *Martin Scorsese: A Journey* (New York: Thunder's Mouth Press, 1991), 121–123.

4. "Creating a Brutal Film Hero."

5. Ellen Stern, *New York Daily News*, Manhattan Section, 5 December 1980, M 2–3.

6. Judy Klemesrud, "That I Had Never Acted Helped Me to Be Natural," *New York Times*, 15 November 1980, 13.

7. Johnson, "What's Black & White"; Kelly, *Martin Scorsese: A Journey*, 125.

8. *Ibid.*

9. Jack Kroll, Review of *Raging Bull* (United Artists movie), *Newsweek*, 24 November 1980, 128.

10. Kelly, *Martin Scorsese: A Journey*, 126.

11. Joel Siegel quoted by D. Bartholomew, *Cinefantastique*, 21 November 1980.

12. Robert Hatch, "Raging Bull Resurrection," *Nation*, 13 December 1980.

13. *American Cinematographer*, May 1981.

14. *Ibid.*, 127.

15. *Ibid.*, 132.

16. Richard Corliss, "Animal House," *Time*, 24 November 1980, 100.

17. Kelly, *Martin Scorsese: A Journey*, 132.

18. Ibid, 136.

19. Kroll.

20. Joseph Gelmis, Review of *Raging Bull* (United Artists movie), *Newsday*, 14 November 1980, Part II, p. 7.

21. Pauline Kael, "Religious Pulp, or the Incredible Hulk," *New Yorker*, 8 December 1980, 222.

22. *In Cinema*, 1980, no. 2, p.7.

23. "Creating a Brutal Film Hero."

24. John Coleman, Review of *Raging Bull* (United Artists movie), *New Statesman*, 2 February 1981, 23.

25. "Creating a Brutal Film Hero."

26. Lorenzo Carcaterra, "The Bull Takes a Swing at the Movies," *New York Daily News*, 12 September 1979, 25.

27. "Creating a Brutal Film Hero."

28. Carcaterra, "The Bull Takes a Swing."

29. Dan Yakir, "Two Sticklers and a Slugger," *After Dark*, November 1980, 30.

30. Robert Edelman, Review of *Raging Bull* (United Artists movie), *Films in Review*, January 1981, 54.

31. Kroll.

32. "Creating a Brutal Film Hero."

33. Robert Asahina, Review of *Raging Bull* (United Artists movie), *New Leader*, 1 December 1980, 18.

34. Jay Gould Boyum, Review of *Raging Bull* (United Artists movie), *Wall Street Journal*, 28 November 1980.

35. *New York Daily News*, Showtime, 30 July 2000, 5.

36. Johnson, "What's Black & White."

Requiem for a Heavyweight (1962)

Columbia Pictures, Drama, B & W, 85 minutes (some television prints 100 minutes)

Producer: David Susskind. *Director*: Ralph Nelson. *Screenplay*: Rod Serling, adapted from his own teleplay. *Film Editor*: Carl Lerner. *Photography*: Arthur J. Ornitz. *Music*: Laurence Rosenthal.

Anthony Quinn (Mountain Rivera), Jackie Gleason (Maish Rennick), Mickey Rooney (Army), Julie Harris (Grace Miller), Stan Adams (Perelli), Madame Spivy (Ma Greeny), Herbie Faye (Bartender), Jack Dempsey (Himself), Cassius Clay (Ring Opponent), Steve Belloise (Hotel Desk Clerk), Lou Gilbert (Ring Doctor), Arthur Mercante (Referee).

The Kraft Television Theater and *Playhouse 90* were staples of the medium of live television which flourished in New York City during the 1950s. They also served as a forum where new artists could display their talents. Representative of this group was Rod Serling, a young New York writer and former amateur boxer. Serling wrote an original script for a 1955 *Kraft Theater* broadcast entitled *Patterns* and was awarded an Emmy for his teleplay.[1] Not surprisingly, when *Playhouse 90* went on the air the following year, producer David Susskind anxiously snatched up Serling's latest script entitled *Requiem for a Heavyweight*.[2]*

Outwardly adorned with boxing paraphernalia, *Requiem*'s underlying premise as developed by Serling was a human character study. "I wanted to analyze a human being who fought for a living but who was nonetheless a human being," the author explained. Aired on October 11, 1956, the poignant examination of a man coming to grips with his own devaluation by society was the hit of the television season. Among the accolades bestowed upon the production, which still ranks as one of television's most honored, was the Emmy Award for best single show of the year. Other Emmys went to Serling for best teleplay, Ralph Nelson for best director, Jack Palance for best single performance by an actor, and Albert Heschong for best art direction.[3]

In 1962, when Columbia Pictures brought *Requiem* to the screen, the film might have been doomed to an inevitable unfavorable comparison to the original. Columbia, however, strove to recapture the brilliance of the television version by tapping into the genius of the earlier production through Susskind, Nelson, and Serling. The film's utilization of this trio, coupled with an unusually talented cast of actors, resulted in another artistic triumph.

For the lead of Mountain Rivera, Columbia cast Serling's first choice, Anthony Quinn.[4] At the apex of his career, Quinn had already won Academy Awards for his dynamic performances in *Lust for Life* and *Viva Zapata*, and was a character actor *par excellence*. He also could rely on personal experience to play his role since he had boxed professionally in the Los Angeles area as a young man.[5] For a spell, Quinn worked out at the Main Street Gym with Mushy Callahan and Newsboy Brown. He even sparred with heavyweight champion Primo Carnera when the Italian trained at Echo Park.[6]

Julie Harris, an Academy Award nominee for best supporting actress in *The Member of the Wedding*, was selected for the critical female lead. The role of Maish, Rivera's morally soft manager, went to the multi-talented Jackie Gleason. Gleason was already an established personality as a nightclub star and television comic, and with a recent Academy Award nomination for his portrayal of Minnesota Fats in *The Hustler*, the brash entertainer had served notice of his gift for drama as well. In the role of Army, Mountain's loyal guardian, Columbia astutely cast Mickey Rooney in what proved to be one of his finest adult performances.

Requiem for a Heavyweight is a compelling and moving drama centered upon the relationships of a fighter, his manager, and his trainer. Mountain Rivera (Quinn), is a ring-worn boxer whose deeply scarred face and cauliflower ears are a visual testimony to his prizefighting experience. His long-time trainer is the weak-willed and posturing Maish Rennick (Gleason). Unbeknownst to his charge, Maish bets that Mountain cannot last four rounds in a bout against a hot prospect (Clay). Ma (Spivey) a gangster, also bets against Mountain on Maish's assurances. When the fighter's courage takes him beyond the expected limit, Maish is given an ultimatum to pay back the lost money or suffer dire consequences. However, the increasingly unnerved Maish is left without a meal ticket to rescue him from retribution when the Boxing Commission demands Mountain retire due to an eye injury.

The slow-witted fighter struggles to begin anew with the paternalistic guidance of his loving trainer Army (Rooney) and a

---

*Like other television productions of the day, the sponsor of *Requiem*, Ronson Lighters, looked to exploit the telecast to its advantage. Not surprisingly, the lighter manufacturer was perturbed at the line "Have you got a match?" and requested that Serling change it to the more apropos "Have you got a light?" Serling agreed to the suggestion, and then sarcastically added that at the end of the show "instead of having wrestling matches we'll have wrestling lighters." With Ronson's request withdrawn, the scene proceeded as originally scripted.

gentle and caring woman for the unemployment office named Ms. Miller (Harris). Ms. Miller recognizes the hoarse-voiced fighter's inherent goodness and helps secure him a job interview for a sports counselor position. However, despite the pleading of Army, Maish arranges for Mountain to engage in wrestling exhibitions to raise money, and then shamefully undermines the counseling job.

Mountain, who has been stripped of everything but his pride, clings to the remainder of his self-worth. Although he idolizes the undeserving Maish, he refuses to wrestle, exclaiming to his manager: "I'll do anything for you, but don't ask me to be a clown."[7] However, when the physical assault of Maish becomes imminent, Mountain makes the ultimate sacrifice. Crowned by a shameful Indian headdress and gripping a phony tomahawk, Mountain symbolically performs his own death dance in the center of the ring amidst the boos and catcalls of an unfeeling audience.

Poignant and hard-hitting, the film possesses some of the most pointed and insightful dialogue ever written for the screen. The characters are rich and deeply human and take the viewer on a roller coaster exploration of pride, loyalty, sacrifice, self-worth and unconditional love.

Requiem was applauded by the critics. Walter J. Carroll of *The Villager* found the film to be a "totally genuine document of human greed, suffering, and compassion." Speaking comparatively, Carroll noted, "Some films live in the beauty of their images, others in a fluid cinematic form. This one lives in the brilliance of its characterizations."[8] While Richard Mallet of *Punch* felt the characterizations were "simple and broad," he nevertheless conceded that the film still made "its dramatic effect triumphantly."[9]

If the film's characters were in any way caricatures, director Nelson's aggregate product seemed to overshadow that deficiency. As observed by the critic of *The New Yorker*, "Ralph Nelson has encouraged the actors to squeeze the last drop of good from their tried-and-true roles."[10]

Indeed, the individual portrayals are the film's true strength. The critics lauded Quinn's performance. Robe of *Variety*, observing the diversity of the portrayal, wrote, "Quinn's punchy, inarticulate behemoth is so painfully natural that one winces when he feels pain, whether to his body or to his feelings."[11] Richard L. Cole of *The Washington Post* felt the role was one of Quinn's finest, "A fascinating meeting of the physical and spiritual ... worthy of next spring's Oscar."[12] *Cue* magazine expressed similar sentiments, finding that Quinn played the part "with Oscar-winning brilliance."[13]

Gleason's performance was also heralded. The critic for *Variety* credited Gleason with an unpredictability stemming from his freshness at serious acting, finding his performance "amazingly fine."[14] *Punch* and *The Washington Post* both pegged the portrayal as "first-rate," with Bosley Crowther of *The New York Times* describing his effort as "brilliantly underplayed."[15] The *Post* observed, "Gleason's achievement is that he makes you understand why the manager is such a heel." The *Post* also applauded Rooney, finding that his "silent suffering reaches us through knowing skill."[16]

A testament to the film's true power to engross is the fact that Quinn is never seen throwing a punch in the ring, yet one is not even conscious of this fact, nor does it detract from the film as a boxing movie. While not a film concerning boxing as a sport, *Requiem* is the ultimate boxing picture in regard to the all too human personage of the fight game.

The appearance of Muhammad Ali, then known as Cassius Clay, was an interesting addition to the film, which has since grown in a significance proportional to Ali's own persona. Joining Ali in the film were an impressive roster of fighters and ex-fighters including Willie Pep, Barney Ross, Jack Dempsey, Gus Lesnevich, Abe Simon, Steve Belloise, Paoli Rossi, Rory Calhoun, and Alex Miteff.

The opening fight scene is still one of the most artistic ever filmed. Shot from the perspective of Mountain Rivera, we see the world through his eyes, including that of an attacking Cassius Clay. The level of consciousness of the besieged and unseen Rivera is conveyed to the audience by simulating a blurry view similar to that offered through water-drenched glass. When Clay lands his knockout blow, we are given a temporary freeze frame of Clay, Rivera's last vision before he temporarily loses consciousness. The camera then turns sideways and scans in an arch-like fashion to simulate the knockdown of Mountain, where the details of the boxer's ringside surroundings seem to intensify in a dream-like state.

1. Judine Mayerle, "Requiem for a Heavyweight and Playhouse 90, an Age Had Come to an End," *Journal of Popular Film and Television*.
2. Ibid.
3. Mayerle, "Requiem for a Heavyweight."
4. Gordon F. Sander, *Serling: The Rise and Twilight of Television's Last Angry Man* (New York: Dutton, 1992), 177.
5. Anthony Quinn, Daniel Paisner, *One Man Tango* (New York: HarperCollins Publishers, 1995), 69–70.
6. Ibid., 71.
7. *Requiem for A Heavyweight*, produced by David Susskind, directed by Ralph Nelson, 87 minutes, 1962.
8. Walter J. Carroll, Review of *Requiem for a Heavyweight* (Columbia Pictures movie), *Villager*, 13 December 1962.
9. Richard Mallet, Review of *Requiem for a Heavyweight* (Columbia Pictures movie), *Punch*, 27 February 1963, 314.
10. Review of *Requiem for a Heavyweight* (Columbia Pictures movie), *New Yorker*, 20 October 1962.
11. Robe, Review of *Requiem for a Heavyweight* (Columbia Pictures movie), *Variety*, 12 September 1962
12. Richard L. Cole, "The Midlands and the Ring." Review of *Requiem for a Heavyweight* (Columbia Pictures movie), *Washington Post*, 9 November 1962, C6.
13. Review of *Requiem for a Heavyweight* (Columbia Pictures movie), *Cue*, 20 October 1962.
14. *Variety*.
15. *Punch*; *Washington Post*; Bosley Crowther, *New York Times*, quoted in William A. Henry III, *The Life and Legend of Jackie Gleason* (New York: Doubleday, 1992), 4–5, 213–214.
16. Washington Post, C6.

Ring of Passion (1978)

Twentieth Century-Fox Studio, Television Movie, Bio-Drama, Color, 100 minutes

Producer: Lou Morheim. *Director*: Robert Michael Lewis. *Screenplay*: Larry Forrester. *Film Editor*: Jules Brenner. *Director of Photography*: Sidney M. Katz, A.C.E. *Music*: Bill Conti. *Boxing Coordinator*: Sonny Shields.

Bernie Casey (Joe Louis), Stephen Macht (Max Schmeling), Brit Ekland (Anny Ondra), Denise Nicholas (Marva Louis), Alan Garfield (Damon Runyon), Joseph Campanella (Paul Gallico), Beah Richards (Lilly Brooks), Norman Alden (Max Machon), Julius Harris ("Chappie" Blackburn), Mordecai Lawner (Joe Jacobs), Percy Rodrigues (John Roxborough), Mel Stewart (Julian Black), Al Lewis (Mike Jacobs), Dan Avery (Blow-by-Blow Announcer), Jack Bernardt (Mr. Weisman), Shaka Cumbuna (Honey Bear), Sarina C. Grant (Vunies), Tom Kelly (Newsman #1), Jimmy Lennon (Ring Announcer), Allan Malamud (Newsman #2), David Moody (Wellwisher), Joni Palmer (Emmarell), Stephen Roberts (Franklin D. Roosevelt), Clement St. George (German Commentator), Wonderful Smitty (Minister), George Latka (Referee Donovan), Patrick O'Hara, (Tom O'Rourke).

By the summer of 1938, Adolf Hitler was persecuting Jews in Europe with an alarming vigor and the Nazis had begun their territorial expansion. In the United States, Third Reich supporters such as the German-American Bund clashed with their adversaries in the Anti-Nazi League. Doctrines of racial and ethnic superiority were being advanced through both rhetoric and acts of hatred, from the streets of Berlin to the streets of New York, and Americans began to look inward, questioning their own racial and religious prejudices at home.

Embroiled in this political intrigue and social unrest were two prizefighters: Joe Louis, a black American, and his German counterpart, Max Schmeling. Unfortuitous circumstance had endowed these two individuals with a public significance disproportionate to their trade. For better or worse, Schmeling became a symbol of Nazism and racial superiority and Joe Louis the torchbearer for Democracy and social justice. When the two stepped into a boxing ring on the evening of June 22, 1938, a world of ever-increasing discord followed them, culminating in the most politically charged sporting event of the century.

Ring of Passion, a television movie from Twentieth Century-Fox Studio, details the convergent worlds of sport and politics, beginning with Schmeling's stunning upset of Louis in June of 1936. The film touches upon Hitler's snub of Jessie Owens at the Berlin Summer Olympics, America's triumph over Germany at Wimbledon, and concludes with Louis's savage knockout of Schmeling in defense of his heavyweight championship two years after their first encounter.

The picture earnestly strives to present the uneasiness and trepidation of the period through a diverse set of lenses. The Jewish-American perspective is seen through the eyes of promoter Mike Jacobs, and Schmeling's manager Joe "Yussel" Jacobs. Louis represents the interests of both black America and a portion of white America, including American Jews. Enigmatically, Schmeling is simultaneously depicted as a German hero, a symbol of Nazism and a champion to white America's racists.

Ring of Passion adopts a sentimental tone. Portraying both of the fighters in a favorable light, they emerge from beneath the world's microscope with their reputations unscathed. The depiction of Louis is, by and large, historically accurate, although the presentation of his responses to complex issues are sometimes oversimplified. Louis is shown condemning racism and having concerns about the racial violence which his fights sometimes engender, while still being aware of his bout's potential to advance the interests of his race. He principally desires to defeat Schmeling in their rematch to reverse his loss and achieve personal redemption. However, if Schmeling must be conquered for ideological reasons, Louis is willing to represent American interests, and humble the symbol of Nazism.

Arguably, world events laid a heavier burden on the shoulders of Schmeling than those of Louis. Schmeling faced pressure from Adolf Hitler and the Nazi party and feared repercussions against his wife, actress Annie Ondra, who was not a German, but a Czech.*

Schmeling maintained the position that he was not a Nazi, or when prudence dictated, he tactfully avoided discussion of the issue altogether. The film goes to great lengths to present Schmeling as a sportsman proud of his German heritage who is unfairly labeled as a Nazi sympathizer by the American press. Max also remained loyal to his Jewish manager "Yussel" Jacobs and was sympathetic to the plight of German Jews. However, on occasion, the film goes too far to make its point. In one unrealistic scene Schmeling takes a hard position with the Fuhrer on the issue of Jacobs's management and in another he is shown giving a German-Jewish couple a free pair of tickets to his first match against Louis. Indeed, Hitler

---

Schmeling's wife, Annie Ondra, was a film star in Germany. In 1936, she starred with Max in a German language boxing film entitled Knock-out *which was released just prior to Schmeling's spectacular upset of Louis. The film also ran in United States theaters in German-speaking neighborhoods including the Seventy-ninth Street Theater in New York City. Critiquing the former heavyweight champion's acting ability, Wear of* Variety *wrote, "'Knock-out' proves that Max Schmeling is still clever with his mitts but that the acting in the family will be done by his wife Annie Ondra.... Schmeling in this film, lacks even the basic elements of showmanship. Appears natural only when doing his fistic training or actually in the ring heaving punches."*

had presented Schmeling with his autographed photograph, which the boxer displayed in his study. It is the omission of Schmeling's less favorable associations with the Nazis that unbalance his portrayal, tipping it into the realm of quasi-fiction.

Kate Kelly of the *New York Post* offered a fair assessment of the film when she wrote, "This is not great drama but it is an honorable attempt at taking a small piece of history—in this case both sports history and political history—and trying to dramatize it."[1] Honest performances also lent credibility to the story. Bernie Casey, who has a facial resemblance to Louis, does an excellent job duplicating Louis's relaxed demeanor and simple manner of speaking. Stephen Macht does a nice job showing Schmeling as both analytical and compassionate. Kaye Gardella of the *New York Daily News* found their performances "touching" and "believable."[2]

The fight scenes in *Ring of Passion* are unique and adopt an intellectual approach. During the ring action, voice-overs of both Casey and Macht are added to the soundtrack, giving the audience a window into the fighters' minds as they move around the ring and exchange blows. This technique is achieved by using slow motion and facial close-ups during the moments in which the fighters' thought processes are examined. The voice-overs are effective in creating insight, though at the sacrifice of hard-core ring action.

Astute boxing fans will note a number of inaccuracies in the picture. A voice-over by the ringside radio broadcaster mistakenly references Schmeling's defeat of Jack Sharkey as occurring in 1935 rather than 1930. The film also incorrectly attributes the famed reference to Joe Louis as "a credit to his race—the human race" to Franklin D. Roosevelt, rather than to sportswriter Jimmy Cannon.

As with most business ventures involving the great Joe Louis, the "Brown Bomber" found himself on the short end of *Ring of Passion's* financial stick. The film had a budget of $1.2 million, but according to the ex-heavyweight champion, he received only $7,000 in a deal made without legal assistance.[3]

1. Kate Kelly, *New York Post*, 3 February 1978, 60.
2. Kay Gardella, "Ring of Passion Is Not a Knockout," *New York Daily News*, 4 February 1978, 36.
3. Bob Williams, "Joe Louis Seeks Better Film Fee," *New York Post*, 30 March 1978, 55.

Ringside Maisie (1941)

Metro-Goldwyn Mayer, Comedy, B & W, 96 minutes

Producer: J. Walter Ruben. *Director*: Edwin L. Marin. *Screenplay*: Mary C. Mccall, Jr. *Photography*: Charles Lawton. *Film Editing*: Frederick Y. Smith. *Music*: David Snell.

Ann Sothern (Maisie Ravier), George Murphy (Skeets Maguire), Robert Sterling (Terry Dolan), Virginia O'Brien (Herself), Natalie Thompson (Cecelia Reardon), Margaret Moffat (Mrs. Dolan), Maxie Rosenbloom (Chotsie), Jack La Rue (Ricky Du Prez), "Rags" Ragland (Vic), Oscar O'Shea (Conductor), John Indrisano (Peaches), Roy Lester (Jitterbug), Eddie Simms (Jackie-Boy Duffy), Jonathan Hale (Dr. Kramer), Purnell Pratt (Dr. Taylor).

Like all prominent newspapers of its day, the *Philadelphia North American* dispatched one of its staff to Reno during the summer of 1910, to cover the much-ballyhooed Jack Johnson–James J. Jeffries fight. Their assigned reporter, Mike Murphy, with the help of his son Thorne, quickly made a scoop. It seemed that challenger Jeffries had adopted an unorthodox regimen of roadwork. After a run of about a mile, the "Boilermaker" would typically stop to fish at the Truckee River and then hop a lift most of the way back to training camp. The last half a mile of the scheduled run was then finished off in a sweaty jog for appearance's sake.[1]

Murphy wrote a story exposing Jeffries's training scam and Tex Rickard, the fight's promoter, personally attempted a pay-off to prevent the story's publication. Murphy not only refused the bribe, but he verbally attacked Rickard, branding him a "crooked son-of-a-bitch." After having the promoter bodily removed, Murphy proceeded with the story.[2]

At the time Murphy had another son, an eight-year-old named George. While George Murphy played no role in exposing Jeffries's lax training, he would later gain fame as one of the men who danced with Shirley Temple, and as the first actor elected to the U. S. Senate.[3] Eventually, George had his own liaison with the prize ring, appearing in a pair of boxing films during his successful career on the silver screen.

In 1934, George Murphy starred in *Jealousy*, a Columbia release which was adapted for the screen by Joseph Moncure March. March also penned the poem *The Set-Up*, from which Robert Ryan's boxing classic of the same name was later spawned. In preparation for his role in *Jealousy*, Murphy boxed with heavyweight contender Lee Rampage, just prior to Rampage's bout with Joe Louis.[4]* Louis easily dispatched Rampage, but Murphy faired better in his efforts, with the *Los Angeles Times* writing that he was "good" in his role as a prizefighter named Larry.[5]

In his other boxing feature, *Ringside Maisie*, Murphy portrayed a boxing manager, opposite the attractive Ann Sothern. The film was the fifth entry in the popular MGM series starring the feisty blonde. The typical Maisie picture found Ms. Sothern plunging headlong into one predicament or another, only to extricate herself by the film's conclusion.

In *Ringside Maisie*, Maisie (Sothern) is a dime-a-dance girl and singer. By chance, she meets a boxer doing roadwork named Terry Dolan (Sterling) whom she befriends. She also develops a hot-and-cold romance with his manager Skeets Gallager (Murphy). Skeets is on the verge of steering Dolan into title contention but Dolan has a distaste for boxing.

Earning enough money to purchase a grocery store, Dolan plans an early retirement. With Maisie's support, Dolan reveals his plans to hang up the gloves, only to have his manager threaten legal action. The fighter is forced into one more bout against top contender Jackie-Boy Duffy (Simms). Dolan is knocked out and his head hits the canvas causing him to lose his sight. Abandoned by his fiancée (Moffat), he is supported by Maisie who stands vigil in the hospital. Maisie initially denounces Skeets, but then reunites with him when she learns that he secured the eye surgeon who restores Dolan's sight.

Archer Winsten of the *New York Post* noted that "George Murphy makes a mighty good fight manager," but most critics harped on the fact that *Ringside Maisie* was beneath the abilities of his co-star Ms. Sothern.[6] Gilbert Kanour, of the *Evening Sun, Baltimore* expressed typical critic sentiment noting that Sothern "is a grand performer, and it is a pity her talents are being wasted in such Hollywood *fol-de-rol*."[7]

Several years earlier, "Yussel" Jacobs, the manager of Max Schmeling, bemoaned, "I shoulda stood in bed" immediately after Jack Sharkey had received a gift decision over his fighter Max Schmeling. Borrowing from Jacobs, critic Lee Mortimer of the *Daily Mirror* quipped, "They shouldha stood in bed," in an unfavorable review of those involved in the Sothern vehicle.[8]

---

*Louis knocked Rampage out in Chicago in 8 rounds on December 14, 1934, and again in Los Angeles in 2 rounds on February 21, 1935.

True, the film may not have been on par with the talents of its stars, but to the benefit of boxing fans, *Ringside Maisie*, as explained by *Variety*, is "more about fighting and its evils than about Maisie and her hard times."[9]

Like many boxing films, *Ringside Maisie* portrays the sport of boxing as a racket, although its fight scenes are honest efforts. Sterling adopts a stand-up boxing style that puts him up on his toes, probing with the jab. Occasionally wooden, Sterling's hooks and right crosses are a bit awkward, but apparently without hindrance to his punching power. Co-star Murphy claimed that Sterling was good enough to have knocked out a professional fighter during the shooting of the film.[10]*

The picture features two professional fighters of note, Maxie Rosenbloom and Eddie Simms, both of whom presented themselves nicely. Critiquing the boxer-thespians, Archer Winsten of the *New York Post* wrote that the pair "lend their authentic phizzes to the fight sequences" and Edgar Price of the *Brooklyn Citizen* noted, "There is some fast ring action and there are any number of good laughs, furnished for the most part by Maxie Rosenbloom."[11]

Simms, who was knocked out by Joe Louis in one round in Cleveland on December 14, 1936, is now a footnote to boxing history. His film career is similarly slight, but for a boxer he was not a bad actor. Writing of his performance in *Ringside Maisie*, *Variety* observed that "he shows some ability as an actor in a bedside sequence."[12]†

1. U.S. Senator George Murphy with Victor Lasky, "*Say ... Didn't You Used to Be George Murphy?*" (New York: Bartholomew House Ltd., 1970), 9.
2. Ibid., 9–10.
3. Ibid., 399.
4. Ibid., 201.
5. "'Jealousy' Screened at Warner Downtown Theater." *Los Angeles Times*, 23 November 1934.
6. Archer Winsten, "'Ringside Maisie' Opens at the Capital Theatre," Review of *Ringside Maisie* (MGM movie), *New York Post*.
7. Gilbert Kanour, "'Ringside Maisie' at the Century; Ann Sothern in the Title Role," Review of *Ringside Maisie* (MGM movie), *Baltimore Evening Sun*, 9 August 1941.
8. Lee Mortimer, Review of *Ringside Maisie* (MGM movie), *New York Daily Mirror*, 11 August 1941.
9. Review of *Ringside Maisie* (MGM movie), *Variety*, 11 August 1941.
10. Murphy, "Say ... Didn't You," 231.
11. Winsten, "Ringside Maisie Opens"; Edgar Price, Review of *Ringside Maisie* (MGM movie), *Brooklyn Citizen*, 1 August 1941.
12. *Variety*.

Rocky (1976)

United Artists, Drama, Color, 119 minutes

Producers: Robert Chartoff & Irwin Winkler. *Director*: John G. Avildsen. *Screenplay*: Sylvester Stallone. *Film Editing*: Scott Conrad, Richard Halsey. *Photography*: James Crabe. *Music*: Bill Conti.

Sylvester Stallone (Rocky Balboa), Talia Shire (Adrian), Burt Young (Paulie), Carl Weathers (Apollo Creed), Burgess Meredith (Mickey Goodwin), Thayer David (Jergens), Joe Spinell (Gazzo),

---

*Sterling also packed a wallop with Sothern, whom he later married.
†Simms's respectable performance in the film undoubtedly led to his casting in Sunday Punch *(1948), a Warner Brothers film that was released the following year. Simms appeared in a brief ring scene, but let the stars William Lundigan and Dan Dailey do the rest of the boxing. To prepare Lundigan and Daily for their boxing sequences, the pair were coached by former heavyweight champion Max Baer and ex-boxer turned actor/technical advisor John Indrisano.*

Jimmy Gambina (Mike), Bill Baldwin, Sr. (Fight Announcer), Al Salvani (Cutman), George Memmoli (Ice Ring Attendant), Jodi Letizia (Marie), Diana Lewis (T.V. Commentator), George O'Hanlon (T.V. Commentator), Larry Carroll (T.V. Interviewer), Tony Burton (Apollo's Trainer), Joe Frazier (Himself).

As much as Rocky Balboa may symbolize the American dream, it is debatable whether the character, or its creator, Sylvester Stallone, deserves to be called its true embodiment. Metaphorically, Sly and Rocky can be equated, though Stallone's journey to fame was the more arduous.

A product of the tumultuous Hell's Kitchen section of New York City, Stallone spent his first 29 years as a vagabond, without much to show for his travels. Early career attempts included studying to become a beautician in Maryland, a stint at the American College in Switzerland, and a couple of years at a drama school in Miami, where he never completed the program.[1]

Later, in New York, as an actor struggling to make ends meet, Stallone cleaned the lion cage at the Central Park Zoo. He also ushered at the Baronet Theater, until he was dismissed by the owner for scalping tickets for a production of *M*A*S*H*.[2] With his acting career at a virtual standstill in the mid-seventies, Stallone turned his hand to screenwriting. Sly earned his first writing credit in 1974 for additional dialogue for *The Lords of Flatbush*, but was still miles from a reputation.

March 24, 1975, would prove to be a pivotal day in the life of Sylvester Stallone.[3] While watching a closed-circuit broadcast of the heavyweight championship match between Muhammad Ali and a courageous underdog named Chuck Wepner, Stallone was struck by "The Bayonne Bleeder's" gallant effort to survive the fifteen-round distance. In Wepner's performance Stallone found inspiration worthy of a film premise. Basic enough to later be described as "pouring old wine into new bottles," but with a universal appeal which ultimately captured ten Academy Award nominations, the tale of Rocky Balboa had unexpectedly begun.[4]

Assisted by his wife Sasha, who would periodically slap herself in the face to remain awake, Stallone worked around the clock to churn out his first draft of *Rocky* in just three and a half days. His agent obtained an initial offer from United Artists (UA) to purchase the screenplay for $75,000, with subsequent negotiations driving the bid up to $245,000.[5]

Stallone, who had $106 in the bank, was in no position to turn down the studio, but did so, in spite of its increasing offers. The major bone of contention was not the price, but Stallone's insistence that he star in the film. The standoff continued, with the deal finally reaching the upper echelon of UA. When the smoke had cleared, the studio was the owner of both a script and its star. The million dollar investment would prove to be one of its soundest.[6]

Rocky is the inspiring story of a Philadelphia club fighter and part-time loan shark enforcer named Rocky Balboa (Stallone). While brutish in his appearance, Rocky has a sensitivity which belies his guttural voice and the hardened surroundings of his South Philadelphia neighborhood. His repressed sensitivity finds a means of expression in a relationship with a painfully shy pet shop worker named Adrian (Shire), the sister of Rocky's friend Paulie (Young), a gruff and inarticulate meat-processing employee. As Rocky draws Adrian into self-awareness, he is presented with his own opportunity for self-fulfillment — a chance to fight the bombastic heavyweight champion of the world, Apollo Creed (Weathers).

The championship match also represents a last chance for an aged trainer Mickey Goodwin (Meredith) to realize his life dream of training a champion. Despite Rocky's cantankerous relationship with Mickey, he recognizes his own tale of woe in the ex-pug, and gives Mickey an opportunity to prepare him for the fight of his life. A prohibitive underdog, Rocky desires only to go the distance with the great champ, to remove the stigma that he is just another "bum from the neighborhood." Although Rocky loses the fight, he embraces his newfound self-worth, and as the ring announcer bellows "and still heavyweight champion of the world, Apollo Creed," Rocky and Adrian confirm their love for one another in celebration of their own personal victories.[7]

While the plot of *Rocky* is generic, the strength of the film lies in its character's development and the depth of their interpersonal relationships. All of the movie's principals possess the capacity for warmth and sensitivity. Engaging and real, they also exhibit their own unique brand of suffering and hope. The script is laced with witty dialogue and memorable images: a sleepy Balboa gulping raw eggs before his pre-dawn run, the fighter pounding slabs of raw meat in a refrigerator, and his triumphant ascension to the top of the steps of the Philadelphia Art Museum.

Perhaps the most memorable scenes of all are also the film's most poignant: Rocky and Adrian's humorous and tender skating date, their awkwardly-sweet yet emotionally charged first kiss, Rocky's gut-wrenching rebuke of Mickey's desperate plea to train him, and Paulie and Adrian's tense and explosive denunciation of their own tortured relationship.

Rocky was the darling of the 1976 Academy Award ceremonies. Nominated for ten Oscars, the film ultimately triumphed as best picture, as did Stallone for best screenplay, and Richard Hasley for best film editor. Other nominees from the film included Burgess Meredith for his role as the sour but sympathetic trainer, and Talia Shire as Rocky's introverted but morally sound girlfriend.[8]

Rocky marked a return to the days of "Capra-corn."* Of the film, Pat Aufderheide of *Cineaste* wrote, "Rocky offers us sweet dreams, and they're confected delightfully. Stallone's proven that old-fashioned themes and gambits are as good as ever."[9] The critic for *Film Heritage* concurred, opining that *Rocky* "revives the old verities about the American Dream and dignity, about the regenerative powers of love and self-respect."[10] *Playboy* credited director Jon Avildsen with adding just the right dose of sentiment, claiming that he "hit on exactly the right chemistry throughout, carefully balancing the toughness and poetry of a story that is full of opportunities to become conventionally or cheaply heartwarming."[11]

Commenting on Stallone's vision of Rocky, John Simon of *New York* magazine wrote that he "has imagined him with intense, bristling love, and plays him with relaxed affection."[12] Robert Asahina of *The New Leader* found, as many others did, that the Academy Award-winning script was "sincerely conceived," and Simon agreed, writing that the dialogue "never sounds out of lowly character yet manages also to be artistic. The words encompass their objectives by their very inarticulateness."[13]

To prepare for his role as the "Italian Stallion," Stallone trained for five months prior to the film's production. His regimen included five-mile runs on the beach, as well as gym workouts.[14] The opening scene of the film is atmospheric and the fighters capture the realistic off-beat tempo so typical of heavyweight club fighters. Training scenes are sprinkled with humor and intensified when desired, as the entire film is, by the driving musical score by Bill Conti.

The film's climactic fight scene was choreographed punch for punch, filling 14 pages of the script, and is still one of Hollywood's best.[15] The action possesses a natural rhythm of fighting, mostly lost in later *Rocky* films, which featured a somewhat artificial increased tempo and punching accuracy. Rocky's cry of "cut me, Mick" between the 14th and 15th rounds has become a part of cinematic lore, as has its speaker, an inarticulate fighter who spoke volumes.

---

*"Capra-corn" is a reference to the style of director Frank Capra reflecting a sentimental tone which some call "corny."

1. Louise Farr, "It Could Be a Contender," *New York Magazine*, October 18, 1976; Judy Klemesrud, "Rocky Isn't Me But We Both Went the Distance," *New York Times*, 28 November 1976; Sylvester Stallone, "Rocky and Me: Sylvester Stallone's Own Story."
2. Klemesrud, "Rocky Isn't Me."
3. Nat Loubet and John Ort, comps., *The 1979 Ring Boxing Encyclopedia and Record Book* (New York: The Ring Book Shop, 1979).
4. Review of *Rocky* (United Artists movie), *Jump Cut*, August 1978, no. 18.
5. Sylvester Stallone, "Rocky and Me: Sylvester Stallone's Own Story."
6. Ibid.
7. *Rocky*, produced by Irwin Winkler, directed by John G. Avildsen, 121 minutes, 1976.
8. Robert Osborne, *50 Years of Oscar: The Official History of the Academy of Motion Picture Arts & Sciences* (La Habra, Calif.: ESE California, 1979).
9. Pat Aufderheide, "Rocky." Review of *Rocky* (United Artists movie), *Cineaste*, 1977, vol. 8, no. 1.
10. "Rocky," Review of *Rocky* (United Artists movie), *Film Heritage*, Spring 1977, vol. 12, no. 3.
11. Review of *Rocky* (United Artists movie), *Playboy*, January 1977.
12. John Simon, "Stallone Ring of Truth," Review of *Rocky* (United Artists movie), *New York Magazine*, 29 November 1976.
13. Robert Asahina, "The Performing Self," Review of *Rocky* (United Artists movie), *The New Leader*, 22 November 1976, 27; Simon, "Stallone Ring of Truth."
14. Klemesrud, "Rocky Isn't Me."
15. Ibid.

Rocky II (1979)

United Artists, Drama, Color, 119 minutes

Producers: Irwin Winkler. Robert Chartoff. *Director*: Sylvester Stallone. *Screenplay*: Sylvester Stallone. *Film Editing*: Stanford C. Allen, Danford B. Green, Janice Hampton, James R. Symons. *Cinematographer*: Bill Butler, *Music*: Bill Conte.

Sylvester Stallone (Rocky Balboa), Talia Shire (Adrian), Burt Young (Paulie), Carl Weathers (Apollo Creed), Burgess Meredith (Mickey), Tony Burton (Apollo's Trainer), Joe Spinell (Gazzo), Leonard Gaines (Agent), Sylvia Meals (Mary Anne Creed), Frank McRae (Meat Foreman), Al Silvani (Cutman), John Pleshette (Director), Stu Nahan (Announcer), Bill Baldwin, Sr. (Commentator), Jerry Ziesmer (Salesman).

A sequel to *Rocky*, a box office giant, was a fiscal natural. For Sylvester Stallone, *Rocky II* was also an opportunity for artistic redemption. In his two films subsequent to *Rocky*, Sly portrayed labor leader Johnny Kovak in *F.I.S.T.*, and wrote, directed and starred in *Paradise Alley*, a tale of three brothers from Hell's Kitchen. Both films were dismal failures and Stallone soon returned to his proven commodity.

A seamless continuation of its predecessor, *Rocky II* begins where *Rocky* concluded, in the ring with Apollo Creed. After the match, both fighters take a trip to the hospital where Creed denigrates Balboa and demands a rematch, though privately he admits to Rocky that he had given him his best. Balboa, however, has other plans and promises Adrian that his ring career is over.

The pair marry, purchase a new home and car, and soon thereafter announce Adrian's pregnancy. Rocky intends to support his new family by making commercials, but his lack of literacy foils the prospect. Uneducated and unskilled, Rocky takes a job at Paulie's meat-processing plant. However, he is soon laid off, forcing Adrian to return to her job at the pet shop.

Fearful that another bout will aggravate Rocky's seriously injured eye, Mickey discourages his ring return. Rocky still feels a compulsion for the fight game and starts to work at Mickey's gym, but carrying a spit bucket and sweeping the ring prove painfully humbling. Creed continues to goad Rocky through the press. Ultimately, a steamed Mickey and prideful Rocky agree to a rematch over Adrian's objections.

Adrian's worry results in Rocky's guilty feelings, and consequently his lackluster training. Work at the pet shop and the stress of the impending fight eventually brings on Adrian's collapse and hospitalization. When Adrian gives birth to a premature but healthy son, she lapses into a coma. Rocky and Mickey stand vigil until Adrian reawakens, at which time she offers her support for the fight.

Rocky then rededicates himself to training. Mickey devises a ploy in which Rocky will fight from a right-handed stance for the majority of the fight to protect his eye and then switch to a lefty stance to surprise Creed. Employing Mickey's strategy, Rocky adopts the southpaw stance in the 15th round to score a climactic come-from-behind knockout to win the championship.

Rocky II possesses the charm of the original, but lacks *Rocky's* emotional clout. Stallone successfully pokes fun at his creation and Rocky's self-deprecating humor helps the film along. However, the domestic challenges of Rocky and Adrian are not nearly as stirring as the personal struggles offered in *Rocky*, nor is the love story as touching. Adrian's coma is potentially more dramatic then any event in the first film, but its delivery falls short of the ambitious material.

Comparisons aside, *Rocky II* was generally well received, but critics disagreed as to the film's level of originality. Jim Robbins of *Box-office* found Burgess Meredith's Mickey "the only expanded characterization in the film," but conceded that "even if 'Rocky II' is mostly a replay, that's what Rocky's fans will be coming to see."[1] However, Susan Sylvers of *Shooting* credited Stallone for developing the characters "into deeper, more meaningful dimensions that everyone can relate to," noting in particular that "Carl Weathers now brings substance to the character of Apollo Creed whose sinewy physique is displayed with accommodating aplomb while carrying a dignified shrewdness."[2]

Production work in the ring was not easy for Stallone. Many of the shots with Carl Weathers were not faked. The pounding Stallone received from the larger man resulted in a number of broken bones as well as a stiff neck caused by Weather's machine-gun like jabs, delivered to Sly's head in 1/24 of a second.[3] Of his ring encounters with Weathers, Stallone bemoaned, "It was the most grueling thing I've ever been through."[4]

To physically prepare for the film, Stallone weight-trained with Frank Columbo. Columbo was the former lightweight boxing champion of Italy, before he embraced the sport of bodybuilding. Unfortunately, the rigors of Columbo's training resulted in an injury to the film's star. If not for the fact that Stallone's muscle tear occurred at a time in the filming when Rocky Balboa switches to punching from a southpaw stance, the picture might have been sidetracked or canceled.[5]

To develop the movie's fight sequences, Stallone studied numerous fight films, including those of Rocky Marciano, Joe Louis, Rocky Graziano, Marcel Cerdan, Muhammad Ali and Sonny Liston.[6] The fight sequences are equal to the action of any of these real-life counterparts, and faster paced than the first film, while still maintaining most of the naturalness exhibited in the original. *Rocky II* marks the beginning of Stallone's direction in the series, and it is at this juncture that his fascination with slow motion begins. Here the technique is used sparingly and effectively.

The film's conclusion, which features Rocky and Apollo simultaneously knocking one another to the canvas, may not at first seem credible. However, the 'double-knockdown' has occurred on several occasions in boxing history, including the Ad Wolgast–Joe Rivers lightweight championship match.* The more far-fetched part of the ring finale

---

*The bout, which was the nation's featured Fourth of July boxing extravaganza of 1912, was held in Vernon, California. Champion Wolgast retained his title by a 13th round knockout in a bout in which objective reporters claim the biased referee assisted Wolgast in rising from his knockdown.

was having Rocky fight from a stance to which he was unaccustomed, a most difficult task indeed.* However, having Rocky wait until the final round to revert to his favored position to steal the fight is even more implausible. Undoubtedly, Stallone was aware that Hollywood fairy tales are allowed improbable conclusions.

1. Jim Robbins, "Rocky II," Review of *Rocky II* (United Artist movie), *Box Office*, 2 July 1979, 21.
2. Susan Sylvers, Review of *Rocky II* (United Artist movie), *Shooting*, July 1979, 72.
3. Red Smith, *New York Times*, 13 June 1979.
4. Roger Ebert, Review of *Rocky II* (United Artists movie), *New York Post*, 21 June 1979.
5. Smith.
6. *Ibid.*

Rocky III (1982)

United Artists, Drama, Color, 99 minutes

Producers: Irwin Winkler, Robert Chartoff. *Director*: Sylvester Stallone. *Screenplay*: Sylvester Stallone. *Film Editing*: Mark Warner, Don Zimmerman. *Cinematography*: Bill Butler. *Music*: Bill Conti.

Sylvester Stallone (Rocky Balboa), Talia Shire (Adrian Balboa), Burt Young (Paulie), Carl Weathers (Apollo Creed), Burgess Meredith (Mickey), Mr. T (Clabber Lang), Tony Burton (Duke), Ian Fried (Rocky Junior), Al Silvani (Al), Wally Taylor (Clabber's Manager), Hulk Hogan (Thunderlips), Jim Hill (Sportscaster), Don Sherman (Andy), Dennis James (Wrestling Commentator), Ray Dedeon (Wrestling Referee).

If United Artists had any reservations about bringing Rocky Balboa to the screen for a third time, they were ultimately quelled. Almost simultaneous with the film's strong box-office opening, the Chicago based rock 'n' roll band Survivor released "Eye of the Tiger," the movie's theme song. Reaching number one on the charts, "Eye of the Tiger" drummed and strummed *Rocky III* into the public consciousness.[1]

Described by Stallone as a "psychodrama," rather than a fight film, *Rocky III* picks up the Balboa story following his championship win over Apollo Creed.[2] After Rocky makes ten defenses of his title over a three-year period, he announces his retirement. However, Clubber Lang, the anti-social, number-one contender, publicly challenges Rocky's manhood, and the "Italian Stallion" is compelled to box him.

Mickey has been protecting Rocky during his title reign by handpicking his opponents to guard his health. He senses that a fight against an opponent of Lang's caliber would be disastrous. To persuade Rocky not to fight, Mickey reveals the truth about Rocky's previous opponents. His plan backfires. Rocky, no longer feeling that his championship is valid, demands to fight Lang to prove his legitimacy.

During the pre-fight histrionics, Mickey suffers a heart attack, and Rocky is forced to face the brooding Lang without Mickey. Having lost his composure, Rocky is quickly knocked out. He then rushes back to the dressing room where Mickey dies in his arms. Balboa is distraught over Mickey's death and the loss of his title. However, his hope is soon renewed by Apollo Creed. Creed, who has a personal grudge against the disrespectful Lang, offers to train Rocky for a rematch. Creed plans to help Balboa recapture his edge by training in Apollo's

---

*As a 4-1 underdog, Sugar Ray Leonard defeated Marvelous Marvin Hagler for the middleweight championship of the world. Southpaw Hagler was unsuccessful in his attempt to confuse Leonard in several of the rounds by boxing from an orthodox position.

old gym in Los Angeles, where the fighters are still hungry, and to teach him a slick new boxing style that will enable him to offset Lang's superior power. Rocky, however, is haunted by his personal demons and has lost faith in himself. He is unable to focus on the fight until Adrian offers the proper perspective and emotional support needed to overcome his fears. Redoubling his efforts, Rocky becomes schooled in Creed's fighting style. Wearing the trunks Apollo wore in their first match, Balboa survives Lang's powerful blows and befuddles his angry opponent with his boxing acumen, regaining the heavyweight championship.

Central to the plot of *Rocky III* was the conversion of Rocky Balboa's fighting style from crude slugger to slick boxer. "I tried to fight like Sugar Ray Leonard," Stallone explained.[3] To enhance the effect of Balboa's new smooth fighting style, Stallone underwent his own physical metamorphosis. From a beefy 210 pounds Stallone pared down to a waif-like 155. He then packed ten pounds of muscle onto his 5 foot 10 inch frame to produce an Atlas-like physique: 47½ inch chest, 29½ inch waist with an inhuman 4½ percent body fat.[4]

To achieve his body beautiful Stallone endured a 10-month training regimen that included a daily workout of two miles of running, two hours of weightlifting, and 18 rounds of sparring. Training was supplemented by a diet of 45 daily vitamins, 10 raw eggs (five more than Rocky Balboa!), whole-grain bread, no sugar and no dinner. Every third day Sly treated himself to a piece of fruit.[5]

Stallone wanted his body streamlined but preferred his fight scenes robust. In the first film, the fighters throw 35 punches in the final round; in the rematch the count increased to 75. *Rocky III* would provide a blitzkrieg of 130 blows in the final canto.[6] The result is fast-paced action which may lack the natural tempo of most real fights, but which makes up for the deficiency in pure excitement. The final round of the second bout is on par with any other boxing match ever filmed for its frenzied pace and climactic effect. Another enhancement technique Stallone relies on throughout the film is the montage, particularly in the training and fight scenes. Individually, these neatly packaged vignettes are effective, but as noted by Tom Milne of *Monthly Film Bulletin*, when viewed collectively, "one begins to feel one is watching a compilation film."[7]

Rocky III marks the introduction of Mr. T. as Clubber Lang, Rocky's central nemesis in the film, and perhaps the most memorable supporting character of the entire series. Stallone originally hired heavyweight contender Earnie Shavers to portray Lang, operating under the assumption that it is easier to teach a boxer to act, then an actor to box. Shavers, while not especially physically imposing, carried one of the hardest right-hand punches in boxing history. After having tasted Shavers's power during one of their sparring sessions, Stallone later commented, "I machoed it out all the way to the men's room before I threw up."[8]

Subsequent to the incident, Shavers was dismissed and Mr. T. a/k/a Lawrence Tero, the former bodyguard of both Muhammad Ali and Leon Spinks, was given the role. Sheila Benson of the *Los Angeles Times* described the new character as "sensational," and "not only larger than life, but larger than Rocky." Ms. Benson also observed that Mr. T. portrayed the mean-spirited Clubber Lang "to the snarling hilt."[9] The added presence of Mr. T., along with wrestling star Hulk Hogan, who faces Rocky in a charity match, pleased the film's large audiences, who for the most part enjoyed the picture. The critics were disappointed, but they could do little to dissuade prospective viewers.

Some critics were brutal in their candor. "*Rocky III*, which Stallone wrote and directed, is the most crudely demagogic of all of the *Rocky* movies," chided David Denby of *New York* magazine.[10] Judith Christ assailed the Balboa character with equal vigor. "He has evolved into a completely one-dimensional cartoon figure, his frame-by-frame progress toward completing the cycle (or so we hope) as tediously predictable as it is blood-spattered."[11]

Still, other reviews found the film praiseworthy. Andrew Sarris of the *Village Voice* expressed his opinion that the film was "richer in irony, satire, and humor" than Stallone's first two efforts, and Joseph Gelmis of *Newsday* credited the film for "maintain [ing] the bumptious humor, sentimentality, [and] simple gratifications" of its predecessors.[12] "While the movie ... will not improve anyone's mental health, it will not kill anyone either," noted Christopher Sharp of *Women's Wear Daily*.[13] Perhaps Robert Asahina of the *New World Leader* summed up most succinctly the appeal of *Rocky III* and its predecessors when he wrote, "For better or worse ... Stallone has created a persona that has taken hold of the popular imagination as firmly as it has his career."[14]

1. Andrew Slater, "Thanks to the Rocky III Hit 'Eye of the Tiger,' This Rock Group Proves It's a Real Survivor," *People*, 30 August, 1982.

2. Harriet Choice, *New York Sunday News*, 9 May 1982.
3. *Ibid*.
4. *The Aquarian Manhattan*, 19–26 May 1982; "Winner and Still Champion," *Time*, 14 June 1982.
5. *Ibid*.
6. "Winner and Still Champion," *Time*, 14 June 1982.
7. Tom Milne, Review of *Rocky III* (United Artists picture), *Monthly Film Bulletin*, August 1982, 174.
8. "Winner and Still Champion," *Time*, 14 June 1982.
9. Sheila Benson, Review of *Rocky III* (United Artists picture), *Los Angeles Times*, 28 May 1982, calendar, p. 1.
10. David Denby, Review of *Rocky III* (United Artists picture), *New Yorker*, 31 May 1982, 80.
11. Judith Crist, Review of *Rocky III* (United Artists picture), *Saturday Review*, June 1982, 64.
12. Andrew Sarris, Review of *Rocky III* (United Artists picture), *Village Voice*, 8 June 1982, 47; Joseph Gelmis, Review of *Rocky III* (United Artists picture), *Newsday*, 28 June 1982, Part II , p. 7.
13. Christopher Sharp, Review of *Rocky III* (United Artists picture), *Women's Wear Daily*, 25 May 1982, 18.
14. Robert Asahina, Review of *Rocky III* (United Artists picture), *New Leader*, 14 June 1982.

Rocky IV (1985)

United Artists, Drama, Color, 91 minutes

Producers: Irwin Winkler, Robert Chartoff. *Director*: Sylvester Stallone. *Screenplay*: Sylvester Stallone. *Film Editors*: Don Zimmerman, John W. Wheeler. *Director of Photography*: Bill Butler. *Music*: Vince Dicola.

Sylvester Stallone (Rocky Balboa), Talia Shire (Adrian), Burt Young (Paulie), Carl Weathers (Apollo Creed), Brigitte Nielsen (Ludmilla), Tony Burton (Duke), Michael Pataki (Nicoli Koloff), Dolph Lundgren (Ivan Drago), R.J. Adams (Sports Announcer), Al Bandiero (American Commentator #2), Dominic Barto (Russian Government Official), Danial Brown (Rocky Jr.'s Friend), James Brown (The Godfather of Soul), Rose Mary Campos (Maid), Jack Carpenter (KGB Driver), Mark De Alessandro (Russian Cornerman), Marty Denkin (Russian Referee), Lou Filippo (Las Vegas Referee), James "Cannonball" Green (Manuel Vega), Dean Hammond (Interviewer), Rocky Krakoff (Rocky Jr.), Sergei Levin (Russian Ring Announcer), Anthony Maffatone (KGB Agent), Sylvia Meals (Mrs. Creed), Dwayne McGee (Limo Driver), Stu Nahan (Commentator #1), Leroy Neiman (Ring Announcer), George Pipaski (Caretaker), George Rogan (Igor Rimsky), Barry Tompkins (American Commentator #1), Warner Wolf (Commentator #2 in Las Vegas).

"I'm calling *Rocky III* the last part of my Rocky trilogy, because that is in fact, what it is. After this, Rocky is no more," Stallone erroneously predicted in 1982.[1] Released in 1985, *Rocky IV* became the highest grossing film for a three-day weekend, earning nearly $20 million.[2] On Friday, December 20, 1985, the movie appeared on a record-breaking 2,232 screens across the U.S. and in Canada.[3] Nearly 10 years after its inception, the Rocky phenomenon was as strong as ever. Rocky clothes, dolls, puzzles, video games and stationery flooded the market, capitalizing on the character's enduring appeal.[4]

Filmed at the MGM Studios, and in Canada, Jackson Hole, Wyoming, and Las Vegas, *Rocky IV* begins with the Soviet Union entering professional boxing.[5] Its heavyweight champion, Ivan Drago, comes to the United States to test his prowess against Western competition. Apollo Creed, who has been in retirement for almost five years, envisions a bout with the Russian as an opportunity to vent his innate combativeness and recapture the spotlight that he dearly misses. Creed also views the Soviets as the enemy and wants to prove the superiority of the United States.

Rocky and Adrian have reservations about the inactive Creed fighting again, and their worst fears are realized when an indifferent Drago mortally wounds Apollo in the ring. Rocky is stunned by the death of his friend and feels guilty for not halting the match as Apollo's second.

Desiring to avenge Apollo's death, Rocky pursues the only means available: his own match against Ivan Drago. A fight is scheduled on Christmas Day in Moscow, and Rocky leaves a disapproving Adrian behind to train in the frozen Russian tundra. His wife unexpectedly arrives later to offer her full support. Despite the Soviet's physical advantages, Rocky's personal fortitude helps him overcome the Russian, knocking him out in the 15th round.

Rocky IV is a metaphor contrasting stereotypical aspects of Eastern and Western societies. Rocky is portrayed as natural and representing rugged American individualism. He trains in the great outdoors, running through snow and streams, up mountains; chopping wood; pulling sleds and dragging stone. Drago is rigid and symbolizes the uniformity of Eastern culture. He trains with the latest mechanical and scientific apparatus, and uses steroids, an unnatural drug. In the end, American ingenuity triumphs over Russian science.

In *Rocky IV,* Stallone unabashedly thrusts Rocky Balboa into the political arena. Not only does the film broadly assault Soviet ideology, but it attempts to portray the Soviet Premier himself, through a shameful impersonation of Mikhail Gorbachev. At the film's conclusion, Rocky grabs the microphone and speaks to the Russian crowd. "I guess two guys killing each other is better than twenty million," Rocky tells the crowd through a translator.[6] The audience, initially hostile, now implausibly cheers the American.

The film's expected Cold War backlash ensued. A group of Soviet cultural officials denounced American films in general and *Rocky IV* and Stallone's companion political piece, "*Rambo First Blood II*," in particular. The secretary of the Soviet Writers Union, Genrikh Borovik, assailed Hollywood for "using art to sell hatred and fear," to create in the words of his comrade George A. Ivanov, a deputy minister of culture, "a new type of hero, a killer with ideological convictions." Another prominent Soviet called Stallone films a "deliberate propaganda campaign to portray Russians as cruel and treacherous enemies." Despite these and other verbal retaliations, the Stallone films continued to do brisk business on the Soviet black market.[7]

Continuing the infusion of new characters into the series, Stallone introduces Rocky's latest nemesis, Ivan Drago, the human incarnation of "the evil empire." Gene Siskel described the character as "a winner," noting the believability of Drago as "a machine-tooled, steroid-injected fighting machine of major proportion."[8] Portraying Rocky's robot-like opponent was 26-year-old Dolph Lundgren, a European kickboxing champion and the son of an economist for the Swedish Parliament. In the role of Drago's wife, Ludmilla, Stallone cast his real-life girlfriend, the luscious model Brigitte Nielsen.

Lundgren's appeal notwithstanding, the film failed to receive favorable notices. If a faction of film critics appeared mutinous against Captain Sly over *Rocky III*, their disdain of *Rocky IV* constituted a full-blown critical insurrection. Christopher Sharp of *Women's Wear Daily* found the film to be "the silliest movie Stallone has yet made, or that anyone has ever made."[9] David Edelstein of the *Village Voice* wrote, "*Rocky IV* is the filmmaking equivalent to painting by numbers; it makes the Bond movies look like a series of loose improvisations."[10]

The Creed-Drago fight was filmed on stage at the MGM Grand Hotel in Las Vegas, while Rocky's bout against the Russian was shot in Vancouver, Canada, in front of 10,000 people.[11] The fight sequences are similar in tempo to those in *Rocky III*, with the "Rock'em-Sock'em Robot" effect taken to new heights. Director Stallone also employs the split-screen and uses superimposing to enhance the Rocky-Drago bout. In actuality, the first punch delivered by Lundgren in the final fight is real. Stallone's diaphragm was pushed up into his heart, he was forced into the hospital, and the film's production was halted for two weeks.[12]

Stallone's skill to manipulate the public could not be denied. As observed by Richard Schickel of *Time*, the *Rocky* movies "are now rituals, Low Masses celebrating what their star-creator assumes to be, on the basis of his past successes, the values of the least common denominator ... Any audience could chant the lines along with the archetypal figures on the screen, as if it were participating in a responsive reading."[13] Rex Reed, writing for the *New York Post*, may have best summed up Rocky's enduring ability to go the distance with his audiences when he wrote, "For a legion of Rocky fans who grew up with the big lug, it's now quite pleasant to grow old with him, too."[14]

1. Peter Stack, *San Francisco Chronicle*, 26 May 1982.
2. *Variety*, 11 December 1985.
3. *Variety*, 25 December 1985.
4. Janet Maslin, *New York Times*, 8 November 1985.
5. Bob Fisher, "Rocky IV a Photographic Dazzler," *American Cinematographer*, February 1986.
6. *Rocky IV*, produced by Irwin Winkler, directed by Sylvester Stallone, 91 minutes, 1985.
7. Philip Taubman, "Soviet Pans 'Rocky' and 'Rambo Films," *New York Times*, 4 January 1986.
8. Gene Siskel, "Rocky IV Produces a Villain You'll Love to Hate." Review of *Rocky IV* (United Artists movie), *Chicago Tribune*, 27 November 1985.
9. Christopher Sharp, Review of *Rocky IV* (United Artists movie), *Women's Wear Daily* 27 November 1985, 13.
10. David Edelstein, Review of *Rocky IV* (United Artists movie), *Village Voice*, 10 December 1985, 67.
11. Gene Siskel, "'Rocky' sequel full of family, feisty fists," *Chicago Tribune*, quoted in *Fort Wayne Sentinel*, 28 November 1985.
12. *Ibid*.
13. Richard Schickel, Review of *Rocky IV* (United Artists movie), *Time*, 9 December 1985.
14. Rex Reed, Review of *Rocky IV* (United Artists movie), *New York Post*, 27 November 1985, 38.

Rocky V (1990)

United Artists, Drama, Color, 104 minutes

Producers: Irwin Winkler, Robert Chartoff. *Director*: John G. Avildsen. *Screenplay*: Sylvester Stallone. *Film Editors*: John G. Avildsen, Michael N. Knue. *Photography*: Steve Livingston. *Music*: Bill Conti.

Sylvester Stallone (Rocky Balboa), Talia Shire (Adrian), Burt Young (Paulie), Sage Stallone (Rocky

Jr.), Burgess Meredith (Mickey), Tommy Morrison (Tommy), Richard Gant (George W. Duke), Tony Burton (Tony), James Gambina (Jimmy), Delia Sheppard (Karen), Michael Sheehan (Merlin Sheets), Michael Williams (Union Cane), Kevin Connolly (Chickie), Elisabeth Peters (Jewel), Hayes Swope (Chickie's Pal), Nicky Blair (Fight Promoter), Jodi Letizia (Marie), Chris Avildsen (Druggy), Jonathan Avildsen (Druggy), Don Sherman (Andy), Stu Nahan (Fight Commentator), Al Bernstein (Fight Commentator), James Binns (Himself), Meade Martin (Las Vegas Announcer), Michael Buffer (Fight Announcer, 3rd fight), Albert J. Myles (Benson), Jane Maria Robbins (Gloria), Ben Geraci (Cab Driver), Clifford C. Coleman (Motorcycle Mechanic), Lou Filippo (Referee), Frank Cappuccino (Referee), Lauren K. Woods (Conference Reporter), Robert Seltzer (Conference Reporter), Albert S. Meltzer (Conference Reporter), John P. Clark (Conference Reporter), Stanley R. Hochman (Conference Reporter), Elmer Smith (Conference Reporter), Henry D. Tillman (Contender #), Stan Ward (Contender #2), Brian Phelps (Reporter), Mark Thompson (Reporter), Paul Cain (Reporter), Kent H. Johnson (Reporter), Cindy Roberts (Reporter), Patricia Cronin (Dr. Rimlan), Helena Carroll (Drinker), Tony Munafo (Drinker), Bob Vazquez (Drinker), Richard "Dub" Wright (Drinker), Susan Persily (Drinker), Lloyd Kaufman (Drinker), Gary Compton (Drinker), John J. Cahill (Drinker), Leroy Neiman (Fight Announcer), Michael Pataki (Nicolo Koloff), Jennifer Flavin (Delivery Girl), Tricia Flavin (Delivery Girl), Julie Flavin (Delivery Girl), Bob Giovane (Timmy), Carol A. Ready (Russian Woman), Katharine Margiotta (Woman in Dressing Room).

Rocky V was Sylvester Stallone's final effort to wring the public's emotional towel for sympathy and money. One of the film's characters, the bombastic fight promoter George W. Duke, ironically states what Stallone may have been thinking when he wrote the final installment. "Sell it while there are still buyers."[1]

Indeed, much had transpired in the five years since the release of the popular though critically besieged *Rocky IV*. Most notably, the Reagan era had ended, and the Soviet Union was dismantled. The theme of a Superpower standoff in *Rocky IV* had already become passé, and perhaps symbolically so.

Having already exhausted the domestic villains and international demagogues within (and plausibly beyond) his creation's orbit, Stallone decided to spill his remaining conviction in the main character. He would complete Rocky Balboa's life cycle by returning him to his roots. Originally, Stallone had scripted the final chapter of the film series to result in Balboa's death. After taking a beating in a Philadelphia street fight, Rocky, already weakened from his many ring contests, would die in his beloved Adrian's arms. While United Artists' management may not have been indoctrinated — at least as much of the public was — to sincerely believe in Balboas invincibility, they did have their own instincts for guarding a film's bottom line. They successfully convinced Stallone to let his hero live on in perpetuity.[2]

In the final and filmed version of *Rocky V*, the "Italian Stallion" returns home from his victory over Ivan Drago to enjoy the fruits of his labor. However, in Rocky's absence, Paulie had mistakenly provided Rocky's accountant with an unfettered power of attorney. The power is abused to facilitate the investment of Rocky's fortune in an unsuccessful real-estate transaction, driving the Balboas into bankruptcy.

Promoter George W. Duke desires that Rocky fight contender Union Caine, but Rocky's doctors discover that he has sustained irreversible brain damage and he is not permitted a license. The Balboas auction off their remaining possessions and return to South Philadelphia, with Rocky reopening Mickey's gym, his sole remaining possession. Rocky begins to manage a hungry boxer named Tommy Gunn, who becomes his successful protégé, while Duke continues to hound Rocky to come out of retirement.

Domestically, the Balboas are making a difficult transition to their new lifestyle. Rocky has become preoccupied with Tommy Gunn, whom he vicariously lives through. This causes a rift between Rocky and Rocky, Jr., who resents the intrusion and the fact that he has lost his father's support during this critical time.

Although Tommy Gunn is successful

under Rocky's tutelage, he gains the emasculating reputation of being Rocky's puppet. Understanding that Gunn desires greater independence, Duke coaxes him away from Rocky by promising him a shot at the title, now held by Caine. Duke's ulterior motive is to have Gunn win the title and then draw Rocky out of retirement by playing on his emotions. After Gunn defeats Caine, he delivers the final blow to his mentor by thanking Duke rather than Rocky for his success.

Duke then stirs Gunn's feeling of resentment toward his teacher, leading Gunn to publicly harass Rocky in a local neighborhood bar before rolling news cameras. Rocky refuses to entertain Gunn's challenge in the ring. However, when his pupil knocks Paulie to the bar floor, Rocky tells Gunn to step outside, where he gives him a lesson in street fighting, with the locals cheering on Balboa one final time.

Rocky V marked the return of the original director of the series, John Avildsen, and the critics applauded his return. Comparing Stallone's directorial work in the middle of the series with Avildsen's bookend efforts, Edmond Grant of *Films in Review* wrote, "The ever-so-brief ring scenes here have the nicely composed quality and raw power that could never have been captured with Stallone's heavy hands at the editing table."[3] Matthew Flamm of the *New York Post* wrote that *Rocky V*, which was "directed by the director of the original *Rocky*, John Avildsen, does not disappoint," finding the film "the sweetest and the liveliest" since the original.[4]

Whereas *Rocky IV* was overt in its political and social overtones, critics found *Rocky V* to possess a subliminal domestic message. Hoberman of the *Village Voice* found that the film offered "a startling downbeat allegory of the Reagan era. Rocky wins the Cold War only to come home and discover that he's been bankrupted by the S & L scandal."[5] Michael Wilmington of *The Los Angeles Times* observed, "*Rocky V* signals what may be a shift in American self-perception. No longer bellicose or swaggering, the movie suggests the mood all around us."[6]

To portray Balboa's protégé, Stallone selected a heavyweight boxer named Tommy Morrison. The reputed, and sometimes disputed, great grand-nephew of John Wayne had started in "tough man" contests at the age of 13, fighting all the way to the Olympic trials as an amateur. The Oklahoma native was a promising prospect with a record of 23-0 at the time of the film's release and would, several years later, capture the WBO heavyweight championship in a bout against George Foreman.[7]

In the true tradition of the *Rocky* series, Morrison broke one stuntman's jaw and fractured his replacement's eye socket during the filming of a fight scene. Predictable litigation followed.[8] To add further realism, Stallone worked Morrison's corner in one of his pro fights, and then incorporated that footage into the picture. The fight's sequences are primarily video-like montages in which Morrison appears as the professional that he is.

The character of Tommy Gunn, however, lacked the charm of a Creed, the menace of a Clubber Lang, or the chill of an Ivan Drago. Morrison "wrestles unsuccessfully with the role of Tommy Gunn, a poorly developed character that would defeat even the most seasoned of actors," wrote critic Philip Wuntch of *The Dallas Morning News*.[9] The more engaging, though uncreative addition to *Rocky V* was George W. Duke portrayed by Richard Gant. Duke was a virtual clone of promotional impresario Don King. "The hustler here is a Don King caricature, and since that makes the role a caricature of a caricature, Richard Gant can't very well be faulted for overacting," noted Terry Kelleher of *Newsday*.[10]

Stallone goes to great lengths to recapture some of the magic of his original story in this, its closing chapter. Rocky returns to the mean streets of Philadelphia, where Andy's bar, Mickey's gym, Adrian's pet shop and the steps of the Philly Art Museum are all revisited. Rocky's trademark black hat, coat, leather gloves and black rubber ball are resurrected, as is Mickey, who appears in one of Rocky's smoke-hued recollections. To a limited degree the film does succeed in mimicking *Rocky*'s effective depiction of human relationships, but as noted by Thomas Wolfe, "You can't go home."

1. *Rocky V*, produced by Irwin Winkler and Robert Chantoff, directed by John G. Avildsen, 144 minutes, 1990.
2. Gene Siskel, "Rocky RIP," *Chicago Tribune*, 2 December 1990.
3. Edmond Grant, Review of *Rocky V* (United Artists movie), *Films in Review*, March-April 1991, 118.
4. Matthew Flamm, Review of *Rocky V* (United Artists movie), *New York Post*, 16 November 1990, 47.
5. J. Hoberman, Review of *Rocky V* (United Artists movie), *Village Voice*, 27 November 1990, 105.
6. Michael Wilmington, Review of *Rocky V* (United Artists movie), *Los Angeles Times*, 16 November 1990, calendar, p.1.
7. United Artists Program for *Rocky V*.
8. Richard Johnson, *New York Post*, 26 April 1990.
9. Philip Wuntch, Review of *Rocky V* (United Artists movie), *The Dallas Morning News*, 16 November 1990.
10. Terry Kelleher, Review of *Rocky V* (United Artists movie), *Newsday*, 16 November 1990, Part II, p.13.

Rocky Marciano (1999)

Metro-Goldwyn Mayer, Drama, Color, 99 minutes.

Producer: Rob Cowan. *Director*: Charles Winkler. *Screenplay:* Larry Golin, Charles Winkler, Dick Beebe. *Editor*: Clayton Halsey. *Director of Photography*: Paul Sarossy, C.S.C. *Music*: Stanley Clarke.

Jon Favreau (Rocky Marciano), Penelope Ann Miller (Barbara Cousins — Rocky's wife), Judd Hirsch (Al Weil), Tony Lobianco (Frankie Carbo), Duane Davis (Joe Louis), Rhoda Gemignani (Pasquelina Marchegiano), Rino Romano (Allie Columbo), George C. Scott (Pierino), Aron Tanger (Charlie Goldman), Noah Danby (Vingo), Gil Filar (Young Rocky), Jerome Silvano (Young Allie).

Boxing greats, perhaps more than their counterparts in other sports, are confronted by their greatest foe *after* retirement: historical comparison. Every boxing great who once laced on a pair of gloves is stripped of the promise of temporary toil, and forced center stage to swap punches with present champions and ghosts of boxing past. Former heavyweight champion Rocky Marciano has been no exception.

Undoubtedly, you can still find a few pot-bellied *pisans* who expound the greatness of "the Rock," boasting of his feats against Charles and Walcott across a checkered tablecloth spread with antipasto and wine. However, by and large, Marciano has been downgraded like a speculative stone that has met the master jeweler's eyepiece; a used auto relegated to the back lot, as favor courts this year's model.

Even though Marciano's relative position in the pantheon of great heavyweights has been under ever increasing scrutiny, his status as an iconoclastic hero of the 1950s and his place in American social history are secure. A clear illustration of this fact is that the United States post office recently issued a commemorative postage stamp in Marciano's honor. The stamp was released in the same month as a television bio-pic, *Rocky Marciano*, which also pays homage to the boxer.[1] Under these circumstances, it is a more acute disappointment that *Rocky Marciano* fails to convey to the public Rocky's historical reputation as a great fighter.

Rocky Marciano attempts to recreate the boxing career of the undefeated heavyweight champion from Brockton, Massachusetts, from his childhood to his tragic death in a plane crash in Des Moines, Iowa, on August 31, 1969. The picture focuses on several prominent but stereotypical themes of the Marciano legend, including his immigrant roots, his desire to escape the shoe factories of his hometown, his fear of poverty, and his contentious relationship with his manager Al Weil.

While the portrayal of Marciano as parsimonious is tiresome, and his greatness as a fighter is never really established, the most severe impediment to enjoyment for the fan is the film's numerous and often reckless factual blunders. As noted by boxing writer Jon Saraceno, "Factual errors pop up like ugly welts on a beaten fighter."[2] Case in point, at the end of the match against fellow contender Carmine Vingo, Marciano is absurdly depicted carrying an injured Vingo while still in his fighting trunks. In truth, Marciano was in his dressing room when he learned that Vingo was taken to the hospital after six brutal rounds at Madison Square Garden.[3] Rocky arrived at the hospital shortly thereafter, and held vigil, while Vingo underwent brain surgery. This was a more than sufficient dramatic moment to show Marciano's empathy and, appropriately, it was used in the film. However, there was no reason for altering sports history by adding the ludicrous stretcher scene.

This scene is the tip of the iceberg. When he knocked out his boyhood idol Joe Louis in eight rounds, Marciano was genuinely saddened to end Louis's career. However, Marciano's initial refusal to take the fight, as depicted in the film, is unsubstantiated. Further, it is true that Rocky maintained a great affection for the former heavyweight champion, but the scene in which Marciano visits Louis in a mental hospital later in life, and delivers a bag of cash to improve his care, is a complete fabrication. Louis was committed to a Denver hospital in May 1970, many months after Rocky had died.[4]

Another error occurs in the Louis bout when Joe refers to his corner man as "Chappie," the nickname of his earlier trainer Jack Blackburn, who had died several years before the Marciano match. Even the hair of these fighters is inaccurate. Somehow, Louis no longer has a bald spot in the Marciano fight, while Rocky, who was very sensitive about his baldness, and wore a toupee later in life, is without it in several scenes.

The film was originally a Columbia Pictures project, but it was acquired by MGM, which produced it for Showtime. Rocky's son, Rocky, Jr., reported that the Marciano family was not consulted by either studio on the project. Further, both MGM and Showtime Entertainment failed to ask boxing officials at Showtime to check the accuracy of the script. The Marciano family was not pleased with the completed project. "Just about every scene was fictionalized or the chronology was wrong," explained Rocky, Jr. Not unexpectedly, after seeing an advance copy of the film, Marciano's brother Lou refused to help promote the picture. The family was also perturbed at the portrayal of Rocky as a dupe for crime figure Frankie Carbo. "The Italian mob was proud of Rocky," noted Michele Gilbert, a Marciano estate representative, "Carbo was told to lay off Rocky."[5]

Ample time is dedicated to fight vignettes in the picture. Jon Favreau is a bit too pumped up to portray Marciano who typically weighed 180-185 pounds. While he is unable to master the unusual low-crouching style that Marciano exploded from to annihilate his opponents, flashes of Marciano are evident in the recreation of the Louis fight. The actor does capture something of Marciano's true grit. As noted by Graham Houston, writing for *Boxing Monthly*, "To be fair, actor Favreau does attempt in jaw-clenching manner, to communicate the intense determination that Marciano brought to the ring."[6]

Judd Hirsch, as manager Al Weil, Tony

Lo Bianco as Frankie Carbo, and George C. Scott as Rocky's father, give sturdy performances, serving as strong braces for a picture otherwise constructed with some missing floorboards and very creaky timber.

1. Graham Houston, "A Rocky Horror?" *Boxing Monthly*, June 1999, 32.
2. Jon Saraceno, *USA Today*, quoted in Charlie Huisking, *Sarasota Herald-Tribune*, 28 May 1999.
3. Houston, "A Rocky Horror?" 35.
4. Richard Sandomir, "A Marciano Docudrama Gets Much of It Wrong," *New York Times*, 30 April 1999, sec D, p.5.
5. *Ibid*.
6. Houston, "A Rocky Horror?" 35.

The Set-Up (1949)

RKO Pictures, Drama, B & W, 72 minutes

Producer: Richard Goldstone. *Director*: Robert Wise. *Screenplay*: Art Cohn, based on a poem by Joseph Moncure March. *Film Editor*: Ronald Gross. *Cinematography*: Milton R. Krasner.

Robert Ryan (Stoker), Audrey Totter (Julie), George Tobias (Tiny), Alan Baxter (Little Boy), James Edwards (Luther Hawkins), Wallace Ford (Gus), Percy Helton (Red), Hal Fieberling (Tiger Nelson), Darryl Hickman (Shanley), Kenny O'Morrison (Moore), David Clarke (Gunboat Johnson), Phillip Pine (Souza), Edwin Max (Danny).

On the heels of William Holden's strong showing in Columbia's *Golden Boy*, Paramount Studios geared up for the production of a modest fight picture entitled *Golden Gloves*. Holden was the dual property of Columbia and Paramount and the latter considered capitalizing on the newcomer as a prizefighter as well. Although Paramount ultimately cast William Denny in the film's lead, the studio nevertheless used *Golden Gloves* to develop its own boxing film property by the name of Robert Ryan.[1]

Ryan, who was discovered by Paramount scouts while studying at Max Reinhardt's Hollywood Dramatic School, was a graduate of the prestigious Dartmouth College. A fine collegiate amateur boxer, he was also the heavyweight champion of Dartmouth for four consecutive years.[2]

In contrast to the handsome Ryan, *Golden Gloves* director Edward Dmytryk deliberately cast a score of extras with pug noses, cauliflower ears and ill-fitting clothes. The director also utilized a number of ex-boxers including Joe Glick, Baby Joe Gans, Abie Bain, and three ex-fighters who later became Los Angeles Golden Gloves referees: Frankie Van, Tommy Herman and Charlie Randolph.[3]

Despite a pugnacious cast, *Golden Gloves* was a critical failure. While Ryan would later nostalgically reflect upon the picture as a "good little B," Hobe of *Variety* objectively assessed the film at the time of its release as a "tawdry little yarn," possessing "some of the most hackneyed dialogue of the season," featuring a number of subplots which appeared to "have been written with stencils."[4]

In spite of the weak reception of the film and the fact that Ryan had only one speaking line in the picture, his performance was strong enough to win him a long-term movie contract with Paramount.[5] Following his film debut in *Golden Gloves*, Ryan would solidify his name as a respected actor during the '40s. He appeared in such films as *Crossfire*, for which he was Oscar-nominated, and concluded the decade playing the lead in *The Set-Up*, now considered a boxing film classic.

The Set-Up, boxing's signature contribution to poetry, was written by Joseph Moncure March, a former college boxer. March drew inspiration for his story from a painting by his friend artist James Chaplin. The work depicts a black boxer sitting in his corner surrounded by his handlers.[6] First published in 1928, March's 184-page narrative poem is rooted in ethnic and racial stereotypes.

The Set-Up relates the woeful tale of a black fighter named Panzy Jones. As penned by March, "Panzy had the stuff, but his skin was brown; and he never got a chance at the middleweight crown."[7] Manipulated by MacPhail and Cohn, "ring lice" masquerading as managers, Panzy is offered as the "set-up" in a match against Sailor Gray.[8]

MacPhail and Cohn allow Panzy to win the bout, double-crossing Gray's manager, Morelli, in the process. Morelli mistakenly believes Panzy is part of the betrayal and seeks retribution. "Panzy, you better look out fer dat wop," Cohn warns. "A wop fights dirty; I know dat breed." Pursued by Morelli and Gray, Panzy ultimately falls from a platform and is struck by an oncoming train.[9]

In fashioning the movie version of *The Set-Up* (which is inspired by the poem although not faithfully based upon it), screenwriter Art Cohn* neutered March's version by stripping away its ethnic diversity and accompanying stereotypes. However, by leaving the concept of the "set-up" intact and drawing equally unsavory characters, Cohn provided himself with a skeleton upon which to construct his screenplay.

Robert Wise, previously nominated for an Oscar for his editing work on *Citizen Kane*, had migrated to directing, but was still primarily handling "B" pictures. He was assigned by Dore Schary, head of RKO's production, to direct Cohn's screenplay. However, after only two weeks' work, Howard Hughes, Hollywood's wealthiest player, took over the studio and dismissed Schary, placing the project's future in jeopardy. Fortunately, Sid Rogell, RKO's new head of production, had the foresight to persuade Hughes to allow the film to proceed.[10]

In *The Set-Up*, Stoker Thompson (Ryan) is a twenty-year boxing veteran who has been reduced to fighting in preliminary bouts in tank towns. His chances for the big-time have all but ebbed, yet his dreams of boxing success remain vivid. Aware of Stoker's decline, his manager Tiny (Tobias) offers his fighter as a set-up in a match against "Tiger" Nelson. A gangster known as "Littleboy" (Baxter) financially backs Nelson upon Tiny's assurances of victory. Confident that Stoker will assuredly lose, Tiny forgoes advising his fighter of the scam. Stoker, fixated upon victory, boxes better than expected, forcing Tiny to reveal the fix midway through the contest. Despite possible recriminations from "Littleboy," Stoker proceeds to win the match. Trapping Stoker in an alley after the fight, Littleboy's henchmen break his hand, ending his career. Though Stoker is physically violated, his pride and self-respect remain intact.

The Set-Up is told in real time, a difficult approach which proves successful due to Wise's craftsmanship in the rapid development of engaging characters. Gilb of *Variety* found *The Set-Up* "compact and suspenseful," while T.M.P. of *The New York Times* called the film a "sizzling melodrama."[11] *The New York Times* credited Robert Wise's "shrewd directing" and Art Cohn's "understanding, colloquial dialogue" for bringing "to vivid, throbbing life, ... the great expectations and shattered hopes" of the film's prizefighters.[12]

Wise and Cohn develop their boxers in the locker room — the modern-day equivalent of a gladiator holding pen — where a fighter dreams and rationalizes as his pre-fight confidences and fears manifest themselves. Off-screen, the fighter's expectations

---

*Art Cohn also scripted two other boxing films. *Glory Alley* (1952) starred Ralph Meeker as prizefighter Socks Barbarrosa, who is determined to prove his worth to the father of the woman he loves. The film also featured Leslie Caron and Louis Armstrong. Critics panned the picture, including Bosley Crowther of *The New York Times*, who wrote in his review of July 30, 1952: "Every now and then, Louis Armstrong sticks his broad, beaming face into the frame and sings or blasts a bit of his trumpet. That makes the only sense in the whole film."

are quickly realized or dispelled in the ring. The audience then views the returning participant in the locker room, where his exultation or heartbreak is openly paraded in front of the other boxers awaiting battle. They offer congratulations or pity, understanding that they will soon box and return to evoke a similarly pointed reaction from their rank and file.

Variety praised Wise for his "skillful direction." Wise, with the assistance of cameraman Milton Krasner, exploited the characters of the fight crowd to add a "lustre of realism" to the film.[13] Boxing fans are depicted by Wise and Krasner as craving violence as a form of entertainment. Their blood lust for ring mayhem is a complementary indulgence to the food, beer, cigars and bets they voraciously consume while watching the matches. For one attendee, the fighter's blood and sweat alone cannot quench his desires, so he derives further satisfaction through a baseball game on his portable radio. Still, for many fans, they need only vicariously feed off the brutality, which they do with a disturbing singularness. Even a blind fan achieves emotional satisfaction through a friend's graphic description of the carnage which unfolds before his sightless eyes. "Close the other eye," the fan ironically demands as he works himself into a frenzy.[14] As noted by the critic for *Cue* magazine, "No film in years has so effectively stripped the phony cloak of glamour from the prizefight racket, and shown it for the brutal, body-and-brain-busting business it is, as this taut and thrilling ringside drama."[15]

The Set-Up was principally filmed at the studio's back lots in Culver City known as the RKO Pathe, a 40-acre stretch that was replaced by an industrial complex after RKO's unfortunate demise. A ring was built at the studio, and all of the fight scenes were shot at that location. The tension-filled scene in which Ryan traverses the empty arena after his bout was shot in the interior of the Ocean Parkway Arena in Brooklyn.[16]

The Set-Up features one significant fight scene near the film's end. The lengthy boxing vignette is expertly choreographed. Realism is achieved through attention to detail and the careful reproduction and placement of natural occurrences that come to the fore during a boxing match. On occasion the boxers are found talking to one another during the nicely spaced clinches that give the fight its realistic tempo. A backhand, a low blow, a punch after the bell and a dose of heeling are buried within professionally stylized punching exchanges. The pace and ferocity of the bout is nicely offset by the parallel action in the fight crowd which adopts a similar tempo.

Ryan appears in the ring in superb physical condition, expertly bends at the waist and displays other technical skills that he learned during his amateur career. Otis L. Guernsey, Jr. wrote, "Robert Ryan's fighter is very nearly a flesh-and-blood characterization of pathetic courage."[17] *Cue* magazine also found Ryan's portrayal "excellent," and *Variety* credited Ryan with "carrying off top honors in a moving portrayal."[18] Co-star Audrey Totter, who portrayed Ryan's wife, was also complimented for her performance, with *Variety* adding that "Miss Totter is equally effective as the sympathetic wife."[19]*

While *The Set-Up* did not make money for Hughes, it helped Wise's career greatly, paving the way for the editor turned director, who would later display unmatched directorial range by making boxing films such as *Somebody Up There Likes Me* and classic musicals with the same ease. For his work on

---

Several years later, Totter would appear as the female lead in another boxing film for Republic Pictures entitled Champ for a Day. Champ for a Day, *which was released by Republic Pictures in 1953, combined the fight angle with a mystery story. Directed by William Seiter and starring Alex Nichol as a boxer named George Wilson, the film also features Henry Morgan, Charles Winninger and Grant Withers. The picture was based upon a* Saturday Evening Post *story entitled "The Disappearance of Dolan," by William Fay. Irving Schulman adapted the story for the screen. Also the author of* Amboy Dukes, *Schulman wrote a boxing novel entitled* The Square Trap, *which was published the same year of the film's release.*

both *West Side Story* and *The Sound of Music*, Wise earned Academy Awards for best director.[20] For Robert Ryan, *The Set-Up* would prove to be one of his most memorable roles, and also his favorite. A still photograph from the film hung for many years in the actor's living room next to another of his prized possessions, an autographed picture of presidential candidate Adlai Stevenson.[21]

1. Studio Publicity for *Golden Gloves*.
2. Jeanne Stein, "Robert Ryan Unlike Most Handsome Actors, He Was Willing to Be a Heavyweight," *Films in Review*, January 1968.
3. Studio Publicity for *Golden Gloves*.
4. Stein, "Robert Ryan Unlike Most Handsome Actors;" Hobe, Review of *Golden Gloves* (Paramount Pictures Movie), *Variety*, 28 August 1940.
5. Stein, "Robert Ryan Unlike Most Handsome Actors."
6. John V. Gromach, *The Saga of the Fist* (Cranbury, N.J: A.S. Barnes and Company, 1997), 136.
7. Joseph Moncure March, *The Set-Up* (New York: Stratford Press, 1928), 3.
8. Ibid., 16.
9. Ibid., 166, 183.
10. Samuel Stark, "Robert Wise Began as a Cutter and Has Retained a Cutter's Cunning," *Films in Review*, January 1963, vol. 14, no. 1.
11. Gilb, Review of *The Set-Up* (RKO Pictures movie), *Variety*, 23 March 1949; T.M.P. Review of *The Set-Up* (RKO Pictures movie), *New York Times*, 30 March 1949.
12. T.M.P. Review of *The Set-Up*.
13. Gilb.
14. *The Set-Up*, produced by Richard Goldstone, directed by Robert Wise, 72 minutes, 1949.
15. Review of *The Set-Up* (RKO Pictures movie), *Cue*, 2 April 1949.
16. *American Cinematographer*, March 1980.
17. Otis Guernsey Jr., Review of *The Set-Up* (RKO Pictures movie), *New York Herald-Tribune*, 30 March 1949.
18. Review of *The Set-Up* (RKO Pictures movie), *Cue*, 2 April 1949; Gilb.
19. Gilb, Review of *The Set-Up* (RKO Pictures movie), *Variety*, 23 March 1949.
20. Stark, "Robert Wise Began as a Cutter."
21. Stein, "Robert Ryan Unlike Most Handsome Actors."

Snake Eyes (1998)

Paramount Pictures, Drama, Color, 98 minutes

Producer: Brian De Palma. *Director*: Brian De Palma. *Screenplay*: Brian De Palma, David Koepp. *Film Editor*: Bill Pankow. *Cinematography*: Stephen H. Burum. *Music*: Ryuichi Sakamoto.

Nicolas Cage (Rick Santoro), Gary Sinise (Commander Kevin Dunne), John Heard (Gilbert Powell), Carla Gugino (Julia Costello), Stan Shaw (Lincoln Tyler), Kevin Dunn (Lou Logan), Michael Rispoli (Jimmy George), Joel Fabiani (Charles Kirkland), Luis Guzman (Cyrus), David Anthony Higgins (Ned Campbell), Mike Starr (Walt McGahn), Tamara Tunie (Anthea), Chip Zien (Mickey Alter), Michaella Bassey (Tyler's Party Girl #2), Paul Joseph Bernardo (Casino Security #1), Jernard Burks (Tyler's Bodyguard), Mark Camacho (C.J.), Desmond Campbell (Arena Security), Jean-Paul Chartrand (Ring Announcer), Chip Chuipka (Zietz — Drunk), Deano Clavet (Arena Security), Tara Ann Culp (Lady at Elevator), Kelly Deadmon (Blonde Reporter), Frederick De Grandpre (College Boy #1), Adam C. Flores (Jose Pacifico Ruiz), George Fourniotis (Blue Shirt #3), Kristina Fulton (Round Girl), Kenneth Glegg (Referee), Sebastien Delorme (College Boy #4 as Sebastien Delorme), Alain Goulem (PPV Director), Dean Hagopian (Latecomer), Jayne Heitmeyer (Serena), Eric Hoziel (Rabat—Assassin), Byron Johnson (College Boy #2), Guy Kelada (Blue Shirt), Sylvain Landry (Remote Producer), Carl Lawrence (Powell's Aide), Robert Norman Lemieux (FBI Agent), Richard Lemire (Agent #2), Christopher B. McCabe (Couple #2, as Christopher McCabe), Sylvain Masse (Cop #1), William J. Mckeon III (Anthea's Cameraman), Patrick McDade (Lawyer, as Patrick F. McDade), Peter McRobbie (Gordon Pritzker), Christian Napoli (Michael Santoro), Lance E. Nichols (Cop #3), Jason Nuzzo (Coin Cup Grabber), Patrick Parent (Detective), Peter Patrikios (Coin Cup Decoy), Jacynthe Rene (Couple #1), Stephen Spreekmeester (College

Boy #3), Eva Tep (Tyler's Party Girl #1), John Thaddeus (Cop #2), Jim Whelan (Mayor — as James Whelan), Brian Anthony (Casino Security #2 — as Brian A. Wilson), Richard Zeman (Agent #1), Gerard Max Desilus (Tyler's Party Crash Guy), Max Pricskett (Photographer Extra).

"Fight Night." It has served as the stage for some amusing, bizarre, and even dangerous evenings. Hysterical mothers have entered the ring and attacked their sons' opponents with the heel of their shoes. The so-called "Fan Man" parachuted out of a Las Vegas sky into the ring during the second Holyfield-Bowe bout in an attempt to join the fracas. The foul-ridden second Riddick Bowe–Andrew Golota fight, at Madison Square Garden, created a rancor that spilled out into the audience and erupted into a full-scale riot.

The boxing ring has been at the epicenter of just about every scenario imaginable, and thanks to a few screenwriters in Hollywood, it has even served as the crime scene for murder. Early in 1938, Republic pictures released a "B" picture entitled *Hollywood Stadium Mystery* starring Neil Hamilton, Evelyn Venable, and Jimmy Wallington. In the film, a fighter is murdered before entering the ring with the champ. Char of *Variety* wrote that the movie was "a fairly acceptable whodunit" in which "Jimmy Wallington impressively plays a sports commentator, guilty of the slaying."[1]

That same year, Twentieth Century-Fox began production on a Charlie Chan vehicle entitled *Charlie Chan at Ringside*. Filming commenced on January 10, 1938, and with a third of the scenes shot in just a week, Chan star Oland Warner took ill and was replaced by Peter Lorre. Several of the lines in the script were revised, and the title of the picture was changed to *Mr. Moto's Gamble*.[2] In the film, Lorre (Mr. Moto) portrays a Japanese friend of Charlie Chan, who teaches a course in criminology. His students include Lee Chan (Keye Luke), Charlie Chan's Number One Son, and Horace Wellington, portrayed by former boxing champ Maxie Rosenbloom.

The picture is an above-average whodunit, in which Lorre, with the assistance of Luke and Rosenbloom, solves the murder of a fighter poisoned in the ring. The film is notable from a boxing fan's perspective, for the extensive speaking role which Rosenbloom has in the picture. Ward Bond, who appeared in boxing films such as *Conflict* with John Wayne, and *Gentleman Jim* with Errol Flynn, portrays the fictional heavyweight champ.

Some 50 years later, director Brian DePalma resurrected the ringside murder plot in his creatively filmed but flawed thriller entitled *Snake Eyes*, starring Nicolas Cage and Gary Sinise. The film, which was largely shot at the old Forum in Montreal, centers around the murder of the U.S. Defense Secretary at ringside of a heavyweight championship match in Atlantic City. Integral to the murder scheme is the heavyweight champion (Shaw) who, in order to clear his casino debts, agrees to throw a match that the Secretary is attending. The dive is used to create a diversion exploited by security officer Kevin Dunn (Sinise), who is behind the conspiracy to commit the murder. Nicolas Cage (Santoro) portrays the wheeling-dealing Atlantic City police officer who must solve the murder and bring down his one-time friend played by Sinise.

Snake Eyes offers multiple points of view, replaying the assassination from various perspectives, as Cage and the audience engage in the deconstructive/reconstructive process, attempting to unravel the mystery. The picture is most memorable for its opening scene: a single twenty-minute take which follows Cage around the arena. The scene, shot with a Steadicam, was praised by the critics. "It takes nerves of steel as well as skill for a filmmaker to plan a shot like that," noted David Kehr for the *Daily News*. "As a stylist, DePalma has few contemporary rivals."[3] "Great credit must go to cinematographer Stephen H. Burum," wrote Stephen Holden for *The New York Times*.[4]

However, as pointed out by Stuart

Klawans writing for *The Nation*, "Nothing in the rest of the picture lives up to that opening shot."[5] The plot is often implausible, as illustrated by the scene in which the recently dethroned heavyweight champion of the world is found beating Cage's character to a pulp at the behest of the assassins. "Nearly every element in the film is contrived or superficial," pointed out Todd McCarthy for *Variety*.[6]

The single boxing scene in the film is fragmented, often serving as a backdrop for the film's numerous flashbacks. Only when the champ recounts his version of the fight do we actually see the one-round battle. However, his opponent is poorly cast, the feel of the scene is artificial, and the overall result is sub-par. As noted by critic Holden, the boxing vignette "looks and sounds transparently fake."[7]

The strong acting of Sinise and flamboyance of Cage keep one engaged, but Philip French, the critic for the *London Observer*, best summed up the experience when he wrote, "Only when we climb out at the end do we notice we've been happily immersed in something two inches deep. The title *Snake Eyes* refers to the lowest score in craps, meaning you lose and the house wins."[8]

1. Char, Review of *Hollywood Stadium Mystery* (Republic Pictures movie), *Variety*, 2 March 1938.
2. Charles P. Mitchell, *A Guide to Charlie Chan Films* (Westport CT: Greenwood Press, 1999), 171–2.
3. David Kehr, Review of *Snake Eyes* (Paramount Pictures movie), *New York Daily News*, 7 August 1998, 57.
4. Stephen Holden, Review of *Snake Eyes* (Paramount Pictures movie), *New York Times*, 7 August 1998, E12.
5. Stuart Klawans, Review of *Snake Eyes* (Paramount Pictures movie), *Nation*, 7 September 1998, 44.
6. Todd McCarthy, Review of *Snake Eyes* (Paramount Pictures movie), *Variety*, 10 August 1998.
7. Holden.
8. Philip French, Review of *Snake Eyes* (Paramount Pictures movie), *Observer* (*London*), 8 November 1998, review section, 6.

Somebody Up There Likes Me (1956)

Metro-Goldwyn Mayer, Drama, B & W, 113 minutes

Producer: Charles Schnee. *Director*: Robert Wise. *Screenplay*: Ernest Lehman, based upon the autobiography of Rocky Graziano by Graziano and Rowland Barber. *Film Editor*: Albert Akst. *Photography*: Joseph Ruttenberg. *Music*: Bronislau Kaper.

Paul Newman (Rocky), Pier Angeli (Norma), Everett Sloane (Irving Cohen), Eileen Heckart (Ma Barbella), Sal Mineo (Romolo), Robert Loggia (Frankie Peppo), Steve McQueen (uncredited), Harold J. Stone (Nick Barbella), Joseph Buloff (Benny), Sammy White (Whitey Bimstein), Arch Johnson (Heldon), Robert Lieb (Questioner), Theodore Newton (Commissioner Eddie Egan), Judson Pratt (Johnny Hyland), Matt Crowley (Lou Stillman), Harry Wismer (Announcer), Sam Taub (Announcer), Donna Jo Gribble (Yolanda Barbella), Robert Easton (Corporal Quinbury), Ray Strictlyn (Bryson), John Rosser (Detective), Frank Campanella (Detective), Ralph Vitti (Shorty).

Boxing historians readily concur that Rocky Graziano was not the best middleweight of his era. Indeed, such contemporaries as Sugar Ray Robinson, Tony Zale and Jake La Motta were all Graziano's ring superiors. Rocky, however, was undeniably the biggest crowd-pleaser of his generation. Displaying an unchecked fury and reckless abandon that had not been seen since the days of Stanley Ketchel, "Rock-a-bye Rocky" packed fans to the rafters everywhere he fought. From St. Nicholas Arena to Yankee Stadium, Graziano created mayhem within the roped square, displaying his explosive persona and casting a shadowy reflection on his frequently turbulent personal life.

Hollywood producers of the day were sure to have found Zale banal, La Motta too stand-offish and Robinson the wrong color. Graziano, however, was an engaging character with a storied past worthy of biographical exploitation. Selecting James Dean to portray Rocky, MGM would tell the Graziano story. A fresh face, Dean had rocked Hollywood in his film debut in *East of Eden* and had two more blockbusters in waiting. The timeless *Giant* and *Rebel Without a Cause* had both already been filmed, but not released.[1]

Before production on Rocky's bio began, Dean was also to star in a television special based on an Ernest Hemingway story about a boxer entitled *The Battler*. While rehearsing for *The Battler*, Dean contacted Graziano to make arrangements to meet and review some preliminaries for the film that was to be entitled *Somebody Up There Likes Me*. The personal introduction never occurred. On September 30, 1955, Dean died tragically in a car wreck at the tender age of twenty-four.[2] Accolades for Dean's last two films would come posthumously.

As Dean's replacement in the television program, another young actor named Paul Newman was selected. When Robert Wise, the director of *The Battler*, also agreed to direct *Somebody Up There Likes Me* (which he did "on the strength of the book alone"), he championed Newman, whom all agreed was impressive as Hemingway's boxer.[3]

Somebody Up There Likes Me is a quality film production which nicely blends lighthearted and dramatic elements to effectively capture the tumultuous personal and professional life of Rocky Graziano. Notwithstanding the standard exercise of Hollywood license, screenwriter Lehman and director Wise remain faithful to the Graziano autobiography of the same name. The fighter's troubled adolescence is conveyed through episodes of thievery, a rooftop gang fight, and his stint in reform school. Child abuse at the hand of his alcoholic father, an ex-fighter, is candidly addressed. Graziano's dishonorable discharge for punching out a corporal and going AWOL is also documented, as is the revocation of his boxing license in New York State for failure to report a bribe.

Newman's strong portrayal of Graziano effectively conveys the diverse emotional range of the film's subject. Newman's Graziano has a short fuse. The actor expertly depicts Rocky's discontent through his smug and wise attitude, a thin veneer that too often fails to cloak his anger, frustration, and violence. This expression of anti-social behavior is expertly balanced against Newman's believable portrayal of Graziano as a decent, and at times even tender individual, related through the fighter's relationships with his mother and wife.

To indoctrinate Newman into Graziano's world prior to filming, the pair became inseparable, visiting Graziano's old haunts such as Stillman's Gym and Tenth Street pool halls. They played cards, went out drinking and caroused together.[4] While bonding, Newman observed Graziano's physical habits. Hands perpetually stuffed in his pockets, shoulders sloped forward and face tilted downward, Newman, in effect, became Graziano. Commenting on the effects of his tutelage, Graziano later stated, "He plays me so good I thinks he's my brudda."[5]

The critics concurred. Bosley Crowther of *The New York Times* wrote that Newman "is funny, tough and pathetic in that slouching, rolling, smirking Brando style, but with a quite apparent simulation of the mannerisms."[6] Jesse Zunser of *Cue* magazine opined that Newman "is excellent as Rocky — with his hunched, half-crouched, rolling gait and Italo-New Yorkese accent."[7] Brog of *Variety* found Newman to have made a real character study of his work writing that "his talent is large and flexible."[8] Newman would admit to Rocky that the role helped his career more than any other acting assignment.[9]

Critics felt that the film captured the essence of Graziano, both the man and his story. *Variety* wrote that the film was "a superbly done, frank and revealing film probe of Rocky Graziano," with *Cue* opining that the film successfully captured "much of the exciting color, brisk, colloquial dialogue and rich dramatic feeling of Rocky's book."[10] Joan Beaufort of *The Christian Science Monitor* found the writing and acting to be "pungent, racy, and down-to-asphalt" and *The New York Times* noted, "Robert Wise's direction is fast, aggressive and bright, and the picture is edited to give it a tremendous crispness and pace."[11]

Supporting players in the film were also well received. Arthur Knight of *Saturday Review* found Eileen Heckart "superb as [Graziano's] long-suffering mother," and *Variety* wrote that Harold J. Stone was "almost uncomfortably real as the wine-sodden father."[12] *Cue* found Pier Angeli "cute, appealing, and quite believable" in the role of Rocky's wife-to-be.[13]

Indoor filming was made at an MGM studio on Fifty-seventh Street, in New York City.[14] Many of the outside scenes, which were filmed in a brief ten days, were shot in Graziano's old lower East Side neighborhood in New York. Director Wise was of the opinion that outdoor sets did not look real in daylight, but photographed fine during the night, and arranged his shoots accordingly.[15]

The film also serves an historical purpose, preserving the interior of Stillman's Gym, which closed its doors in the early 1960s. Stillman's was one of the most famous boxing gyms of all time. Every heavyweight champion from Jack Dempsey to Floyd Patterson is said to have trained there. Astute boxing fans may also observe at ringside Nat Fleischer, the editor and publisher of *The Ring* magazine; blow-by-blow announcer Sam Taub, a pioneer in boxing radio broadcasting who personally witnessed every heavyweight champion from Jeffries to Ali; and legendary trainer Al Silvani, who frequently appeared in boxing movies, including the *Rocky* series.

Paul Newman proves athletic, believable and in all respects worthy of the task of portraying Graziano in the ring. Regarding Newman's boxing ability, the fighter himself commented, "When he punches the light or heavy bag, he does it better than a lotta pros, and when I spar with him he t'rows some pretty good punches."[16]

The climactic scene in the film, Graziano's rematch against Zale, still ranks as one of the best boxing vignettes put on film. The fight scenes are realistic and well choreographed, utilizing frequent and effective close-ups. In spirit they are representative of the classic Graziano-Zale trilogy, which is often lauded as the greatest in boxing history. Shamefully, the first two matches between Graziano and Zale were never filmed.

To portray Graziano's arch ring nemesis Tony Zale, MGM gave no quarter in the department of authenticity and cast the boxer to portray himself. However, once upon the set, it became apparent that either Zale could not grasp the nuances of Hollywood boxing or could not resist beating up a movie star. After doubling Newman over, knocking him to the canvas, and bruising his ribs, Zale's realistic services were dismissed. By pure coincidence, an MGM employee knew a barkeep who was an ex-boxer, and the spitting imagine of Zale, broken nose and all. In an instant, the bartender was substituted for Zale![17]

1. Rocky Graziano and Ralph Corsel, *Somebody Down Here Likes Me, Too* (New York: Stein & Day, 1981), 127–128.
2. *Ibid.*
3. Samuel Stark, *Films in Review*, January 1963, vol. 14, no. 1.
4. Graziano, *Somebody Down Here Likes Me, Too* 129–132.
5. *Ibid.*
6. Bosley Crowther, Review of *Somebody Up There Likes Me* (MGM movie), *New York Times*, 6 July 1956.
7. Jesse Zunser, "Rocky Graziano's Movie, Too, Scores a K.O." Review of *Somebody Up There Likes Me* (MGM movie), *Cue*, 14 July 1956.
8. Brog, Review of *Somebody Up There Likes Me* (MGM movie), *Variety*, 4 July 1956.

9. Graziano, *Somebody Down Here Likes Me*.
10. *Variety*; "Rocky Graziano's Movie," *Cue* 14 July 1956.
11. John Beaufort, "Portrait of a Fighter." Review of *Somebody Up There Likes Me* (MGM movie), *Christian Science Monitor*, 31 July 1956; *New York Times*.
12. Arthur Knight, Review of *Somebody Up There Likes Me* (MGM movie), *Saturday Review*; *Variety*.
13. "Rocky Graziano's Movie."
14. Graziano, *Somebody Down Here Likes Me, Too*, 129–132.
15. *Films in Review*.
16. Graziano, *Somebody Down Here Likes Me, Too*, 127–128.
17. Ibid., 127–128.

Spirit of Youth (1937)

Globe Pictures Corp., distributed by Grand National Films, Inc., Drama-Musical, B & W, 65 minutes

Producer: Lew Golder. *Director*: Harry Fraser. *Screenplay*: Arthur Hoerl. *Film Editor*: Carl Pierson. *Cinematography*: Robert Cline. *Original Score*: Clarence Muse, Williot Carpenter.

Joe Louis (Joe Thomas), Anthony Scott (Joe as a Child), Edna Mae Harris (Mary Bowden), Mae Turner (Flora Bailey), Mantan Moreland (Crickie Fitzgibbons), Cleo Desmond (Nora Thomas), Clarence Muse (Frankie Walburn), Clarence Brooks (Speedy — Trainer), Tom Southern (Mr. Bowden), Jules Smith (Duke Emerald), Jesse Lee Brooks (Jeff Thomas), Marguerite Whitten (Eleanor Thomas), Plantation Boys Choir, Creole Chorus, Big Apple Dancers.

Spirit of Youth has become the subject of historical retrospectives as an example of the "race" film, which subsisted for decades in the giant shadow of "white" Hollywood. At the time of its release, however, it was a timely effort by producer Lew Golder to financially capitalize upon Joe Louis's ascension to the heavyweight championship.[1]

The second African-American to win the coveted title, by the late 1930s Louis was emerging as the most important black in America. The first athlete of his race to tightrope-walk the color line to achieve universal appeal, Louis had already proved his economic power in the ring. By testing the champ's financial draw in the entertainment world, Golder was now taking the next logical step in exploiting Louis's broadening acceptability.

Nevertheless, the use of the medium of film to mirror newfound racial tolerance was laced with irony. In 1910, Jack Johnson, the first African-American to win the heavyweight title, defeated a white challenger, the former champion James J. Jeffries. Race riots ensued and Congress immediately passed a law prohibiting the transfer or distribution of the film of their fight, a ban still in effect at the time *Spirit of Youth* was produced.[2] Paradoxically, while the United States government continued its policy of prohibiting the public viewing of Johnson's symbolic dismantling of white supremacy, filmmakers freely recreated and distributed Louis's title winning defeat of another Caucasian, which was then seen by millions.

Distribution, however, came with a warning label. PCA director Joseph Breen informed Globe Pictures Corp. that the movie was "questionable from the standpoint of policy, because it shows, among other things, several scenes of a black man victorious in a number of fistic encounters with white men." Breen also cautioned one of the film's producers Edward Shanberg of the "serious difficulty" that the film's distribution potentially faced, "especially in a number of states in the South."[3]

Despite the inherent risks in the project, the picture's production was raced to completion to capitalize on the free publicity being generated by Louis's bout with

Nathan Mann.[4] Premiering on January 20, 1938, the film debuted at the Central Theater on Broadway in New York City, and was soon showing in numerous theaters in Detroit, Kansas City, Washington, D.C. and other locations that could be counted on to be receptive to the film's subject matter.[5]

Spirit of Youth is loosely based on the life of the "Brown Bomber." Louis's alter ego is Joe Thomas, an Alabama country boy from a family-oriented home. Joe leaves his girlfriend Mary (Harris) behind and travels North for work. With the encouragement of his co-worker Crickie (Moreland) he enters the Detroit Golden Gloves. Ultimately winning the tournament, he turns pro under the tutelage of Crickie's boss Frankie (Muse).

Joe becomes involved with a showgirl named Flora (Turner) who is beholden to a nightclub owner named Duke (Smith). Duke, an avid gambler, uses Flora to soften up Joe, so he can win a long shot bet on one of Joe's opponents. The boxer spends late nights out with the entertainer at the expense of his training regimen. Despite efforts by Mary and Frankie to alter the course set by Duke, Joe is knocked out. Determined not to waste his talent, Joe rededicates himself to the sport and obtains a title shot. Fighting listlessly, Joe is rejuvenated upon the estranged Mary's eleventh hour arrival at ringside, rallying to win the championship.

The factual portions of *Spirit of Youth* touch upon Louis's southern origins, his love for his mother and his start in the Detroit Golden Gloves. His setback to Max Schmeling is also covered, and Louis's many romantic interferences are symbolized by Flora. Frankie is an emotional substitute for the champ's beloved trainer "Chappie" Blackburn. The remainder of the story is pure fiction.

Several established black actors of the day were assembled to surround the champion in his film debut. Edna Mae Harris, who regularly appeared in Hollywood features including *Bullets or Ballots* and *Garden of Allah*, portrayed Joe's leading lady. Clarence Muse, a veteran of over 300 films, who had appeared in *Cabin in the Cotton*, *Show Boat*, and the boxing story *The Life of Jimmy Dolan*, not only portrayed Joe's manager, but also co-authored the film's score and sang one of its tunes.[6]

Consistent with many films of the day that punctuated drama with musical interludes, *Spirit of Youth* served up several musical numbers. Catering to black audiences, the film assembled a virtually all-black cast, including the talented Savoy Ballroom dancers, featuring Roberta Reeves, Gladys Wilson, Maddie Kendal and Rubberneck Homes.[7]

All the supporting talent in the world, however, could not alter Louis's expressionless demeanor, which did not translate well on the screen. Odec of *Variety* wrote, "What keeps the unintended humor down to a minimum is that Joe Louis isn't called upon to act too often." Offering Louis a backhanded comment, Odec also wrote that the film "isn't so bad, considering the handicaps entailed in the star's lack of facial and lingual mobility."[8]* Taking a different tack, Wanda Hale of the *New York Daily News* approached the boxer's film debut with a twinkle in her eye, writing, "Where Louis

---

*Light-heavyweight champion Billy Conn, one of Louis's opponents, proved to be Louis's near equal in the ring, but may have actually surpassed the "'Brown Bomber" for worst acting laurels. Conn starred as himself in the aptly titled boxing yarn, The Pittsburgh Kid, which co-starred Jean Parker. Despite being surrounded by a number of boxers, including former middleweight champion Freddie Steele and three-division titleholder Hammerin' Henry Armstrong, Conn proved painfully out of place on screen.

Bosley Crowther of The New York Times, in a review entitled "Conn and Pros," wrote "As an actor, the Kid is a dud. When he is sparring with Henry Armstrong or other congenial partners he is a little bit all right. When he is sparring with Miss Parker, however, or those of the Screen Actors Guild, he looks bad — very bad." "It's one continuous monotone," wrote Herb of Variety lamenting over Conn's verbal delivery. "Conn should stick to the light-heavyweight division. Joe Louis and the movies do nothing to enhance his reputation," added Howard Barnes of the New York Herald-Tribune.

does not have the aplomb of Clark Gable, he makes up with his fists," adding that the film "moves along more quickly than its star but not as gracefully."[9]

Working as technical advisors on the film were three prominent Blacks: Louis's attorney John Roxborough, Roxborough's brother, who was a former state senator, and Julian Black, a prominent Chicago businessman, who, with Roxborough, guided Louis to the championship. To keep in line with the fictionalization of the film, no actual film footage of Louis's bouts is included in the picture. The fight sequences include training, sparring and several bouts which were filmed at the Hollywood Legion Stadium.

One of Louis's screen opponents, Willie Callahan, a New Jersey heavyweight, purportedly staggered the champion while attempting to knock him out during filming. Callahan believed a knockout of the champion could secure him a real title shot. Louis paid Callahan back for his indiscretion by K.O.'ing him on the set.[10]

The fight scenes in *Spirit of Youth* are well-choreographed with a mixture of close-ups, overhead angles and upward shots from between the ring ropes. Of course Louis is the real attraction, and the champ goes through the paces with the same deadpan efficiency he used in real life.

An unprecedented ten years after winning the title, Louis remained the heavyweight champion. With his public appeal still intact, an early independent black filmmaker named Bill Alexander called Louis back to the screen to star in his second boxing vehicle entitled *The Fight Never Ends*.

The film co-starred Ruby Dee, who felt that the film was as "good as anything that Hollywood had to offer."[11] Unfortunately, the picture was beset with financial problems from the get-go. In trouble with creditors, Alexander was forced to borrow $5,000 from Dee to keep the film in production. Eventually, lawsuits caused filming to halt. Months after the film was finally finished it was seized by creditors, and Alexander went on the lam. Over the next two decades Dee unsuccessfully tried to locate both Alexander and the film![12]

1. Patricia King Hanson, *The American Film Institute Catalog of Motion Pictures Produced in the United States, Volume F3, Feature Films, 1931–1940* (Berkeley: University of California Press, 1993), Film Entries M-Z, 2025.
2. Nat Loubet and John Ort, comps., *The 1979 Ring Boxing Encyclopedia and Record Book* (New York: The Ring Book Shop, 1979), 156.
3. Hanson, *The American Film Institute Catalog*, 2025.
4. *Film Daily*, 2 March 1938.
5. *Ibid.*, 6.
6. "'Stompin' at the Savoy Gives Way to Agitatin' the Big Apple in New Joe Louis Feature Film." Globe Pictures Corp. Publicity for *Spirit of Youth*.
7. *Ibid.*
8. Odec, Review of *Spirit of Youth* (Globe Pictures Corp. movie), *Variety*, 5 January 1938.
9. Wanda Hale, Review of *Spirit of Youth* (Globe Pictures Corp. movie), *New York Daily News*, 26 February 1938.
10. "'Spirit of Youth' Had Aid of Louis Fight Managers," Globe Pictures Corp. Publicity for *Spirit of Youth*.
11. Hanson, *The American Film Institute Catalog*, 2025.
12. Ozzie Davis and Ruby Dee, *With Ozzie & Ruby: In This Life Together* (New York: William Morrow, 1998), 172–176, 196.

The Square Jungle (1955)

Universal-International, Drama, B & W, 86 minutes

Producer: Albert Zugsmith. *Director*: Jerry Hopper. *Screenplay*: George Zuckerman. *Film Editor*: Paul Weatherwax. *Photography*: George Robinson, *Music*: Heinz Roemheld.

Tony Curtis (Eddie Quaid/Packy Glennon), Pat Crowley (Julie Walsh), Ernest Borgnine (Bernie Browne), Paul Kelly (Jim McBride), Jim Backus (Pat Quaid), Leigh Snowden (Lorraine Evans), John Day (Al Gorski), Joe Vitale (Adamson), John Marley (Tom Dillon), David Jannsen (Jack Lindsay), Kay Stewart (Mrs. Gorski), Barney Phillips (Dan Selby), Frank Marlowe (Kane), Joe Louis (Himself), Carmen Mcrae (Singer).

For the handsome but un-established Tony Curtis, the first chance to showcase his acting abilities came in the offbeat role of a deaf-mute boxer in Universal-International's *Flesh and Fury*. Directed by Joseph Pevney, who had recently helped Rock Hudson toward movie stardom in another boxing film, *Iron Man*, *Flesh and Fury* co-starred Jan Sterling and Mona Freedman as Curtis's competing love interests and Wallace Ford as his manager.

As pointed out by H.H.T. of *The New York Times*, the film was "an obvious attempt to launch the studio's current bobby-soxer idol, Tony Curtis, as a full-fledged emoter," which "strives with fair success, to be different."[1] Indeed, the premise of *Flesh and Fury* is fairly unique, though not without precedent. Providing a providence for the film's concept was Eugene "Dummy" Hairston, a deaf-mute man from the Bronx, New York, who was a bona fide middleweight contender during the late 1940s and early 1950s.*

The critics for *Kinematograph Weekly* and *Motion Picture Herald* acknowledged Curtis's thespian abilities in *Flesh and Fury*. The former also complimented the actor on his ring acumen, writing that he "distinguishes himself in the ring," while the latter expressed admiration for the actor's boxing skill "in some very convincing fight scenes."[2]

Curtis, however, learned his new trade for a price. Many years later, the actor recalled the repeated beatings he took during rehearsals, and the moment he attempted to exact revenge upon his ring opponent: "I saw my opening and knocked him flat on his ass ... He looked up at me and said 'Kid, is that as hard as you can hit?' Kind of flattered, I said, 'Well yeah.' And he said, 'Stay out of bars.'"[3]

If Curtis had a powder-puff punch, audiences were blissfully unaware; and several years later Universal-International cast the increasingly popular actor in a more traditional fight picture entitled *The Square Jungle*. In *The Square Jungle*, Eddie Quaid (Curtis) is the son of a proud but depressed alcoholic (Backus), who is locked up after a bar fight. To raise bail money Eddie enters the ring. His success spawns a boxing career under his father's old fight moniker, "Packy Glenn," inspiring dad to kick his drinking habit.

Guiding Packy's career is an ex-fighter turned philosopher named Bernie Brown (Borgnine) who simultaneously attempts to develop his charge's fighting ability and moral fiber. Caught in Packy's tumultuous personal voyage is his girl Julie (Crowley). Packy wins the middleweight championship, but loses the title in the return match, maligning the referee for stopping the contest prematurely. He regains the belt in the rubber match, but his opponent Al Gorski is seriously injured, when the same referee, heeding Packy's prior complaints, lets the match go too far.

To divorce himself from his Packy Glenn persona, the guilt-ridden boxer ironically turns to alcohol and goes into seclusion. Packy eventually finds a kindred soul in Bernie, who coaxes him into attending a boxing match where Gorski is to appear. Joining the ailing Gorski at the ring microphone, Packy expounds some of Bernie's philosophy for the audience, beginning his journey towards self-forgiveness.

Critiquing *The Square Jungle*, M.E. of *The New York Times* quipped, "The drama and the prizefighter are both middle-

---

*Hairston campaigned professionally from 1947 to 1952 with a final record of 45-13-5. He defeated Paul Pender and "Kid" Gavilin and fought a draw with Jake La Motta.

weights."⁴ Without question, portions of the script are weak and at times implausible, but Borgnine and Curtis kept the drama firm enough, earning themselves nice reviews in the process. Brog of *Variety* noted that Borgnine "gives a quiet, able performance as the trainer," in a role which P.V.B. of *The Herald-Tribune* acknowledged for "lifting the picture a notch or two above itself."⁵* *Variety* praised Curtis, noting that he "responds well to the directorial demands of Jerry Hopper," while *The Motion Picture Herald* wrote that the actor "piles up a telling score of points for himself as a performer and a box-office power."⁶

Frankie Van, who also fashioned the fight scenes for *Iron Man* (1951), acted as the film's boxing technical advisor. Van applies his keen sense of ring generalship and boxing technique to choreograph credible and entertaining boxing vignettes, which are enhanced by his use of detail. The fighters feint as a precursor to their offensives. On defense, they not only duck blows, but parry and block them as well.

The ring action is often furious, but it is realistically punctuated with moments of repose, where the fighters circle, backpedal or occasionally fall into a clinch. Van's boxers are equipped with jabs, and the ability to in-fight, throw combinations and body-punch, creating a multi-dimensional arsenal befitting of the championship-caliber fighters being portrayed. Curtis nicely assimilates Van's tools and techniques as does his ring nemesis John Day, who had already shown his boxing ability in *Champion, Abbott and Costello Meet the Invisible Man* and *City of Bad Men*.

Following *The Square Jungle*, Curtis would go on to exhibit his ever-growing acting diversity in a wide range of roles in such films as *The Sweet Smell of Success*, *Spartacus* and *Some Like It Hot*. Film stardom earned during the 1950s and '60s later ebbed, with Curtis eventually fading into semi-obscurity. During the 1960s, Curtis found his way to another fight picture entitled *Title Shot*, a low-budget Canadian film that unsuccessfully attempts to build a thriller around a heavyweight championship fight. A pro surrounded by amateurs, even Curtis's star quality could not overcome the picture's poor acting, unintentionally humorous script, and lame fight scenes.

1. H.H.T. Review of *Flesh and Fury* (Universal-International Pictures movie), *New York Times*, 28 March 1952.
2. *The Kinematograph Weekly*, quoted in Allan Hunter, *Tony Curtis: The Man and His Movies* (New York: St. Martin's Press, 1985), 37; *Motion Picture Herald*, quoted in Allan Hunter, *Tony Curtis: The Man and His Movies*, 37.
3. Tony Curtis and Barry Paris, *Tony Curtis: The Autobiography* (New York: William and Morrow Company, Inc., 1993), 106.
4. M.E. Review of *The Square Jungle* (Universal-International Pictures movie), *New York Times* 31 December 1955.
5. Brog, Review of *The Square Jungle* (Universal-International Pictures movie), *Variety*, 30 November 1955; P.V.B. Review of *The Square Jungle* (Universal-International Pictures movie), *New York Herald-Tribune*, 31 December 1955.
6. *Variety*, quoted in Allan Hunter, *Tony Curtis: The Man and His Movies*, 59; *Motion Picture Herald* quoted in Allan Hunter, *Tony Curtis: The Man and His Movies*, 59.

---

*The Square Jungle *boasted Ernest Borgnine in his first screen appearance following his Oscar-winning role as a Bronx butcher in* Marty, *the Academy's best picture of 1955. The picture was the first of several boxing films for Borgnine. In 1971, the actor appeared with Robert Blake in* Un Uomo dalla pelle dura, *a film which carried numerous English titles including* Counterpunch *and* Ripped Off. *Borgnine portrays a police captain who pursues Blake, an ex-con turned boxer suspected of murdering his manager. In 1976, the veteran actor landed the role of trainer Angelo Dundee in the Muhammad Ali biography entitled* The Greatest. *Borgnine also portrayed an ex-fighter and trainer in* The Opponent *(1987), a class D production, in which Borgnine was the film's only redeeming quality.*

The Sting II (1982)

Universal Pictures, Comedy, Color, 102 minutes

Producer: Jennings Lang. *Director*: Jeremy Paul Kagan. *Screenplay*: David S. Ward. *Cinematography*: Bill Butler. *Music*: Lalo Schifrin.

Jackie Gleason (Gondorff), Mac Davis (Hooker), Terri Garr (Veronica), Karl Malden (Macalinski), Oliver Reed (Doyle Lonnegan), Bert Remsen (Kid Colors), Kathalina Veniero (Blonde with Kid Colors), Jose Perez (Lonnegan's Guard), Larry Gellecher (Lonnegan's 2nd Guard), Frank Mccarthy (Lonnegan's Thug), Richard C. Adams (Lonnegan's Thug), Ron Rifkin (Eddie), Harry James (Band Leader), Frances Bergen (Lady Dorsett), Monica Lewis (Band Singer).

Even the "Great One," Jackie Gleason, had to earn his reputation. As a young entertainer in Los Angeles, the transplanted Brooklynite hustled to make it in Hollywood. In the early 1940s, while a contract player at Warner Brothers, Gleason landed a gig as a comic, regularly appearing on stage at "Slapsie Maxie's," a nightclub owned by former light-heavyweight champion Maxie Rosenbloom.[1]

The nightlife perfectly suited Gleason's boisterous personality and, like Rosenbloom, Jackie was not bashful about enhancing his reputation with his fists. One incident back East was particularly memorable. One evening, after a heated exchange, Jackie called out a New Jersey barkeep named Tony to test his skill against the barrel-shaped proprietor. Gleason was knocked out cold. Only afterwards did Gleason learn that he had challenged "Two Ton" Tony Galento, a boxer who had once knocked down the great Joe Louis, coming within a ten-count of winning the heavyweight title.[2]

Unlike Galento, who refused to compromise his appetites to make weight, Gleason, at least privately, was perturbed that his eating and drinking binges prevented him from better physical health. During the 1950s he appealed to heavyweight champion Rocky Marciano for assistance. Gleason purchased about $17,000 in workout equipment and then joined Marciano at his training camp. Gleason accompanied Marciano in doing his roadwork, but only made it through a quarter of the regimen. Later, in a gesture of resignation, he donated his training equipment to a boys' orphanage.[3]

Despite his penchant for fighting and his many acquaintances from the boxing world, the portly Gleason was no more likely to be cast as a boxer on-screen than as a romantic lead. However, the Irishman's burgeoning dramatic talents were eventually put on display in a fight-oriented story when he was cast in the role of a fight manager in *Requiem for a Heavyweight*. *Requiem* turned out to be a screen classic and one of his greatest roles. A couple of decades later, in the twilight of his film career, Gleason appeared in one more boxing film, *The Sting II*.

The Sting II is the sequel to the Redford-Newman classic. It is now almost ten years later and grifters Jake Hooker (Davis), and Fargo Gondorff (Gleason) are out to con a Brooklyn racketeer named Macalinski (Malden). Lonnegan (Reed), who was the victim in *The Sting*, is working a counter-sting to enact revenge against Hooker and Gondorff. Naturally, the con is connected to a fixed fight.

Based upon the screenplay of David S. Ward, who also penned the first film, the critics felt that *The Sting II* lacked originality. Berg, the critic for *Variety*, noted "similar types of plot twists and character devices" between the sequel and the original.[4] The picture "copies the first film shamelessly," wrote Janet Maslin of *The New York Times*.[5] Another drawback in the film was the basic premise itself, which unrealistically required that the audience accept Davis and Gleason as the older versions of Redford and Newman.

The film's best attribute is the pairing of Gleason and Malden. It is a pleasure to watch these two old pros at their craft. Gleason has an innate ability to add the right nuance at the right moment, is a master of understatement and offers just enough bite to his character to position him as a con artist. Malden is engaging and entertaining as a sport who is the victim of the sting.

To add realism to the film's fight sequences the talents of Academy Award winning designer Ed Carfagno were utilized. The Los Angeles Variety Arts Theatre, originally built in 1923 for musicals and operas, served as a fight club — mimicking a common practice of the 1940s in which legitimate theaters doubled as boxing venues to stave off bankruptcy.[6]

Some of the film's gym sequences were shot at the Main Street Gym in Los Angeles. A keen eye will note that the life-size, cut-out figures of several heavyweight champions that appear in the background are identical to those featured in Mickey Goodwin's gym in *Rocky*. The venerable gymnasium was left unaltered for *The Sting II*. "We did nothing except remove the modern-day fighters," noted Carfagno.[7]

Appearing in the film are veteran referee Marty Denkin, and U.S. Senator John Tunney, who portrays his father former heavyweight champion Gene Tunney. The climactic fight sequence was filmed at the Olympic Auditorium by cinematographer Bill Butler, who was also behind the lens for *Rocky* and *Rocky II*. Mac Davis, who portrays the grifter-boxer, had done some boxing in high school, but in the picture, he is mostly called upon to be at the receiving end of his opponent's blows. "I got banged up but I did it myself," explained Davis. "I was trying to make a slow-motion shot look terrific — there's a place in the fight where I get knocked down, so I went flying through the air and landed on my rib cage. I broke a rib. It was my own fault ... I was overacting," he added with a smile. "But it's the old story — it only hurts when you laugh."[8]

1. William A. Henry, III, *The Great One — The Life and Legend of Jackie Gleason* (New York: Double Day, 1992), 62–63.
2. Episode of the television series *The Main Event* starring Rocky Marciano.
3. Henry III, *The Great One*, 170.
4. Berg, Review of *The Sting II* (Universal Pictures movie), *Variety*, 19 January 1983.
5. Janet Maslin, Review of *The Sting II* (Universal Pictures movie), *New York Times*, 18 February 1983.
6. The Sting II — Production Notes, 8 February 1982, 4.
7. *Ibid.*, 3.
8. *Ibid.*, 5.

Streets of Gold (1986)

Twentieth Century-Fox, Drama, Color, 95 minutes

Producers: Joe Roth, Harry Ufland. *Director*: Joe Roth. *Screenplay*: Heywood Gould, Richard Price, Tom Cole, based on a story by Dezso Magyar. *Film Editor*: Richard Chew. *Director of Photography*: Arthur Albert. *Music*: Jack Nitzche.

Klaus Maria Brandauer (Alek Neuman), Adrian Pasdar (Timmy Boyle), Wesley Snipes (Roland Jenkins), Angela Molina (Elena Gitman), Elya Baskin (Klebanov), Rainbow Harvest (Brenda), Adam Nathan (Grisha), John Mahoney (Linnehan), Jaroslav Stremien (Malinovsky), Dan O'Shea (Vinnie), Mike Beach (Sonny), Al Bernstein (Announcer).

Filmmakers have been quick to recognize that redemption is not only elemental to the human experience but also a very serviceable theme for their art. For filmmakers of the boxing genre, however, the notion of redemption has further metamorphosed.

Once a useful theme for the screenwriter's consideration, redemption has evolved into something more akin to a mandated element of their story. In fact, with strikingly predictable regularity, fight films have utilized a boxer's fistic redemption as the essence of their story. *Streets of Gold*, a tale of amateur boxing, illustrates this trend, but offers a twist — a trainer rather than a boxer is the protagonist striving for redemption.

In *Streets of Gold*, Alek Neuman (Brandauer) is a former Russian national amateur champion who immigrates to the United States. Though he was a national hero in Russia, he is only a dishwasher in his adopted home in the Russian enclave of Brighton Beach, Brooklyn. A cynic who is often drunk, Alek is also filled with self-pity. His condition is partially a result of his reduced station in life, but mostly due to the fact that his opportunity to fight in the Olympics was denied him due to anti-Semitism.

Alek's journey to redemption begins when he becomes acquainted with two amateur boxers. Timothy Boyle (Pasdar) seeks out Alek to train him after witnessing Alek give another amateur boxer named Roland (Snipes) a boxing lesson in a street altercation. Alek unenthusiastically takes on Timmy as his pupil. While Alek trains Timmy, the pair engage in parallel feuds with Roland, who is angry at Alek for showing him up and jealous of Timmy, who is receiving Alek's valuable tutelage. After Alek takes on Roland as his second boxer, the two fighters' distrust and mutual contempt eventually give way to respect and friendship. Training the fighters rekindles Alek's spirit, which is further bolstered by a romance he develops with his beautiful neighbor Elena (Angela Molina).

Alek's chance at redemption arrives when the Russian's national team is to fight an American squad, and Roland and Timmy qualify for the competition. The rival Russian team is led by Alek's former coach, whom Alek holds responsible for thwarting his Olympic dreams. However, when Roland's hand is injured, Timmy, clearly the less talented of the pair, becomes Alek's sole deliverer. Despite his underdog status, Timmy stages a come-from-behind knockout to provide Alek his victory over his one-time coach.

Streets of Gold replaces the all too familiar theme of a fighter boxing to redeem himself, for the less used but no less clichéd theme of a boxer using his fists to allow another to vicariously achieve his redemption. In fact, *Streets of Gold* is filled with clichés. There is the black boxer who breaks away from his drug-dealing environment in search of money, the underdog American fighter battling the more experienced and elder Russian foe, and a potpourri of racial, religious, and ethnic prejudices and rivalries. Stating it succinctly, Kim Newman of *Monthly Film Bulletin* wrote, "*Streets of Gold* is clichéd as its title suggests."[1] Allen Barra of the *Village Voice* found the clichés to be an unavoidable assault on the audience writing, "If clichés were punches, no one would be admitted to *Streets of Gold* without headgear."[2]

But notwithstanding the film's numerous discomforting familiarities, some critics were endeared to the picture. Leo Seligsohn of *Newsday* found the film to be "good, old-fashioned chicken soup for the soul," presumably subscribing to the theory that corny pictures can still be enjoyable pictures if they move you and make you feel good.[3]

The film's use of rundown Brighton Beach night spots, underground boxing venues and sparse tenements all nicely complement the oppressed personal lives of Alek and his fighters. As Michael Wilmington of the *Los Angeles Times* observed, "At its best, [the film] seethes and vibrates with low, gritty passion."[4]

At the heart of the film's successful elements is the performance of Brandauer, fresh off his Academy-Award-winning role the previous year in *Out of Africa*. The Austrian actor in his first English-speaking film is dead-on as a Russian émigré. He can act believably disheveled and charming in the same moment and he can oscillate between being lethargic and intense with great fluidity and ease. Leo Seligsohn applauded his performance, writing, "He displays the subdued, electric intensity common to all his performances. Let the others act; Brandauer reacts — his face in effect always a clear mirror of his thoughts and feelings." Michael Wilmington observed that "as Alek, Brandauer dominates, working in great leaping arcs of tension."5

Snipes and Pasdar, as Braudauer's charges, received predominately strong reviews. Wilmington found them "perfect as his fighters," and C.M. Fiorillo of *Films in Review* wrote that Pasdar demonstrates "great emotional depth," while Snipes is "a feast for the senses."6

The picture also provides ample boxing footage with numerous training scenes. In the gym we see it all. Push-ups, sit-ups, the heavy bag and the double-ended bag, the medicine ball and sparring. Most importantly, we see the commanding but compassionate instruction of Alek, and his two competitive fighters who eagerly assimilate his knowledge.

The fight scenes, which were coordinated by Jimmy Nickerson, have that artificial "Rockyesque" quality, where the fighters heads move uniformly with the punches landed. But on the positive side, they also possess their compact choreography, their high electric energy, and plenty of connecting power punches for the viewers' pleasure. But it is the training scenes in which Pasdar and Snipes seem most natural and athletic, as they pound away in combination on their trainer's hand pads. Both actors are in excellent condition, particularly the buff Snipes, who sports six-pack abdominal muscles.

The astute boxing fan should be able to spot former lightweight contender Edwin Viruet as a corner man. Also featured from the fight fraternity is Al Bernstein at the mike and Marty Denkin handling referee chores. The competition against the Golden Gloves champions was held at the famous Gleason's Gym.

1. Kim Newman, Review of *Streets of Gold* (Twentieth Century-Fox movie), *Monthly Film Bulletin*, June 1987, 187.
2. Allen Barra, Review of *Streets of Gold* (Twentieth Century-Fox movie), *Village Voice*, 25 November 1986, 64.
3. Leo Seligsohn, Review of *Streets of Gold* (Twentieth Century-Fox movie), *Newsday*, 14 November 1986, Part III, 3.
4. Michael Wilmington, Review of *Streets of Gold* (Twentieth Century-Fox movie), *Los Angeles Times*, 15 November 1986, Calendar, 5.
5. *Ibid.*
6. C.M. Fiorillo, Review of *Streets of Gold* (Twentieth Century-Fox movie), *Films in Review*, January 1987, 47.

The Superfight (1971)

Warner Productions, Inc., Drama, Color, 70 minutes

Producer and Director: Murry Woroner. *Film Editors*: Oscar Barber, William Hallahan, Ralston Prince. *Photography*: Howard Winner, Willard Jones, Oscar Barber, Richard Schwartz, Rick Anderson, Egon Stephan.

Rocky Marciano (Himself), Muhammad Ali (Himself), Chris Dundee (Promoter), Angelo Dundee (Ali's Second), Mel Ziegler (Marciano's Second), Dr. Ferdie Pacheco (Ring Physician), Mel Wolfe (Ring Announcer), Murry Woroner (Color Commentator and Narrator), Guy Lebow (Announcer), Off Camera Voices: James J. Braddock, Jack Sharkey, Jersey Joe Walcott, Max Schmeling, Jack Kearns, Jr., Nat Fleischer.

One of the inalienable rights of the sports fan is indulging in the comparison of athletes from different eras. Boxing, more so than most sports, lends itself well to this imaginative digression, since it pits individuals in direct competition with one another. Boxing aficionados spiritedly debate the outcome of matches between fighters of different generations engaging one another, matching such legends as Jack Dempsey and Joe Louis or Harry Greb and Sugar Ray Robinson.

Recognizing the enormous appeal of these unsatiated fantasies, a Miami promoter named Murry Woroner combined computer technology with staged fisticuffs to bridge fantasy and reality in *The Superfight*. Woroner's ambitious goal was to create the illusion that Rocky Marciano and Muhammad Ali were boxing one another for the all-time heavyweight championship.

Marciano-Ali is a fight fan's fantasy possessing all the requisite angles: two undefeated champions, the stoic hero of the fifties against controversial upstart of the sixties, the slugger against the boxer, with the belabored white versus black issue thrown in for good measure. However, in 1969, the task of bringing the two legendary fighters together in the same boxing ring appeared insurmountable. Marciano was already 45 years of age, had not been in the squared circle in 14 years and was almost 50 pounds over his fighting trim. While only twenty-seven, Ali was also inactive. A boxing exile who had been stripped of the heavyweight championship, the self-proclaimed Greatest had more serious considerations and was appealing his conviction as a draft-dodger of the Vietnam War.

Deprived of his livelihood, Ali was desperate for cash, and for the paltry sum of $999.99 the erstwhile Cassius Clay was seduced by Woroner's project. Marciano's motivation was two-fold. The $10,000 payday was another welcome *hors d'oeuvre* for Marciano's unyielding craving for money. More importantly, the opportunity to train for one more fight, although a staged match, was highly appealing to "The Rock."[1]

Marciano sweated and sacrificed with the same vigor he had exhibited as an active professional. By July, 1969, he had dropped nearly 50 pounds, recapturing some of the physical condition and hardened appearance that he possessed during his prime.[2] The still youthful Ali underwent no particular preparation, and for the first time in his career, his sinewy-muscled physique included an uncharacteristic roll around his midriff.

The first portion of *The Superfight* features pre-fight training sequences, which are complemented by voice-overs of former champions offering their fight predictions. James J. Braddock and Max Schmeling favored Ali, citing his superior speed and movement. Even Jersey Joe Walcott, whom Marciano defeated twice, predicted Ali as the winner. Joe Louis, however, pegged Marciano the victor, explaining that his former foe would eventually catch the fleet-footed Ali.

The fighters shared their own reflections as well. Ali, in typical cocky fashion, bellowed, "I'm not going to knock him out, I'm gonna whup him," and Marciano, holding to his usual modest form, reasoned "Perhaps, if I can corner him, and that would take some doing, I perhaps could knock him out."[3]

The fight scenes comprised the entire second half of the film, and were created by editing seventy one-minute rounds which Marciano and Ali boxed at a gym in North Miami Beach. On occasion, Ali would knock Marciano's hairpiece off during shooting, and Marciano would warn Ali to "watch the piece." Nevertheless, in between their spirited sparring sessions, the two great fighters became friends. As explained by Ali, "Our work is phony but our friendship has become real." Ali, in fact, commented that he "felt closer" to Marciano than to any other white fighter.[4]

The film was produced in secrecy, with only twenty or so persons in attendance. The match was filmed with seven different endings, some featuring Ali as the winner, others with Marciano. So clandestine was the outcome that neither Ali or Marciano knew the result prior to the film's release.

Purportedly, an NCR 315 computer was fed three years of researched information. The computer then utilized four million formulae to calculate the fighters' condition, the number of punches thrown and landed and other variables such as cuts, knockdowns, and of course, the ultimate result of the match.[5] In support of the film, Marciano applauded the use of the computer, but privately, as perhaps others did, he held a different view on how the bout's result was derived. The older champion purportedly told Ali that "the fight will be rigged to come out the way it'll make the most money for the promoter."[6]

From a boxing fan's perspective, seeing Ali and Marciano fight, even a simulated match, is a special treat. The punches to the head are all pulled, but as with any good artistic creation the shots that whiz by the fighters' faces within a whisker of landing look real. "The flurry of action, at times furious, belies any pulling of punches," wrote Prim of *Variety*.[7] The body shots are legitimate and as forceful as those thrown in sparring sessions.

Variety credited producer Woroner for putting "together a novel and exciting punch fest," in which the realism exceeded the staged aspect.[8] However, what does detract from the fight is the shooting of the ring action against a black backdrop. No audience surrounded the fighters, presumably to prevent Woroner's closely held secret from leaking to the public before the production reached the theaters. Without a live audience, the element of authenticity is somewhat eroded, even with the enhancement of dubbed crowd noise and synchronized audio to simulate the sound of leather against flesh.

One does get a sense of what the pair of fighters might have looked like in the ring together. Particularly impressive is the size differential between the five foot, ten and one half inch Marciano, posited even lower in a crouching position, and Ali, standing fully erect at more than six feet, three inches. Looks can be deceiving though, and Ali even admitted to his trainer Angelo Dundee that Marciano "was a lot harder to hit with a jab than he looked."[9]

Just three weeks after production was completed, on August 31, 1969, Marciano was tragically killed in a plane crash in Des Moines, Iowa. While no one but Woroner was to have known the result of the fight, Marciano's brother Peter claims that Rocky had revealed to him the actual result before meeting his untimely end.[10] Whether Rocky's communiqué to his brother was based upon actual knowledge, or was just a hunch portentously plucked from the seven possible endings, will never be known. Ali would later claim that he condoned the use of the ultimate version.[11]

On January 20, 1970, *The Superfight* simultaneously opened in theaters across the world for a one-time showing. In the 13th round Rocky Marciano, bloodied, and trailing on the scorecards, scores a knockout over Muhammad Ali. Marciano-Walcott had been revisited and Marciano's unbeaten record preserved. It was advertised that after the film's showing, bonded guards would pick up the prints of the motion picture and destroy them, but this proved nothing more than a publicity maneuver.[12] Luckily for historians and boxing buffs alike, *The Super-Fight* remains a boxing fantasy come alive.

1. Muhammad Ali with Richard Durham, *Greatest: My Own Story* (New York: Random House, 1975), 297.
2. Ibid.
3. *The Superfight*, produced by Murry Woroner, directed by Murry Woroner, 70 minutes, 1970.
4. Everett M. Skehan, *Rocky Marciano: Biography of a First Son* (Boston: Houghton Mifflin Company, 1977), 341; Ali and Durham, *Greatest*, 297.
5. *The Superfight*.
6. Ali and Durham, *Greatest*, 297.
7. Prim, Review of *The Superfight* (Woroner's Productions, Inc. movie), *Variety*, 31 December 1969.
8. Ibid.
9. Skehan, *Rocky Marciano*, 340.
10. Ibid., 361–362.
11. Ali and Durham, *Greatest*, 297.
12. Prim.

They Made Me a Criminal (1939)

Warner Brothers, Drama, B & W, 92 minutes

Producer: Warner Bros. *Director*: Busby Berkeley. *Screenplay*: Sig Herzig, based upon a novel by Bertram Millhauser and Beulah Marie Dix. *Film Editor*: Jack Kilifer. *Photography*: James Wong Howe. *Music*: Max Steiner. *Musical Director*: Leo F. Forbstein.

John Garfield (Johnnie Bradfield alias Jack Dorney), Claude Rains (Detective Phelan), Gloria Dickson (Peggy), May Robson (Grandma), Billy Halop (Tommy), Huntz Hall (Dippy), Leo Gorcey (Spit), Bobby Jordan (Angel), Barbara Pepper (Budgie), Ward Bond (Lenihan), Gabriel Dell (T.P.), Bernard Punsley (Milt), Ann Sheridan (Goldie), Robert Gleckler (Doc Ward), John Ridgely (Magee), William Davidson (Ennis), Robert Strange (Malvin), Louis Jean Heydt (Smith), Frank Riggi (Rutchek), Cliff Clarke (Manager), Dick Wessel (Colossi), Raymond Brown (Sheriff), Sam Hayes (Fight Announcer).

While John Garfield was still a stage actor in New York and a member of The Group Theater, Clifford Odets scripted a play entitled *Golden Boy* with the dark-haired youngster in mind to play the prizefighter lead. However, when the theater's leader, Harold Clurman, chose Lou Adler to portray the boxer, Garfield was left the comedic role of Siggie the cabdriver.[1] Just a short year later, Garfield made the successful transition from stage to screen. Fresh from his Academy Award nomination for best supporting actor in *Four Daughters*, Warner Brothers was eager to showcase their new star.

Douglas Fairbanks, Jr., had previously starred for the studio in a boxing film entitled *The Life of Jimmy Dolan*. Garfield, like Fairbanks, possessed swarthy good looks and ample screen magnetism and was an ideal candidate to reprise the Fairbanks role. Remaking the Fairbanks vehicle as *They Made Me a Criminal*, Garfield atoned for his missed opportunity in *Golden Boy* in his very first leading role in Hollywood.

In the film, Johnny Bradfield (Garfield), the new light-heavyweight champion, projects an all-American persona for the public, but he is actually immoral and self-interested. While celebrating his championship victory, Johnny's manager (Clarke) kills a newspaper reporter and flees with Johnny's girlfriend Goldie (Sheridan). The pair then die in an auto accident, and the charred male corpse is believed to be Bradfield. Unsure whether he himself killed the newsman while inebriated, Bradfield capitalizes upon his "deceased" status and goes underground under the alias Jack Dorney. However, a shrewd detective name Phelan (Rains) believes that Bradfield is still alive, and launches a one-man search to locate the boxer.

Alias Jack eventually arrives hungry and exhausted at an Arizona date farm established to rehabilitate juvenile delinquents (The Dead End Kids). The street-wise pug readily blends with the wayward youths and bonds with them by giving boxing lessons. Jack also pursues Peggy (Dickson), the sister of one of the boys, who is put off by Jack, finding him a less than ideal role model for the boys. When one of the boys almost drowns in an irrigation tank, Jack's heroic role in the incident comes to the fore and he wins Peggy's respect and romantic interest.

Beginning to grasp the value of giving, Jack looks to alleviate the farm's mounting financial crisis by entering a boxing tournament. However, when Phelan arrives in town, Jack bows out.

Jack is branded a coward by the boys and resigns to leave in shame, but ultimately decides he'd rather risk capture than lose face.

During his fight, Jack attempts to deceive Phelan by abandoning his southpaw stance. Consequently, he suffers a beating, but stays enough rounds to win the prize money. A hero to Peg and the kids, he is taken into custody by Phelan. Phelan, sensing Jack's metamorphosis, ultimately releases him.

A lull in musical productions at Warner Brothers at the time propelled Busby Berkeley, the renowned director of musicals, into the unlikely role of fight picture orchestrator. Here he proved the diversity of his talents. "Busby Berkeley's direction has punch, both in the quieter moments and such rousing scenes as the prizefights," noted Hobe of *Variety*.[2] Irene Thirer of the *New York Post* opined that "Busby Berkeley's swift direction of this one puts the erstwhile dance master in the top ranks."[3]

The casting of the film was on par with its direction. The Dead End Kids, straight from their stint in *Dead End*, were an ideal match for fellow native New Yorker John Garfield.

The picture rated good reviews, and Garfield, receiving excellent write-ups, seemed to make the difference. "It is a thoroughly good melodrama, lifted to distinction by Mr. Garfield's performance," observed Bland Johaneson of *The New York Daily Mirror*.[4] Offering a concurring opinion, B.R.C. of *The New York Times* wrote, "It is always Mr. Garfield, with his sublime self-confidence, the unhandsome attractiveness of his greasy, round, gamin face, who carries the show along."[5]

Hobe of *Variety* found Garfield's performance "stunning," a display of "insight, study, sincerity and restraint."[6] Herbert Cohn of the *Brooklyn Daily Eagle* said of Garfield: "He is living his part. What he does is always natural, always sure and definite, always sensitively shaded, always convincing."[7] If *Four Daughters* had put Garfield on the map as a supporting player, *They Made Me a Criminal* confirmed that his talents were transferable to a lead role. Garfield was dubbed "a rising star" by *The New York Times* and an "important screen personality" by the *New York Journal-American*, who in the words of *Variety*, "could scarcely miss becoming a major star."[8]

Garfield's rugged good looks and staccato voice were well-suited for the prizefighting character. While not particularly muscular, Garfield offers a trim physique and his omnipresent masculinity and tough-guy demeanor are fully convincing. Boxing sequences are limited to a brief but well-done opening scene, several shots of Garfield engaging in horseplay with the Dead End Kids, and the climactic fight scene toward the film's conclusion. The fight finale is realistic, despite the fact that the Garfield character purposefully refrains from exhibiting his boxing acumen in order to conceal his identity. When Garfield switches back to southpaw and fights in earnest, audiences get a preview of what is to follow in *Body and Soul*.

1. George Morris, *John Garfield* (New York: Jove Publications, Inc., 1977), 25.
2. Hobe, Review of *They Made Me a Criminal* (Warner Bros. movie), *Variety*, 25 January 1939.
3. Irene Thirer, "'They Made Me a Criminal' With John Garfield at Strand." Review of *They Made Me a Criminal* (Warner Bros. movie), *New York Post*, 21 January 1939.
4. Bland Johaneson, "John Garfield Gives Exciting Show in Debut as Star," Review of *They Made Me a Criminal* (Warner Bros. movie), *New York Daily Mirror*, 21 January 1939.
5. B.R.C. "The Warners Present John Garfield in 'They Made Me a Criminal' at the Strand-Three Foreign Films," Review of *They Made Me a Criminal* (Warner Bros. movie), *New York Times*, 21 January 1939.
6. Hobe.
7. Herbert Cohn, "John Garfield, a Fine, Impressive Actor, Stars in 'They Made Me a Criminal,' at N.Y. Strand; Drummond Film at B'klyn Strand," Review of *They Made Me a Criminal* (Warner Bros. movie), *Brooklyn Daily Eagle*, 21 January 1939.
8. B.R.C.; Rose Pelswick, "They Made Me a Criminal Filled with Action," Review of *They Made Me a Criminal* (Warner Bros. movie), *New York Journal-American*, 21 January 1939; Hobe.

Triumph of the Spirit (1989)

Columbia Pictures, Drama, Color, 120 minutes

Producers: Arnold Kopelson, Shimon Arama. *Director*: Robert M. Young. *Screenplay*: Andrzej Krakowski, Laurence Heath. *Film Editor*: Arthur Coburn. *Director of Photography*: Curtis Clark. *Music*: Cliff Eidelman.

Willem Dafoe (Salamo), Edward James Olmos (Gypsy), Robert Loggia (Poppa), Wendy Gazelle (Allegra), Kelly Wolf (Elena), Costas Mandylor (Anram), Kario Salem (Jacko), Edward Zentara (Janush), Hartmut Becker (Major Rauscher), Burkhard Heyl (Aid to Rauscher), Sofia Saretok (Momma), Grazyna Kruk-Schejbal (Sister, Julie), Karolina Twardowska (Benuta), Juranda Krol (Sarah), Wiktor Mlnarczyk (Beppo), Jerzy Gralek (Kapo Kyr), Mieczyslaw Budzynski, Krzysztof Tadak, Josef Lis, Evan Kopelson (Boxers), Teddy Atlas (Boxer, Boxing Choreographer and Trainer), Mickey Duff (Boxing Consultant).

The success of *Schindler's List* and *Life Is Beautiful* have proven that films about the Holocaust can be both financially and artistically successful. Yet not long ago, the studios avoided the subject. During the early 1980s, producer Arnold Kopelson met with traditional resistance when he attempted to make a film about an Auschwitz survivor. It was only later that the success of Kopelson's *Platoon* elevated him to a position from which he could bring his project to the screen.[1]

As noted by critic Stanley Kaufmann writing for *The New Republic*, Kopelson's film, *Triumph of the Spirit*, is the belated response to Leni Riefenstahl's *Triumph of the Will*, the powerful Nazi propaganda piece that subjugated human spirit in the name of nationalism.[2] Salamo Arouch, a Greek Jew from Thessalonski, and the middleweight boxing champion of the Balkans, served as the film's subject. In 1943, Arouch was interned by the Germans at Auschwitz-Birkenau concentration camp along with tens of thousands of other denizens of Thessalonski.

Triumph of the Spirit begins with Arouch's (Dafoe) joyous win of his boxing title, which he celebrates with his beloved father (Loggia), brother and fiancée. The anticipation of their impending relocation by the Nazis soon turns to the confusion and fear found with actual internment at Auschwitz. The film powerfully details the dehumanization process at the camp, where identity is stripped in favor of uniformity. Heads are identically shaved, names are eliminated and replaced by numbered tattoos burned into the skin. Privacy is nonexistent. Forced labor, gnawing hunger, and deplorable living conditions are for the survivors; the weak and disfavored go "up the chimney," victims of the Nazi's human crematorium.[3]

Arouch is distinguished from his fellow prisoners by his boxing ability. After winning a fistfight with another prisoner, he gains favor with a high-ranking German officer, and is given the opportunity to fight in the ring as entertainment for S.S. officers who bet on the matches. "How many rounds?" Arouch asks before his first match. "No rounds," a German official replies. "You fight until one goes down and can't get up."[4]

Winners in the ring are rewarded with a loaf of bread. Arouch shares the precious prize with his loved ones while others claw for their crumbs. Losers in the ring are subject to a death sentence. Arouch achieves no redemption in his ring victories, only survival. His boxing courts him limited favor; it cannot save his father or brother from death.

The carnage at Auschwitz-Birkenau was unimaginable. It is believed that four million were put to death there.[5] The film drives toward the essence of the tragedy, feeding the viewer the experience vicariously. By filming on location the picture establishes integrity. Most of the film's interiors were shot at Birkenau.⁶ Dafoe described the sensation of arriving at the concentration camp as "terrific numbness."⁷

Other authentic filming locations included a Gestapo headquarters and the infamous cellblock 11, where the film's finale occurs. Forty-five members of the cast received instruction on life in the camp from ex-prisoners, including Arouch himself, who told Willem Dafoe, "After this ordeal, life is a gift."⁸

The picture boldly recreates Arouch's experience. Rex Reed wrote that the film was "powerful and compelling. A life-reaffirming motion picture that will touch your soul."⁹ "A film of high-purpose and overwhelming power, brilliant cast and beautifully acted," observed Michael Medved of *Sneak Previews*.¹⁰ "Disturbingly authentic film," noted Tom O'Brien of *Commonweal*.¹¹

Dafoe was similarly praised. "As the battered, world-weary boxer, Dafoe is just right," wrote Jeffrey Lyons for *Video Review*.¹² Dafoe portrays Arouch as steady and resilient, cognizant of the hollow nature of his ring victories and the reality that surrounds him, yet resolute in the possibilities of human hope. "Willem Dafoe is excellent," noted Bruce Williamson of *Playboy*.¹³

To prepare for his role in the ring, Dafoe trained for two weeks beforehand, and then throughout the shooting of the film.¹⁴ D.B. of *Film Journal* wrote that Dafoe was "convincingly pumped up to look like a middleweight champion."¹⁵ The actor, in fact, had added several pounds of sinewy muscle to his ultra-slim frame for the film. The results perfectly suited the role: a physique of a finely tuned and muscular athlete whose excessive leanness reflected the onset of deterioration. Regarding his training experience Dafoe noted: "The boxing, since it engages you physically and there was a genuine transformation, was a real pleasure."¹⁶

The fight vignettes in the picture are brief, but are done with an artistry that makes them compelling and memorable. Dafoe expertly conveys the life-and-death tension of his matches and the mixture of humility and hatred he experiences in their immediate aftermath. Slow motion is used with great effect, particularly in a montage that features graphic knockout sequences. The ring is also a poignant metaphor for the Nazis' human denigration, where boxers are displaced for follow-up entertainment featuring a small bow-wearing dog who jumps over a streamer.

The fight scenes for *Triumph of the Spirit* were choreographed by boxing trainer Teddy Atlas, who trained recent heavyweight champions Mike Tyson and Michael Moorer. Atlas, who was once a fighter under the tutelage of Cus D'Amato, appears as one of Dafoe's opponents as well.

The experience of making the picture affected all involved. Atlas said, "I went down to one of the crematories. When I got down there, I saw all these fresh flowers laid on top of the ovens. That's when everything became real to me. There were people who were still alive who remember. People who are still suffering."¹⁷

1. *New York Times*, 17 March 1989.
2. Stanley Kaufmann, Review of *Triumph of the Spirit* (Columbia Pictures movie), *The New Republic*, 25 December 1989.
3. *Triumph of the Spirit*, produced by Arnold Kopelson, directed by Robert M. Young, 120 minutes, RCA/Columbia Home Video, videocassette.
4. *Ibid*.
5. David Heuring, "Triumph of the Spirit: Survivors at Any Cost," *American Cinematographer*, February 1990.
6. *Ibid*.
7. Steve Oney, "Willem Dafoe, Looking for Characters with Possibility," *Sunday New York Times*, 3 December 1989.
8. Matthew Flamm, "Death Camp Ring Leader" *New York Post*, 5 December 1989; Harry Haun, "'Hard Fought' Triumph," *Sunday New York Daily News*, 3 December 1989.
9. Rex Reed, as quoted in *New York Post* advertisement, 15 December 1989, 47.
10. Michael Medved, Review of *Triumph of the Spirit* (Columbia Pictures movie), *Sneak Previews*.
11. Tom O'Brien, Review of *Triumph of the Spirit* (Columbia Pictures movie), *Commonweal*, 12 January 1990.

12. Jeffrey Lyons, Review of *Triumph of the Spirit* (Columbia Pictures movie), *Video Review*, June 1990.
13. Bruce Williamson, *Playboy*, as quoted in *New York Post* advertisement, 15 December 1989, 47.
14. Haun.
15. D.B., Review of *Triumph of the Spirit* (Columbia Pictures movie), *Film Journal*, January 1990.
16. Haun.
17. Mark DiIonnio, "*Triumph of the Spirit*, Atlas Bears Witness," *New York Post*, 4 December 1989.

Undisputed (2002)

Miramax Films, Drama, Color, 94 minutes

Producer: David Giler, Walter Hill, Brad Krevoy, Andrew Sugarman. *Director:* Walter Hill. *Screenplay:* David Giler Walter Hill. *Film Editor:* Freeman Davies. *Cinemaphotography:* Lloyd Ahern. *Music:* Stanley Clarke.

Wesley Snipes (Monroe Hutchens), Ving Rhames (Iceman Chambers), Peter Falk (Mendy Ripstein), Michael Rooker (A.J. Mercker), Jon Seda (Jesus "Chuy" Campos), Wes Studi (Mingo Pace), Fisher Stevens (Ratbag Dolan), Dayton Callie (Yank Lewis), Amy Aquino (Darlene Early), Johnny Williams (Al), Joe D'Angerio (Vinnie), Nils Allen Stewart (Vern Van Zandt), Denis Arndt (Warden Lipscom), Tawnee Rawlins (Rose Rollins), Jim Lampley (himself), Master P. (himself), George Christy (himself), Maureen O'Boyle (herself).

The idea that a heavyweight champion of the world might spend time incarcerated in prison is neither fanciful nor new. From the time when Jack Johnson surrendered to the authorities for violation of the Mann Act, the tone was set for legal scrutiny of the antics of future bearers of the crown.

Jack Dempsey, Muhammad Ali and Sonny Liston have all had significant entanglements with the law. Dempsey's "slacker trial" and Ali's refusal to serve in the Armed Forces during the Vietnam War are now part of American history and boxing lore. While Dempsey couldn't fight and Ali wouldn't, Liston followed his own personal call to arms. He was a St. Louis Mafia enforcer who eventually served time for armed robbery.

However, the conviction of Mike Tyson for the rape of beauty contestant Desiree Washington escalated Heavyweight depravity to a new level, further linking violence and the sport of boxing in the public's mind.

Undisputed, the latest entree of writer-director Walter Hill, examines the fictious journey of "Iceman" Chambers (Rhames), the reigning Heavyweight champion, who, like Tyson, is sent to prison for rape. The prison already has its own Heavyweight champion, Monroe Hutchens (Snipes). A lifer, Hutchens sports an undefeated record, and has little interest in having his position usurped by "Iceman." However, when aged mobster Mendy Ripstein (Peter Falk) brokers a match which will yield both financial gain for Hutchins and an early prison release for Chambers, the battle for the prison's undisputed champion is set.

Undisputed director Walter Hill, who made his 1975 directorial debut with *Hard Times*, an examination of the underground bare-knuckle fight scene of the Depression-era, has a knack for recreating the masculine world. As Robert Koehler of *Variety* noted in his review of *Undisputed*, "his universe of hardened men living by their own rules outside society's mainstream has rarely received better expression."[1] Arnold White, writing for the *New York Press*, credited Hill for making "*Undisputed* the most unpretentious, yet sociologically insightful b-movie since — well, since his 1979 film, *The Warriors*."[2]

Ving Rhames had previously given one

of the greatest performances in a boxing film in his magnificent portrayal of promoter Don King in *Don King: Only in America*. In *Undisputed*, Rhames provides another fine performance, prompting John Anderson of *Newsday* to write, "Wesley Snipes may be the punitive lead of the film, but it's Ving Rhames who carries the water."[3] Jack Matthews of *Newsday* found Rhames's character to be "genuinely scary," sporting "a glare as menacing as any seen in a ring since Sonny Liston."[4] Critic John Koehler recognized the superior work of Snipes, who also previously appeared in the boxing film *Streets of Gold*. Koehler writes that Snipes's performance was "distinguished" amongst an "impeccably cast ensemble," which included Peter Falk "in his most colorful role in years."[5]

The fight scenes in the picture take a departure from the Marquess of Queensberry rules, as the bout for the championship is a fight to the finish with no referee. Robert Koehler reported that the final fight vignette was "one of the most physically intense fight sequences since *Raging Bull*— and one in which Snipes and Rhames visibly did all the fighting."[6]

Fight aficionados will enjoy the appearance of HBO boxing analyst Jim Lampley, and hip-hop fans will equally embrace the appearance of Master P and the musical score featuring Cash Money Millionaires.

1. Robert Koehler, "*Undisputed*: Boxing Saga Pulls No Punches," Review of *Undisputed* (Miramax Pictures Movie), *Variety*, 28 August 2002.
2. Arnold White, *New York Press*, August 21-27 2002, 42.
3. John Anderson, "Droll with All Its Punches," Review of *Undisputed* (Miramax Pictures Movie), *Newsday*, 23 August 2002.
4. Jack Mathews, "Even Behind Bars, They're Lords of the Ring," Review of *Undisputed* (Miramax Pictures Movie), *New York Daily News*, 23 August 2002.
5. Robert Koehler, "*Undisputed*: Boxing Saga Pulls No Punches."
6. *Ibid*.

When We Were Kings (1996)

DAS Films, Ltd., Documentary, Color, 87 minutes

Producers: Leon Gast, David Sonenberg, Taylor Hackford. *Director*: Leon Gast. *Film Editors*: Leon Gast, Taylor Hackford, Jeffrey Levy-Hinte, Keith Robinson. *Concert Producers*: Stewart Levine, Hugh Maserela, Lloyd Price. *Cinematography*: Maryse Alberti, Paul Goldsmith, Kevin Keating, Albert Mayes, Roderick Young.

Muhammad Ali, George Foreman, Don King, James Brown, B.B. King, Mobutu Sese Seko, Spike Lee, Norman Mailer, George Plimpton, Thomas Hauser, Malik Bowens, Lloyd Price, The Spinners, The Crusaders, Miriam Makeba.

When Leon Gast envisioned making a documentary about an African musical festival he could have scarcely imagined his project culminating 23 years later as an Academy Award-winning film about the personalities, politics and pageantry that converged at the George Foreman–Muhammad Ali fight. Yet from its inception, everyone and everything that touched Gast's project was extraordinary. A conglomeration of colorful and unique characters and unpredictable influences steered his film to its artistic finality with an almost collective willfulness.

The threads of Gast's tapestry began to take hold in 1974. As an encore to the liberation of the erstwhile Belgian Congo, Mobutu Sese Seko, the ruthless leader of Zaire, was determined to catapult his nation into world public consciousness. At that same time, another new ruler, the brooding and seemingly invincible heavyweight champion George Foreman, was anxious to exploit new capitalistic opportunities. At Foreman's heels was the former heavyweight crown-bearer, the irrepressible Muhammad Ali. Time to recapture his old scepter was waning, and Ali was desperately posturing for an opportunity to dethrone Foreman. Waiting in the wings was ex-convict and fledgling entrepreneur Don King. Determined to live up to his surname by establishing his own boxing promotional fiefdom, King did not shy away from strange bedfellows when his ambitions were at issue.

All roads would meet in Kinshasa, Zaire. In one of the greatest leveraged promotions in sports history, Don King, with the assistance of Mobutu, his unlikely patron and the fight's eventual host, facilitated the guarantee of $5 million to both Foreman and Ali to box one another for the championship.[1] The fight would not only provide the power-drunk Mobutu with unimaginable publicity and Foreman the greatest purse in boxing history, but it would give Ali a chance to reinvent himself and King the forum to gain a reputation overnight.

Incidental to the promotional extravaganza was the potential subject of Gast's film documentary, an African music festival which was to be staged over the three days prior to the fight. Scheduled performers included the likes of James Brown, B.B. King, the Spinners, and the Pointer Sisters. As Gast prepared his documentary, fate interceded. With the swing of a spar mate's blow, Foreman incurred a nasty gash over his eye, which not only prevented him from further sparring, but forced a six-week delay in the fight. With time on their hands Gast and his crew quickly shifted their cameras' focus to the fighters' good-will tours, promotional appearances, and training sessions.

A four-to-one underdog, Muhammad Ali's defeat of George Foreman for the heavyweight championship of the world was heralded as one of the great sports comebacks. A jubilant Ali returned to the United States, as did Gast, who assuredly was overwhelmed by the 300,000 feet of film he had in tow.[2] Ironically, attendance fees earmarked by Gast to cover post-production costs were severely reduced when Mobutu persuaded a free admission policy after the turnout for the festival's first day was dismal.[3] The extra 100,000 feet of film shot during the delay compounded Gast's expenses, forcing him to spend the next 15 years paying off his film lab processing fees. Six more years were spent editing and re-editing the impossible volume of film into eight separate film versions.[4]

The ultimate product was made possible with the financial assistance of David Sonenberg. The resulting documentary, aptly entitled *When We Were Kings*, is a thought-provoking and entertaining mix of politics, sports, music and culture as captured on the eve of one of sports' most memorable events.

To keep Kinshasa safe for the many foreigners he desired to impress, Mobutu utilized the recesses of his newly built boxing stadium as a detention center for criminals and even held executions there, until it was explained to the zealous revolutionary that such repression would do little to court international favor.[5] Through the use of clips illustrating his past and present strong-arm tactics, Gast documents the heavy hand of Mobutu, which hung omnipresently above the seemingly festive atmosphere surrounding the match.

Gast captures the throngs of natives warmly embracing Ali, as they supportively shout "Ali bomaye" ("Ali kill him"). This starkly contrasts with the locals' cool reception of Foreman, who unwittingly attended a press conference with his pet police dog — the symbol and practical arm of Belgian Colonialism.* The film also serendipitously

---

*Perhaps Foreman was destined to play the role of "the bad guy." Most Zairians did not even know who he was prior to his arrival, and they had assumed the American heavyweight champion was a white man. Foreman could not understand their kinship with Ali, exclaiming, "I'm blacker than Ali."

documents the origins of the frighteningly charming and ceaselessly verbal Don King, who was just beginning to prove that self-confidence and "street smarts" can substitute for a formal education.

Gast complements the telling of Ali's love affair with Africa, and Foreman's pre-fight misfortunes, with an assortment of boxing scenes. The filmmaker visits Ali's training camp, where the challenger spars with Larry Holmes, and later calls upon Foreman, where the champion displays unequaled raw power punishing the heavy bag.

Laced with anecdotal stories that both charm and amuse, the film's narration is provided by authors Norman Mailer and George Plimpton who lend a thoughtful and humorous voice-over to many of the film's varied clips. During one piece, Odessa Clay, Ali's mother, affectionately recalls how the theft of her son's bicycle led to a fighting career. In another, Howard Cosell smugly predicts a Foreman victory. Author Thomas Hauser details the amazing financial and promotional aspects of the fight, director Spike Lee waxes political on Ali's stance on Vietnam and his role as a hero, and Ali's corner man Bundini Brown champions Ali as a prophet. The boxing vignettes and retrospective interviews are cleverly punctuated with well-placed out-takes from the music festival which help to set the film's pace, while providing the cultural backdrop for the event and the musical soundtrack for the picture.

When the film originally played at the Sundance Film Festival it copped the "Special Jury Prize" and 17 offers to distribute the film followed. After the film's general release, the critics embraced it. Will Joyner of *The New York Times* dubbed the picture "a verite study of Muhammad Ali's unlikely recovery of boxing's top title."[6] Todd McCarthy of *Variety* noted, "Tightly made and populated by a uniformly larger-than-life cast of characters, pic is a total delight for every second of its running time."[7]

Gast's incredible journey culminated with unparalleled reward. The film captured best documentary awards from the New York Film Critics Circle, Los Angeles Film Critics Association and the National Society of Film Critics.[8] As its crowning achievement, *When We Were Kings* went on to become the first sports documentary to garner an Academy Award, winning in the category for best non-fiction film, feature-length documentary.[9]

1. *When We Were Kings, The True Story of the Rumble in the Jungle*, Production notes, 11.
2. *Ibid.*, 16.
3. Jack Mathews, "Finally, a Knockout. Leon Gast's Rumble in the Jungle Film Wins a Spot in Oscar's Ring," *Newsday*, 12 February 1997, sec. B, p.3.
4. *When We Were Kings, The True Story of the Rumble in the Jungle*, Production notes, 16.
5. Dave Anderson, "When Ali Performed a Knockout on Film," *Sunday New York Times*, 23 February 1997, sec. 8, p. 2.
6. Will Joyner, "The Fight Took 8 Rounds, the Film 22 Years," *Sunday New York Times*, 16 February 1997, sec. 2, p. 11.
7. Todd McCarthy, Review of *When We Were Kings* (DAS Films, Ltd. movie), *Variety*, 12–18 February 1996.
8. Anderson, "When Ali Performed a Knockout," 2.
9. Claude Bradesser, "Lawsuits over Ali Pic Ready to Rumble," *Daily Variety*, 1 September 1998.

When's Your Birthday? (1937)

RKO Radio Pictures, Comedy, B & W (with color cartoon), 76 minutes

Producer: David Loew. *Director*: Harry Beaumont. *Screenplay*: Harry Clork, adaptation by Harvey Gates, M.S. Boylan, S.M. Pike.

Joe E. Brown (Dusty Willoughby), Marian Marsh (Jerry Grant), Fred Keating (Larry Burke), Edgar Kennedy (Mr. Basscombe), Maude Eburne (Mrs. Basscombe), Suzanne Kaaren (Diane Basscombe), Margaret Hamilton (Mossy), Minor Watson (Regan), Frank Jenks (Lefty), Don Rowan

(Steve), Granville Bates (Judge O'Day) Charles Judels (Head Waiter), Corky (Zodiac).

Perhaps best known for his gallant but failed attempt to capture heavyweight laurels from Jack Dempsey in 1921, light-heavyweight champion Georges Carpentier was already making inroads into the film industry a year before he even met the "Manassa Mauler" when he starred in *Wonderman*. A decade later, capitalizing on the enduring popularity of the French war hero, Warner Brothers cast Carpentier in another prizefighter role in the early sound boxing film *Hold Everything* (1930). The musical comedy also starred the rubbery-faced Joe E. Brown as a preliminary fighter, boxing on the card headlined by Carpentier. Several years later, when the Fred Ballard play *When's Your Birthday?* was brought to the screen by RKO, Brown would make his own cinematic return to the ring.

When's Your Birthday? is a vehicle for the slapstick antics of Joe E. Brown. Brown portrays Dusty Willoughby, an unlikely prelim boxer whose real love is astrology. He uses his astrological acumen to predict the misfortune of a judge named O'Day (Bates). Dusty also successfully predicts the result of a dog race for the judge's companion Lefty (Jenks). However, before Lefty's boss Regan (Watson) can offer Dusty a job as a prognosticator, he disappears.

Dusty secures a job as a fortuneteller. He also begins a relationship with a pretty young assistant named Jerry (Marsh). He is eventually arrested for telling fortunes without a license, but he has the good luck of going before Judge O'Day, who puts him in contact with Regan.

Regan places a bet on the Salvador Slayer in his bout against Cracker Craven. Later, Dusty advises him that the planets indicate that the Slayer can't possibly win. Consequently, Regan presses Dusty to fight in his place.

Without the moon in the proper position, Dusty barely survives the first couple of rounds. However, when the moon finally rises, a rejuvenated Dusty scores a knockout. When Dusty and Jerry leave the stadium their future is revealed in the moon, which has taken the shape of a baby's face.

Rose Pelswick of the *New York Evening Journal* described the picture as featuring "typical Joe E. Brown material, a farcical assortment of gags and tumbles."[1] But most of the slapstick, at least outside of the squared circle, failed to create mirth. By today's standards, glasses falling off trays, a potted plant breaking off a head, and the star dressed in drag all fail to achieve their desired effect. Apparently, at least to some, the gags were no more humorous when the picture was released. As Scho of *Variety* bluntly observed, "A good portion of the slapstick is dated."[2] Still, Brown's advocates stood up to be counted, with the critic for the *New York Daily News* writing, "The story provides situations in which Joe E. Brown is at his mighty best."[3]

To be accurate, one must draw a clear distinction between the majority of the movie and the slapstick that occurs in the ring in the final scene of the picture. While the former was lacking, the latter provides some good entertainment. "If nothing else," wrote critic Wanda Hale, "*When's Your Birthday?* is worth seeing for this last fight. It sets a record as the goofiest of all goofy matches on the screen or in the ring."[4] Several of the gags in the boxing ring, while not of the sidesplitting variety, certainly qualify as amusing. Granted Brown benefited from the previous ring antics of two great predecessors, Chaplin and Keaton, but there was not a great body of work to draw from when fashioning his own ring skits, which prove to have a good deal of originality.

In one funny scene Brown has his gloves on the wrong hands. When his corner man removes them to switch hands, Brown crosses his arms, thus presenting the wrong fists for the gloves when they are to be re-fitted. In another, Brown clings in desperation to a giant microphone as he is dragged around the ring prior to the commencement of the bout. The standard gag involving the complications of removing his fight robe, a thumb caught in his trunk knot, and tickling by his corner man come off with varying degrees of success. But throughout it all, Brown is good at wearing a perplexed face etched with great concern.

Film buffs may also enjoy the uncredited appearance of Ward Bond, who portrays a cop in this film, but is better known for his portrayal of another policeman in *It's a Wonderful Life*. Equally enjoyable is the brief appearance and unforgettable voice of Margaret Hamilton, who had not yet given her famous portrayal of the wicked witch of the West in *The Wizard of Oz*.

1. Rose Pelswick, "Joe E. Brown Film Premiere Reviewed," Review of *When's Your Birthday?* (RKO Radio Pictures movie), *New York Evening Journal*, 19 March 1937.
2. Scho, Review of *When's Your Birthday?* (RKO Radio Pictures movie), *Variety*, 24 March 1937.
3. Review of *When's Your Birthday?* (RKO Radio Pictures movie), *New York Daily News*, 19 March 1937.
4. Wanda Hale, Review of *When's Your Birthday?* (RKO Radio Pictures movie), *New York Daily News*, 19 March 1937.

Winner Take All (1932)

Warner Brothers, Drama, B & W, 67 minutes

Producer: Roy Del Ruth (Uncredited). *Director*: Roy Del Ruth. *Screenplay*: Robert Lord, Wilson Minzer, adapted from the story *133 at 3* by Gerald Beaumont. *Editor*: Thomas Pratt. *Photography*: Robert Kurrle. *Music*: Vitaphone Orchestra conducted by Leo F. Forbstein.

James Cagney (Jim Kane), Marian Nixon (Peggy Harmon), Guy Kibbee (Pop Slavin), Dickie Moore (Dickie Harmon), Virginia Bruce (Joan Gibson), Alan Mowbray (Forbes), Ester Howard (Ann), Clarence Muse (Rosebud the Trainer), Clarence Wilson (Ben Issacs), Ralph Harolde (Legs Davis), John Roche (Roger Elliot).

In just over a decade, James Frances Cagney, Jr. went from an unknown stage player to the apex of his profession. *Public Enemy* (1931) brought the actor early public recognition, and further critical acclaim was earned in *Angels with Dirty Faces* (1938). *Yankee Doodle Dandy* (1942) would eventually elevate him to the status of entertainer *nonpareil*.

On his way to film stardom Cagney portrayed a prizefighter on several occasions. *City for Conquest*, a tale of ambitious New Yorkers, proved to be the most enduring of these efforts. Conversely, *The Irish in Us*, a simple comedy tenuously held together by the celtic camaraderie of Cagney and his off-screen pals Pat O'Brien and Frank McHugh, has all but been forgotten.

Cagney's first opportunity to box on the screen, which came in a Warner Brothers production entitled *Winner Take All*, has likewise been pushed off the late show and into obscurity.

In *Winner Take All*, Jim Kane (Cagney) is a gruff-talking prizefighter from New York, who is sent out West by his manager Pop (Kibbee) to be cleansed of nightclubs, booze, and women. There he meets and begins a romance with Peggy (Nixon), a sweet girl. Kane fights a "winner take all" match to help Peggy meet her bills, but their relationship is abruptly interrupted when he is called back to New York to resume his career in earnest.

The lightweight boxer then meets a Park Avenue socialite named Joan (Bruce) who fancies the fighter with his mashed nose and cauliflower ears, finding him something of a curiosity. Kane, however, believes it's love and has plastic surgery to impress his sophisticated partner. To protect his new countenance, the fighter adopts a defensive fighting style which causes him to fall out of favor with both fight fans and Joan, who no longer finds Kane physically unique.

When Peggy arrives in New York, she learns that Kane plans to wed her competition. Joan, however, has other plans and skips Jim's championship fight to take a cruise to Havana. Kane makes quick work of the titleholder and races to the pier only to discover Joan with another man. The new champion then returns to Peggy, who welcomes him with open arms.

Winner Take All finely illustrates Jimmy Cagney's ability to carry the most routine of stories. As reported by the *Times (London)*, "Mr. Cagney gives such a fascinating picture of the boxer's conceit and stupidity that the original plot, which might have come from a novelette, is lost in the intricacies of his character."[1] *Time* magazine wrote that Cagney's performance, as in his previous roles, possessed "a quality of effortless authenticity."[2]

Though the film was only the first to depict Cagney as a prizefighter, it was readily apparent that this was another type of character the actor could master. Gerald Breitigam of the *New York World-Telegram* wrote that Cagney "carries with him a veritable smell of the shower room, of sweating body and sodden leather," adding that he could be one "of the lads in Jimmy Johnston's stable at the Garden."[3] Comparatively speaking, Mordaunt Hall of *The New York Times* found Cagney to be "far more convincing than most players who elect to impersonate pugilists."[4] "He is unerring in his portrayal of the 'mug' type," reported the *Hollywood Herald*.[5]

Preparation was instrumental to Cagney's success. The actor trained in Palm Springs for several weeks under the tutelage of former pro boxer Harvey Perry. Perry was once a member of the United States diving team that participated in the 1912 Summer Olympic games.[6] In addition to adhering to a strict diet, Cagney's training regimen included five-mile daily jogs along Palm Springs desert roads, rope jumping and routine engagements with two spar mates.[7]

The picture's screenwriter, Wilson Minzer, was closely connected to boxing as a former manager and promoter, and the fight scenes in *Winner Take All* are among the best filmed during the 1930s. Cagney, an excellent dancer, moves around the ring with confidence as part of the well-choreographed fight vignettes. His fighting style may appear somewhat antiquated by today's standards, but judging by films from the Depression featuring Barney Ross, Tony Canzoneri and Jimmy McLarnin, Cagney got it just right. Tommy Richards, the former Pacific Coast lightweight champion, and an editor at Warner Brothers' First National Studio at the time of the film's production, commented that Cagney "can box with the best of them. He's the best actor-boxer I have seen in ten years."[8] If appraisals of Cagney's ability from observers are unconvincing, perhaps empirical evidence from the actor's sparring partner, pro boxer Billy DeGroot, might convince: A left hook from Cagney sent the boxer to the hospital.[9]

To create a large arena feeling, ample footage of crowd scenes was edited into the boxing vignettes. Robert Kurrle's camera records Cagney in action from three different distances, alternating the use of long, medium, and close-up shots. To further add to the film's authenticity twenty pro boxers from a local Los Angeles gym and other members of the fistic fraternity were featured as extras or advisors.[10] Most prominent of the group was Joe Rivers, former lightweight champion of the world, and fight manager Tom Jones, the pilot of boxing Hall-of-Famers Billy Papke and Abe Attel. Jones is also said to have provided a bit of inspiration for Guy Kibbee's portrayal of Pop.[11]

In 1938, Twentieth Century-Fox produced another fight picture, also bearing the name *Winner Take All*. Directed by Otto Browner, the film was a romantic comedy starring the popular bandleader and crooner

Tony Martin. Martin may not have been appropriate as a boxer in a serious role, but as a lighthearted leather-pusher he seemed to fit the bill. "If it's the picture's intent to kid the prizefight racket, the sheer casting of Tony Martin in the role of the pugilist rates the producer a bull's-eye," noted critic Odec of *Variety*.[12]

1. Review of *Winner Take All* (Twentieth Century-Fox movie), *Times (London)*, 13 September 1932.
2. *Time*, quoted in Homer Dickens, *The Films of James Cagney* (Secaucus, N.J.: Citadel Press, 1972), 65.
3. Gerald Breitigam, Review of *Winner Take All* (Twentieth Century-Fox movie), *New York World-Telegram*, 17 June 1932.
4. Mordaunt Hall, *New York Times*, quoted in Homer Dickens, *The Films of James Cagney*, 65–66.
5. *Hollywood Herald*, quoted in Homer Dickens, *The Films of James Cagney*, 66.
6. "Former Champion Acted as Technical Advisor for 'Winner Take All.'" Studio Publicity for *Winner Take All*.
7. "James Cagney Underwent Rigors of a Training Camp for 'Winner Take All.'" Studio Publicity for *Winner Take All*.
8. "Cagney Changed Jeers of Extras to Cheers When He Showed He Can Box." Studio Publicity for *Winner Take All*.
9. "Cagney's Earnestness in 'Winner Take All' Scenes Tough on Sparring Mate." Studio Publicity for *Winner Take All*.
10. "Pugs on the Set Made Cagney Self-Conscious While at Work in 'Winner Take All.'" Studio Publicity for *Winner Take All*.
11. "Tom Jones, Manager of Champions Is Used as Extra in 'Winner Take All'" Studio Publicity for *Winner Take All*.
12. Odec, Review of *Winner Take All* (Twentieth Century-Fox movie), *Variety*, 5 April 1939.

Woman-Wise (1937)

Twentieth Century-Fox, Comedy, B & W, 71 minutes

Producer: Sol M. Wurtzel. *Director*: Allan Dwan. *Screenplay*: Ben Markson. *Photography*: Robert Planck.

Rochelle Hudson (Alice Fuller), Michael Whalen (Tracey Brown), Thomas Beck (Clint DeWitt), Alan Dinehart (Richards), Douglas Fowley (Stevens), George Hassell (John DeWitt), Astrid Allwyn ("Bubbles" Carson), Chick Chandler (Bob Benton), Pat Flaherty (Duke Fuller).

While Allan Dwan's claim that he directed as many as 1,800 films was clearly an exaggeration, he was undoubtedly one of the most prolific directors in screen history.[1] As one of a handful to bark instructions from the bullhorn during the silent epoch of one-reelers, as well as the post–studio system era of the 1950s, Dwan left a long trail of lost or forgotten films. Still, the indefatigable director left a modest film legacy. In addition to his unsurpassed productivity, Dwan possessed a creative streak. He invented the equipment utilized for the famed crane shot in *Intolerance*, and introduced the "dolly shot" in *David Harum* when he filmed the strolling William H. Crane from a Ford vehicle.[2]

During the late 1930s, Dwan was making "B" movies for Twentieth Century-Fox. One of the pictures he ground out of his celluloid assembly line was *Woman-Wise*. The film's first treatment was entitled *The Sporting Editor*.[3] Later, screenwriter Ben Markson's yarn about a crusading newspaperman's fight against corruption in amateur boxing adopted its more alluring title.

Norwegian skating star Sonja Henie was originally slated to appear in the film. Skating scenes incidental to the fight story were to be written into the script to justify her character, but the movie ultimately proceeded without Henie. The pretty blonde nevertheless secured her own footnote in boxing history, not through a cameo appearance in a routine fight flick, but as a sexual conquest of heavyweight champion Joe Louis.[4]

In *Woman-Wise*, Tracey Brown (Whalen) is a sportswriter who seeks to expose a racket run by a corrupt fight manager named Richards (Dinehart) and an immoral sports editor named Stevens (Fowley). Richards and Stevens have been exploiting downtrodden boxers by featuring them in set-ups and then capitalizing on the fixed matches through a betting scam.

One of the prostituted fighters is named Duke Fuller (Flaherty). Brown takes on Duke in the ring and defeats him, gaining first hand knowledge of the prearranged bouts. Duke has a daughter named Alice (Hudson). Brown is attracted to Alice and he engages her to assist him in his crusade. Under his threat to expose the racket, Brown assesses a tax against the crooked parties and uses the acquired money to establish a relief fund for ex-fighters. Richards's son Clint (Beck), however, attempts to portray the benevolent Brown as an extortionist. Ultimately, Richards and Stevens are discredited and Brown's misconception that Alice is in love with Beck rather than himself is dispelled.

Wear of *Variety* found the film a "humorous version of [the] prize-fight ring." Wear also noted the "Sports scribe-newspaper background rings true because of a nice writing job by Ben Markson, adept direction by Allan Dwan and uniformly trim performances." Of the film's star Wear wrote, "Whalen … impresses here as the sports editor."[5]

Before becoming an actor, Michael Whalen was a model for both photographers and artists. Appearing in many ads and illustrations, Whalen posed before a number of famous artists including James Montgomery Flagg.[6] Incidentally, Flagg made a memorable contribution to the fight game himself by painting a giant picture of Jack Dempsey crouched before a towering Jess Willard. The picture hung in Dempsey's restaurant on Broadway in New York City for many years. The piece now hangs in the Smithsonian Institution, remaining one of the most famous pieces of boxing art ever created.[7] One of Dempsey's contemporaries, Fidel LaBarba worked on *Woman-Wise* as technical advisor. LaBarba trained Michael Whalen for three weeks to prepare him for his ring scenes. Others of the fight game to assist director Allan Dwan with the filming of the fight scenes were nationally known referee George Blake, heavyweight contender Bob Perry, and Joe Glick, an extra in numerous boxing movies.[8]

Those from the fight game were not the only ones responsible for the fisticuffs on the set. In one scene, the script called for Rochelle Hudson to slug Michael Whalen. The actress hit her co-star with such force that she sprained her wrist. Apparently the studio felt that this scene was empowering women and sought to exploit it as part of a promotional stunt. Twentieth Century-Fox's publicity material suggested that theaters set up a punching bag machine in the theater lobby and have the likeness of Whalen's face painted on the bag. Ticket-holding females entering the theater could then be invited to take a free swing at the star's face, just as Rochelle Hudson did in the movie![9]

1. Michael Barson, *The Illustrated Who's Who of Hollywood Directors Volume I: The Sound Era* (New York: Farrar, Straus and Giroux, 1995), 128.
2. *Ibid.*
3. Patricia King Hanson, *The American Film Institute Catalog of Motion Pictures Produced in the United States, Volume F3, Feature Films, 1931–1940* (Berkeley: University of California Press, 1993), Film Entries M–Z, 2463.
4. *Ibid.*; Joe Louis, Art Rust, Jr., Edna Rust, *Joe Louis: My Life* (New York: Harcourt Brace, 1981), 142,144.
5. Wear, Review of *Woman-Wise* (Twentieth Century-Fox movie), *Variety*, 20 January 1937.
6. "Male Tyros Beat Girls in Movie Rivalry," Studio Publicity for *Woman-Wise*.
7. "Whalen Shows 'Piano' Punch in Film Debut," Studio Publicity for *Woman-Wise*.
8. "Ex-Headliners Lend Hand on Sport Picture," Studio Publicity for *Woman-Wise*.
9. "Punching Bag Stunt." Studio Publicity for *Woman-Wise*.

Wonderman (1920)

No information available.

Seeking the heavyweight championship held by Jack Dempsey, the former light-heavyweight king, Frenchman Georges Carpentier, traveled to New York via the ocean liner *Savoie* in 1920. With his new bride Georgette, and his masseur and manager in tow, Carpentier, often besieged by seasickness, made his way across the Atlantic in anticipation of his boxing exhibition tour arranged by American promoter Jack Curley.

The purpose of the tour was to make Carpentier's name known to the American public, which in turn would make him a financially viable opponent for Dempsey's title. In addition to the boxing tour, publicity was to be generated through Carpentier's appearance as a boxer in a film entitled *Wonderman*.[1]

Arriving in New York, Carpentier boxed an impromptu exhibition with Major Drexel-Biddle, president of the International Sporting Club, took in the Ziegfeld Follies, and experienced Enrique Caruso at the Metropolitan Opera House. Shortly thereafter, Georges was leaving the Biltmore Hotel every morning at 8 A.M. and heading for a film studio across the Hudson River in New Jersey. He was regularly accompanied by his manager Descamps and his masseur Gus Wilson.[2]

The handsome Carpentier portrayed the lead in *Wonderman*, a French, non-commissioned officer who was on a secret mission in the United States. Carpentier was charged with tracking down an American traitor in cahoots with the Germans. Carpentier, who had won the Croix de Guerre during World War I, was required to do three things in the film. The first two, being a war hero and a boxer, came naturally. The third, which was to speak his lines, was not as easy. In spite of knowing that the audience would never actually hear his lines in a silent motion picture, Carpentier was still on edge while delivering them. Many years later he would explain, "The profession of film actor never appealed to me." Nevertheless, the compensation was welcome. In addition to the publicity generated, Carpentier earned $45,000 for just twenty-five days of work.[3]

Carpentier would go on to gain his shot at Jack Dempsey for the heavyweight championship on July 2, 1921, at Boyles Thirty Acres, in Jersey City, New Jersey. The match drew the first live million-dollar gate in boxing history. It was also the first boxing match ever broadcast over the radio. Carpentier was dispatched by Dempsey in four rounds, and though he never won the heavyweight championship, he continued to box for several years.

Despite his uneasiness with the acting profession, Carpentier would again appear on screen. He had met Arthur Loew, vice-president of MGM, in Paris in 1929, and would spend the holiday with him in Glenn Cove, Long Island, with such film luminaries as Mary Pickford, Douglas Fairbanks, Douglas Fairbanks, Jr., and his wife Joan Crawford.[4]

Shortly afterwards, Carpentier was given a small role in Jack Warner's *Show of Shows*, a film that not only featured the new invention of sound, but also was made in Technicolor. In the picture, Carpentier portrayed a professor of "physical culture" and his chief responsibility was to display his physique. Carpentier felt that he faired well in front of the camera, but "felt a bit out of place on the vast sets at Hollywood with their forests of apparatus and their rings of glaring lights." Nevertheless, the fighter accepted another Warner assignment to appear in *Hold Everything*, in which he starred with the rubbery-faced comic Joe E. Brown. Georges was offered the important role instead of accomplished actor Grant Withers, because the film required an ample amount of boxing scenes.[5] Carpentier took the role seriously, later noting, "Filming isn't such hard work as boxing, but all the same you have to be in reasonably good physical condition."[6]

Carpentier appeared in two other minor roles in American films, and concluded his film career in the 1934 French boxing film *Tobaggan*, in which Georges portrayed a fighter on the comeback trail, who loses both his come-back bid and the girl.[7]

1. Georges Carpentier, *Carpentier by Himself*, trans. Edward Fitzgerald (London: Hutchinson & Co. [Publishers] Ltd., 1955) 123–124.
2. *Ibid.*, 125–126.
3. *Ibid.*, 126
4. Carpentier, *Carpentier by Himself*, 187.
5. *Ibid.*, 188–189.
6. *Ibid.*, 193.
7. *Ibid.*, 197.

Selected Bibliography

Books

Ali, Muhammad, with Richard Durham. *The Greatest: My Own Story*. New York: Random House, 1975.

Anderson, Chris, Sharon McGehee, and Jake LaMotta. *Raging Bull II: Continuing the Story of Jake La Motta*. Secaucus, N.J.: Lyle Stuart Inc., 1986.

Armstrong, Henry. *Gloves, Glory and God*. Westwood, N.J.: Fleming H. Revell Company, 1956.

_____. Preface to *20 Years of Poems, Moods and Meditations*. n.p., 1954.

Ayleworth, Thomas G., and John S. Bowman. *The World Almanac Who's Who of Film*. New York: Bison Books, 1987.

Bankes, James. *Jack London: Stories of Boxing*. Dubuque, IA: Wm. C. Brown Publishers, 1992.

Barson, Michael. *The Illustrated Who's Who of Hollywood Directors Volume I: The Sound Era*. New York: Farrar, Straus and Giroux, 1995.

Baxter, John. *Stanley Kubrick: A Biography*. New York: Carroll and Graf Publishers Inc., 1997.

Buford, Kate. *Burt Lancaster: An American Hero*. New York: Alfred A. Knopf, 2000.

Cannon, Robert C. *Van Dyke and the Mythical City of Hollywood*. New York: Garland Publishing, 1977.

Carpentier, Georges. *Carpentier by Himself*. Trans. Edward Fitzgerald. London: Hutchinson & Co. Ltd., 1955.

Carpozi, Jr., George. *The John Wayne Story*. Westport CT: Arlington House, 1979.

Chaiton, Sam, and Terry Swinton. *Lazarus and the Hurricane: The Freeing of Rubin "Hurricane" Carter*. New York: St. Martin's Griffin, 2000.

Clayton, Rose, and Dick Heard. *Elvis Up Close, in the Words of Those Who Knew Him*. Atlanta: Turner Publishing, Inc., 1994.

Clinch, Minty. *Burt Lancaster*. New York: Stein and Day, 1984.

Cooper, Jackie, with Dick Kleiner. *"Please Don't Shoot My Dog": The Autobiography of Jackie Cooper*. New York: William Morrison & Company, Inc., 1981.

Corbett, James J. *The Roar of the Crowd*. Garden City, N.Y.: Garden City Publishing Company, 1925.

Costello, Chris, with Raymond Strait. *Lou's on First*. New York: St. Martin's Press, 1981.

Curtis, Tony, and Barry Paris. *Tony Curtis: The Autobiography*. New York: William And Morrow Company, Inc., 1993.

Davis, Ozzie, and Ruby Dee. *With Ozzie & Ruby: In This Life Together*. New York: William Morrow, 1998.

Dempsey, Jack, and Barbara Piatelli Dempsey. *Dempsey*. New York: Harper and Row Publishers, 1977.

Dickens, Homer. *The Films of James Cagney*. Secaucus, N.J.: Citadel Press, 1972.

Dixon, Wheeler W. *The "B" Directors: A Biographical Directory*. Metuchen, N.J.: The Scarecrow Press, Inc., 1985.

Douglas, Kirk. *The Ragman's Son: An Autobiography*. New York: Simon and Schuster, 1988.

Essoe, Gabe. *Tarzan of the Movies: A Pictorial History of More Than Fifty Years of Edgar Rice Burrough's Legendary Hero*. New York: The Citadel Press, 1968.

Fairbanks, Jr., Douglas. *A Hell of a War*. New York: St. Martin's Press, 1993.

Fishgall, Gary. *Against Type: The Biography of Burt Lancaster*. New York: Simon and Shuster, Inc., 1995.

Fleischer, Nat. *The Glamour Boy of The Ring*. New York: n.p., 1970.

Flynn, Errol. *My Wicked Wicked Ways*. Cutchogue, N.Y.: Buccaneer Books, 1976.

Franklin, Joe. *Classics of the Silent Screen: A Pictorial Treasury*. New York: The Citadel Press, 1959.

Goldman, Herbert, ed. *1984 Record Book and Boxing Encyclopedia*. New York: The Ring Publishing Corp., 1984.

Graziano, Rocky, and Ralph Corsel. *Somebody Down Here Likes Me Too*. New York: Stein & Day, 1981.

Gromach, John V. *The Saga of the Fist*. Cranbury, N.J.: A.S. Barnes and Company, 1977.

Hanson, Patricia King. *The American Film Institute Catalog of Motion Pictures Produced in the United States. Volume 3, Feature Films, 1931–*

1940. Berkeley: University of California Press, 1993.

Heimer, Mel. *The Long Count*. New York: Athenaeum, 1969.

Henry, William A., III. *The Great One—The Life and Legend of Jackie Gleason*. New York: Doubleday, 1992.

Hirsch, James S. *Hurricane: The Life of Rubin "Hurricane" Carter, Fighter*. London: Fourth Estate Limited, 2000.

Hunter, Allan. *Tony Curtis: The Man and His Movies*. New York: St. Martin's Press, 1985.

Huston, John. *An Open Book*. New York: Da Capo Press, 1980.

Isenberg, Michael T. *John L. Sullivan and His America*. Urbana and Chicago: University of Illinois Press, 1988.

Jones, James Earl, and Penelope Niven. *Voices And Silences*. New York: Charles Scribner's Sons, 199.

Kaminsky, Stuart. *John Huston: Maker of Magic*. New York: Houghton Mifflin, 188.

Kelly, Mary Pat. *Martin Scorsese: A Journey*. New York: Thunder's Mouth Press, 1991.

Kramer, Stanley, with Thomas M. Coffey. *A Mad Mad Mad Mad World: A Life in Hollywood*. San Diego: Harcourt Brace & Company, 1997.

La Motta, Jake, Joseph Carter, and Peter Savage. *Raging Bull: My Story*. Englewood Cliffs, N.J.: Prentice Hall, 1971.

LoBrutto, Vincent. *Stanley Kubrick: A Biography*. New York: Penguin Publishing Group, 1997.

Loubet, Nat, and John Ort, comps. *The 1979 Ring Boxing Encyclopedia and Record Book*. New York: The Ring Book Shop, 1979.

Louis, Joe, Art Rust, Jr., and Edna Rust Jr. *Joe Louis: My Life*. New York: Berkley Books, 1981.

Madsen, Axel. *John Huston: A Biography*. New York: Doubleday & Company, Inc., 1978.

March, Joseph Moncure. *The Set-Up*. New York: Stratford Press, 1928.

Marx, Arthur. *The Nine Lives of Mickey Rooney*. New York: Stein and Day, 1986.

McCabe, John. *Cagney*. New York: Albert A. Knof, 1997.

McGilligan, Patrick. *The Actor as Auteur*. New York: Da Capo Press, Inc., 1975.

Meade, Marion. *Buster Keaton: Cut to the Chase*. New York: HarperCollins, 1995.

Mellow, James R. *Hemingway, A Life Without Consequences*. New York: Houghton Mifflin, 1992.

Mitchell, Charles P. *A Guide to Charlie Chan Films*. Westport CT: Greenwood Press, 1999.

Mitchell, Ray. *Ray Mitchell's Boxing Quiz Book #1*. Horwitz Publications, Inc., 1966.

Morris, George. *John Garfield*. New York: Jove Publications, Inc., 1977.

Mullally, Frederic. *Primo: The Story of 'Man Mountain' Carnera*. London: Robson Books Ltd., 1991.

Murphy, George, with Victor Lasky. *"Say ... Didn't You Used to Be George Murphy?"* New York: Bartholomew House Ltd., 1970.

Nown, Graham. *The English Godfather Owney Madden*. London: Ward Lock Limited, 1987.

Odd, Gilbert. *The Fighting Blacksmith: The Story of Bob Fitzsimmons*. London: Pelham Books, 1976.

Oppenheimer, Jerry, and Jack Vitek. *Idol, Rock Hudson: The True Story of an American Hero*. New York: Villard Books, 1986.

Osborne, Robert. *50 Years of Oscar: The Official History of the Academy of Motion Picture Arts & Sciences*. La Habra, Calif.: ESE California, 1979.

Parrish, James Robert, and Gregory Mank. *The Best of M-G-M: The Golden Years 1929-1959*. Westport, CT: Arlington House, 1981.

Phillips, Gene D. *Stanley Kubrick: A Film Odyssey*. New York: Popular Library Publishers, 1975.

Pratley, Gerald. *The Cinema of John Huston*. A.S Barnes Co., Inc., 1977.

Quinn, Anthony, with Daniel Paisner. *One Man Tango*. New York: HarperCollins, 1995.

Quirk, Lawrence J. *Bob Hope: The Road Well-Traveled*. New York: Applause Books, 1998.

Quirk, Lawrence. *Fasten Your Seatbelts: The Passionate Life of Bette Davis*. New York: Signet, 1990.

Quirk, Lawrence J. *The Films of Robert Taylor*. Secacus: Citadel Press, 1975.

Reynolds, Michael. *Hemingway: The 1930s*. New York: W.W. Norton & Company, 1997.

Robbins, Jan. *Inka Dinka Doo: The Life of Jimmy Durante*. New York: Paragon House, 1991.

Roberts, Randy. *Papa Jack: Jack Johnson and the Era of White Hopes*. New York: The Free Press, 1983.

Robinson, David. *Buster Keaton*. Bloomington and London: Indiana University Press, 1969.

Ross, Barney, and Martin Abramson. *No Man Stands Alone: The True Story of Barney Ross*. Philadelphia: J.B. Lippincott Company, 1957.

Sander, Gordon F. *Serling: The Rise and Twilight of Television's Last Angry Man*. New York: Dutton, 1992.

Shepherd, Donald, and Robert Slatzer with Dave Grayson. *Duke: The Life and Times of John Wayne*. Garden City, N.Y.: D-Day and Company, 1985.

Skehan, Everett M. *Rocky Marciano: Biography of a First Son*. Boston: Houghton Mifflin Company, 1977.

Spada, James. *Streisand: Her Life*. New York: Crown Publishing, 1992.

Sperber, A.M., and Eric Lax. *Bogart*. New York: William Morrow and Company, Inc., 1997.

Spoto, Donald. *Stanley Kramer: Film Maker*. New York: G.P. Putnam's Sons, 1978.

Stine, Whitney. *Mother Goddam: The Story of the*

Career of Betty Davis. New York: Berkley Books, 1974.

Swanberg, W.A. *Citizen Hearst*. New York: Charles Scribner's Sons, 1961.

Thomas, Bob. *King Cohn: The Life and Times of Mogul Harry Cohn*. New York: McGraw-Hill Publishing Co., 1990.

_____. *Golden Boy: The Untold Story of William Holden*. New York: St. Martin's Press, 1983.

Thomas, Tony, Rudy Behlmer, and Clifford McCarty. *The Films of Errol Flynn*. Secaucus, N.J.: Citadel Press, 1975.

Wayne, Jane Ellen. *Clark Gable: Portrait of A Misfit*. New York: St. Martin's Press, 1993.

Wiles, Buster. *My Days With Errol Flynn: The Autobiography of Stuntman Buster Wiles*. Santa Monica, C.A.: Roundtable Publishers, 1988.

Zucker, Harry Marc, and Lawrence J. Babich. *Sports Films: A Complete Reference*. Jefferson, NC: McFarland, 1987.

Articles

Anderson, Dave. "When Ali Performed a Knockout on Film," *New York Times* (23 February 1997): sec. 8, p.2.

Anderson, Jon. "'Heart of a Champion' Plot Doesn't Have Knockout Punch," *Chicago Tribune* (1 May 1985): sec. 2, p.7.

Asahina, Robert. "Summer Fun and Games," *New Leader* (2 July 1979): 21.

Baram, Marcus. "He Spars No Effort," *New York Daily News* (12 November 1997): 14.

Barra, Allen. *New York Times* (14 November 1999): sec.2, p.13.

_____. "Michael Mann and Will Smith in the Ring with Ali," *New York Times* (9 September 2001): sec 2, p.56.

Beck, Marilyn. "TV Traumas," *New York Daily News* (13 August 1979): 8.

Borden, Martin. "Gossett's Film a Real Workout," *New York Post* (12 August 1992).

Boxer, Tim. "'Boom Boom' Boos Blake," *New York Post* (30 April 1985): 74.

Bradesser, Claude. "Lawsuits over Ali Pic Ready to Rumble," *Daily Variety* (1 September 1998): 1.

Buckley, Tom. *New York Times* (13 July 1979): sec. c, p. 10.

Carcaterra, Lorenzo. "The Bull Takes a Swing at the Movies," *New York Daily News* (12 September 1979): 25.

Choice, Harriet. *New York Sunday News* (9 May 1982).

Corlis, Richard. "Animal House," *Time* (24 November 1980): 100.

_____. "An Indie Knockout," *Newsweek* (2 October 2000).

Crewe, Regina. *New York American* (7 August 1938).

Crist, Judith. *TV Guide* (13 October 1979): A-7.

_____. *TV Guide* (16 October 1982): A-6.

D.D., *The New Yorker* (17 January 2000): 19.

Dawson, James P. *New York Times* (28 May 1934).

Denby, David. "Rough Stuff," *New Yorker* (2 October 2000): 148.

DiIonnio, Mark. "Triumph of the Spirit, Atlas Bears Witness," *New York Post* (4 December 1989).

Dixon, Campbell. "Harold Lloyd at His Best," (London) *Daily Observer* (4 March 1936).

Dominguez, Robert. "Mancini Tackles Heavyweight Role with Body & Soul Remake," *In Focus, New York Vue, New York Daily News*, 8.

Farr, Louise. "It Could Be a Contender," *New York Magazine* (18 October 1976).

Fisher, Bob. "Rocky IV a Photographic Dazzler," *American Cinematographer* (February 1986).

Flamm, Matthew. "Death Camp Ring Leader," *New York Post* (5 December 1989).

Flanders, Harry. "TV Choices." Review of *Dempsey* (CBS television movie). *New York Daily News* (28, September 1983) 61.

Frederick, Robert B. "Producer Ruddy Tour—Touts for His Boxing Kangaroo," *Variety* (28 June 1978): 42.

Gardella, Kay. "A Dempsey Treat." Review of *Dempsey* (CBS television movie). *New York Daily News* (23 September 1983): 74.

_____. "'Boom Boom' Mancini Packs Punch as TV Project," *New York Daily News* (26 February 1985): 68.

_____. "Intrique, Incest & Ideals," *New York Daily News* (11 October 1979): 112.

_____. "Marciano Gets Kayoed—by ABC," *New York Daily News* (19 October 1979): 70.

_____. "Ring of Passion Is Not a Knockout," *New York Daily News* (4 February 1978): 36.

Goldstein, Patrick. "Putting on the Gloves," *Newsday*, Sunday (9 December 2001): D6.

Graham, Houston. "A Rocky Horror?," *Boxing Monthly* (June 1999): 32.

Guernsey, Otis L., Jr. "To Make Boxing Films, Follow the Formula," *New York Herald Tribune* (17 April 1949).

Hale, Mark. "A Kings World," *New York Post*, Sunday (23 December 2001): p.63.

Harmetz, Aljeau. *New York Times* (29 April 1978).

Harris, James C. *New York Amsterdam News* (4 December 1997): 52.

Hatch, Robert. "Raging Bull Resurrection," *Nation* (13 December 1980).

Haun, Harry. "'Hard Fought' Triumph," *Sunday New York Daily News* (3 December 1989).

Heuring, David. "Triumph of the Spirit: Survivors at Any Cost," *American Cinematographer* (February 1990).

Hinkley, David. "Sparring with a Myth," *New York Daily News* (16 December 2001): p.4.

Holden, Stephen. "Fighting the Demons Within," *New York Times* (29 December 1999): sec. E, p.3.

Johnson, Hildy. "What's Black & White and Red All Over? Martin Scorsese," *In Cinema* (December 1980).

Johnson, Richard. *New York Post* (26 April 1990).

Johnson, Robert E. "Leon and Jayne Answer Critics About Their Sizzling Photos," *Jet* (20 August 1981): 58.

Jory, Tom. "Dempsey Film Doesn't Pack Enough Punch." Review of *Dempsey* (CBS Television movie). *New York Post* (28 September 1983): 82.

Joyner, Will. "The Fight Took 8 Rounds, the Film 22 Years," *New York Sunday Times* (16 February 1997): sec. 2, p.11.

Kael, Paula. "Religious Pulp, or The Incredible Hulk," *New Yorker* (8 December 1980): 222.

Kelly, Katie. *New York Post* (3 February 1978): 60.

Klemesrud, Judy. "Rocky Isn't Me but We Both Went the Distance," *New York Times* (28 November 1976).

_____. "That I Had Never Acted Helped Me to Be Natural," *New York Times* (15 November 1980): 13.

Levy, Barney. "George O'Brien of Screen Might Have Been Star Had He Entered Ring," New York *Enquirer* (5 June 1927).

Luft, Herbert G. "Mark Robson Did Not Dally Long With Message Films," *Films in Review* (May 1968): 288–291.

Maslin, Janet. *New York Times* (8 November 1985).

Mathews, Jack. A Racial Farce on the Ropes," *Newsday* (3 May 1996): sec. B, p.3.

_____. "Finally, a Knockout Leon Gast's Rumble in the Jungle Film Wins a Spot in Oscar's Ring," *Newsday* (12 February 1997): sec. B, p.3.

Mayerle, Judine. "Requiem for a Heavyweight and Playhouse 90, An Age Had Come to an End," *Journal of Popular Film and Television*.

Millner, Denene. "'Hurricane' Foes Fight Back," *New York Daily News* (9 February 2000): 44.

Moore, Marie. "Divorce-Bound Kennedy Still Tied 'Body and Soul'," *New York Amsterdam News* (28 November 1981): 30.

Naha, Ed. "You Can't Divorce This Body from This Soul," *The New York Post* (24 November 1981): 21.

Natale, Richard. "Goin' Back to Houston," *Women's Wear Daily* (27 July 1972): 12.

Nichols, Joseph C. *New York Times* (12 September 1933).

O'Connor, John J. "Marciano's Story Joins Live 'Sportsworld' Bout," *New York Times* (19 October 1979): C36.

_____. "3 Movies, Comedy on Cable Show," *New York Times* (15 October 1982): sec. c, p.26.

Oney, Steve. "Willem DaFoe, Looking for Characters with Possibility," *Sunday New York Times* (3 December 1989).

Pearlstein, Stephen. "Champion of the Innocents," *The Observer* (9 January 2000): 17.

Pride, Ray. "Raging Bulls," *Time Out New York* (13–17 December 2001): 145.

Rabb, Selwyn, quoted in Kam Williams, "Hurricane Distorts," *New York Amsterdam News* (6–12 January 2000).

Reid, Margaret. "George — As He Is," *Picture Play* (May 1929): 112. "Bob Roberts Sues Over 'Body and Soul'," *Variety* (13 May 1981): 12.

Rodell, Fred. "Everybody Reads the Comics," *Esquire* (March 1945): vol. XXXIII, no. 3.

Rosenthal, Harold. "Cameras Ready to Roll on the Joe Louis Story," *New York Herald Tribune*, Sunday (8 May 1953).

Ross, Barney. "Ross Gets off the Hook," *Toronto Daily Star* (1 June 1957): 27.

Sandomir, Richard. "A Marciano Docudrama Gets Much of It Wrong," *New York Times* (30 April 1999): sec D, p.5.

Sandomir, Richard. "HBO's Movie on King Has Promoter Jabbing," *New York Times* (14 November 1997): sec. C, 5.

Sarris, Richard. *Village Voice* (5 December 1963): 16.

Schallert, Edwin. *Los Angeles Times* (7 July 1933).

Schwartz, Tony. "The Heartbreak Kid," *Newsweek* (23 April 1979): 69.

Siegel, Joel, quoted by D. Bartholomew, *Cinefantastique* (21 November 1980).

Silverman, Stephen M. "O'Neil and Streisand — A K.O at the B.O.," *New York Post* (9 July 1979): 30.

Siskel, Gene. "'Rocky' Sequel Full of Family, Feisty Fists," *Chicago Tribune*, quoted in Fort Wayne *Sentinel* (28 November 1985).

_____. "Rocky RIP," *Chicago Tribune* (2 December 1990).

Slater, Andrew. "Thanks to the Rocky III Hit Eye of the Tiger, This Rock Group Proves It's a Real Survivor," *People* (30 August, 1982).

Smith, Liz. *New York Daily News* (11 July 1979).

_____. "Tears in Ears," *New York Daily News* (23 March 1979): 6.

_____. "What You Didn't Know — Til Now," *New York Daily News* (20 June 1979): 8.

Smith, Red. *New York Times* (13 June 1979).

Springer, P. Gregory. "Where Are All the People?," *Filmmakers Monthly* (August 1979).

Stack, Peter. *San Francisco Chronicle* (26 May 1982).

Stark, Samuel. *Films in Review* (January 1963): vol.14, no.1.

_____. "Robert Wise 'Began as a Cutter and Has Retained a Cutter's Cunning," *Films in Review* (January 1963): Vol. 14, no.1.

Stein, Jeanne. "Robert Ryan: Unlike Most Handsome Actors He Was Willing to Be a Heavyweight," *Films in Review* (January 1968).

Stern, Ellen. *New York Daily News*, Manhattan Section (5 December 1980): M 2–3.

Swaffer, Hannen. *World Film News* (March 1937):7.

Taubman, Philip. "Soviet Pans 'Rocky' and 'Rambo' Films," *New York Times*, 4 January 1986.

Thomas, Bob. *New York Daily News* (16 August 1992).

Turner, Megan. *New York Post* (21 January 2000).

Walcott, James. "M Is for the Many Things She Gave Me…," *The Village Voice* (15 October 1979).

Waters, Harry F. "Does Incest Belong on TV?," *Newsweek* (8 October 1979): 101.

Watts, Jr., Richard. "Some Applause for Charlie Chaplin," Sunday *New York Post* (30 April 1950): sec. M, p.4.

W.B. "'Galahad' Portrays Real Life," *New York World-Telegram* (29 May 1937).

Williams, Bob. "Joe Louis Seeks Better Film Fee," *New York Post*, (30 March 1978): 55.

Williams, Scott. "Ving — Rhames with Ring and 'King,'" *New York Daily News* (12 January 1997): 74.

Yakir, Dan. "Two Sticklers and a Slugger," *After Dark* (November 1980): 30.

Index

A.D.S. 98
A.W. 73, 101, 102, 142
Abbis, Abdullah 45, 55
Abbott, Bud 5
Abbott & Costello Meet the Invisible Man 5, 191
Abel 134
Abrams, Gerald 61
The Abysmal Brute 39
Adler, Luther 12, 198
The African Queen 57
Against the Ropes 6
Alaska Packer Fleet 64
Albertson, Jack 137
Albright, Lola 29, 112
Alexander, Bill 189
Alexander, Jane 73, 74
Alger, Horatio 47
Ali 9, 10, 139, 196, 197
Ali, Muhammad 8, 9, 10, 16, 22, 51, 57, 78, 79, 85, 92, 99, 116, 124, 126, 138, 139, 160, 169, 186, 196, 197, 202, 203, 204, 205
Ali the Fighter 117
The All-American Boy 26
All Good Marines 44, 47, 123
All in the Family 21
Allen, Tom 132
Allwyd, Astrid 121
Allyson, June 90
The Amateur Gentleman 123
Ambers, Lou 106, 125
American Broadcast Company Television 138
American Film Institute 157
American International Pictures 132
American Legion Stadium 55, 113
Anderson, John 147, 148, 150, 203
Anderson, Jon 86,
Andrews, Edward 82
Andrews, Peter 62
Angeli, Pier 186

Angels with Dirty Faces 20, 32, 207
Ansen, David 49, 140
Anti-Nazi League 161
Antoinette Perry Award 73
Apollo Theater 106
Aragon, Art 57, 142
Arbuckle, Fatty 34
Arguello, Alexis 85, 86, 90
Arlen, Richard 121
Armida 90, 91
Armstrong, Henry 103, 104, 105, 106, 125, 137
Armstrong, Robert 97, 98, 143
Arnold, Edward 44
Arouch, Salamo 200
Artis, James 92
Arum, Bob 52, 76, 147
Asahina, Robert 127, 157, 167, 172
Ascension Parish House Gymnasium 70
Atlas, Teddy 148, 201
Attel, Abe 208
Attenborough, Richard 8
Aufderheide, Pat 167
Auld Lang Syne 63
Auschwitz-Birkenau 200, 201
Avildsen, Jon 149, 150, 167, 176
Ayers, Lew 97, 98

B.R.C. 44, 199
Bad Girl 25, 70
Backus, Jim 190
Bacon, Lloyd 95, 96
Baer, Buddy 5
Baer, Max 19, 42, 44, 79, 82, 83, 84, 115, 152, 153, 154
Bain, Abie 112, 121, 122, 179
Ballard, Fred 206
Baltimore Evening Sun 164
Baltimore Sun 30
Bancroft, George 88, 114
Banderas, Antonio 147, 148
Banks, Sonny 139

Bare, Richard 105
Barn 19
Barnes, Howard 20, 23, 44, 45, 68, 109, 111
Barnum, P.T. 51
Baronet Theater 166
Barra, Allen 194
Barrymore, Ethel 29
Barrymore, John 144
Barrymore, Lionel 63
Barthelmess, Richard 145, 146
Basilio, Carmen 71
Bass, Bobby 50
Bates, Granville 206
The Battler 185
The Battling Bellhop 113
Battling Butler 11, 12, 133, 134
Baxter, Alan 180
Baxter, T. 135
Bayne, Al 55
Be Yourself 98
Beacon Communications 93
Beaudine, William 135
Beaufort, Joan 186
Beaumont, Gerald 53
Beck, Thomas 210
Beedle, Bill, Jr. 68
Beery, Noah, Jr. 98
Beery, Wallace 24, 25, 26, 98, 107
Bell, Alexander Graham 71
Bello, Alfredo 92
Belloise, Steve 160
Benedict, Richard 137
Benson, Shelia 171
Berenger, Tom 61, 62
Berg 192
Berg, Peter 76, 77
Berkeley, Busby 107
Berlenbauch, Paul 125
Bernard, Jamie 94, 141
Bernstein, Al 147, 195
Bernstein, Armyan 93
Bettina, Melio 70
The Big House 24
Bige 144, 153

219

Biltmore Hotel 211
Biroc, Joseph 27
Black, Julian 189
Blackburn, Jack "Chappie" 101, 102, 178, 188
Blake, George 210
Blake, Robert 85, 86
Blondell, Joan 27, 109
Bloom, Phil 96, 112, 121
Bloom, Willie 112
Blue Eagle 53
Blue Veil 27
Blythe, Betty 136
Boasberg, Al 11
Body and Soul 12, 13, 14, 15, 16, 17, 21, 33, 60, 106, 199
Boehnel, William 20, 33, 68, 96, 111, 112, 120, 144, 153, 154
Bogart, Humphrey 20, 83, 84, 111, 112, 114
Bogdanovich, Peter 57
Bon 95, 96
Bond, Ward 64, 109, 183, 207
Bonnie & Clyde 26
Boone, Richard 37
Borgnine, Ernest 190, 191
Born to Fight 18, 19, 21, 142
Borovik, Genrikh 173
Borzage, Frank 25, 70
Boston Daily Record 30
Boston Phoneix 127
Bowe, Riddick 71, 183
Bowery Blitzkrieg 20, 21, 142
Bowery Boys 19, 20, 21, 136
Box Office 151, 169
Boxing Kangaroo 132
Boxing Monthly 178
Boyles Thirty Acres 211
Boyum, Jay Gould 157
Braddock, James J. 42, 100, 196
Bradley, Bill 92
Bramble, Livingstone 86
Brandauer, Klaus Maria 194, 195
Brando, Marlon 33, 57, 66, 185
Breen, Joseph 187
Breitigam, Gerald 208
Brian, May 54
Brice, Fanny 98
Bridges, Jeff 57, 58
Bridges, Lloyd 37
Briggs, Donald 55
Britton, Barbara 72
Britton, Jack 96, 106, 115
Brix, Herman 41, 42

Broadway Melody 107
Brockovich, Erin 7
Brodetsky, Julian 68
Brog 20, 21, 59, 70, 191
Broken Blossoms 145
Bronson, Charles 80, 81, 112
Brooklyn Citizen 165
Brooklyn Daily Eagle 39, 96, 109, 112, 114, 129, 134, 146, 199
Brooks, Hazel 13
Brouillard, Lou 106
Brown, Abe "Newsboy" 45, 159
Brown, Charles D. 121
Brown, Drew "Bundini" 139, 205
Brown, James 204
Brown, Joe E. 107, 206, 211
Brown, Tom 56
Brown v. Board of Education 102
Browner, Otto 208
Browning, Tod 97
Bruce, Virginia 207
Bryan, Jane 111
Bryant, William 106
Buchinsky, Charles 80
Buchman, Sidney 89
Buckingham, Steve 91
Buffer, Michael 91, 147
Bullets or Ballots 188
Bupp, Tommy 39
Burdett, Winston 96, 134
Burkeley, Busby 199
Burnett, W.R. 97, 98
Burns, Tommy 39, 74, 128
Burroughs, Edgar Rice 42
Burum, Stephen H. 183
Butler, Bill 193

Cabin in the Cotton 188
Cage, Nicolas 183, 184
Cagnegata, Leonard L. 106
Cagney, James 20, 32, 33, 59, 95, 96, 112, 207, 208
Cagney, William 33, 143, 144
Cahn, Sammy 108
Cain and Mabel 22, 23, 107
Calhoun, Rory 160
Callahan, Mushy 30, 74, 96, 110, 113, 114, 159
Callahan, Willie 189
Callam, Alex 136
Calleia, Joseph 68
Cameron, Kate 23, 33, 69, 96, 120
Canby, Vincent 27, 50, 57, 127, 132

Cannes Film Festival 57, 66
Cannon, Jimmy 163
Cannon Group 15
Canzoneri, Tony 134, 208
Caplan, Bill 147
Capone, Alphonse 137
Captain Blood 64
Carbo, Frankie 21, 178
Carfagno, Ed 193
Carlson, Richard 129
Carlton Theater 135
Carnegie, Andrew 71
Carnera, Primo 19, 82, 83, 84, 152, 153, 154, 159
Carpentier, Georges 14, 47, 206, 211, 212
Carpentier, Georgette 211
Carr, Trem 40
Carroll, Kathleen 132
Carroll, Walter J. 160
Carruth, Milton 98
Carruthers, Jimmy 128
Carson, Jack 64
Carter, Rubin 92, 93
Cartier, Walter 117
Caruso, Enrique 211
Casey, Bernie 163
Cash Money Millionaires 203
Cassavettes, John 61, 62
Ceder, Ralph 121
Central Park Zoo 166
Cerdan, Marcel 71, 155, 169
Chaiton, Sam 93
Chalmette Railroad Yards 81
The Champ 24, 26, 27, 86, 107, 127, 128
Champion 28, 29, 30, 31, 34, 35, 38, 121, 133, 191
Chandler, Jeff 98
Chaney, Lon 97
Chaplin, Charles 34, 35, 108, 123, 133, 206
Chaplin, James 180
Chapman, Michael 156
Char 109, 120, 183
Charles, Ezzard 22, 177
Charlie Chan at Ringside 183
Chase, Borden 98
Chayefsky, Paddy 27
Chesire, Godfrey 76
Chester, Hal 103
Chic 59
Chicago Golden Gloves 71
Chicago Hope 77
Chicago Magazine 27
Chicago Post 53
Chicago Stadium 71
Chicago Sun-Times 86

Chicago Tribune 86
Chicago Tribune Charities, Inc. 71
Chiklin, Michael 17, 19
Chinatown 26
Chips 90
Chissel, Kid 55
Choyinski, Joe 64
Christian Science Monitor 20, 79, 140, 186
Chute, David 127
Cianelli, Eduardo 103, 104
Cineaste 79, 167
Citizen Kane 29, 180
City for Conquest 32, 33, 34, 59, 207
City Lights 25
City of Badmen 36, 37, 60, 191
Clarence Derwent Award 73
Clark, Frank Howard 87
Clarke, Cliff 198
Clarke, Robin 151
Clay, Cassius 9, 10, 78, 138, 139, 159, 160, 161, 196; see also Ali, Muhammad
Clay, Odessa 205
Clayton, Lou 143, 144
Clayworth, June 70
A Clockwork Orange 117
Clork, Harry 108
The Clown 25
Club Durant 145
Clurman, Harold 198
Cobb, Lee J. 59, 68, 69
Cobb, Randall 28, 49, 50
Coburn, James 81
Cockell, Eustace 80
Cohn, Art 80, 180
Cohn, Harry 12, 67, 68
Cohn, Herbert 109, 112, 199
Cohen, John S., Jr. 120, 125, 154
Cokes, Curtis 57
Colasanto, Nicholas 58
Cole, Al 141
Cole, Lester 98
Cole, Richard L. 160
Coleman, John 157
Colina, Bert 57
Collier, William, Sr. 124
Columbia Broadcasting System (CBS) 61, 86, 131
Columbia Pictures 12, 78, 82, 89, 159, 178
Columbia Studios 67, 68
Columbo, Allie 130
Columbo, Frank 169
The Comeback 121

Coming Home 26
Comiskey, Pat 83, 84
Commonweal 201
Conflict 123, 183
Conn, Billy 64, 70, 95
Conrad, Robert 13
Conte, Richard 59, 60
Conti, Bill 107, 167
Conway, Tim 151, 152
Cooper, Jackie 24, 25, 26
Corbett, James J. 22, 36, 37, 38, 46, 47, 55, 60, 62, 63, 64, 72, 123
Corby, Jane 129
Corliss, Richard 66, 156
Cornstalk Hotel 81
Corona, Paolo 147
Cosell, Howard 28, 41, 205
Costa, Al 104
Costello, Lou 5
Courtenay, Bryce 149
Courtney, Peter 36, 63
The Cowboy and the Prize-Fighter 59
Crabbe, Buster 41, 42
Crain, Jeanne 37
Crane, William W. 209
Crawford, Joan 153, 211
Creelman, Eileen 23, 55, 111, 129
Crewe, Regina 18, 96, 134, 144
Crisp, Donald 114
Crist, Judith 61, 62, 90
Criterion Pictures, Ltd. 123
Croix de Guerre 211
Crosby, Bing 72
Crossfire 179
The Crowd Roars 40, 43, 44, 45, 114, 119
Crowley, Pat 190
Crowther, Bosley 13, 33, 37, 83, 108, 116, 160
Cue 30, 61, 160, 181, 185, 186
Curley, Jack 211
Curtis, Tony 190, 191
Curtiz, Michael 112
Cutler, Grace 146

D.B. 201
D.C. 79
D.D. 93
Dafoe, Wilhem 200, 201
Daily Mirror 40, 164
Daily News 49, 55, 79, 120, 131, 183
The Daily Worker 14, 33
Daku 86
Dallas Morning News 30, 176

D'Amato, Cus 201
Daniels, Bebe 123
D'Arbanville, Patti 127
Darcy, Les 128
DareDevil Jack 46
Darnell, Linda 72
Darro, Frankie 18, 19, 21, 142
David Harkum 209
Davidovitch, Lolita 147
Davies, Marion 22, 23, 107
Davis, Amy 150
Davis, Bette 111
Davis, Cathy "Cat" 132
Davis, Mac 192, 193
Day, John 38, 191
Day of the Fight 117, 118
Dead End 20, 199
Dead End Kids 19, 20, 198, 199
Dean, James 185
Deauville Film Festival 66
Dee, Ruby 189
DeGroot, Billy 208
De Havilland, Olivia 95, 96
Dekker, Albert 116
Delaney, Jack 125
Delehanty, Thorton 25, 120, 144
Del Rio, Dolores 90
Demange, Frenchy 82
Dempsey, Jack 14, 22, 46, 47, 48, 53, 54, 63, 99, 106, 107, 110, 115, 123, 140, 142, 144, 146, 153, 154, 160, 186, 196, 202, 206, 210, 211
Dempsey Returns 47
Denby, David 66, 140, 171
De Niro, Robert 49, 75, 128, 140, 141, 155, 156, 157
Denkin, Marty 91, 193, 195
Denny, Reginald 39
Denver Post 146
DePalma, Brian 183
Derek, John 90
Dern, Bruce 49, 50
Descamps, Francois 211
Desert Fury 116
Desperate Journey 63
Devil Dogs of the Air 96
Devine, Andy 121
Diab, Mohammad Ali 7
Diamond, Legs 144
Dickson, Gloria 198
Diggstown 49
Dinehart, Alan 210
Dixon, Bob 58
Dmytryk, Edward 179
Dr. Jekyll and Mr. Hyde 25

Dr. Strangelove 117
Dolan, Frankie 55
Dolan, Jimmy 112
Don King: Only in America 51, 203
Donlevy, Brian 45
Donlin, Mike 124
Don't Pull Your Punches 111
Dorff, Stephen 149, 150
Doty, Douglas 121
Douglas, Kirk 29, 30, 31, 34
Dove, Billie 53
Downs, Cathy 105
Doyle, Jimmy 88
Drama Critics Award 73
Drew, Roland 42
Drexel-Biddle, Major 211
Duffy, "Big" Bill 82
Dunaway, Faye 26, 28
Dundee, Angelo 9, 10, 139, 197
Dundee, Johnny 96, 125
Dundee, Vince 45, 106
Dunn, James 45, 70
Dunphy, Don 131
Duran, Roberto 16, 128
Durante, Jimmy 143, 144
Dwan, Allan 53, 209, 210

E.C. 144
E.J.B. 104
Eagle-Lion 59, 70
East of Eden 185
East Side Kids 19, 20
Eastside, Westside 53, 54
Eaton, Eileen 6
Ebling, George 73
Edelman, Robert 157, 174
Edga 40
Edison, Thomas 36, 63, 71
Edwards, James 102
Einstein, Albert 35
Enterprise Productions 12
Epperson, Lee 131
Epps, Omar 7
Epps, Robbie 16
Errol, Leon 103, 104
Erwin, Stuart 143, 144
Estrada, Erik 90, 91
Esquire 115
Evening Post 25
Ever Since Eve 54
Ex-Champ 55
Eye of the Tiger 170

Fairbanks, Douglas, Jr. 122, 123, 198, 211
Fairbanks, Douglas, Sr. 42, 122, 123, 211

Falk, Peter 202, 203
Falke, Evelyn 129
Famechon, Johnny 128
Farber, Jim 58
Farnol, Jeffery 123
Farolino, Audrey 49
Fat City 57, 58
Favreau, Jon 178
Fear and Desire 118
The Fear Fighter 72
Fenech, Jeff 128
Fenton, Simon 149, 150
Fidler, Jimmy 30
Fields, Jackie 43, 56, 154
Fields, Stanley 109
Fifty Grand 115
The Fight Never Ends 189
The Fighter 59
Fighting Champ 59
Fighting Fools 21
Fighting Heart 53
Film Heritage 167
Film Journal 201
Films in Review 57, 131, 157, 176, 195
Fiorillo, C.W. 195
Firpo, Luis Angel 47, 110
First Artists 126
First National Pictures 33, 70, 145
Fisher, Ham 103, 143
F.I.S.T. 168
Fitzsimmons, Bob 22, 36, 37, 38, 39, 46, 60
Flagg, James Montgomery 210
Flaherty, Pat 210
Flamm, Matthew 176
Flanders, Judy 48
Fleischer, Nat 186
Flesh and Blood 61, 62, 127
Flesh and Fury 190
Flin 44
Flood, Paddy 72
Flying Fists 42
Flynn, Errol 63, 64, 65, 114, 183
Fonda, Jane 86
For the Love of Pete 103
Ford, John 39, 40, 53, 55
Ford, Wallace 107, 190
Foreman, Carl 29
Foreman, George 9, 10, 51, 52, 77, 78, 148, 176, 204, 205
Forrest Gump 8
Fort Wayne Sentinel 145
Foster, Darrel 9, 148
Four Daughters 198, 199
Fowley, Douglas 121, 210

Fox, Billy 14
Fox Film Corp. 70, 88, 12
Fox Studios 53, 54
Frankenstein 97
Frawley, William 55, 64
Frazier, Harry 121
Frazier, Joe 116, 124
Freaks 97
Free Milk Fund for Babies 134
Freedman, Mona 190
Freedman, Tommy 106
Freeman, Morgan 149, 150
French, Lloyd 103
French, P. 149
Freund, Karl 69
Frias, Art 85, 86
Fulks, Sarah June 114
Funny Girl 126

G.M.C. 40
Gable, Clark 22, 23, 43, 189
Galento, Tony 5, 192
Gallico, Paul 70, 132
Gambina, Jimmy 28, 86
The Game 39
Gandhi, Mohandas 8
Gans, Joe 101, 179
Gant, Richard 176
Garcia, Alex 50
Garcia, Ceferino 103, 104
Garcia, Frankie 112
Gardella, Kay 62, 131, 163
Garden of Allah 188
Gardner, Ava 29, 116
Gardner, Leonard 57
Garfield, John 12, 13, 14, 18, 67, 69, 108, 198, 199
Gargan, William 43, 98, 133
Gast, Leon 9, 203, 204, 205
Gaynor, Janet 53
Gelb, Philip 103
Gelmis, Joseph 156, 172
Gene 84, 138
Gentleman Jack 63
Gentleman Jim 63, 183
Gentleman Joe Palooka 104
George, Gorgeous 138
George, Nelson 79
George Raft Caravan 106
German-American Bund 161
Gerstad, Harry 30
Giant 185
Giardello, Joey 93, 94
Gibson, Julie 42
Gielgud, John 150
Gilb 5, 21, 180
Gilbert, Lou 73
Gilbert, Michele 178

The Girl from Monterrey 90, 108
Girlfight 65, 66
Gleason, Jackie 138, 159, 160, 192, 193
Gleason, James 88, 89, 122
Glick, Joe 55, 96, 112, 114, 121, 179, 210
Globe Pictures Corp. 187
Goebels, Hermann 103
Goff, Lloyd 13
Golden, Mickey 121
Golden Boy 12, 13, 40, 67, 68, 69, 73, 179, 198
Golden Globe Award 94
Golden Gloves 179
The Golden Gloves Story 70, 71
Golder, Lew 187
Goldstein, Abe 96
The Goldwyn Girls 108
Golota, Andrew 183
Gonley, Sondra 14
Gorbachev, Mikhail 173
Gorcey, Leo 19, 20, 21
Gordon, Dan, III 93
Gordon, Robert 101
Gorman, Cliff 140
Gossett, Louis, Jr. 49, 50
Gottschalk, Norman 103
Gould, Elliot 132
Grace, Meyers 104
The Graduate 73
Gramercy Gym 157
Grandetta, Frank 55
Grange, Red 46
Grant, Edmond 176
Graziano, Rocky 169, 184, 185, 186
Grease 48
The Great John L. 72
The Great Sinner 29
The Great White Hope 73, 74, 85, 120
The Great White Hype 76
The Greatest 8, 78, 79, 85
Greb, Harry 124, 125, 196
Green, Abe 116
Green, Cannonball 68, 69
Griffith, D.W. 97, 145
Griffith, Emile 94
Gross, Laura 86
Grossinger's Gym 102
Group Theater 73, 198
Grusin, David 27
Guernsey, Otis L., Jr. 30, 38, 59, 102, 116, 129, 142, 181
Guffey, Burnett 83
Guild Films 104

Guilty by Suspicion 140
Guinness Book of World Records 8
Gunga Din 123

H.T.T. 59, 190
Haade, William 111, 112, 114
Hacienda Hotel and Casino 147
Haggerty, Dan 37
Hairston, Eugene 190
Hale, Alan 64
Hale, Wanda 114, 129, 188, 206
Hall, Huntz 20, 21
Hall, Mourdant 123, 144, 145, 146, 153, 208
Hamil, Peter 60, 61
Hamilton, Margaret 207
Hamilton, Neil 183
Har 151
Hard Times 80, 81, 202
The Harder They Fall 21, 82, 83, 84
Harlow, Jean 97, 153
Harrelson, Woody 147, 148
Harrington, Hamtree 106
Harris, Edna Mae 188
Harris, Genevieve 53
Harris, James C. 51
Harris, Julie 159, 160
Harris, Phil 107
Harris, Steve 139
Harron, Robert 145
Hasley, Richard 167
Hatch, Robert 156
Hauser, Thomas 205
Hearns, Thomas 6
Heart of a Champion: The Ray Mancini Story 85, 86, 87, 99
Heart Punch 87, 88
Hearst, William Randolph 22, 134
Heaven Can Wait 27, 89
Heckart, Eileen 186
Hellinger, Mark 116
Hemingway, Ernest 115, 116, 185
Henie, Sonja 101, 209
Henley, Hobart 39
Henney, Tom 128
Henning, Ted 151
Henry Armstrong Youth Foundation 106
Hepburn, Katharine 126
Herald-Tribune 25, 84
Herb 114, 212

Here Comes Mr. Jordan 89
Here Comes the Navy 96
Herman, Tommy 179
Hernandez, Fred 147
Herzfeld, John 52
Heschong, Albert 159
Hialeah Park Race Track 27
Hift 102
High Noon 31
Hill, Roy 81
Hill, Walter 202
Hippodrome 115
Hirsch, Judd 178
Hit Me with Your Best Shot 6
Hitler, Adolf 100, 161, 162
Hobe 179, 199
Hoberman 176
Hogan, Eddie 114
Hogan, Hulk 171
Hold Everything 206, 211
Holden, Stephen 93, 183, 184
Holden, William 40, 68, 69, 179
Holliman, Earl 80
Hollywood Herald 208
Hollywood Legion Stadium 189
Hollywood Reporter 106
Hollywood Stadium Mystery 183
Holmes, Larry 50, 52, 128, 205
Holmes, Rubberneck 188
Holyfield, Evander 52, 183
Home Box Office (HBO) 52, 203
Home of the Brave 102
Honest Hearts and Willing Hands 72
Honey Boy 90
Hope, Bob 142
Hope, Leslie 141, 142
Hopkins, Bernard 125
Hornaday, Ann 7
Horne, Lena 101
Horse Soldiers 40, 41
Horton, Edward Everett 89
Houck, Leo 54
Houston, Graham 178
Howard, Shemp 103, 121
Howard, Terrence 138
Howe, James Wong 14, 59, 60
Hud 73
Hudson, Rochelle 210
Hudson, Rock 98
Hughes, Carol 136
Hughes, Howard 180, 181
Hughes, Lloyd 87

Hughes, Rupert 33, 145
Hull, Chuck 91
Hume, Cyril 42
Hurley, Jack 55, 87
The Hurricane 93, 94
The Hustler 159
Huston, John 57, 58
Huston, Walter 57, 153

I Got Lucky 112
I Love Lucy 55
The Idol of Millions 47
In Cold Blood 86
In Living Color 77
In the Money 20
Indrisano, John 21, 44, 72
The Informer 55
The Insiders 8
International Boxing Federation (IBF) 6
International Sporting Club 211
Intolerance 97, 145, 209
Intruders in the Dust 102
The Irish in Us 32, 33, 95, 96, 207
The Iron Horse 53
Iron Man 97, 98, 99, 143, 190, 191
Is Zat So? 53, 88, 89, 122, 143
It's a Wonderful Life 207
Ivanov, George A. 173

J.D.B. 20
J.T.M. 23
Jack and the Beanstalk 5
Jackson, Eddie 143, 144
Jackson, Jessie 92
Jackson, Peter 128
Jackson, Samuel L. 76
Jacobs, Joe 100, 162, 164
Jacobs, Mike 140, 162
James, Bobby 117
James, Steve 100
The Jazz Singer 105
Jealousy 164
Jeffries, James J. 39, 63, 74, 109, 154, 163, 164, 186, 187
Jenkins, Allen 95
Jenkins, Lew 85
Jenkins, Steve 140
Jenks, Frank 206
Jennings, Whitey 141
Jewison, Norman 93
Joan of Arc 6
Joe and Max 99, 100
The Joe Louis Story 101, 102
Joe Palooka, Champ 103, 104

The Joe Palooka Story 104
Jofre, Eder 90
Johaneson, Bland 40, 44, 109, 112, 144, 199
Johannson, Ingemar 40
Johnny Belinda 114
Johnson, Jack 39, 46, 55, 63, 74, 76, 85, 124, 128, 163, 187, 202
Johnson, Mae 106
Johnston, Jimmy 208
Jolo 123
Jolson, Al 105
Jones, Bobby 46
Jones, Ed "Too Tall" 50
Jones, James Earl 73, 74
Jones, Tom 87, 208
Jordan, Bobby 20
Jory, Tom 48
Journal-American 18
Joyner, Will 205

Kael, Pauline 74, 81, 156
Kallen, Jackie 67
Kandel, Aben 32, 59
Kane, Irene 118
Kanour, Gilbert 164
Kanter, Hal 142
The Karate Kid 149
Kass, Henry 17
Katz, Michael 148
Kaufman, Stanley 200
Kaye, Danny 21, 108
Kazan, Elia 26, 32, 33
Keach, Stacey 57, 58
Kearnan, Johnny 121
Kearns, Jack "Doc" 47, 48
Keaton, Buster 11, 21, 133, 206
Keep Punching 106
Kehr, David 183
Kelleher, Terry 176
Kelly, Albert 121
Kelly, Kate 163
Kelly the Second 119
Kendall, Maddie 188
Kennedy, Arthur 12, 29, 31, 32, 33, 34
Kennedy, Jayne 15, 16
Kennedy, Leon Issac 13, 15, 16, 17
Kent, Dorothea 98
Ketchel, Stanley 184
Keyes, Evelyn 89
Keystone Productions 34
Khan, Rasho 77
Kibbee, Guy 122, 207, 208
The Kid 133

The Kid Comes Back 109, 111, 112
Kid Dynamite 20
The Kid from Brooklyn 108
The Kid from Kokomo 109, 110, 119
Kid Galahad 80, 109, 111, 112, 113
Kid Nightingale 114
Killer McCoy 45, 70, 142, 145
The Killers 115, 116
Killer's Kiss 73, 118
The Killing 118
Kilran, Jake 72, 148
Kim, Duk Koo 85
Kinematograph Weekly 190
Kiner, Les 40
Kinescope 36, 63
King, Allan 140, 141
King, B.B. 204
King, Don 51, 52, 76, 77, 128, 176, 203, 204, 206
King, Lou 5
King for a Night 119, 120
King Kong 143
King of the Jungle 42
Kirkwood, Joe, Jr. 103, 104, 105
Kitman, Marvin 52, 86
Klawans, Stuart 77, 183, 184
Klien, Izzy 71
Knight, Arthur 186
Knock on Any Door 70
The Knockout 34, 35, 212, 133
Knotts, Don 151
Knox, Elyse 104
Koch, Ed 92
Koehler, Robert 202, 203
Koenekamp, Fred J. 27
Kopelson, Arnold 200
The Kraft Television Theater 158
Kramer, Stanley 28, 29, 30, 31, 38
Krasner, Milton 181
Krieger, Solly 70
Kroll, Jack 74, 79, 156, 156, 157
Kronk Gym 6
Kruger, Otto 153, 154
Kubrick, Stanley 73, 117, 118
Kurosawa, Akira 148
Kurrle, Robert 208
Kusama, Karyn 65, 67

LaBarbara, Fidel 56, 109, 210
Ladd, Allan 49
Lady and Gent 88

Laemmle, Carl 121
LaGuardia, Michael 151
Lamas, Fernando 90
La Motta, Jake 14, 49, 75, 85, 155, 156, 157, 184, 185
La Motta, Joey 155
La Motta, Vicki 155
Lampley, Jim 147, 148, 203
Lancaster, Burt 116, 117
Lane, Johnny 5
Lane, Mike 82, 84
Lange, Jessica 140
Lansing, Hal 103
Lardner, Ring 28
LaRue, Jack 18
Lasky, Art 42, 55, 114
The Last Picture Show 57
The Last Temptation of Christ 8
Lastarza, Roland 131
Latzo, Pete 54
Laughton, Charles 129
Lawrence, Jody 90
Lazarus and the Hurricane 93
Leach, David 57
The Leather Pushers 18, 121
Leather Saint 90
LeBorg, Reginald 104
Lee, Canada 13, 106
Lee, Catherine 87
Lee, Spike 205
Lehman, Ernest 185
Lemrick, Lou 148
LeoGrande, Ernest 79
Leonard, Benny 5, 96, 115
Leonard, Ray 16, 171
Lesnevich, Gus 160
Lester, Vicki 136
Levene, Sam 45, 69, 116
Levy, Emanuel 94
Lewis, Ed "Strangler" 64
Lewis, George 88
Lewis, Ted "Kid" 96
Liberty Magazine 134
Life 74, 138
Life Is Beautiful 200
The Life of Jimmy Dolan 122, 123, 142, 188, 198
Lifeboat 106
Lincoln, Abraham 8
Liston, Charles "Sonny" 9, 10, 21, 22, 79, 139, 159, 202, 203
Little Ceasar 109
Litvak, Anatole 33
Lloyd, Harold 108, 133, 134
Lo Bianco 131, 178, 179
Loew, Arthur 211
Loggia, Robert 200

Lolman, High 55
London, Jack 38, 39, 59, 60, 115
London Observer 149, 184
London Prize Ring Rules 64, 81
London Times 125, 208
Look 117
The Lord in His Corner 80
Lords of Flatbush 166
The Lords Referee 53
Lorre, Peter 183
Los Angeles Film Critic Association Award 205
Los Angeles Times 7, 50, 120, 144, 149, 164, 171, 176, 178, 194
Los Angeles Variety Arts Theatre 193
Louis, Joe 5, 19, 20, 22, 45, 99, 100, 101, 103, 104, 106, 115, 124, 129, 140, 162, 163, 164, 169, 187, 188, 189, 196, 210
Loutzenhiser, James K. 151
Lovitz, John 76
Loy, Myrna 153, 154
Lucky Fella on the Make for Love 154
Lui, Lisa 147
Luke, Keye 183
Lundgren, Dolph 173, 174
Lust for Life 159
Lux Radio 25
Lyons, Jeffery 201

M.B. 95
M.E. 190
M.M. 33
Mabel's Married Life 34
Macht, Stephen 163
Madden, Owney 82
Madison Square Bowl 135
Madison Square Garden 11, 18, 45, 60, 61, 69, 114, 116, 124, 125, 128, 132, 178, 183
The Magnificent Obsession 99
Maher, Peter 36
Mailer, Norman 92, 205
The Main Event 126, 128
Main Street Gym (Los Angeles) 86, 127, 159, 193
Maine, U.S.S. 22
Malden, Karl 192, 193
Mallet, Richard 160
The Maltese Falcon 57
Mamoulian, Rouben 67
The Man from Down Under 129

Mancini, Lenny 85, 86
Mancini, Ray 17, 18, 77, 85, 86
Mann, Michael 8, 9, 10, 139
Mann, Nathan 188
The Mann Act 74, 202
March, Frederic 25
March, Joseph Moncure 80, 164, 179
Marciano 130
Marciano, Lou 178
Marciano, Peter 197
Marciano, Rocky 22, 39, 71, 82, 99, 100, 101, 102, 124, 130, 131, 140, 169, 177, 178, 192, 197
Marciano, Rocky, Jr. 178
Mardik, Martin 155
Maren, Jerry 72
Marill, Alvin H. 131
Marin, Cheech 76
Marion, Frances 25, 26
Markson, Ben 209, 210
Marley, Mike 52
Marquess of Queensberry 16, 203; rules 62, 64, 81
Marsh, Marian 206
Martin, Dewey 70, 80
Martin, Lesara 92, 93, 94
Martin, Tony 209
*M*A*S*H* 166
Maslin, Janet 76, 77, 192
Master P. 203
Masters, Dorothy 40, 42, 55
Masterson, Bat 37
Masterson, Fay 149
Mathews, Jack 76, 141, 203
Matilda 132, 133
Mattewson, Baby-Faced 112
Mattimore, Cornelius Van 121
Maxwell, Marilyn 31, 142
Mayer, Louis B. 22, 25, 153
Mayfair Pictures 87
Mayo, Archie 122
Mayo, Donald 42
Mayo, Virginia 108
Mazurski, Mike 64
McCarthy, Clem 45
McCarthy, Todd 184, 205
McClure, Greg 72, 73
McCoy, Kid 39
McFarland, "Packy" 141
McHugh, Frank 32, 95, 96, 114, 207
McKeon, Doug 85, 86
McKinley, William 22
McLaglen, Victor 53, 54, 55, 56

McLarnin, Jimmy 19, 45, 96, 98, 104, 107, 134, 208
McMahon, Horace 121
McManus, John T. 129
McNaught Syndicate Newspapers 143
McNeeley, Tom 77
McNeely, Peter 77
McVoy, Jock 44
Mead, Eddie 106
Mean Streets 155
Medved, Michael 201
Meltzer, Lewis 67
Member of the Wedding 159
Menjou, Adolph 68, 69, 134
Merchant, Larry 52, 148
Meredith, Burgess 24, 166, 157, 169
Metiff, Alex 160
Metropolitan Opera House 211
The Mexican 39, 59
MGM 22, 24, 25, 26, 27, 29, 43, 44, 45, 46, 70, 77, 90, 107, 108, 152, 153, 154, 164, 173, 178, 185, 186, 211
MGM Grand Hotel 77, 174
Midnight Cowboy 26
The Milky Way 108, 133, 134, 135
Miljan, John 97, 119
Miller, Seton I. 89
Milne, Tom 171
Minzer, Wilson 208
The Miracle Kid 136
Miranda, Carmen 90
The Misfits 57
Mr. Hex 20, 21, 136
Mr. Motto's Gamble 119, 183
Mr. Smith Goes to Washington 67
Mitchell, Cameron 137, 138
Mitchell, Charlie 72
Mitchum, Robert 132
Mix, Tom 53
Mobutu, Sese Seko 203, 204
Moffatt, Margaret 164
Molina, Angela 194
Mona Lisa 51
Monkey on My Back 137, 138
Monogram Pictures 20, 21, 104, 135, 136
Monogram Studios 103
Monroe, Marilyn 90
Montalban, Carlos 83
Montalban, Ricardo 90
Montegna, Joe 17, 18
Montez, Maria 90
Montgomery, Elizabeth 112

Montgomery, Robert 89
Monthly Film Bulletin 171, 194
Moreland, Mantan 188
Moriarity, Cathy 155
Moore, Archie 116, 117, 131
Moore, Constance 55
Moore, Marie 15
Moorer, Michael 52, 201
Moreno, Antonio 90
Moreno, Rita 90
Morgan, Frank 43, 44
Morgan, Gary 132
Morgenstern, Joe 9, 66
Moroz, Ben 104
Morris, Chester 119, 120
Morris, Wayne 109, 110, 111, 112, 116
Morrison, Tommy 176
Mortimer, Lee 164
Motion Picture Herald 88, 98, 190, 191
Mueller-Stahl, Armin 148
Muhammad, Eddie Mustafa 16
Muhammad, Elijah 9
Muhammad Ali: King of the World 138, 139
Mullally, Frederic 82
Murph 79
Murphy, George 164, 165
Murphy, Mike 163
Murphy, Morna 27, 127
Murphy, Thorne 163
Muse, Clarence 188
Musuraca, Nick 69
Mutiny on the Bounty 23, 129
Myhers, John 151

Naha, Ed 16
The Nation 77, 156, 184
Nation of Islam 78
National Broadcasting Company (NBC) 90
National Federation for Decency 61
National Foundation of Arts 73
National Society of Film Critics Award 205
Native Son 106
Nauyoks, Fred 92
Neal, Lex 11
Neal, Tom 136
Nelson, Battling 39
Nelson, Ralph 159, 160
New Leader 127, 157, 167
The New Leather Pushers 72, 121
New Republic 200

New Statesman 157
New World Leader 172
New York 167, 171
New York-American 96, 134, 144
New York Amsterdam News 15, 51, 79
New York Daily Mirror 44, 112, 114, 144, 199
New York Daily News 19, 23, 25, 27, 33, 40, 42, 48, 62, 69, 70, 77, 90, 94, 104, 114, 129, 136, 163, 188, 206
New York District Attorney's Office 14
New York Evening Journal 23, 134, 145, 206
New York Evening Post 120, 144
New York Film's Critic Circle Award 205
New York Herald 39
New York-Herald Tribune 5, 20, 23, 30, 38, 44, 45, 59, 60, 64, 68, 96, 102, 104, 109, 111, 116, 123, 124, 129, 153, 191
New York Journal 22, 23
New York Journal-American 112, 199
New York Morning Telegraph 74
New York Post 7, 16, 18, 23, 33, 35, 40, 44, 49, 57, 79, 81, 86, 109, 111, 112, 114, 132, 136, 141, 148, 149, 163, 164, 165, 174, 176, 199
New York Press 202
New York Sun 23, 44, 55, 56, 96, 111, 120, 125, 129, 144, 154,
The New York Times 13, 23, 27, 30, 33, 37, 44, 45, 50, 55, 56, 59, 60, 61, 63, 64, 66, 69, 73, 76, 77, 83, 90, 93, 95, 98, 101, 102, 104, 108, 116, 120, 123, 127, 131, 132, 142, 144, 145, 153, 160, 180, 183, 186, 190, 192, 199, 205, 208
New York World-Telegram 20, 23, 33, 96, 111, 120, 144, 153, 208
The New Yorker 30, 66, 74, 81, 92, 125, 140, 156, 160
Newfield, Jack 51
Newman, Kim 194
Newman, Paul 185, 186
News Hounds 21, 136

Newsday 52, 76, 86, 141, 147, 150, 156, 172, 176, 194, 203
Newsweek 27, 49, 66, 74, 79, 140, 156
NFL Today 15
Nickerson, James 50, 195
Nielsen, Brigitte 174
Night and the City 140
Nixon, Marion 207
Norris, James D. 140
Norton, Robert 103
Nova, Lou 20, 104
Novarro, Ramon 90
Nugent, Frank 69
Nunn, Michael 6

Oakie, Jack 124, 125
O'Brien, Edmond 116
O'Brien, George 53, 54, 122
O'Brien, Pat 32, 95, 96, 109, 207
O'Brien, Philadelphia Jack 39
O'Brien, Tom 201
Ocean Parkway Arena 181
O'Connor, Carrol 21
O'Connor, John J. 61, 62, 90, 131
Odec 188, 209
Odets, Clifford 12, 67, 68, 198
Oedipus Rex 61
Off Limits 142
An Officer and a Gentleman 49
Olivares, Ruben 90
Oliver, Jim 92
Olympic Auditorium 6, 11, 28, 193
O'Morrison, Kevin 70
On Golden Pond 86
On the Waterfront 21, 33, 82
Ondra, Annie 162
One Step Beyond 80
1000 Eyes Magazine 35
O'Neal, Ryan 26, 126, 127, 128
O'Neil, Sally 11
Ortiz, Manuel 90, 103
O'Sullivan, Mauren 44
O'Sullivan, Michael 7
Otto, Frank 136
Our Gang 24
Out of Africa 194
Owens, Jessie 162

P.M. Reviews 129
P.S.C. 30
P.V.B. 191
Palance, Jack 159
Palermo, "Blinkie" 21
Palmer, Lili 13

Palomino, Carlos 128, 131
Palooka 143, 144
Papke, Billy 124, 154, 208
Paradise Alley 168
Paramount Pictures 88, 90, 142
Paramount Studios 179
Paramount Television 61
Pasdar, Adrian 194, 195
Pat and Mike 126
The Patent Leather Kid 12, 33, 145, 146
Pathe 22, 46
Pathe-Movie Tone 30
Paths of Glory 31
Paton, Stuart 87
Patterns 158
Patterson, Floyd 8, 40, 41, 71, 186
Payne, John 114
Pearl, Jack 44
Pearlberg, William 68
Peck, Gregory 29
Pelswick, Rose 23, 109, 112, 134, 145, 206
Pep, Willie 120, 160
Pepeli, Rocky 50
Perkins, Gil 37, 38
Perroni, Patsy 44, 45
Perry, Bob 210
Perry, Harvey 96, 208
Perry, Jock 96, 112
Persoff, Nehemiah 83
Pesci, Joe 155, 157
Peters, Jon 126
Peters, Lisa 93, 94
Petrella, Peter 155
The Petrified Forest 109
Pevney, Joseph 13, 98, 190
Phantom of the Opera 120
Philadelphia Art Museum 167, 176
Philadelphia North American 163
Pickford, Mary 211
A Piece of Steak 39
Pihodna, Joe 5, 64, 104
Pinky 102
Pirates of Penzance 48
Pivar, Beau 70
Platoon 200
Play It to the Bone 147
Playboy 16, 167, 201
Playhouse 90 158, 159
Pleshette, Suzanne 61
Plimpton, Geore 205
Plunkett, Joseph 146
Pointer Sisters 204

Pollack, Jackson 156
Polo Grounds 47, 134
Polo Grounds Athletic Club 32
Polonsky, Abraham 12, 13
Powell, Dick 90
Power, Tyrone 67
The Power of One 149
The Prado Museum 57
Presley, Elvis 80, 112, 113
Price, Andy 16
Price, Edgar 165
Prim 197
The Private Lives of Henry VIII 129
The Prize Fighter 151
Prizefighter 117
The Prizefighter and the Lady 47, 153, 154
Producers Releasing Corporation 108, 136
Pryor, Tom 45
Public Enemy 32, 207
Pulitzer, Joseph 22
Pulitzer Prize 73
Punch 160
The Punisher 49
Purcel, Dick 19

The Quiet Man 53, 55
Quimby, Fred C. 46
Quinn, Anthony 33, 34, 112, 121, 122, 159, 160

Raab, Selwyn 93
Raft, George 106
Raging Bull 10, 11, 14, 49, 50, 85, 91, 128, 140, 155, 156, 203
Rains, Claude 20, 89, 198
Rambeau, Majorie 143
Rambo: First Blood II 173
Ramirez, Jose Luis 86
Rampage, Lee 164
Randolph, Charlie 179
Rashomon 148
Ray, Nicholas 70
Rayart Pictures 72
Rebel Without a Cause 185
Rector, Enoch J. 36
Red Ryder 59
Redford, Robert 26, 192
Reed, Donna 129
Reed, Oliver 192
Reed, Rex 174, 201
Reeves, Roberta 188
Regan, Ronald 114
Reinhardt, Max 96, 179

Rembrandt 129
Remmick, David 138
Republic Pictures 183
Requiem for a Heavyweight 34, 112, 121, 142, 159, 160, 192
Revere, Ann 13
Revill, Clyde 132
Reynolds, Gene 43
Rhames, Ving 51, 52, 202, 203
The Rialto Theater 20
Rich, Frank 81
Rich, Irene 24
Richards, Tommy 208
Richmond, Kane 18, 121
Richmond, Ray 52
Rickard, "Tex" 140, 164
Riefenstahl, Leni 200
Ride the Rainbow 112
Right Cross 90
The Ring 90
The Ring Magazine 102, 186
Ring of Passion 99, 162, 163
Ring Record Book 104
Ringside Maisie 119, 164, 165
Rios, Lalo 90
Rip Roarin' Buckaroo 59
Ritchie, Joe 112
Ritchie, Michael 50
Ritt, Martin 73, 74
Rivers, Joe 154, 169, 208
RKO 31, 118, 180, 181, 206
Robe 160
Robbins, Jhan 144
Robbins, Jim 169
Roberts, Bob 12, 14, 15
Robertson, Dale 37
Robinson, Edward G. 108, 109, 111, 113
Robinson, Jackie 101
Robinson, Ray 71, 88, 91, 107, 147, 148, 155, 184, 185, 196
Robson, Mark 29, 30, 31, 83, 84
Robson, May 109
Rockefeller, John D. 71
Rocky 13, 24, 61, 86, 91, 107, 140, 149, 150, 151, 166, 167, 168, 169, 171, 174, 176, 186, 193
Rocky II 128, 168, 169, 193
Rocky III 91, 170, 171, 172, 174
Rocky IV 172, 173, 174, 175, 176
Rocky V 175, 176
Rocky Graziano, He's a Good Boy Now 117
Rocky Marciano 177, 178

Rocky Marciano: Biography of a First Son 131
Rodriguez, Michelle 66
Rogell, Sid 180
Rogers, Jean 40
Roland, Roy 45
Roman, Ruth 29
Rooney, Mickey 45, 70, 123, 142, 159, 160
Roosevelt, Franklin Delano 101, 103, 163
Root, Lynn 108
Roots 49
Roper, Jack 64, 65, 104, 114
Rose, Billy 144
Rose, Lionel 128
Rosen, Joe 74
Rosenberg, Aaron 98
Rosenbloom, Maxie 45, 105, 109, 110, 112, 114, 119, 120, 165, 183, 192
Rosenfeld, John 30
Rosofsky, Barnet David 137
Ross, Barney 71, 106, 134, 137, 138, 160, 208
Ross, Wirt 106
Rossen, Robert 13, 14, 15, 17, 33
Rossi, Paoli 160
Roth, Eric 8
Roughneck 53
Roxborough, John 189
Ruggles, Charles 11
Runaway Romany 22
Ruth, Babe 46
Ruth, Daniel 86
Ryan, Meg 7
Ryan, Paddy 72
Ryan, Robert 164, 179, 180, 181, 182
Ryan, Tommy 124

Sackler, Howard 73, 74
St. Nicholas Arena 184
St. Valentine's Day Massacre 137
St. Vincent DePaul Cemetery 81
Salas, Joe 43
Salas, Lauro 90
Salica, Lou 112
San Francisco Chronicle 146
Sanders, Hugh 37
Sands, Dave 128
Santell, Alfred 147
Saraceno, Jon 178
Sarris, Andrew 74, 81, 172
Sarron, Petey 106

The Saturday Review 62, 186
Savage, Peter 155
Savold, Lee 102
Savoy Ballroom Dancers 188
Sax, Sam 103
Schaaf, Ernie 83
Schary, Dore 180
Schindler's List 200
Schmeling, Max 45, 99, 100, 152, 162, 163, 164, 188, 196
Schneible, A.T. 114
Scho 206
Schribner 115
Schroder, Ricky 25, 27
Schulberg, Budd 82, 83
Schwartz, Tony 27
Scorsese, Martin 8, 10, 11, 14, 155, 156, 157
Scott, A.O. 66
Scott, George C. 178
Scott, James 144
Scott, Mabel Jolienne 39
Scott, Randolph 38
Scozza, Lou 119
Screenplays, Inc. 31
Sea Wolf 64
Sedwick, Josie 46
See, Leon 82
Segal, Clancy 79
Seligsohn, Leo 194, 195
Semenoff, Simon 72
Semler, Dean 149
Sennett, Max 34
Serling, Rod 158, 159
Serrano, Pulga 147
The Set-Up 31, 164, 179, 180, 181, 182
Setlickel, Richard 74
Severn, Christopher 129
Shack, Stanley 112
Shampoo 27
Shanberg, Edward 187
Sharkey, Jack 152, 163, 164
Sharkey, Tom 124
Sharp, Christopher 172, 174
Shavers, Earnie 51, 171
Shaw, George Bernard 115
Shaw, Julie 25
Shaw, Stan 183
Shearer, Norma 121, 153
Shelley, Norman 145
Shelton, Ron 76, 147
Sher, Jack 142
Sheridan, Ann 32, 198
Shickel, Richard 79, 174
Shire, Talia 24, 166, 167
Shooting 27, 127, 169

Show of Shows 211
Showtime Entertainment 52, 178
Sid 98
Siddown 17
Siodmak, Robert 116
Siegel, Joel 156
Sight and Sound 57, 140
Siki, "Battling" 134
Silvani, Al 47, 186
Silvera, Frank 118
Simms, Eddie 164, 165
Simon, Abe 160
Simon, John 167
Sinise, Gary 183, 184
Siskel, Gene 173
The Sixteenth Round 92
Skelton, Red 25
Skippy 24
Smith, Alexis 64
Smith, Charles H. 11
Smith, Gunboat 47
Smith, Jamie 118
Smith, Liz 27, 127
Smith, Paul Gerard 11
Smith, Tim 148
Smith, Will 8, 9, 10
Snake Eyes 183, 184
Sneak Previews 201
Snipes, Wesley 194, 195, 202, 203
Society Girl 70
Soho 64
Solomon, King 54
Some Blondes Are Dangerous 98
Some Like It Hot 191
Somebody Up There Likes Me 181, 185
Sonenberg, David 204
Sony Pictures 8, 10
Sothern, Ann 164
The Sound of Music 182
Spartacus 191
Speak Up America 15
The Spectator 79
Spinks, Leon 126
Spinners 204
The Spirit of Youth 106, 187, 188, 189
Spivey, Ma 159
The Spoilers 38
The Sporting Editor 209
The Square Jungle 190, 191
Stage Coach 39
Stahl 30
Stallone, Sasha 166
Stallone, Sylvester 86, 91, 107, 128, 166, 167, 168, 169, 171, 172, 173, 175, 176
Stander, Lionel 44
Stanley, Joe 112
Stanwyck, Barbara 68
Starz 99
Steele, Bob 59
Steele, Freddie 64, 104
Steele, Richard 16, 91
Steiger, Rod 17, 18, 82, 84
Stein, Ron 91
Sterling, Jan 190
Sterling, Robert 164, 165
Sterritt, David 79, 140
Stevenson, Adlai 182
Stevenson, Hayden 39, 121
Stewart, Emanuel 6
Stewart, Paul 29, 31
Stillman's Gym 185, 186
The Sting 49
The Sting II 192, 193
Stone, Harold J. 186
Streets of Gold 194, 203
Streisand, Barbra 126
Stribling, "Ma" 6
Stribling, Young 6
Strike Me Pink 143
Stuart, Dan 36, 37
Sturges, John 90
Styne, Jule 108
Submarine D-1 112
Sugar, Bert Randolph 141
Sullivan, Billy 72, 212
Sullivan, John L. 46, 63, 64, 71, 72, 73, 95, 121, 148
Sundance Film Festival 66, 205
Sunday New York Daily News 96
The Sunday New York Times 57
Superfight 196, 197
Survivor 170
Susskind, David 159
Swaffer, Hannen 23
Swanee River 45
Sweet Smell of Success 191
Swinton, Terry 93
Sylvers, Susan 169

T.M.P. 55, 64, 90, 180
T.S. 129
T.V Guide 61, 90
Taber, Richard 88, 122
Taggart, Ben 136
Tallmer, Jerry 149
Tanis, Hazel 92
Taradash, Daniel 67
Tarzan the Ape Man 42
Taub, Sam 186
Taxi Driver 155
Taylor, Estelle 47
Taylor, John Russell 57
Taylor, Robert 40, 43, 44, 45
Tazelaar, Marguerite 123
Temple, Shirley 164
Tennessee Champ 80
Tero, Lawrence 171
Terris, Sid 96, 125
Thalberg, Irving 22, 42
They Made Me a Criminal 12, 20, 107, 198, 199
Thirer, Irene 25, 112, 199
This Is America 118
This Is Living 112
The Three Stooges 103, 121
Tilden, Bill 46
Time 13, 30, 35, 37, 79, 112, 156, 174, 208
The Times 64
Tiomkin, Dimitri 30
Tirelli, Jamie 66
Title Shot 191
To Have and Have Not 115
Tobaggan 212
Tobias, George 180
Toney, James 6
Tony Award 73
Toronto Film Festival 66
Torres, Jose 47, 58, 127
Totter, Audrey 181
Touchdown 42
Tough Kid 19, 21
Tracy, Spencer 126
Traveling Executioner 57
A Tree Grows in Brooklyn 70
Trinadad, Felix 125
Triple Cross 104
Triumph of the Spirit 200, 201
Triumph of the Will 200
Tube 112
Tunney, Gene 22, 39, 44, 47, 48, 54, 98, 109, 125, 193
Tunney, John 193
Turan, Kenneth 7, 149, 150
Turman, Lawrence 73
Turner, Mae 188
Twelvetrees, Helen 119
Twentieth-Century Fox 37, 60, 67, 73, 74, 77, 162, 183, 208, 209, 210
Two-Fisted 88
Two-Fisted Gentleman 70
2001: A Space Odyssey 117
Tyler, Tom 59

Tyson, Mike 16, 22, 76, 77, 201, 202

Undisputed 202, 203
United Artists 28, 31, 118, 123, 136, 155, 166, 170, 175
Universal International 190
Universal Pictures 98
Universal Studios 54, 55, 56, 59, 87, 121
Uzcudun, Paulino 100

Valdez, Sonny 112
Van, Frankie 28, 98, 179, 191
Vanderbilt, Cornelius 71
Van Dyke, W.S. 42, 153
Van Rooten, Luis 29
Variety 5, 18, 19, 20, 21, 23, 30, 40, 42, 44, 49, 50, 52, 55, 59, 59, 64, 68, 69, 70, 77, 79, 84, 86, 89, 90, 94, 96, 98, 102, 108, 109, 111, 112, 114, 116, 120, 121, 123, 134, 136, 138, 144, 150, 151, 153, 154, 160, 165, 179, 180, 181, 183, 184, 185, 186, 188, 191, 194, 197, 199, 202, 205, 209, 210
Velez, Lupe 90, 143
Venable, Evelyn 183
Vera-Ellen 108
Vernon, Bobby 87
Video Review 58, 201
Vidor, King 24, 25, 27, 107
Vietnam War 78, 79, 196, 202, 206
The Village Voice 61, 81, 132, 172, 174, 176
The Villager 160
Vincent, Sailor 96, 121
Vingo, Carmen 178
Viruet, Edwin 195
Vitaphone Studios 103
Viva Zapata 159
Voight, Jon 25, 26, 27, 28, 86, 128

WABC-TV 156
Walcott, James 61
Walcott, Jersey Joe 71, 84, 131, 177, 196, 197
Walker, Mickey 107, 124
Wall Street Journal 9, 66, 67, 157
Wallace, Coley 102
Wallach, Eli 140, 141
Wallington, Jimmy 183
Walsh, "Happy" 141

Walsh, Raoul 33, 63, 64
Walt 89
Ward, David S. 192
Warden, Jack 27, 140, 141
Warfield, Marlene 73
Warner, Jack 27, 63, 111, 113, 211
Warner, Oland 183
Warner Brothers 12, 32, 33, 63, 64, 96, 108, 111, 113, 114, 192, 198, 199, 206, 207, 208
Warriors 202
Washington, Denzel 62, 94
Washington, Desiree 202
Washington Post 7, 160
Watkins, Eddie 77
Watson, Minor 206
Watts, Richard, Jr. 25, 26, 124, 153
Way Down East 145
The Way We Were 126
Wayans, Damon 76, 77
Wayne, David 151
Wayne, John 38, 39, 40, 41, 89, 123, 176, 183
Wear 210
Weathers, Carl 166, 169
Weaver, Mike 128
Weil, Al 130, 131, 178
Weismuller, Johnny 41, 42
Welles, Orson 29
Wellington, Horace 183
Welsh, Freddie 96, 112
Wepner, Chuck 51, 166
West Side Story 182
Wexel, John 32
Whalen, Michael 210
What's Up Doc? 126
When We Were Kings 10, 203–205
When's Your Birthday? 205–207
White, Alice 119
White, Arnold 202
White Men Can't Jump 76
Wierman, Marie 87
Wildmon, Donald 61
Wiles, Gordon 70
Willard, Jess 47, 48, 55, 74, 87, 154, 210
William Fox Productions 53
Williams, Ike 21
Williams, Larry 45
Williams, Treat 47, 48
Williamson, Bruce 201
Wilmington, Michael 50, 176, 194, 195
Wilson, Gladys 188

Wilson, Gus 211
Wimbledon 162
Winkler, Irving 140
Winner Take All 32, 33, 96, 104, 144, 207, 208
Winsten, Archer 33, 57, 69, 79, 109, 111, 164, 165
Winter Garden Theater 116
Winters, Shelly 80
Wise, Robert 180, 181, 185, 186
Witcher, Guy 148, 150
Withers, Grant 212
Witwer, H.C. 121
Wizard of Oz 72, 207
Wolfe, Thomas 177
Wolgast, Ad 169
Woman-Wise 210
Women's Wear Daily 172, 174
Wonder, Stevie 92
Wonderman 206, 211
Wood 136
Woods, James 49, 50
World Boxing Association (WBA) 86
World Film News 23
World in My Corner 142
World War I 31, 53, 55, 141, 145, 211
World War II 14, 20, 72, 80, 85, 90, 95, 101, 103, 129, 149
Woroner, Murry 196, 197
Wuntch, Philip 176
Wyman, Jane 44, 114

X, Malcolm 9, 79, 139

A Yank at Oxford 43
Yankee Doodle Dandy 32, 207
Yankee Stadium 184
Yanni, Nicholas 61
Yordan, Philip 82, 84
Young, Bert 166
Young, Gig 112
Young, Loretta 122, 123

Zaire 9
Zale, Tony 71, 184, 185, 186
Zanuck, Darryl 67
Zbyszko, Stanislaus 124
Zeffereli 27
Zieff, Howard 126
Ziegfeld Follies 211
Zinsser, William K. 84
Zivic, Fritzie 16
Zsigmond, Vilmos 62
Zuckerman, George 98
Zunser, Jesse 185

www.ingramcontent.com/pod-product-compliance
Ingram Content Group UK Ltd.
Pitfield, Milton Keynes, MK11 3LW, UK
UKHW050532150426
5217IPUK00026B/1901